STREET ATLAS

BRISTOL & AVON

COMPREHENSIVE COVERAGE

CONTENTS

III Key to map symbols

IV Key to map pages

VI Administrative boundaries

1 Street maps

140 Index explanation and abbreviations

141 Index of towns, villages and rural localities

142 Index of street names

TED SMART

First edition published 1995

Ordnance Survey® and	George Philip Ltd, a division of
Romsey Road	Octopus Publishing Group Ltd
Maybush	2-4 Heron Quays
Southampton	London
SO16 4GU	E14 4JP

This edition produced in 1999 for
The Book People Limited
Hall Wood Avenue
Haydock
St Helens WA11 9UL

ISBN 1-85613-503-9

Printed and bound in Great Britain by Bath Press, Bath

Key to map symbols

⮀	**British Rail station**
⊖	**Underground station**
🚂	**Private railway station**
⬤	**Bus or coach station**
Ⓗ	**Heliport**
♦	**Police station** (may not be open 24 hours)
✚	**Hospital with casualty facilities** (may not be open 24 hours)
☐	**Post office**
+	**Place of worship**
◣	**Important building**
P	**Parking**
174	**Adjoining page indicator**
⊠	**No adjoining page**
▬▬	**Motorway**
▬▬	**Dual carriageway**
──	**Main or through road**
A27	**Road numbers** (Department of Transport)
─┬─	**Gate or obstruction to traffic** (restrictions may not apply at all times or to all vehicles)
- - -	**Path, bridleway, byway open to all traffic, road used as public path, dismantled railway etc.**
═══	**Track**

The representation in this atlas of a road, track or path is no evidence of the existence of a right of way

Amb Sta	**Ambulance station**	LC	**Level crossing**
Amb Dpo	**Ambulance depot**	Liby	**Library**
Coll	**College**	Mus	**Museum**
FB	**Footbridge**	Acad	**Academy**
F Sta	**Fire station**	Sch	**School**
Hospl	**Hospital**	TH	**Town Hall or Town House**

```
0        1/4         1/2         3/4       1 mile
0    250m    500m    750m    1 Kilometre
```

The scale of the maps is 3 1/2 inches to 1 mile (1:18103)

The small numbers around the edges of the maps
identify the 1 kilometre National Grid lines

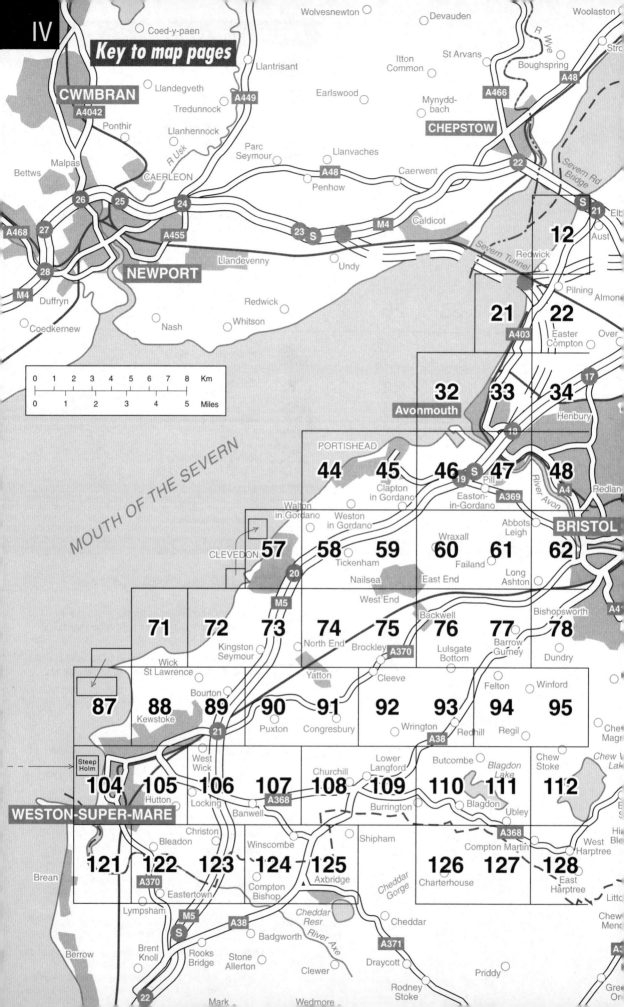

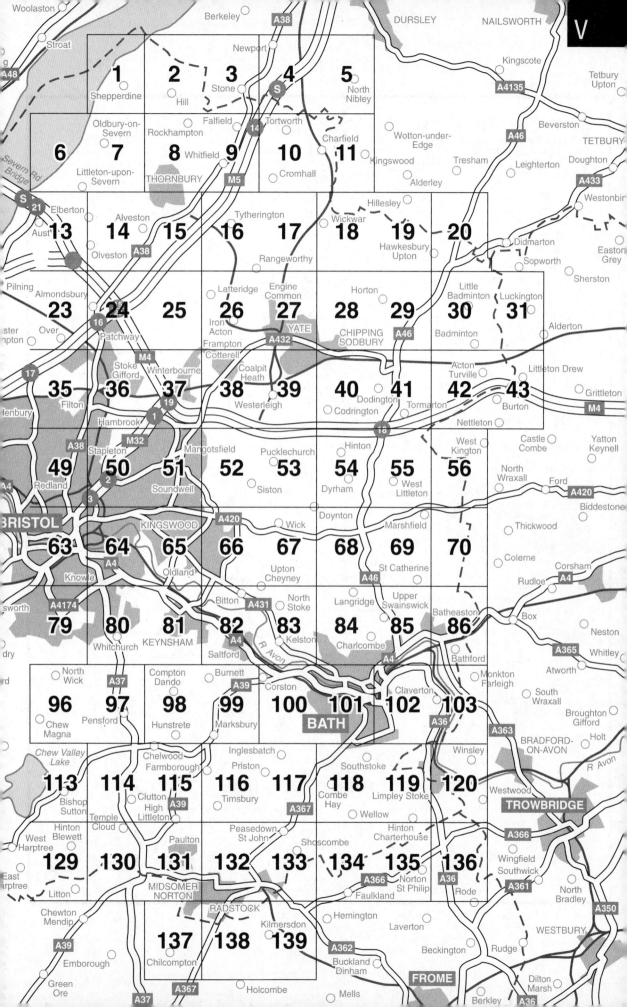

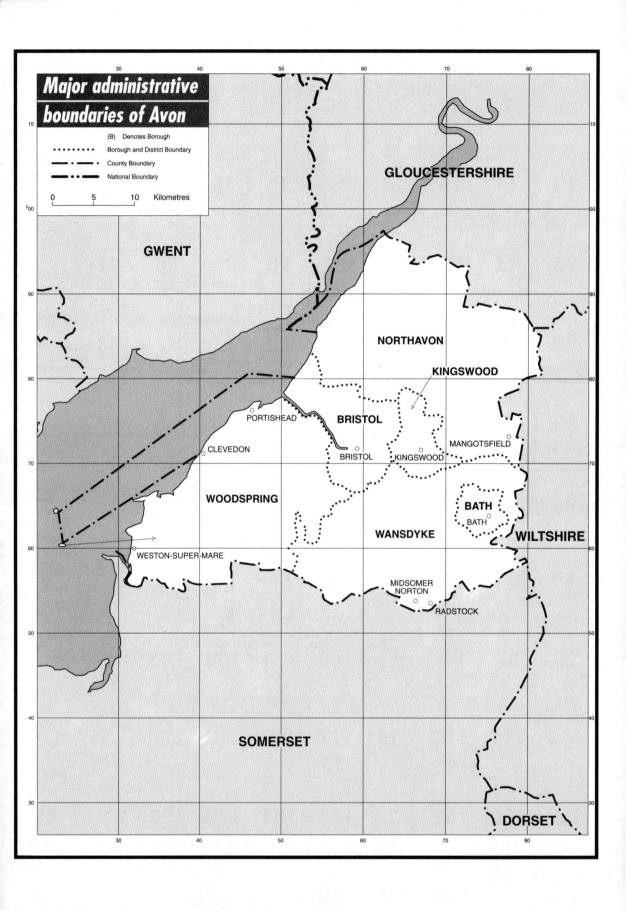

Major administrative boundaries of Avon

(B) Denotes Borough

········· Borough and District Boundary

–·–·–·– County Boundary

–··–··– National Boundary

0   5   10   Kilometres

GLOUCESTERSHIRE

GWENT

NORTHAVON

KINGSWOOD

PORTISHEAD

BRISTOL

CLEVEDON

BRISTOL

KINGSWOOD

MANGOTSFIELD

WOODSPRING

BATH

BATH

WANSDYKE

WILTSHIRE

WESTON-SUPER-MARE

MIDSOMER
NORTON

RADSTOCK

SOMERSET

DORSET

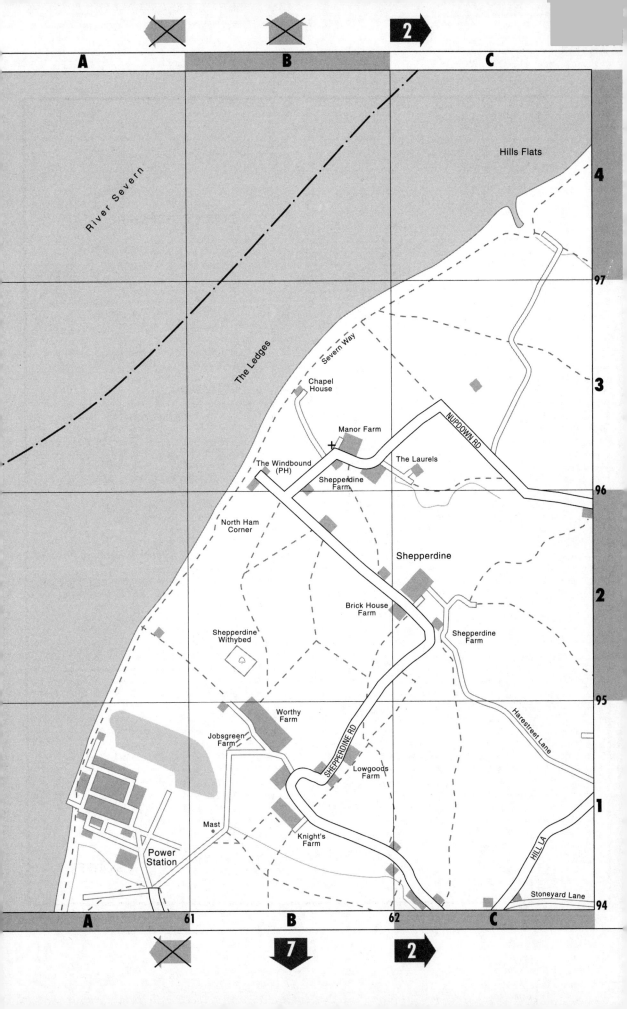

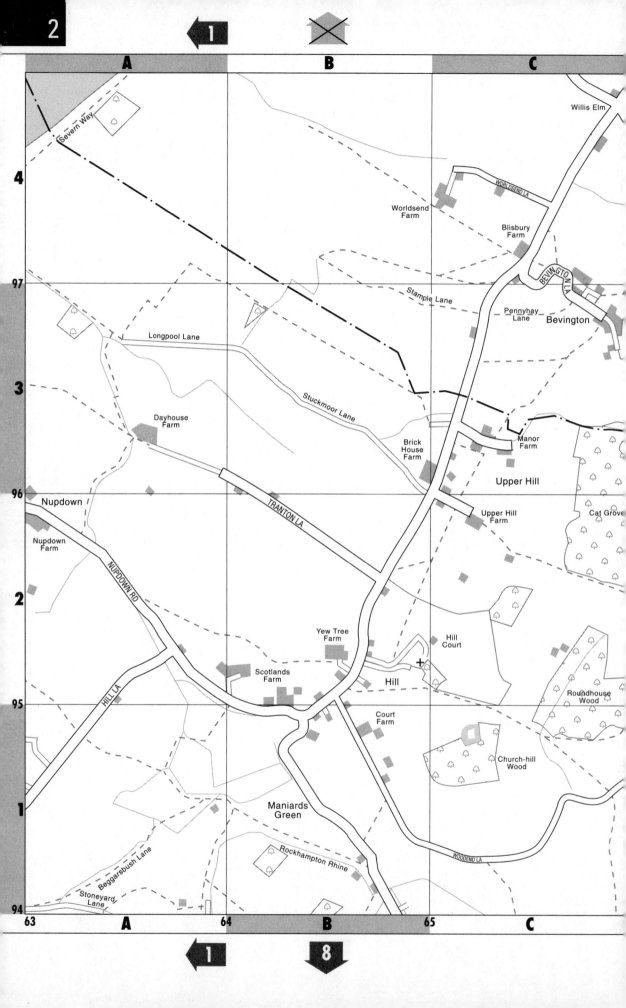

A   B   C

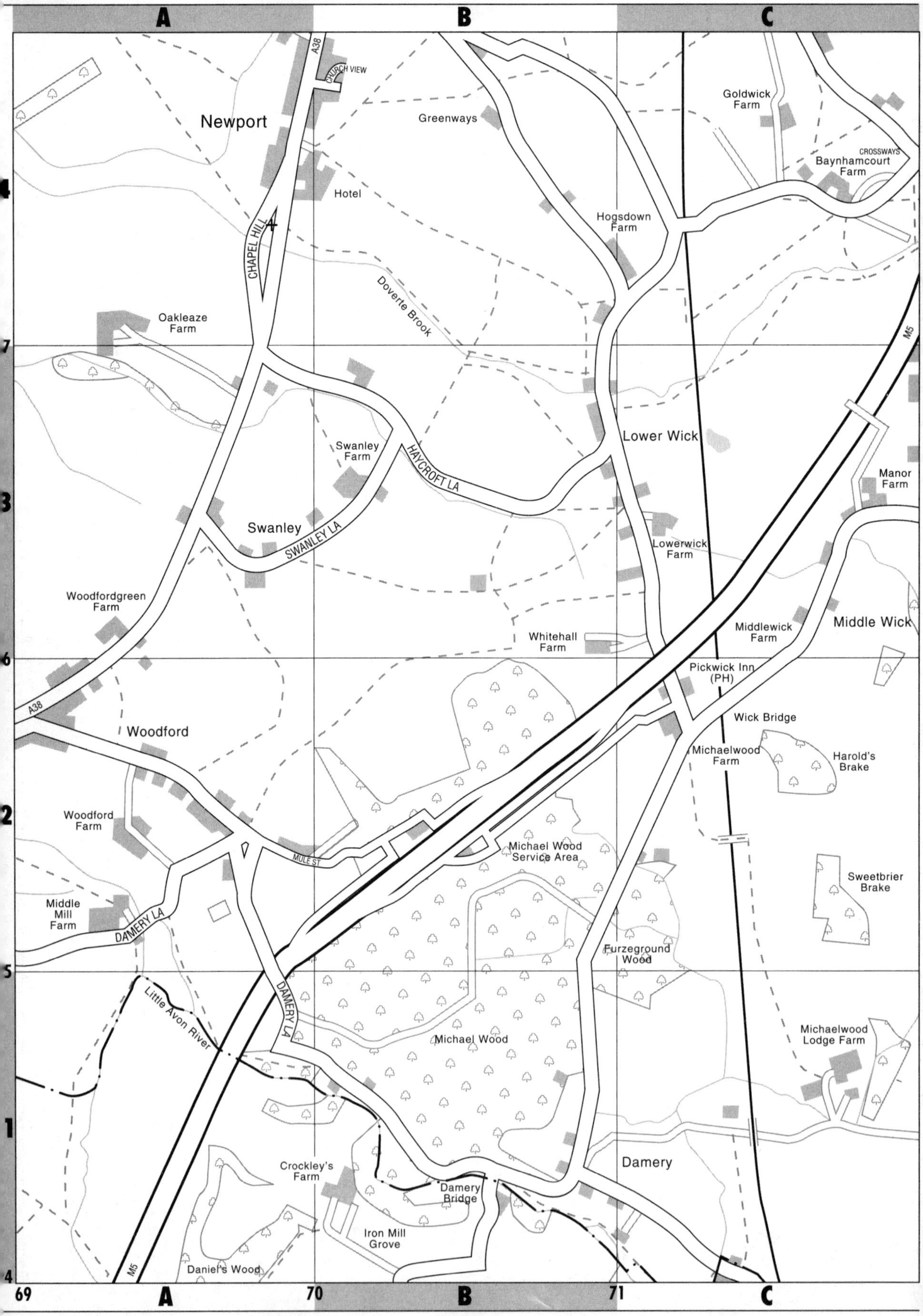

A38

CHURCH VIEW

Newport

Greenways

Goldwick
Farm

CROSSWAYS

Baynhamcourt
Farm

Hotel

Hogsdown
Farm

CHAPEL HILL

Doverte Brook

7

Oakleaze
Farm

M5

Lower Wick

Manor
Farm

HAYCROFT LA

3

Swanley
Farm

Swanley

SWANLEY LA

Lowerwick
Farm

Woodfordgreen
Farm

Middle Wick

Middlewick
Farm

Whitehall
Farm

6

A38

Pickwick Inn
(PH)

Wick Bridge

Woodford

Michaelwood
Farm

Harold's
Brake

2

Woodford
Farm

MULE ST

Michael Wood
Service Area

Sweetbrier
Brake

Middle
Mill
Farm

DAMERY LA

Furzeground
Wood

5

Little Avon River

DAMERY LA

Michael Wood

Michaelwood
Lodge Farm

1

Crockley's
Farm

Damery

Damery
Bridge

Iron Mill
Grove

M5

Daniel's Wood

4

69   A   70   B   71   C

Stinchcombe

Holt's Farm

Fortune Farm

Drakestone House

Stancombe Farm

Stancombe Park

Park Wood

PARK LA

Cotswold Way

Park Farm

Sewage Works

Snitend Bridge

Doverte Brook

Wick House Farm

Burleigh Court

Crowell Brook

Nibley Green

Forthay Farm

Isle of Rhe

FROG LA

Hunt's Court Farm

Forthay

Pitt Court

Sch

THE STREET

INNOCKS EST

WARREN CROFT

BARRS LA

HIGHLANDS DR

Bush Street Farm

Nibley House Farm

North Nibley

NEW RD

Black Horse Inn (PH)

Cotswold Way

Bassett Court

Cemy

Tyndale Monument

Nibley Knoll

Westridge Wood

Millmans Farm

Southend

Southend Farm

Big Ride

Brackenbury Ditches Fort

Katherine's Farm

STUMPWELL LA

Daisy Farm

DAISY GREEN LA

Howley

Bournstream

Kitesnest Farm

Elmcote

Howley Farm

B4060

SWINHAY LA

VERNALS LA

D   73   E   74   F

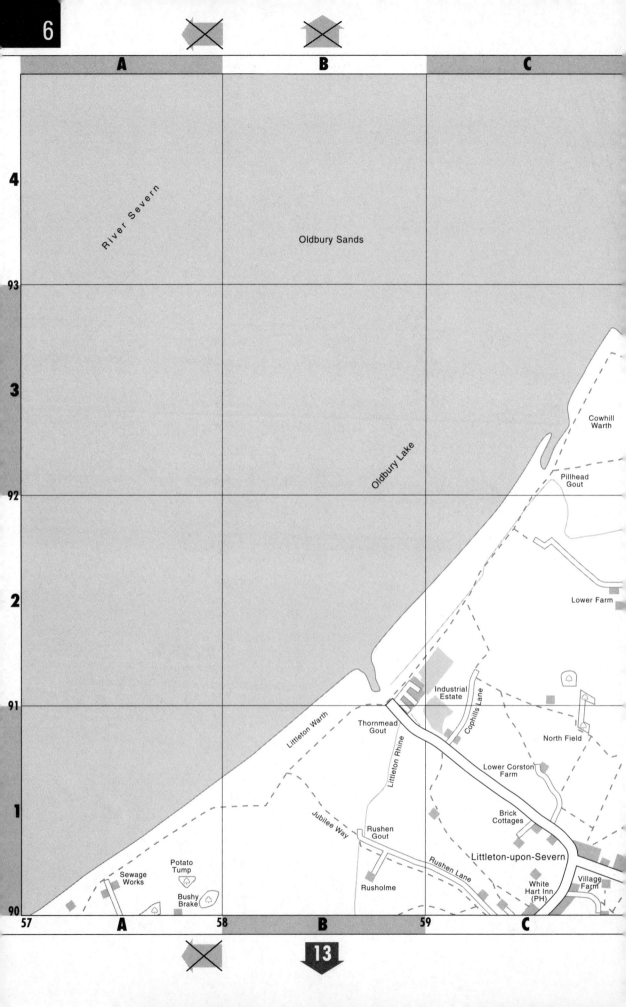

A B C

4

River Severn

Oldbury Sands

93

3

Cowhill Warth

Oldbury Lake

Pillhead Gout

92

Lower Farm

2

Industrial Estate

Cophills Lane

91

Littleton Warth

Thornmead Gout

North Field

Littleton Rhine

Lower Corston Farm

1

Jubilee Way

Brick Cottages

Rushen Gout

Littleton-upon-Severn

Rushen Lane

Sewage Works

Potato Tump

Rusholme

White Hart Inn (PH)

Village Farm

Bushy Brake

90

57 A 58 B 59 C

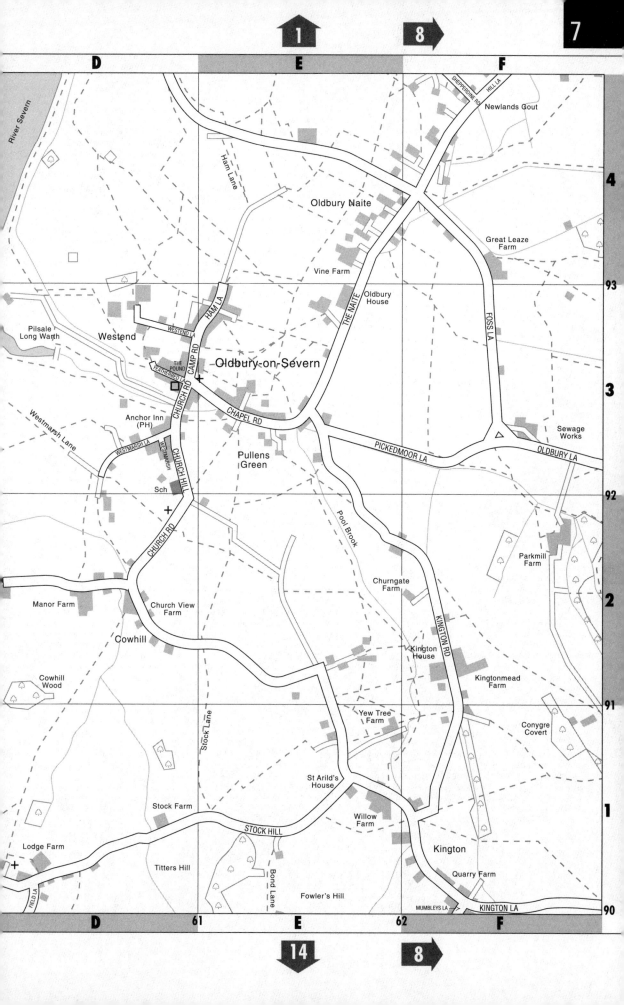

D   E   F

River Severn

Newlands Gout

SHEPPERDINE RD

HILL LA

4

Oldbury Naite

Great Leaze
Farm

Vine Farm

93

THE NAITE

Oldbury
House

FOSS LA

Ham Lane

Pilsale
Long Warth

Westend

WESTEND LA

HAM LA

CAMP RD

Oldbury-on-Severn

THE POUND

FEATHERBED LA

CHURCH RD

3

Anchor Inn
(PH)

CHAPEL RD

Westmarsh Lane

WESTMARSH LA

WESTMARSH

CHURCH HILL

Pullens
Green

PICKEDMOOR LA

Sewage
Works

OLDBURY LA

Sch

92

CHURCH RD

Pool Brook

Parkmill
Farm

Manor Farm

Church View
Farm

Churngate
Farm

2

Cowhill

KINGTON RD

Kington
House

Kingtonmead
Farm

Cowhill
Wood

Stock Lane

91

Yew Tree
Farm

Conygre
Covert

St Arild's
House

Stock Farm

STOCK HILL

Willow
Farm

1

Kington

Lodge Farm

Titters Hill

Bond Lane

Fowler's Hill

Quarry Farm

FIELD LA

MUMBLEYS LA

KINGTON LA

90

D   61   E   62   F

A B C

4

Rockhampton Rhine

Northfield Lane

SUNDAYSHILL LA

The Old Rectory

Rockhampton

Lodge Farm

GULLY LA

Spreyte Comb Farm

Pennywell Farm

The Hollies

93

The Firs

Luce's Farm

Yew Tree Farm

Newton

Groves Gully

Duckhole

3

Longman's Grove

Pound Farm

Lower Morton

Maypole Farm

HORSE LA

Catsbrain Lane

Oak Farm

92

OLDBURY LA

Spring Farm

MORTON ST

Upper Morton

Manor Farm

Yewtree Farm

2

Morton House

Park Farm

BUTT LA

Mile End Farm

The Knapp

PARKLAND WAY

DYRHAM CL

QUEENS WALK

KEMPTON CL

ST JAMES WAY

ROSSLYN WAY

CHARLES CL

PITVILLE

SWALLOW PK

OSPREY PK

Morton

Morton Bridge

VICTORIA CL

ALEXANDRA AVE

HYDE AVE

ROBERTS CL

NORTH PK

NIGHTINGALE

SPEEDWELL

CELANDINE CL

Sch

91

Thornbury Park

Sch

KENSINGTON CL

COSSHAM CL

CHESTNUT CL

WHITFIELD

B4061

JAMES LANE

WALLOW

Knapp Farm

Thornbury Castle

PARK RD

CHANTRY RD

MILBURY

HOWARD RD

F Sta

ROBIN CL

ROBIN CL

CASTLE RD

FALCON WAY

MORTON WAY

Crossways House

COOMBE AVE

THE ROW

CAMPION CL

FOXGLOVE CL

SORREL CL

ARUNDEL CT

WHITEWALL LA

1

WARWICK CL

CHURCH RD

GLOUCESTER RD

EASTLAND RD

DAVIS CT

HARTHORN CRES

PARK VIEW AVE

BLUEBELL

LARKSPUR

ARUNDEL CT

Crossways

THORNBURY

Sch

Hosp

Sch

MAPLE AVE

WOODLEIGH

HIGH ST

WALNUT WK

EASTON HILL RD

Sch

Sch

Schs

HACKET LA

CLAY LA

Cemy

Off

CASTLE ST

STOKEFIELD CL

ORCHARD GRANGE

CARE WALK

THE ROW

MILL LA

HIGH ST

DANDS RD

MAPLE AVE

JANES CRES

OAKLEAZE

ORCHARD AVE

CROSSWAYS RD

KNAPP RD

CUMBERLAND

CLEVELAND

Kington La

ST MARYS WAY

SILVER ST

ST MARYS ST

ROCK ST

GROVESEND RD

PULLEN'S GREEN

P

Sta

CASTLE CT

THE PLAIN

B4061 HIGH ST

JOHN ST

QUAKER LA

P

COLIN

CRISPIN LA

HILL CREST

BLAKES RD

ASHGROVE

FERNDALE

KNAPP RD

SIBLAND RD

PADDOCKS

JUBILEE DR

90

63 A 64 B 65 C

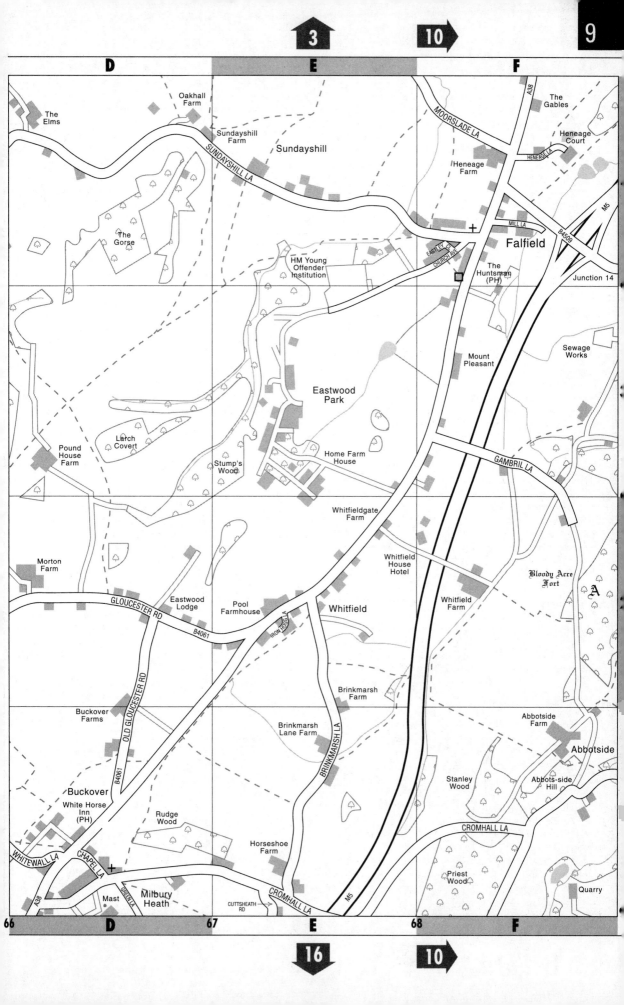

D   E   F

The Elms

Oakhall Farm

Sundayshill Farm

Sundayshill

SUNDAYSHILL LA

The Gorse

HM Young Offender Institution

A38

MOORSLADE LA

The Gables

Heneage Court

HENEAGE LA

Heneage Farm

MILL LA

Falfield

EASTLEY LA

CHURCH AVE

The Huntsman (PH)

B4509

M5

Junction 14

Mount Pleasant

Sewage Works

Eastwood Park

GAMBRIL LA

Pound House Farm

Larch Covert

Stump's Wood

Home Farm House

Whitfieldgate Farm

Whitfield House Hotel

Bloody Acre Fort

A

Morton Farm

Eastwood Lodge

GLOUCESTER RD

B4061

Pool Farmhouse

IRON MILL LA

Whitfield

Whitfield Farm

OLD GLOUCESTER RD

Buckover Farms

Brinkmarsh Lane Farm

Brinkmarsh Farm

BRINKMARSH LA

Abbotside Farm

Abbotside

B4061

Stanley Wood

Abbots-side Hill

Buckover

White Horse Inn (PH)

Rudge Wood

CROMHALL LA

WHITEWALL LA

CHAPEL LA

A38

Mast

GREEN LA

Milbury Heath

CUTTSHEATH RD

Horseshoe Farm

CROMHALL LA

M5

Priest Wood

Quarry

A
B
C

4

Little Avon River

AVENING GREEN

Huntingford
Farm

Old Court
Farm

Little Tortworth
Copse

Huntingford

Hotel

Tortworth

Brook
Farm

Howcroft
Cottages

+
Tortworth
Chestnut

M5

B4509

Sch Old Lodge
Farm

Kennel
Plantation

Tortworth
Copse

Underwood
Farm

3

Gall Pond

Arboretum

Elmtree
Farm

Poolfield
Farm

Tortworth
Court

Tortworth
Green

Sch B4058

Charfield
Hill

WOTTON RD

MANOR LA

The
Lake

+

H M Prison

Tafarn-bach

B4509

The
Old Rectory

2

Leyhill

PARK RD

Cromhall
Quarry

Hammerley
Down

Poundhouse
Farm

WOODLAND RD

Woodend
Farm

Harris's Wood

MEADOW RD

B4509

Tortworth
Park

CHURCHEND LA

Manor
Farm

Parkend

The
Royal Oak
(PH)

Churchend

Wicks' Hill

KNAPP LA

Bibstone

DEVIL'S LA

Church
Farm

1

Sodam Mill

FARLEIGH LA

Brand
Wood

+

TINGWELL

Talbotsend
Farm

Hawley's Lane

CHURCH LA

Talbot's End

B4509

LONGCROSS

Cromhall

Lake Lane

Churchwood
Quarry

Court
Farm

RECTORY LA

BRISTOL RD
B4058

Foxhole
Lane

69
A
70
B
71
C

4

Swinhay
Farm

VERNALS LA

Canonscourt
Farm

GLOUCESTER
ROW

ELLERNCROFT RD

Bradley

Wotton-
under-
Edge

Burrough
Hill
Farm

Bradley
Green

Little
Avon River

Lower Huntingford
Farm

SWINHAY LA

NEW RD

B4058

93

Works

Lower
Barns
Farm

Sewage
Works

Hopyard
Farm

Sch

B4062

Merryford
Farm

B4060

NEW ST

NEW ST

FARMTEES

LONGS VIEW

Park
Farm

Watsome
Bridge

Mill

WOTTON RD

Penn
House

3

Charfield

WOTTON RD

STATION RD

THE
SIDINGS

PH

Charfield
Green

HORSFIELD RD

COTSWOLD VIEW

Elbury
Hill

CHARFIELD RD

Chestnutpark
Farm

B4062

Mill

VINEYARD LA

THE
WALK

Sch
Abbey

ABBEY ST

GOLDEN LA

LAXTON GR

BRAMLEY C

92

KATHRINE
DR

NEWTOWN

DURHAM RD

OLD THAMES

UNDERHILL RD

BERKELEY CL

WILLOW CL

MANOR LA

ORCHARD CL

HAWTHORN CL

MANOR CL

Grange
Farm

Chestnut
Park
Est

Kingswood

OLD RECTORY
RD

PH

ORCHARD

RUSSET C

THE
CHIPPING

Walk
Mills

Hill
House
Farm

WOODLANDS RD

WALK MILL LA

HILLESLEY RD

SOMERSET

VERNON

Walk
Mills

2

LITTLE BRISTOL LA

Little
Bristol

WICKWAR RD

Trench
Farm

WEAVERS CL

Cemy

Charfield
Hall
Farm

Neathwood
Farm

91

Upper
Barns
Farm

DEVIL'S LA

Day
House
Farm

B4060

1

Newhouse
Farm

Southend
Farm

Uppergreen
Farm

Highwood
Farm

90

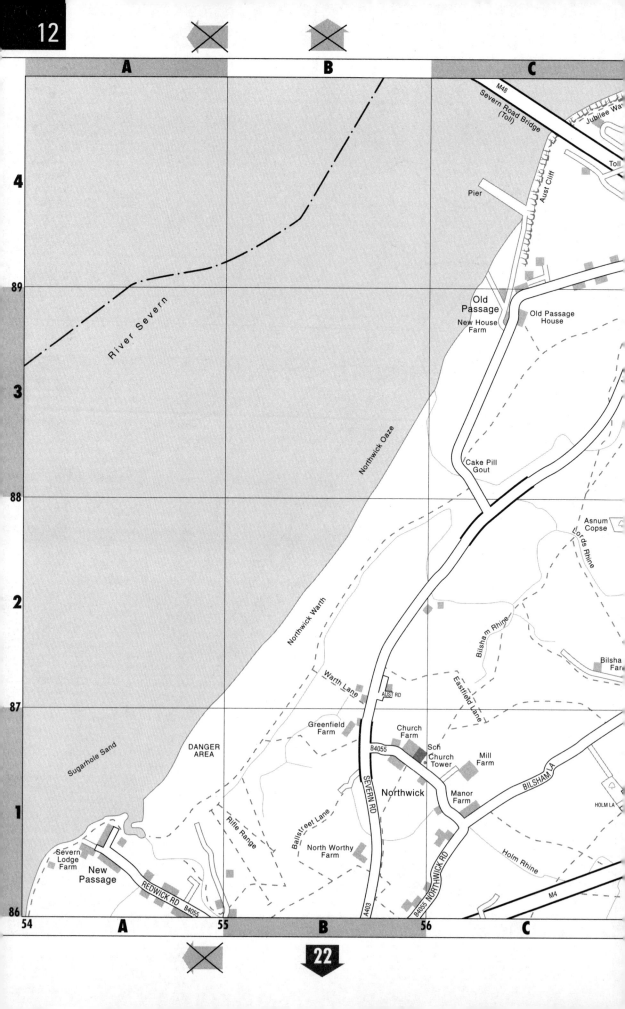

A B C

4

89

River Severn

3

Northwick Oaze

88

2

Northwick Warth

Warth Lane

AUST RD

87

Greenfield
Farm

DANGER
AREA

Sugarhole Sand

1

Rifle Range

Ballstreet Lane

North Worthy
Farm

Severn
Lodge
Farm

New
Passage

REDWICK RD

B4055

86

54 A 55 B 56 C

Severn Road Bridge
(Toll)

M48

Jubilee Wa

Toll

Aust Cliff

Pier

Old
Passage

New House
Farm

Old Passage
House

Cake Pill
Gout

Asnum
Copse

Lords Rhine

Bilsham Rhine

Bilsha
Far

Eastfield Lane

Church
Farm

Sch
Church
Tower

Mill
Farm

BILSHAM LA

HOLM LA

B4055

Northwick

Manor
Farm

SEVERN RD

NORTHWICK RD

Holm Rhine

M4

A403

B4055

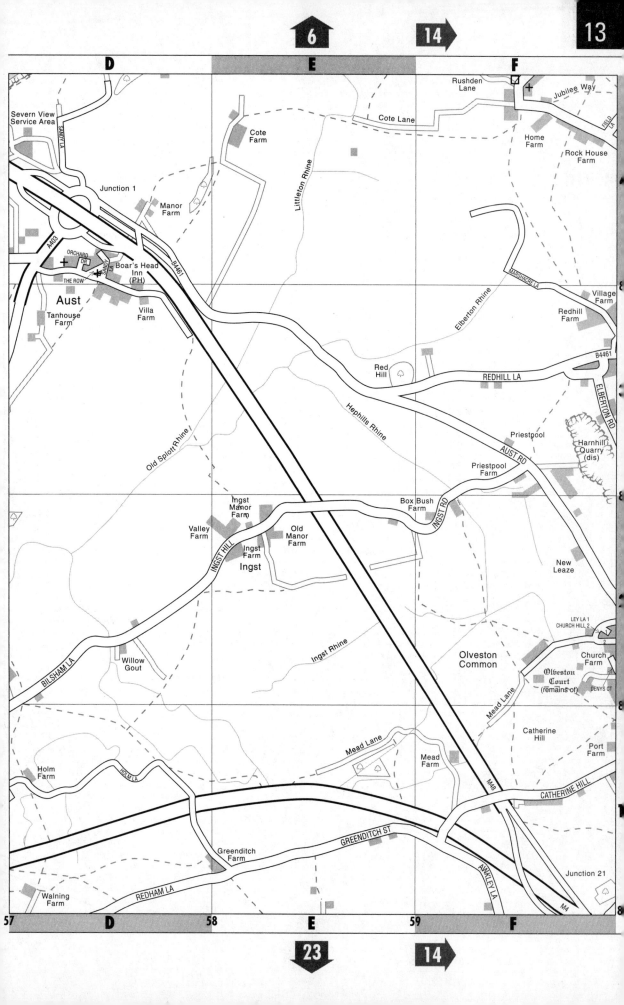

D   E   F

Rushden
Lane
Jubilee Way
Cote Lane
FIELD LA
Severn View
Service Area
SANDY LA
Cote
Farm
Home
Farm
Rock House
Farm
Littleton Rhine
Junction 1
Manor
Farm
MARSHACRE LA
Village
Farm
Elberton Rhine
A403
ORCHARD
DR
Boar's Head
Inn
(PH)
B4461
Redhill
Farm
Redhill
Farm
THE ROW
SANDY LA
B4461
Aust
Villa
Farm
ELBERTON RD
Tanhouse
Farm
Red
Hill
REDHILL LA
Hephills Rhine
Priestpool
Harnhill
Quarry
(dis)
Old Splott Rhine
AUST RD
Priestpool
Farm
Box Bush
Farm
Ingst
Manor
Farm
INGST RD
Valley
Farm
Old
Manor
Farm
New
Leaze
INGST HILL
Ingst
Farm
Ingst
LEY LA 1
CHURCH HILL 2
2
Church
Farm
Olveston
Common
Olveston
Court
(remains of)
DENYS CT
BILSHAM LA
Willow
Gout
Ingst Rhine
Catherine
Hill
Port
Farm
Mead Lane
Holm
Farm
HOLM LA
Mead Lane
Mead
Farm
CATHERINE HILL
M48
Junction 21
Greenditch
Farm
GREENDITCH ST
ANKLEY LA
M4
Walning
Farm
REDHAM LA

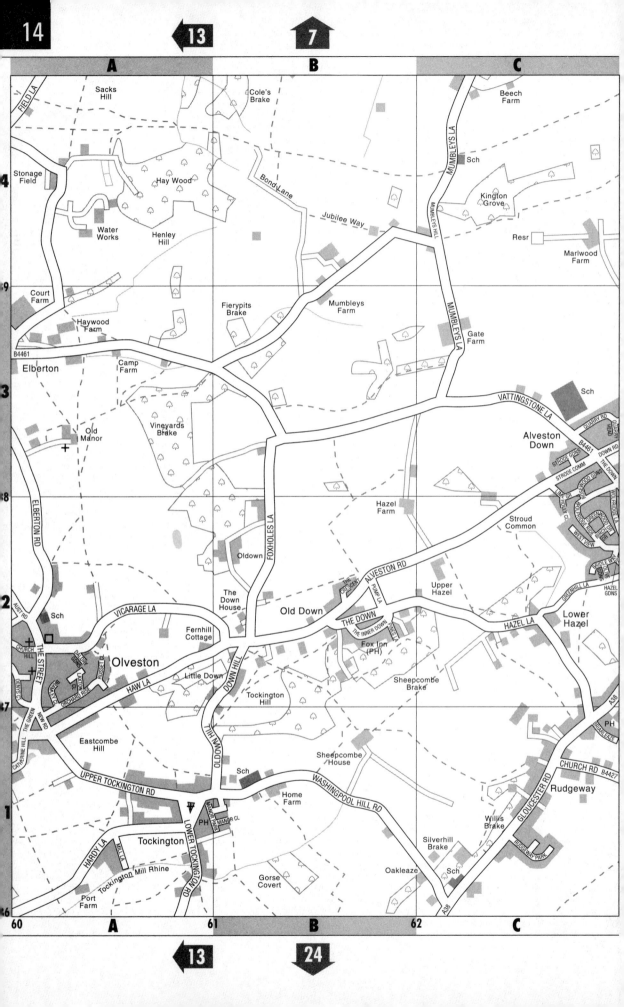

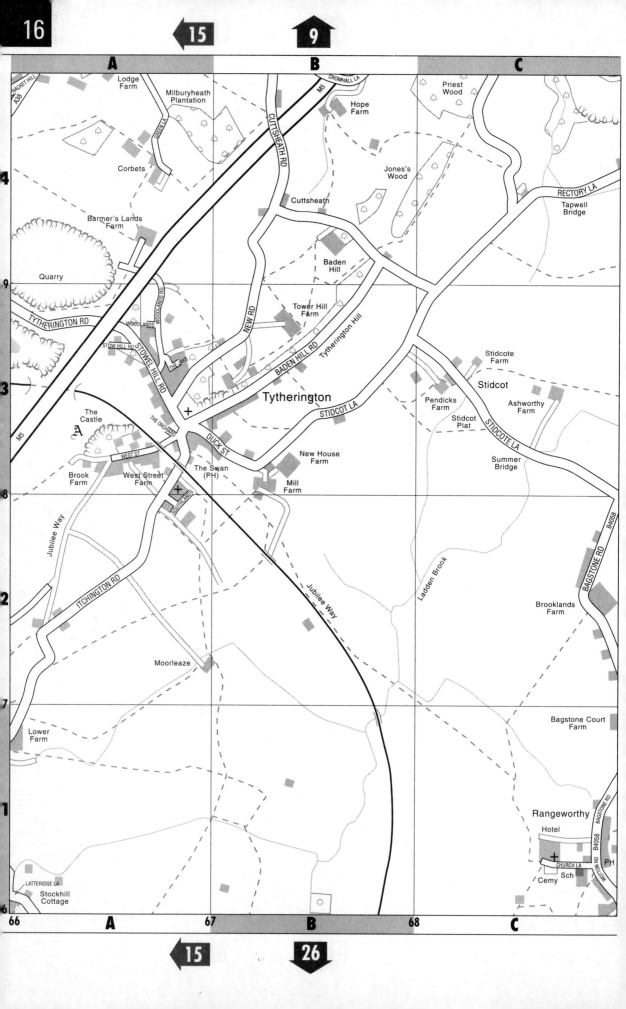

A
B
C

HACKET HILL

A38

Lodge
Farm

Milburyheath
Plantation

GREEN LA

Corbets

CROMHALL LA

M5

Hope
Farm

Priest
Wood

4

Barmer's Lands
Farm

CUTTSHEATH RD

Cuttsheath

Jones's
Wood

RECTORY LA

Tapwell
Bridge

Quarry

9

Baden
Hill

TYTHERINGTON RD

WOODLANDS RD

WOODLANDS

NEW RD

Tower Hill
Farm

BADEN HILL RD

Tytherington Hill

STOW HILL RD

STOWEL HILL RD

THE JAYS

Stidcote
Farm

Stidcot

3

The
Castle

THE ORCHARD

Tytherington

STIDCOT LA

Pendicks
Farm

Stidcot
Plat

Ashworthy
Farm

STIDCOTE LA

M5

DUCK ST

New House
Farm

Summer
Bridge

8

WEST ST

Brook
Farm

West Street
Farm

The Swan
(PH)

SOUTHLANDS

Mill
Farm

Jubilee Way

ITCHINGTON RD

Ladden Brook

BAGSTONE RD

B4058

Brooklands
Farm

2

Jubilee Way

Moorleaze

7

Bagstone Court
Farm

Lower
Farm

1

Rangeworthy

BAGSTONE RD

B4058

Hotel

B4058

CHURCH LA

HOLLOW RD

PH

Sch

LATTERIDGE LA

Stockhill
Cottage

Cemy

6

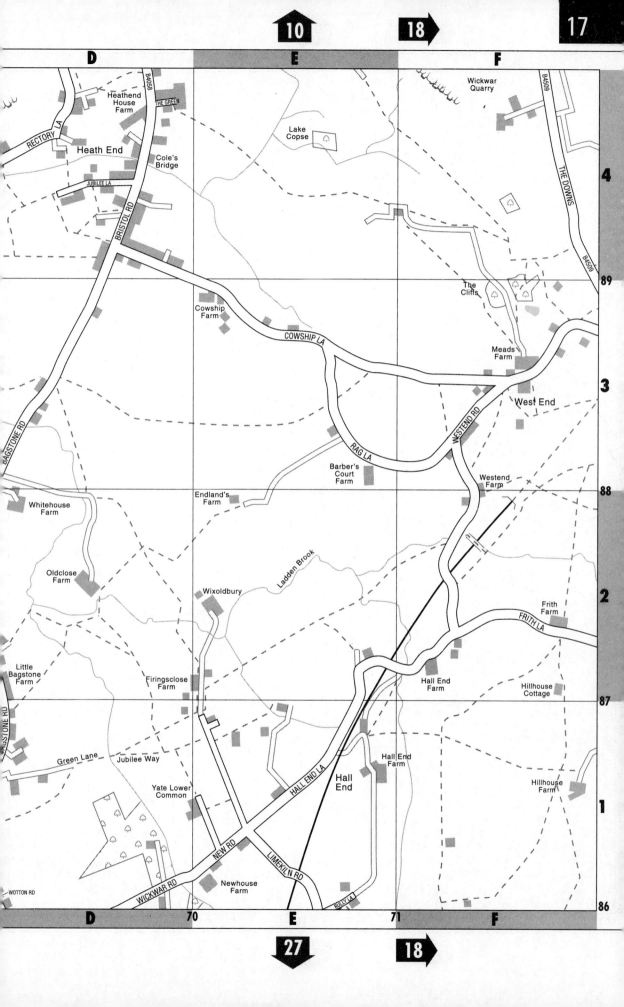

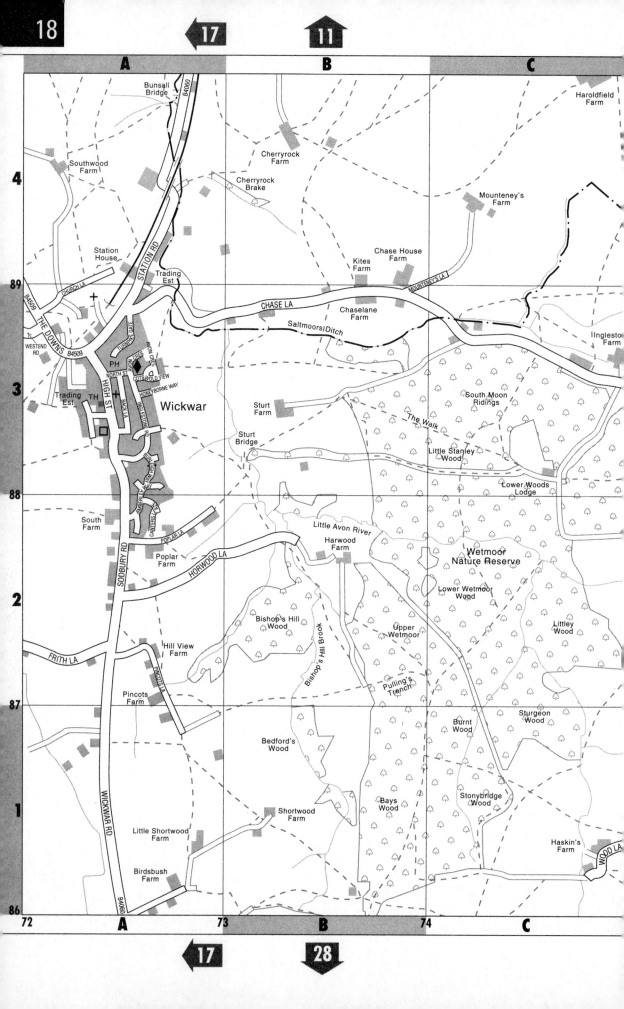

A
B
C

Bunsall Bridge

B4060

Haroldfield Farm

Southwood Farm

Cherryrock Farm

Cherryrock Brake

Mounteney's Farm

Station House

STATION RD

Trading Est

Kites Farm

Chase House Farm

MOUNTENEY'S LA

89

CHURCH LA

CHASE LA

Chaselane Farm

Saltmoors Ditch

Inglesto Farm

THE DOWNS

B4509

WESTEND RD

B4509

TURNPIKE GATE

AVON CRES

GREEN ROW

COTSWOLD VIEW

HONEYBORNE WAY

South Moon Ridings

PH

NORTH ST

HIGH ST

BACK LA

The Walk

3

Trading Est

TH

Wickwar

Sturt Farm

Little Stanley Wood

Sturt Bridge

Lower Woods Lodge

88

ABBEYFIELD WAY

CANTERS LA

South Farm

Poplar LA

Little Avon River

Harwood Farm

Wetmoor Nature Reserve

SODBURY RD

Poplar Farm

HORWOOD LA

Bishop's Hill Wood

Lower Wetmoor Wood

Upper Wetmoor

Littley Wood

2

FRITH LA

Hill View Farm

Bishop's Hill Brook

PINCOTS LA

Pincots Farm

Pulling's Trench

87

Sturgeon Wood

Burnt Wood

Bedford's Wood

WICKWAR RD

Bays Wood

Stonybridge Wood

1

Shortwood Farm

Little Shortwood Farm

Haskin's Farm

WOOD LA

Birdsbush Farm

B4060

86

72
A
73
B
74
C

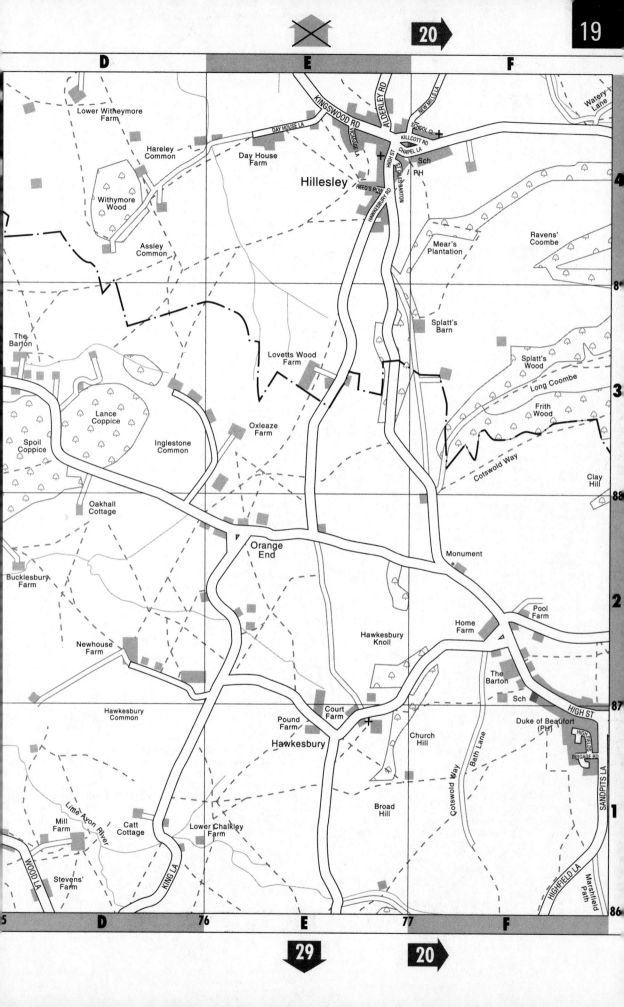

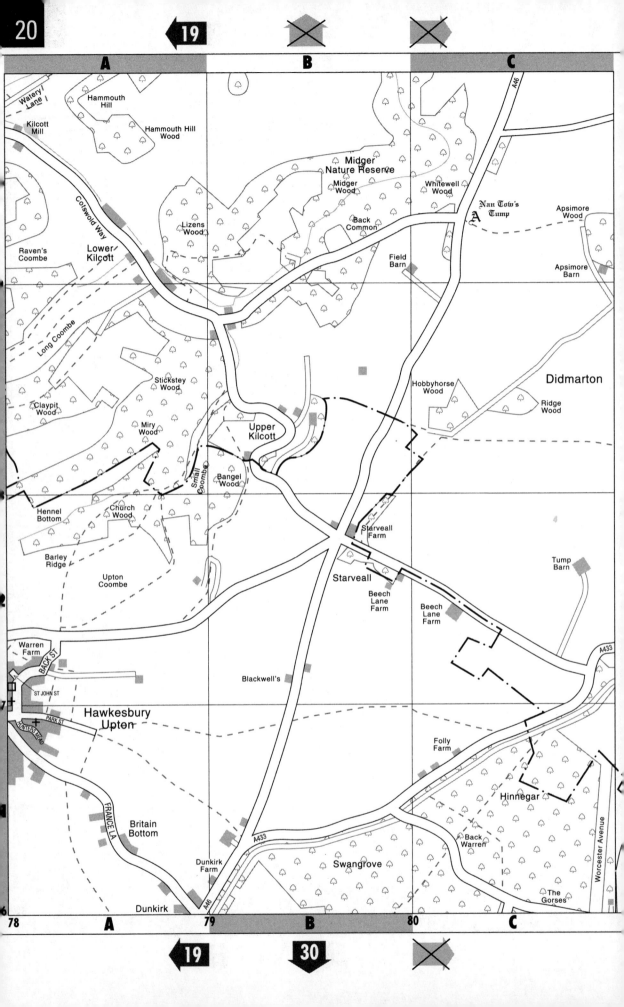

A **B** **C**

Watery Lane

Hammouth Hill

Kilcott Mill

Hammouth Hill Wood

Midger Nature Reserve

Midger Wood

Whitewell Wood

Nan Tow's Tump

Apsimore Wood

Lizens Wood

Back Common

Raven's Coombe

Lower Kilcott

Field Barn

Apsimore Barn

Cotswold Way

Long Coombe

Hobbyhorse Wood

Didmarton

Sticksley Wood

Ridge Wood

Claypit Wood

Miry Wood

Upper Kilcott

Small Coombe

Bangel Wood

Hennel Bottom

Church Wood

Starveall Farm

Barley Ridge

Upton Coombe

Tump Barn

Starveall

Beech Lane Farm

Beech Lane Farm

Warren Farm

BACK ST

ST JOHN ST

Blackwell's

A433

Hawkesbury Upton

PARK ST

HUNTERS MEAD

Folly Farm

Hinnegar

Britain Bottom

FRANCE LA

Worcester Avenue

Dunkirk Farm

A46

A433

Back Warren

Swangrove

The Gorses

Dunkirk

M4

M4

English
Lake

Salmon
Pool

English Stones

The Binn Wall

4

BEACH RD

BEACH
AVE

85

3

A403

84

2

New Pill
Gout

Works

83

Chittening Warth

Red Rhine

Works

SEVERN RD

Tanks

1

A403

Crook's Marsh

82

A B C

4

85

3

84

2

83

1

82

54 A 55 B 56 C

Nursery

Southworthy Farm

Junction 22

PH

Works

REDHAM LA

SHAFT RD

M49

B4064

Redwick

The Pill

NORTHWICK RD

Laurel Farm

A4003

M4

B4055

Salthouse Farm

OSBORNE RD

BEACH RD

BEACH AVE

B4064

GORSE COVER RD

LITTLE GREEN LA

REDWICK RD

WHITEHOUSE RD

WICK RD

CHEESEY PL
KEENS LA
BETTWICK GDNS
THE GLEBE
ENID GASKELL RD

Pilning

St Peter's Farm

East Redham Farm

JACKSON CL

Cross Hands Inn (PH)

B4055 CROSS HANDS RD

WHITBRIDGE CRES

Gumhurn Farm

Torrs Farm

BANK RD

CHURCH RD

Dismantled Railway

PILNING ST

The Plough (PH)

Severn Beach Station

Severn Beach

STRIDE CL
ABBEY RD
ALBERT RD
VICTORIA CRES
Sch
SCHOOL WAY
DENNY ISLE DR
CROSSROCK RD
ABBOTT RD
SEVERNWOOD

ABLETON LA

CHURCH RD

SEVERN RD

Whitehouse Farm

Redwick Common Rhine

Whitehouse Rhine

Ellinghurst Rhine

MARSH COMM

Pilning Station

A4403

Grove Farm

STATION RD

SHAYMOOR LA

Gilslake

Ellinghurst Farm

Marsh Common

Edsleigh Farm

Middle Compton Rhine

Swanmoor Rhine

Creed's Farm

Dyer's Common

Swanmoor Bridge

Avlon Works

Noor Rhine

CENTRAL AVE

ROAD TWO

Severnside Works

Upper Compton Rhine

SPANIORUM VIEW

B4055

THE LANE

Easter Compton

Tower

PROSPECT CL

Compton Farm

FARM LA

Lyde Brook

LC

Brook Farm

ABLETON LA

How Street Rhine

VIMPENNYS LA

Crook's Marsh

M49

BERWICK LA

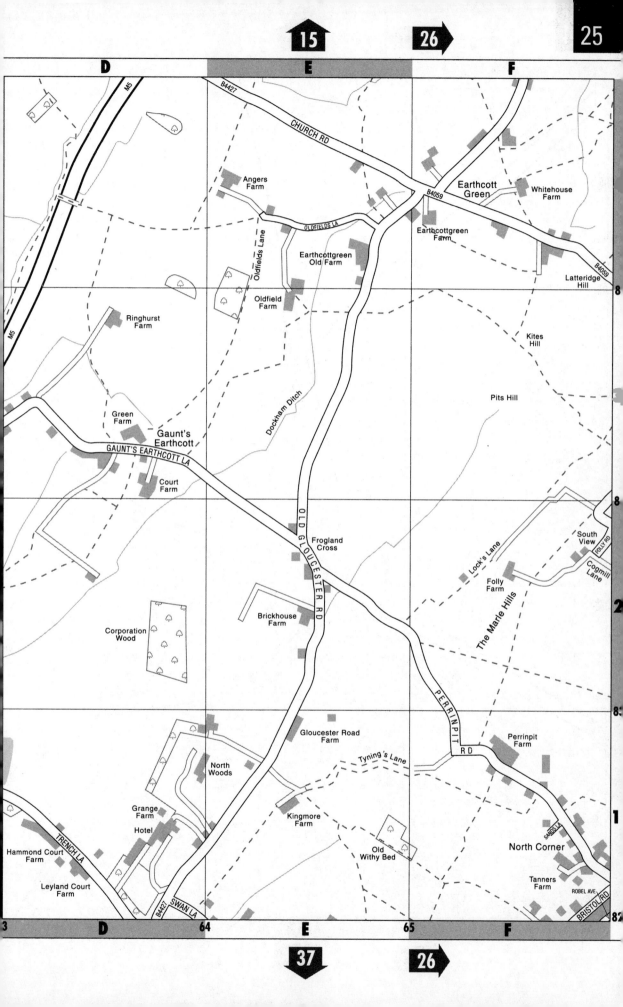

D E F

B4427

CHURCH RD

Angers
Farm

OLDFIELDS LA

Oldfields Lane

Earthcottgreen
Old Farm

Oldfield
Farm

Earthcott
Green

B4059

Earthcottgreen
Farm

Whitehouse
Farm

B4059

Latteridge
Hill

8

Kites
Hill

Ringhurst
Farm

Pits Hill

M5

Dockham Ditch

Green
Farm

Gaunt's
Earthcott

GAUNT'S EARTHCOTT LA

Court
Farm

OLD GLOUCESTER RD

Frogland
Cross

8

South
View

FOLLY RD

Cogmill
Lane

Lock's Lane

Folly
Farm

2

Corporation
Wood

Brickhouse
Farm

The Marle Hills

83

PERRINPIT

Gloucester Road
Farm

RD

Perrinpit
Farm

North
Woods

Tyning's Lane

1

Grange
Farm

Hotel

Kingmore
Farm

Old
Withy Bed

SANDS LA

North Corner

Hammond Court
Farm

TRENCH LA

ROBEL AVE

Tanners
Farm

Leyland Court
Farm

B4427 SWAN LA

BRISTOL RD

82

3 D 64 E 65 F

25
16

A B C

4

Lower Lark's
Farm

El Sub Sta

LARK'S LA

LATTERIDGE LA

Pool
Farm

PATCH ELM LA

Dowells
Farm

B4059

Mudgedown
Farm

85

Latteridge
Hill

NORTHMEAD LA

CHAINGATE LA

Chaingate
House

WOTTON RD

Ladden Bows
Bridge

Latteridge

LC

Two Pools
Farm

3

FOLLY RD

Ladden Brook

Acton
Court

Acton
Lodge

Sheephouse
Farm

84

Hill
House

B4059

B4058

B4059

LC

Iron
Acton

Sch

White Hart
Inn
(PH)

LATTERIDGE RD

PARK ST

Isle of Rhee

WOTTON RD

2

Laddenside
Farm

Elm
Farm

HIGH ST

HOLLY HILL

YATE RD

Cogmill Lane

Rose & Crown
Inn
(PH)

STATION RD

BRISTOL RD

Lavenham
Farm

LC

CHILWOOD CL

ALGARS DR

B405

Ford

River Frome

NIBLEY LA

HOVER'S LA

BRISTOL RD

Brake
Farm

Algars
Manor

Robins
Wood

83

Cog Mill
Farm

Frome Valley Walkway

Hover's Lane

FRAMPTON END RD

Tubb's
Bottom

1

Chestnut
Farm

B4058

PH

CONIFER CL

Frampton
Cotterell

MILL LA

Mayshill

BADMINTON RD

A43

Cemy

ROBEL
AVE

WESTERN AVE

SCHOOL RD

CHURCH RD

A4432

82

66 67 68

A B C

A   B   C

4

Oxwick Farm

B4060

BURY HILL LA

Lattimore Farm

Little Wood

Brinsham Wood

Lady's Wood

The Chase

MAPLERIDGE LA

Horwood Riding Farm

VINNEY LA

Springfield Farm

Horton Bushes

85

Brinsham Farm

Brinsham Bridge

BRINSHAM LA

GRAVEL HILL RD

Home Farm

B4060

Quarry

Quarry

WICKWAR RD

3

Totteroak

84

LOVE LA

Sodbury Common

Star Vale Farm

Totter Farm

CARMARTHEN CL

Jubilee Way

Mead Riding

Golf Qourse

CH

The Windmill

HORTON RD

Newhouse Farm

Little Sodbury End

Winchcom Farm

2

GREENWAYS RD

WILTSHIRE

Quarry (dis)

Stub Riding

Great House Farm

DORSET

WALNUT WAY

83

SOMERSET AVE

Jubilee Way

PORTWAY LA

Harwoodgate Farm

MELROSE CL

BROADWAY

RIDGEWAY

HIGHWAY

Works

Cemy

ST JOHNS WAY

COUZENS CL

Park's Farm

COMMON MEAD LA

1

STATION RD

BOWLING HILL BSNS PK

Mill

BOWLING HILL

Frome Valley Walkway

BARNHILL RD

PC

Chipping Edge Est

HATTERS LA

HORTON RD

ST JOHNS WAY

MANOR WAY

VARGE CL

Frome Valley Walkway

BENNET

STREAMSIDE RD

RIVER RD

MEADOW

THE PARADE

QUARRY RD

MILL LA

ROUNCEVAL ST

HIGH ST Liby

BROAD ST

TH

BROAD ST

BATTEN CT

GRACE CL

FROME RD

BRANDASH RD

WALSHE AVE

WHITEFIELDS

SHERRY RD

WISTARIA AVE

CHESTNUT

CULVERHILL RD

ELM CL

LEMAN CL

Court

Schs

HOUNDS RD

ARNOLD

HORSE ST

MELBOURNE DR

ORLANDS RD

MEAD RD

B4060

HARTLEY CL

NELSON CL

CHIPPING SODBURY

82

72   A   73   B   74   C

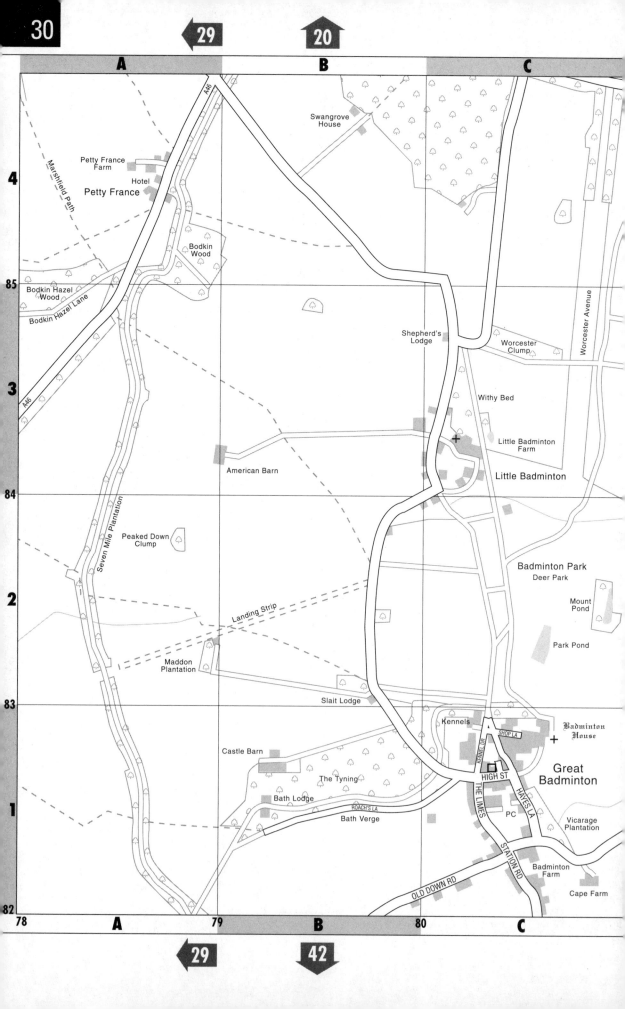

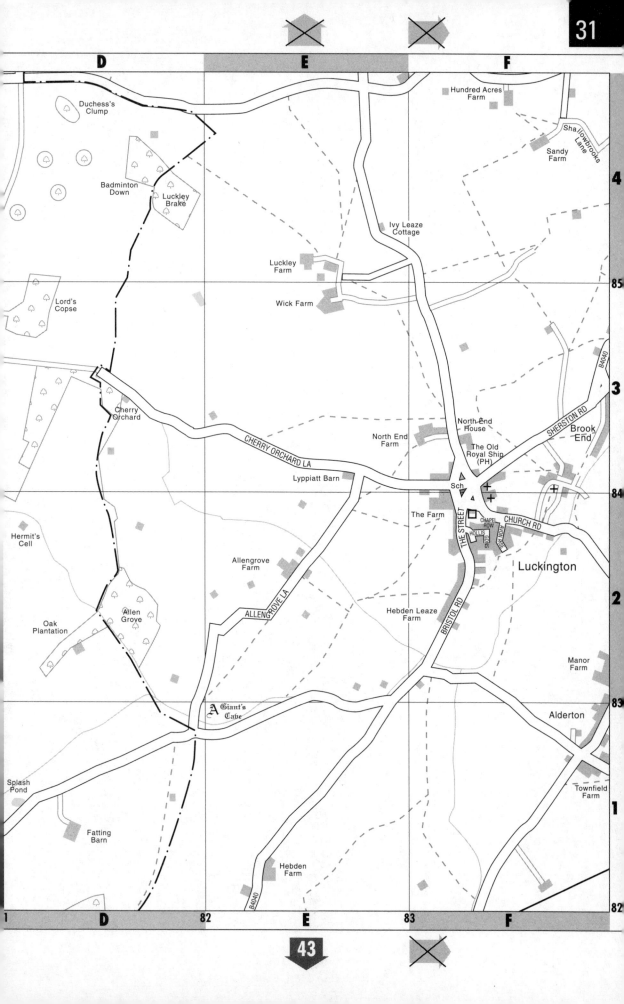

4

81

3

80

2

Jetty
(dis)

Fuel Storage
Depot

79

Piers

Docks

1

King Road

East Pier

River Avon
Swash Channel

Resr

West Pier

SEA BANK RD

RIVER RD

78

33
22

A **B** **C**

M48

Red Rhine

ABLETON LA

MINOR'S LA

Minor's Farm

Works

4

Industrial Estate

Elmington Manor Farm

Spaniorum Farm

Compton Greenfield

BERWICK LA

BOWSTREET LA 1
HOLLYWOOD LA 2

Bisho Farm

Manc Farm

Spaniorum Hill

Hakes Hill Wood

81

SEVERN RD

Stowick Farm

Sampson House

Sampson Farm

Berwick Wood

Berwick Lodge

Camp

3

Hallen Marsh

Hallen Farm

Berwick Farm

Berwick

Berwick Lodge Farm

Norton Farm

THE CLOSE

B4055

A401

CRIBB

Hallen

King William the IVth (PH)

Haw Wood

80

M49

MOORHOUSE LA

Moor House

Wellinghouse Farm

WINDSOR CRES

OAKHILL

Mount Skitham

B4055

2

HALLEN RD

Severn House

NETTLESTONE CL

MEADOWLAND RD

STATION RD

CRANDELL

TORMARTON CRES

LOVERINGE CL

TRATMAN WLK

BICKERTON CL

FITCHE

TREVERDOWE WLK

MARISSAL RD

SILVERHILL

COTRITH GR

DARTALE CL

LANGFIELD CL

DOLMAN CL

MODECOMBE GR

PEVERELL CL

LEWIS CL

VAUGHAN CL

VIMPENY CL

Sch

MARATHON RD

HARMER CL

TRYM CL

WLK

Sch

HENBURY CT

ISON HILL RD 1
SEVERN GRANGE 2
DARLEY CL 3
COUSINS CL 4
GREENSIDE CL 5
GLENEAGLES DR 6

COWLEY

COOMBE CL

INN'S CT DR

WINDMILL

TUBE GR

GREEN DELL WOOD

SCANDRETT CL

HALLEN CL

AVONMOUTH WAY

B4057

BRANDON

DUNDAS CL

BATTERSBY WAY

79

M5

LAWRENCE WESTON RD

Nature Reserve

Sch

Moorgrove Wood

BLAISE HAMLET

WOODGROVE RD

CASTLE CL

Cemy

CHURCH LA

CHURCH RD

PC

Mus

PC

Sch

TRENHOLME CL

HENBURY RD

CROW LA

RICHESON CL

LORAIN WLK

RICHESON WLK

Sch

1

Lawrence Weston

ATWOOD DR

AYLMINTON WLK

Sch

LONG CROSS

GOURNAY CT

KNOWLE CL

BAR GDNS

MANDALE CL

JASMINE GR

CALDICOT CL

NG RD

PRESTON GDNS

GORHAM CL

BERWICK CL

VINCENT CL

DE CLIFFORD RD

STOWICK CRES

LAWRENCE WESTON RD

DEERING CL

HILL CL

Sch

KINGS WESTON RD

P

Hazel Brook

HENBURY GDNS

Henbury

Sch

DURDHAM CL

BLETHWIN CL

ARMIDALE CL

Coll

SALTMARSH DR

PC

TILE HOUSE

BROADLANDS DR

KIRBY RD

COMMONFIELD RD

AWDELETT CL

BENVILLE LANE

LITTLE MEAD

PENDLE

FERNHILL

BEACHLEY WLK

Greenhill Plantation

Nature Reserve

Blaise Castle

Blaise Castle Estate

Coombe Hill

Golf Course

COOMBE WAY

COLLEGE PA

DR

NORTHOVER

B4055

Sch

CHRISTCHURCH

ASTRY CL

BRADELEY

THE BASTION

QUAKERS RD

KINGSWESTON LANE

Off

BROADMEAD

SHORT

REPLE RD

LITTLE MEAD

Limekiln Wood

Goodring Hill

B4057

Sch

CH

WESTOVER RD 1
WESTOVER CL 2
WESTOVER GDNS 3

78

54 A 55 B 56 C

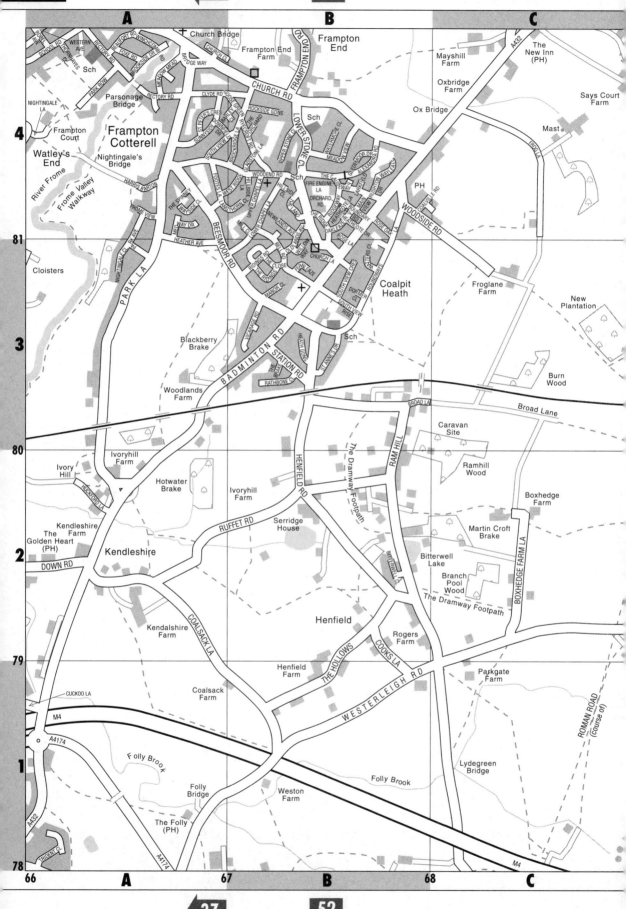

A   B   C

+ Church Bridge
SCHOOL RD   WESTERN AVE   WINCHCOMBE   Frampton End   Frampton End   Mayshill Farm   The New Inn (PH)
BEAUFORT RD   FOXE RD   WOODSIDE DR   Sch   Frampton End Farm
PARK ROW   MEADOW HEAD   BRIDGE WAY   CHURCH CL   Oxbridge Farm   Says Court Farm
Parsonage Bridge   RECTORY RD   CHURCH RD   LOWER STONE CL   A4432
NIGHTINGALE LA   CLYDE RD   ROCKSIDE GDNS   Sch   Ox Bridge   Mast
4   Frampton Court   Frampton Cotterell   SOUTH VIEW   Sch   FRIAR LA   PH
Watley's End   Nightingale's Bridge   UPPER STONE CL   MEADOW   WOODSIDE RD
River Frome   HARRIS BARTON   Woodend Rd   ALEXANDRA   Froglane Farm   New Plantation
Frome Valley Walkway   THE SPINNEY   FOOTES LA   FIRE ENGINE LA   ORCHARD RD
FROME VIEW   WAY DR   NEWLANDS AVE   THE RIDGE   Burn Wood
81   HEATHER AVE   BEESMOOR RD   THE CLOSE   CHURCH LA   Coalpit Heath
Cloisters   PARK LA   RIDINGS RD   SOUTH VIEW CRES   SOUTH VIEW RISE
3   Blackberry Brake   VICARAGE RD   BADMINTON RD   STATION RD   HEATH GDNS   St Anne's Ter   Sch
Woodlands Farm   THE MEWS   RATHBONE CL
BROAD LA   Broad Lane
80   Ivoryhill Farm   HENFIELD RD   The Dramway Footpath   RAM HILL   Caravan Site   Ramhill Wood
Ivory Hill   HUCKFORD LA   Hotwater Brake   Ivoryhill Farm   Boxhedge Farm
Kendleshire Farm   The Golden Heart (PH)   RUFFET RD   Serridge House   Martin Croft Brake   BOXHEDGE FARM LA
2   Kendleshire   COALSACK LA   BITTERWELL LA   Bitterwell Lake   Branch Pool Wood
DOWN RD   Kendalshire Farm   Henfield   Rogers Farm   The Dramway Footpath
79   Coalsack Farm   Henfield Farm   THE HOLLOWS   COOKS LA   Parkgate Farm
CUCKOO LA   WESTERLEIGH RD   ROMAN ROAD (Course of)
M4   Folly Brook   Lydegreen Bridge
A4174   Folly Brook
1   Folly Bridge   Weston Farm
A4432   The Folly (PH)   A4174   M4
TRIDENT CL
78
66   A   67   B   68   C

D E F

Westerleigh Common

WESTERLEIGH RD

Works

Sch

St ANDREW'S

Sch

DURNBURY KENILWORTH

SHACKLETON AVE

P

Kingsgate Park

SCOTT WAY

FINCH RD

BROOKTHORPE

LYDBROOK

ST BRIAVELS DR

HIGHWORTH CRES

TODDINGTON CL

APPLEBY CL

BIRKDALE

ELM WOOD

HOLLAW

SUNNINGDALE

DOVECOTE

Sch

HERON WAY

Sch

KESTREL CL

4

GLENBERRY

LONGFORD

SANDHURST

PRESCOTT

WOODMANCOTE

NORTHS

LANSDOWN

CHATCOMBE

SANDY LODGE

DOVECOTE

DEERHURST

BISLEY

BARNWOOD RD

GLENFALL

HATHERLEY

CHATCOMBE

PITCHCOMBE

HARDWICKE

CRANHAM

CHARLGROVE

P

RODFORD WAY

BREDON

BLAISDON

HARESCOMBE

HARESCOMBE

LITTLEDEAN

RODBOROUGH

WITCOMBE

KERSTON CL

BREDON

BREDON

BLAISDON

WOODCHESTER

Beech Hill

Say's Wood

Elm Farm

Rodford

WESTERLEIGH RD

BROCKWORTH

BROCKWORTH

EDGEWORTH

EDGEWORTH

BADGEWORTH

Sch

Sch

Sch

KINGSCOTE

MAISEMORE

CHEDWORTH

WOODCHESTER

81

Chescombe Farm

ROMAN ROAD (course of)

SHIRE WAY

Pool Farm

Wapley Bushes

Cliff Farm

3

BESOM LA

Grove Farm

Wapley Common

Dodmoor Farm

Dodmoor Farm

Westerleigh

BROAD LA

MILL CRES

NEWMAN CL

PH

THE QUADRANGLE

Wychwell Farm

Church Farm

Wapley

WAPLEY HILL

80

Brice's Farm

Hill House Farm

SHORTHILL RD

Beanwood Farm

Bush's Farm

B4465

2

Bean Wood

Kidney Hill

WESTERLEIGH RD

Westerleigh Hill Farm

79

Westerleigh Hill

Abattoir

Dewshill Wood

Cliff Farm

Burbarrow Lane

1

Gorse Covert

LEIGH LA

Leigh Farm

B4465

78

A   B   C

A432
VIRGINIA
CLIVE LA
DOWNLEAZE DR
BOWLING RD
CULVERHILL RD
KENNEDY WAY
MALLARD CL
WOODMANS
WOODMANS RD
KINGROVE CRES
HORSE ST
HOUNDS RD
WICKHAM
GORLANDS RD
GORLANDS
ST JOHNS WAY
MEAD RD
TWO STONES
WOODMANS VALE
DRAYCOTT
BAUZO
GRASSINGTON DR
GULLIVERS
COTSWOLD RD
Sch
GAUNTS RD
GREEN HAYES
SMARTS GRO
STATION CL
Blanchards Farm
COLTS GREEN
BADMINTON RD
Colt's Green
Frome Valley Walkway
River Frome
ZINCH WAY
HERON WAY
KINGFISHER
ROBIN WAY
LAPUT AVE
PL
Sch
P
Smart's Green
Frome Bridge

4

DODINGTON RD
CLAYPIT HILL
Homestead Farm
Kingrove Farm
KINGROVE LA
Kingrove Common
Lower Kingrove Farm
Fatting House Farm
MILL LA
Bungalow Farm

81

Mouswell Farm
Hamwood Farm
Branchley Farm
DODINGTON LA
Ham Wood
Dodington Manor

3

80

B4465
Lydes Farm
The Grove
The Link

2

Downs Farm
Lean Tom Plantation
Shepherds Close Farm
Long Sands

Codrington
WAPLEY RD
Codrington Arms (PH)
Barleyclose Cottages
Fat Jack Plantation
Sands Court

79

Ostlands Farm
Tyning Farm
Codrington Court

1

Quarry (dis)
Barley Close Farm
River Boyd
Springs Farm

78

72   A   73   B   74   C

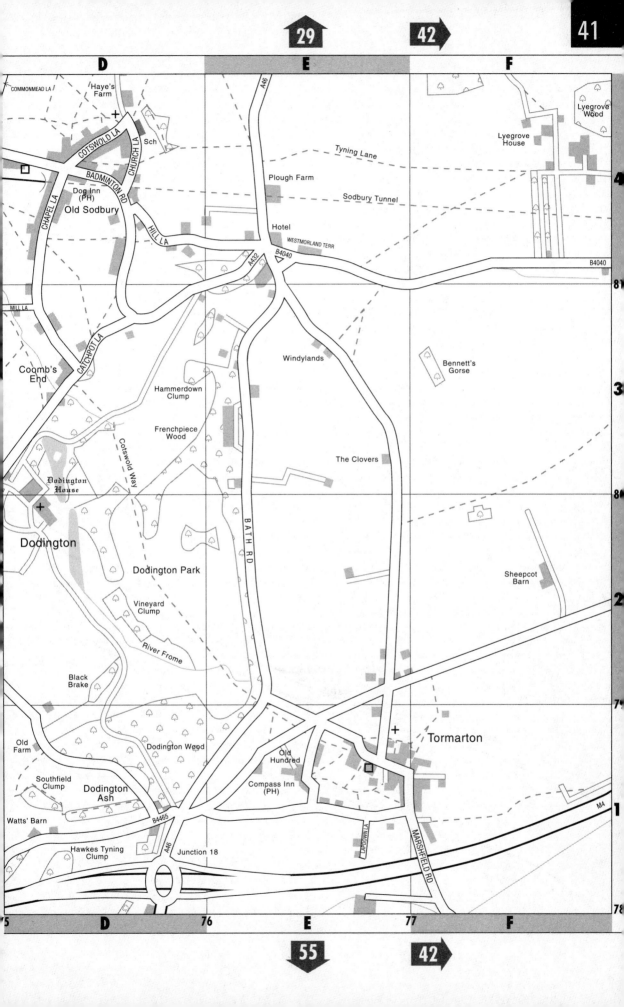

D   E   F

4

Centre Walk
Brake

B4040

Alderton Grove
Farm

Cranhill
Wood

Alderton
Grove

81

HOLLYBUSH CL

Sch

Hollybush
Farm

Goulter's
Gorse

ALDERTON RD

3

Grittleton

Ivy
Leaze

VINER'S LA

Manor
Farm

Littleton
Drew

Withy
Beds

Townsend
Farm

80

Marsh Lane

The Plume of
Feathers
(PH)

New
Town

M4

2

TOLL DOWN WAY

Burton
Farm

Horsedown

The
Gibb

THE MEADS

Burton

NETTLETON RD

PH

EDGECORNER LA

The
Piggeries

Littleworth
Plantation

Goulter's Mill
Farm

Step Hill
Plantation

79

B4039

Sch

By Brook

Fosse
Bridge

Green
Farm

Gatcombe Hill
Plantation

Lugbury

Fosse Way

ROMAN ROAD

Mill

Gatcombe
Hill

A

Priory
Farm

Three Stones
Plantation

Nettleton
Green

Gatcombe
Wood

Hanger
Wood

Elm Tree
Farm

Manor
Farm

Square
Plantation

LONG LEAZE

78

D   82   E   83   F

A B C

4

77

3

Black Nore

SEVERNMEADE
PINE CREST
RIVERLEAZE
HIGHGROVE
NORWOOD GR
GREENWOOD RISE
SEAVIEW
NIGHTBIRD'S WAY

FEDDEN VILLAGE

76

Hang Rock

NORE RD
SOMERSET RD
DEVONSHIRE
HAWTHORN CL
DERBY VIEW
MEADS

BEECHWOOD DR
BEECHWOOD CL
BEECHWOOD RD
ISAR CL
OSRAMS PL
HALLWELL RD
OLIVER'S WAY
HILLCREST RD
MARLON CL
NEWPORT CL
MONMOUTH CL
KINGSTON
BEOWIN CL

Redcliff Bay

LITTLE HALL
NEWHAVEN PL
SEAVIEW RD

Mast

ST AUGUSTINE'S CL
QUEEN'S RD
PANORAMA

DOWN RD

2

HILLSIDE PARK
CLIFF VIEW
NEWHAVEN RD
HILLSIDE RD
PEMBROKE RD
CEDARHURST RD
HILL BAY CL
HOMESTEAD
BRANSCOMBE WAY

Redcliff Bay

REDCLIFFE CL
NORTHFIELD RD
CHESTERFIELD
BADGERS RISE
BROOK END

Nightingale Valley

Caravan Park
Mast PH

HIGHFIELD RD
NIGHTINGALE RISE
BRANSCOMBE WALK

Manor Farm

Charlcombe Bay

Charlcombe Wood

VALLEY RD

75

Weston Down

Black Rock Quarry (dis)

Walton Bay

Black Strip

Weston Lodge

Seven Acre Wood

1

The Ripple

Weston in Gordano

Culver Cliff

Weston Wood

The Conygar

B3124

Pigeon House Bay

Signal Station

Farley

Common Hill Wood

SILVER ST
THE CLOSE
CADBURY HALT
MEADOW DR
WESTON RD

White Hart (PH)

Walton Down

Canon's Wood

B3124

74

42 A 43 B 44 C

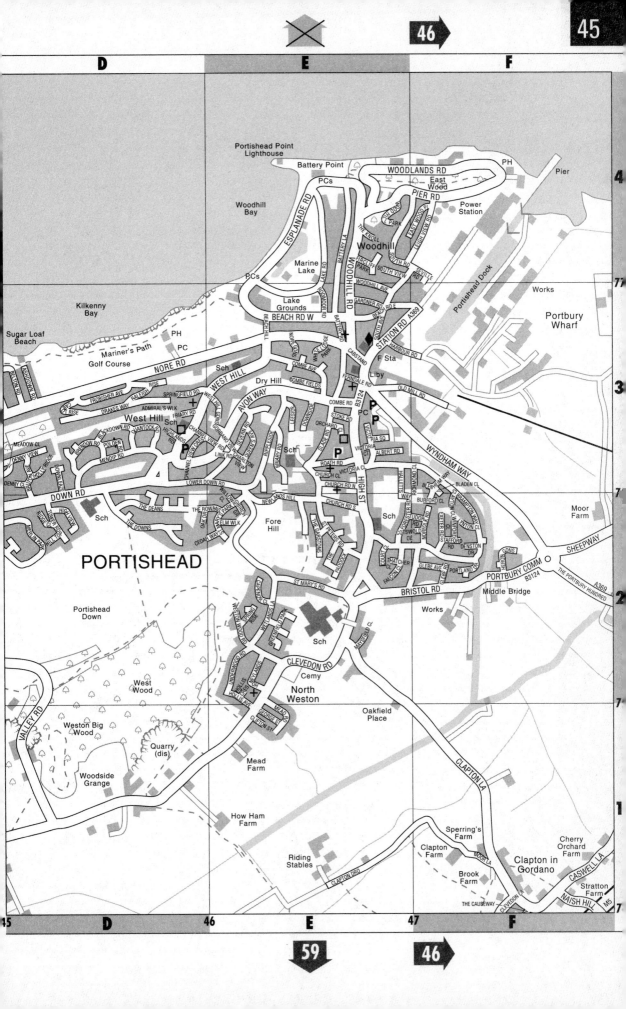

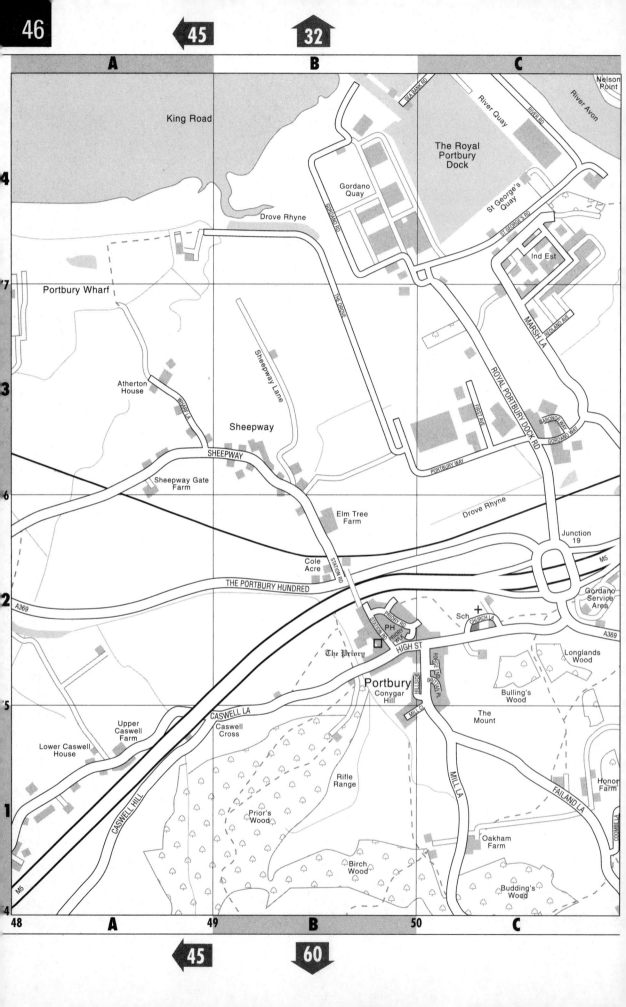

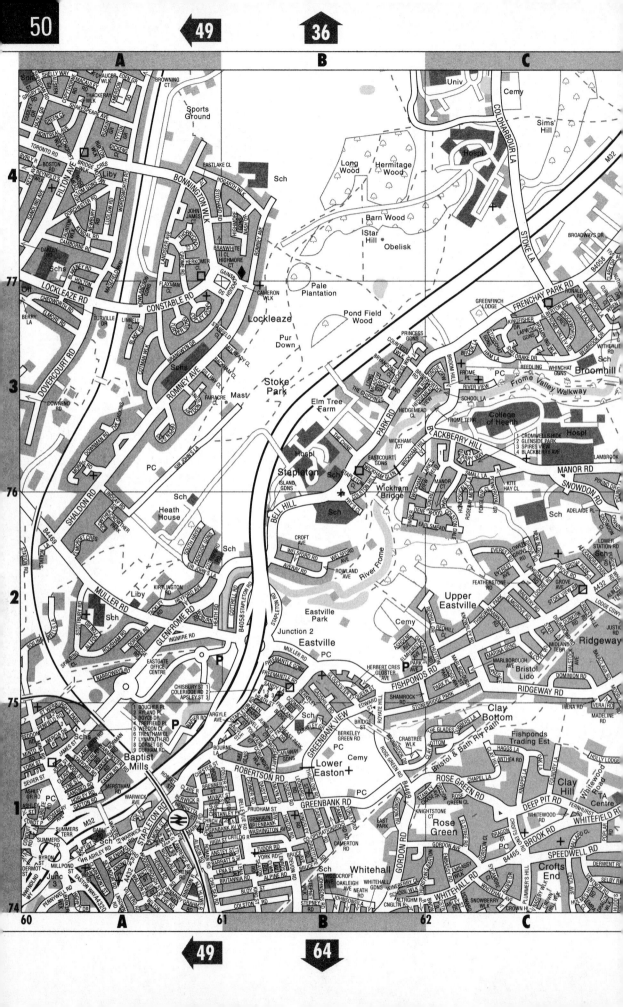

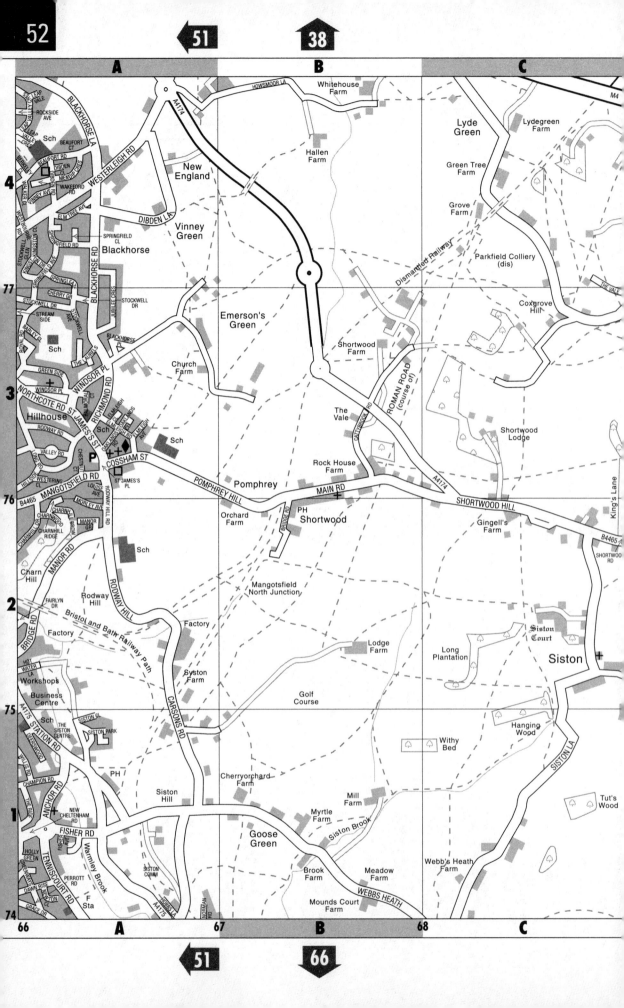

D E F

Park Farm
Ivy Cottage
Parkfield
FIELD RD
THE VALE
PARKFIELD RD
Rose and Crown (PH)
King's Lane
Pucklechurch
WESTERLEIGH RD
B 4465
BATCHFIELD LA
M4
Burbarrow Lane
St Aldam's Ash Farm
Barleyclose Farm
Lower Field Farm
Bridehill Farm
Home Farm
Sch
Cranford Farm
CASTLE RD
EDMUND CT
LANSDOWN RD
HILL VIEW RD
FELTHAM RD
Feltham Farm
Feltham Brook
Marsh Farm
Churchmead Farm
MAPLE WK
HOLLY CR
HAWTHORNE CL
ROSEMARY WAY
BIRCH DR
ORCHARD RD
QUEEN'S RD
WESTERLEIGH RD
DENNISWORTH
SHORTWOOD RD
POPLAR
BECKET CT
ST ALDAM'S DR
HAWKRIDGE
Dennisworth Farm
POLICE STATION HILL
HM Remand Centre
Pucklechurch Trading Estate
OAK TREE AVE
KESTREL DR
MERLIN RIDGE
WOODFINCH CRES
PARTRIDGE RD
GOLDFINCH WAY
EAGLE CRES
HAWTHORNE CL
HODDON LA
COSSHAM RD
SHORTWOOD RD
Back Lane
REDFORD LA
Sewage Works
Redford Lane
ROOKERY LA
Trunkhouse Barn
Telephone Exchange
ABSON RD
Rookery Farm
mrose Wood
Northmead Farm
erscourt Farm
Collin's Farm
Church Farm
Abson
Woodlands Farm
Wilton Farm
LODGE RD
Abson Edith Farm
Bottoms Farm
Wilkes' Farm
Doynton Mill
MILL LA
Boyd Bridge
Cross House Inn (PH)
HIGH ST
Clovermead Farm
CLEEVE LA
Gatherham Farm
HAM LA
River Boyd
Blue Lodge

4
77
3
76
2
75
1
74

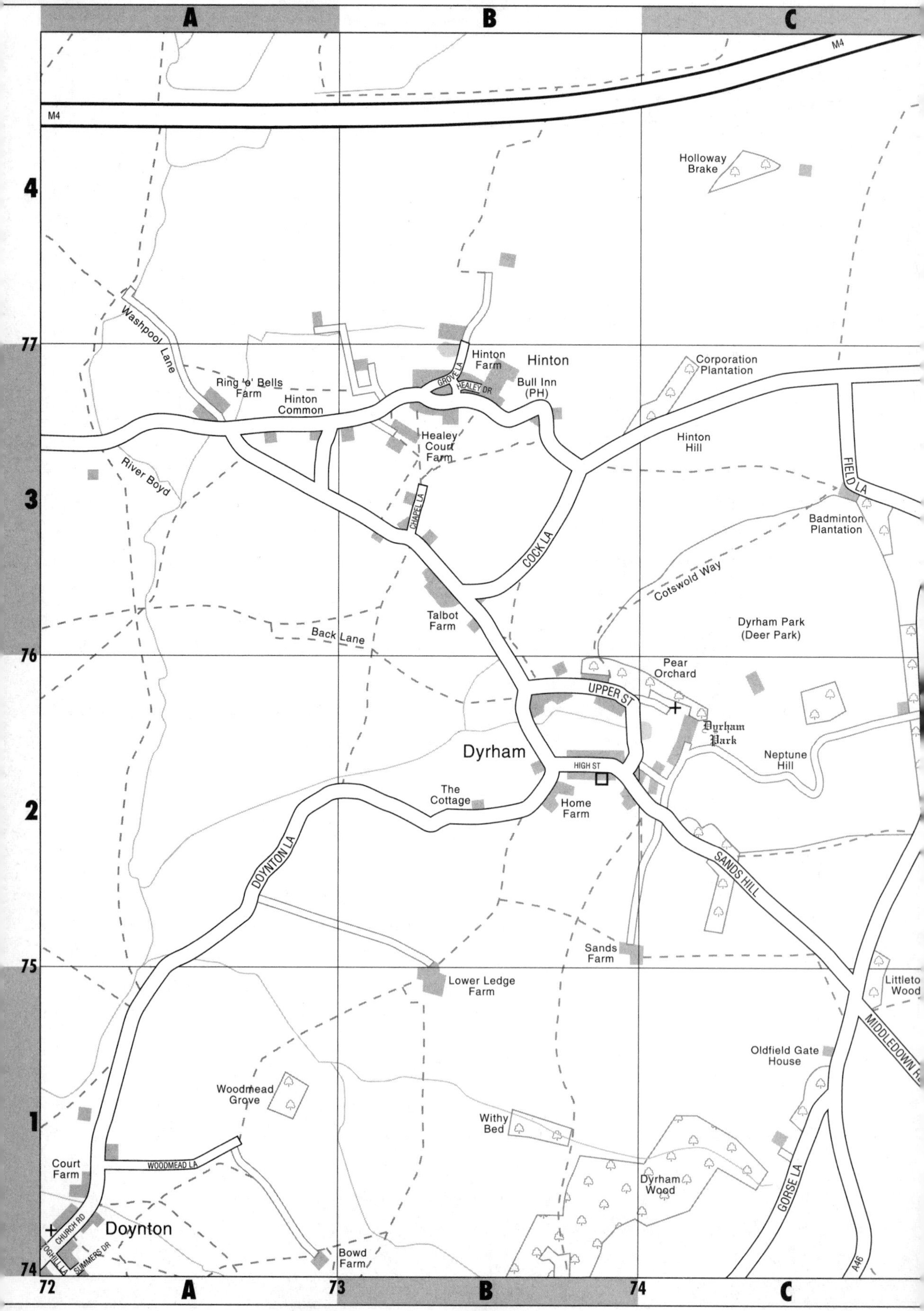

A B C

4

Holloway
Brake

M4

Washpool Lane

77

Hinton
Farm

Hinton

Ring 'o' Bells
Farm

Bull Inn
(PH)

Corporation
Plantation

Hinton
Common

GROVE LA

HEALEY DR

Healey
Court
Farm

Hinton
Hill

FIELD LA

River Boyd

3

CHAPEL LA

COCK LA

Badminton
Plantation

Cotswold Way

Dyrham Park
(Deer Park)

Back Lane

Talbot
Farm

76

Pear
Orchard

UPPER ST

Dyrham
Park

Dyrham

HIGH ST

Neptune
Hill

2

The
Cottage

Home
Farm

DOYNTON LA

SANDS HILL

Sands
Farm

75

Lower Ledge
Farm

Littleto
Wood

MIDDLEDOWN R

Oldfield Gate
House

Woodmead
Grove

1

Withy
Bed

GORSE LA

Court
Farm

WOODMEAD LA

Dyrham
Wood

CHURCH RD

Doynton

ORBILL LA

SUMMERS DR

Bowd
Farm

A46

74

72 A 73 B 74 C

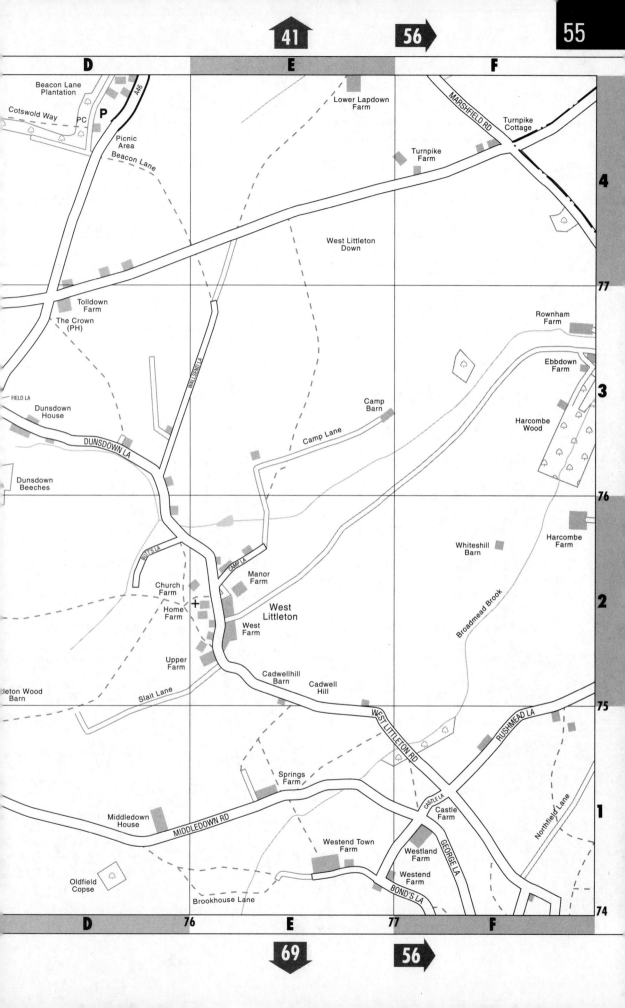

A   B   C

4

NAISH HILL
CASWELL HILL

Bullock's Bottom

Charlton Farm

Sch

The Cleaves

Windmill Hill

MILL LA

Racecourse Farm

73

WHITEHOUSE LA

Moat House Farm

CHARLTON DR

Breach Wood

Old Hill

Quarry (dis)

New Forest

CUCKOO LA

Upgang

White House

Moat Cottages

Higher Farm

Limekiln Cottages

Barn Plantation

The Horse Race

3

B3128

WEST HILL

The Ripple

CLEVEDON RD

PORTBURY LA

Limekiln Plantation

Works

Stoney Steep

The Warren

Court Farm

WRAXALL HILL

Sidelands Cottages

Wraxall Court

The Sidelands

B31

72

TOWER HOUSE LA

West Hill

STONE STEP

HAM LA

Ham Farm

Sch

Rectory

Home Farm

Tyntesfield

TOWER HOUSE LA

Wraxall House

Wraxall

Widdecombe Arms (PH)

Truckle Wood

Tyntesfield Park

2

B3130

Cradle Bridge

THE GROVE

CLEVEDON RD

FRYTH HOUSE 1
NORTHAMPTON HOUSE 2

Hazel Farm

HIGH ST

Land Yeo

St John's House

71

HOLLY CL
THE HAMLET
MAYFLOWER GDNS
BLACKTHORN WAY
BRIAR CL

Elm Farm

Holly Cottage

Lower Lodge

LODGE LA

Tibbington

Orchard Farm

Gable Farm

Vyne's Farm

SPINDLEBERRY GR
BIRCHDENE
SCOTS PINE AVE

1 WINCANTON CL
2 GLASTONBURY CL

Watercress Farm

1

KEMBLE CL

TRENDLEWOOD WAY

Brook Farm

BACKWELL BOW

Watercress Wood

Bathing Pond Wood

CHELVEY RISE
FALMOUTH CL

3 CRICKLADE CT
4 SUNNINGDALE CL
5 GLENEAGLES CL
6 ST ANDREWS CL

BACKWELL COMM

70

48   A   49   B   50   C

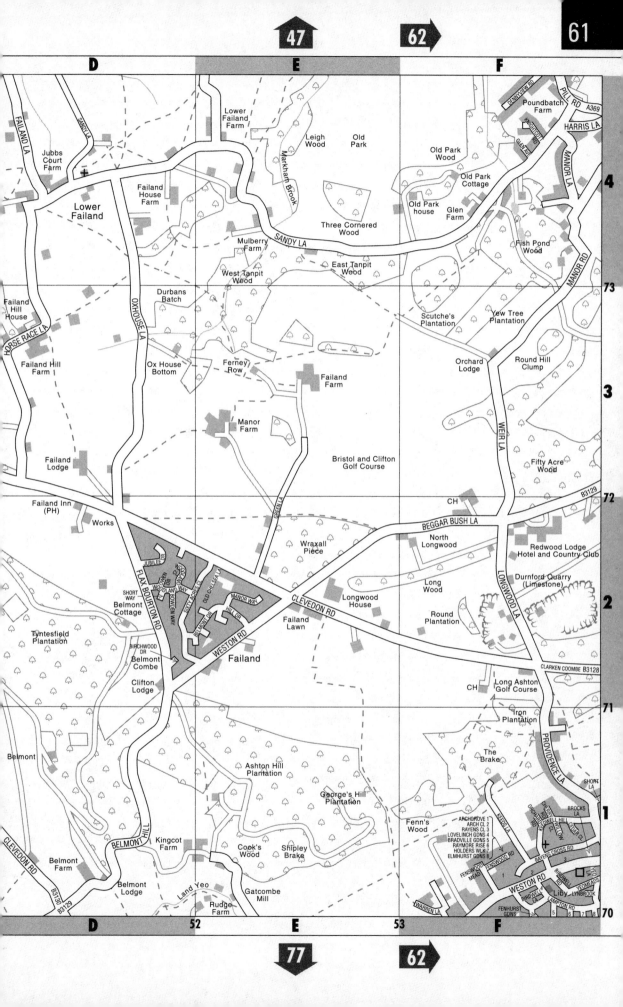

A   B   C

HARRIS LA
PILL RD
CHURCH RD
MANOR RD
PH
Abbots Leigh
THE MANOR CL
A369
Home Farm House
P
4
Leigh Warren
ASHGROVE AVE
HOME FARM RD
Leigh Woods
Avon Gorge Nature Reserve
A
Stokeleigh Camp
Nightingale Valley
New Zig Zag
A4
BRIDGE VALLEY RD
A4176
Coll
PORTWAY
A4176
The Promenade
CLIFTON DOWN
Jack's Hole
Observatory
CLIFTON DOWN RD
CLIFTON CL
NORLAND RD
CAMP RD
GLOUCESTER ST 1
CARTER'S BLDGS 2
JAMES PL 3
WESTFIELD PL 4
WATERLOO ST 5
CECIL RD
WEST MALL

Warren House Plantation
73
ABBOTS LEIGH RD
VALLEY RD
B3129
Leighwoods House
NORTH RD
BROAD OAKS
CHURCH RD
VICARAGE RD
BANNERLEIGH RD
BRIDGE RD
CYPRESS GDNS
Burgh Walls
Suspension Bridge
Toll
CALEDONIA MEWS
BANNERLEIGH LA
River Avon
HOTWELL RD
PRINCESS VICTORIA ST
CALEDONIA PL
ROYAL YORK CRE
YORK PL
OXFORD

Upper Farm
Quarry Plantation
Kingcott Farm
BEGGARS BUSH LA
3
Golf Course
CH
Leighwoods
ST MARY'S RD
B3129
FOYE HOUSE
BURWALLS RD
ROWNHAM HILL
Rownham Plantation
Rownham House
VICTORIA TERR 1
WINDSOR CT 2
CUMBERLAND PL 3
ALBERMARLE ROW 4
SOUTH GREEN ST 5
NORTH GREEN ST 6
DOWRY SQ 7
POLYGON RD 8
CORNWALLIS AVE 9
BRISTOL GATE 10
HUMPHRY DAVY WAY 11
LITTLE CAROLINE PL 12
OLDFIELD PL 13
GRENVILLE PL 14
ASHMEAD WAY 15
CUMBERLAND RD 16
BRUNSWICK PL 17
PC
WINDSOR TR
HINTON
FREELAND PL
CABOT WAY
BENNETT
CUMBERLAND BASIN

72
Summerhouse Plantation
Ashton Court Estate
Deer Park
Ashton Court
Bower Ashton
Coll
KENNEL LODGE RD
CLANAGE RD
A369
P
BRUNEL LOCK RD
MCADAM WAY
CLIFT HOUSE RD
CLIFT HOUSE
LINDERPASS
BRUNEL WAY
A30
MARSH RD

B3129
2
PILL GROVE
CLARKEN COOMBE
Lodge
Church Wood
Lodge
The Smyth Arms (PH)
B3128 ASHTON RD
A370
PARKLANDS RD
COURT LANDS LA
Sch
ROWNHAM WAY
BLACKMOORS LA
WINTERSTOKE UNDERPASS
Sch
A3029
WINTERSTOKE RD
LC
Cala Trading Estate
Ashton Gate Trading Estate

71
Goombe Plantation
Golf Course
Ashton Hill
FOLLY RD
CHESTNUT RD
RIDGEWAY RD
HEATH RIDGE
KEMPE'S CL
WESTWARD
GIBBS LA
COLLEGE RD
The Folly
HOBWELL LA
BEECHFIELD GR
CHURCH LA
Vic
Parsonage Farm
LONG ASHTON RD
GLEBE RD
PARSONAGE RD
HILLSIDE RD
Colliter's Brook
BROOK GATE
Ashton Vale
ST BURY RD
AVEBURY RD
Sch
ASHTON DR
SWISS RD
DALE RD
TREVANNA RD
TREGARTH RD
SOUTH LIBERTY LA

1
SHORT LA
WESTON RD
YEOMEADS
ESTUNE WK
PROVIDENCE LA
GIBBS CL
NORTH
WOOLLARD
BOURTON MEAD
WELL CL
KNEES CROFT
WEYDON WAY
RIVERCROFT RISE
BROOK CL
GARDENERS WK
Long Ashton
YANLEY LA
Ashton Brook
ANGLEY CRES

70
LAMPTON RD
Bridge Farm

54   55   56
A   B   C

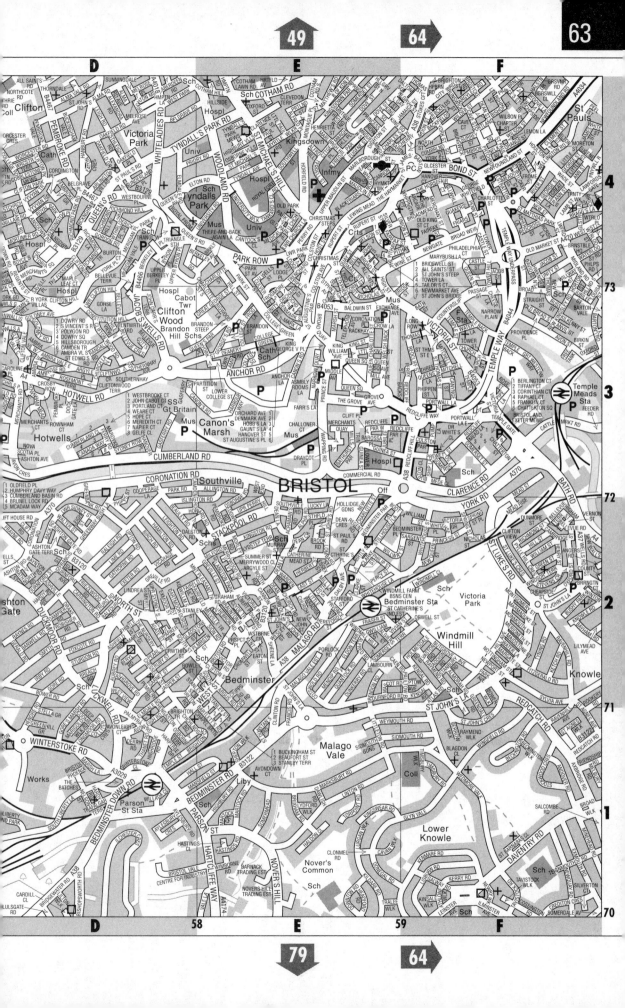

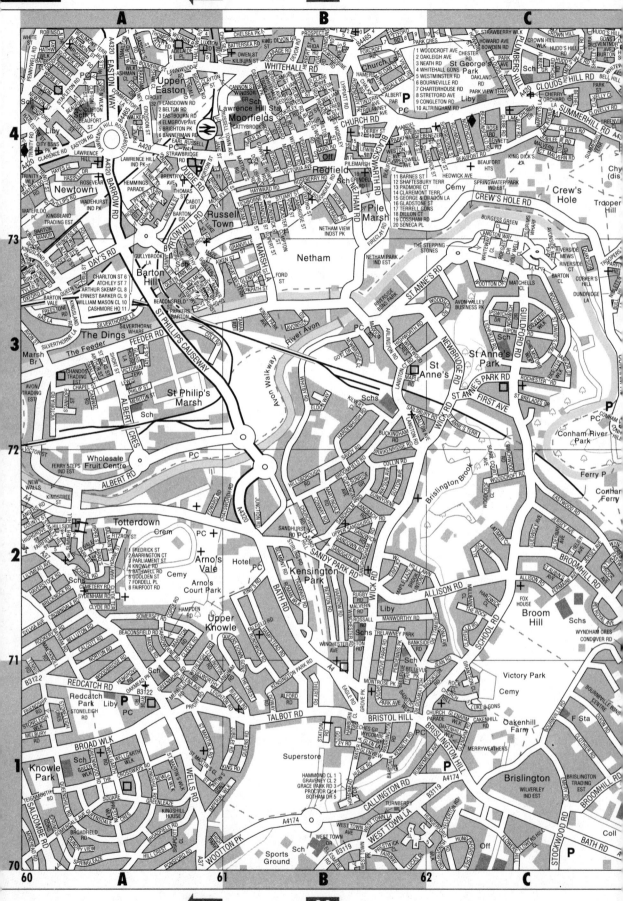

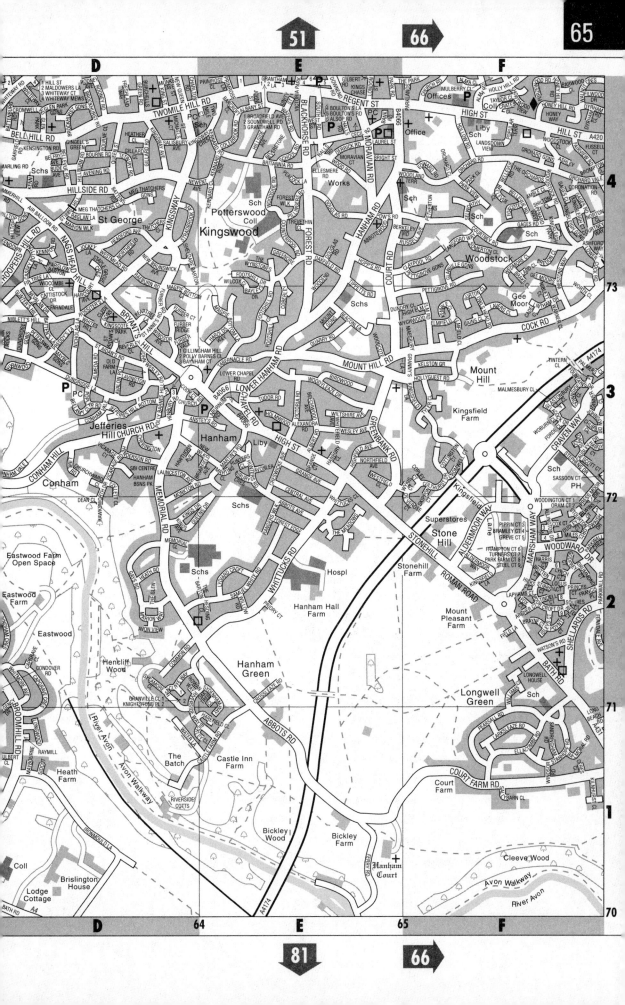

A · B · C

4

Webb's
Heath

Warmley

Bridge
Farm

Oaklodge
Farm

Chavenage
Lynton

Sch

HILL ST A420

DEANERY RD

Playing
Field

White Hart
(PH)

Chesley Hill
Farm

Chesley Hill

Bridgeyate
Common

Springfield
Farm

Chapel

HIGH ST

P

Industrial
Estate

London Rd

PH

Bridgeyate

Grimsbury
Farm

73

Warmley
Tower

Ullswater
Cl

Haweswater

Coniston

Highfield
Farm

Homeapple Hill

Riding Barn

Highfield Lodge
Farm

TOWER LA

Poplar Rd

North
Common

Cann La

Cann
Farm

3

CRAVEN WAY

CADBURY HEATH RD

The Batch

Mill La

Chargrove
Highcroft

Sch

Poplar

Samuel
Wright

Southway Dr

Cann
Brake

Cann
Brake

Cadbury
Heath

Playing
Field

Abbatoir

72

Golf
Course

Siston Brook

Hill View

Schs

Harver's
Lye

West Court
Farm

Oldland

North St

High St

Redfield
Farm

2

California Rd

Court Rd

Oldland
Common

Redfield
Hill

Redfield Hill

Beach Hill

Willsbridge

Long Beach

Cherrygarden
Hill

Cullyhall
Farm

Upper Oullyhall
Farm

Park
Farm

Redfield Lodge
Farm

The
Old Mill

Newpit La

71

Nursery

River Boyd

Golden Valley La

Golden Valley

WILLSBRIDGE HILL

Mill

PH

Kimber
Coombe

Boyd
Farm

Mill La

1

KEYNSHAM RD

BATH RD

A4175 CHERRY GARDEN RD

The
Lons

Hill
Farm

Bitton
Hill

Little
Normeads

70

66 · A · 67 · B · 68 · C

A   B   C

4

Rectory Farm

Beech Farm

WATERY LA

TOGHILL LA

Babwell Farm

Toghill Lane

Woodlands Farm

Shrubbery Farm

Oldfield Farm Cottages

Cotswold Way

GORSE LA

Swan Inn (PH)

Sandy Tyning

Pennsylvania

The White H (PH)

The Folly

73

Highways

Picnic Site

Cold Ashto

The Lynch

3

Tel Ex

A420

Toghill House Farm

Toghill Barn Farm

Tog Hill

Cotswold Way

GREENWAY LA

Shapland's Farm

SLOUGH LA

Toghill Farm

Uplands

St John's Wood

FREEZINGHILL LA

72

Tracy Cottage Farm

Hamswell Farm

Hill Farm

2

Freezing Hill

Hamswell House

Nimlet

Henley Tyni Farm

Vine Cottage

Lower Hamswell

Nimlet Hill

LEIGH LA

Parkfield Farm

HALL LA

Lilliput Farm

71

Hall Lane

HALL LA

Rushmead Wood

Torney's Court Farm

TADWICK LA

GLOUCESTER RD

Noade's Leaze

Manor Farm

The Battlefields

Sir Beyil Granville's Monument

Goudie's Farm

Tadwick

⚔ 1643

Cotswold Way

Manor Farm

1

70

72   A   73   B   74   C

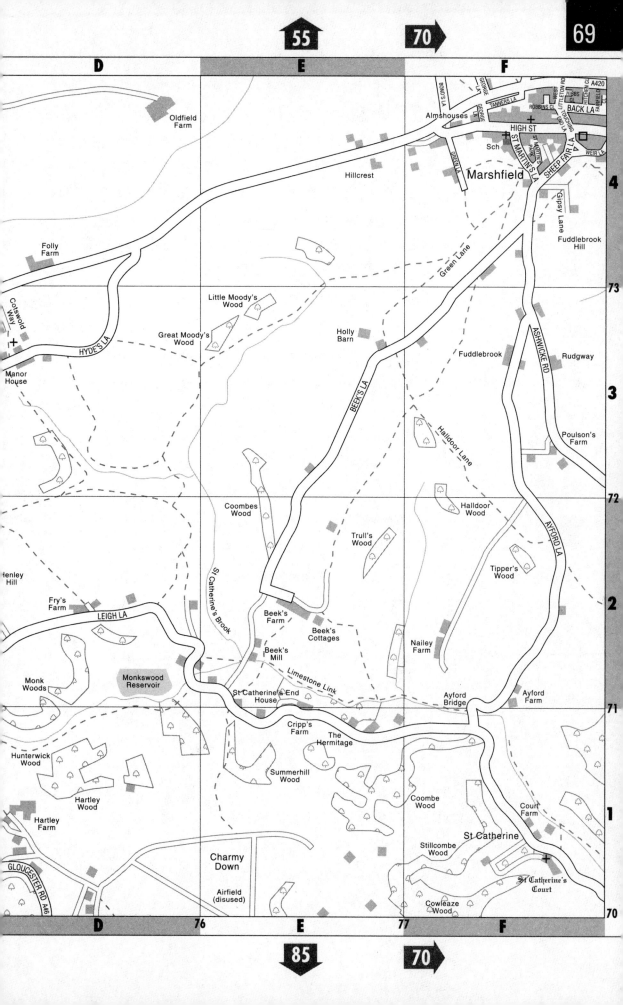

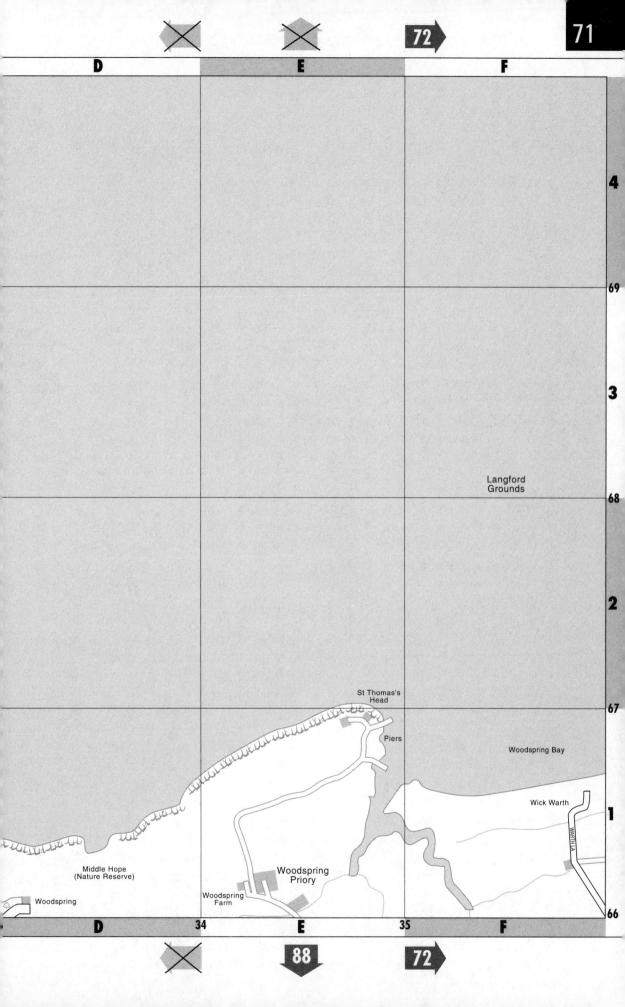

4

69

3

Langford
Grounds

68

2

St Thomas's
Head

67

Piers

Woodspring Bay

Wick Warth

1

WARTH LA

Middle Hope
(Nature Reserve)

Woodspring
Priory

Woodspring

Woodspring
Farm

66

4

69

3

68

2

67

1

66

Clevedon Farm

Carice Gdns

M5

Whitehouse Farm

DAVIS LA

Portbury House

Colehouse Bridge

Drum and Monkey (PH)

Kenn

KENN RD

Kenn St

Stonehouse Farm

Kenn Court Farm

Kenn Est

Thirteen Acre Rhyne

COLEHOUSE LA

Mast

Wireless Transmission Station

STRODE RD

Blind Yeo

Dowlais Farm

Dorsal Farm

LOWER STRODE RD

Lower Farm

Southfield Farm

Colehouse Farm

River Kern

NEW CUT BOW

Poplar Farm

Riverside Farm

Sewage Treatment Works

BACK LA

Pear Tree Farm

Bullock Farm

BULLOCKS LA

Hope Farm

Ham Farm

HAM LA

The Bridge Inn (PH)

NORTH END RD

Smith's Forge Industrial Estate

B3133

Middle Lane Farm

MIDDLE LA

Laurel Farm

Rookery Farm

Kingston Seymour

LAMPLEY RD

Lampley Bow

Lampley Rhyne

Little River

Horsecastle Farm

Britton's Farm

HAM LA

Hope Farm

YEW TREE LA

Moorside Farm

Yewtree Farm

M5

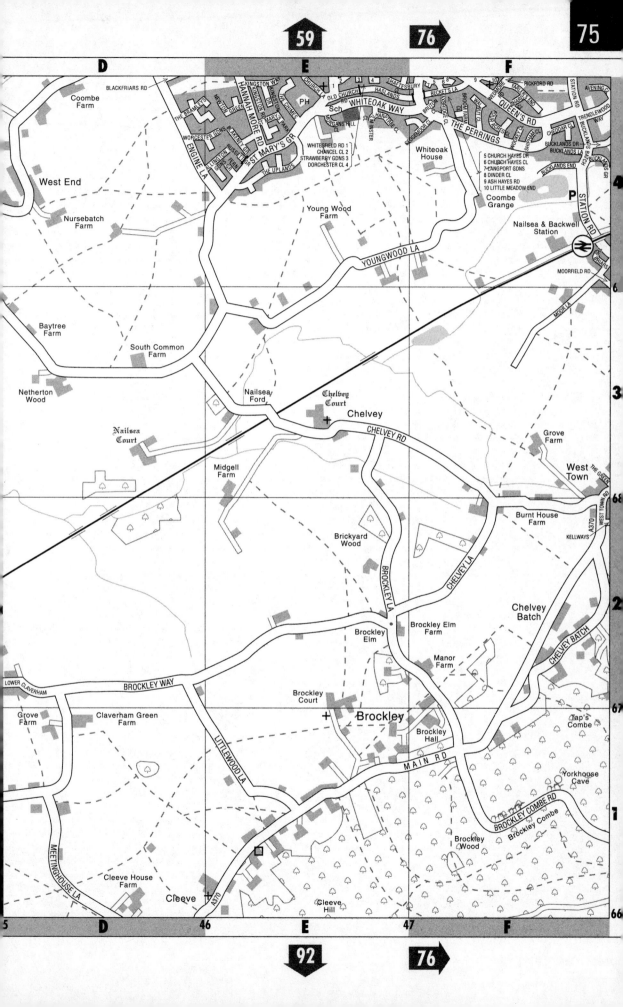

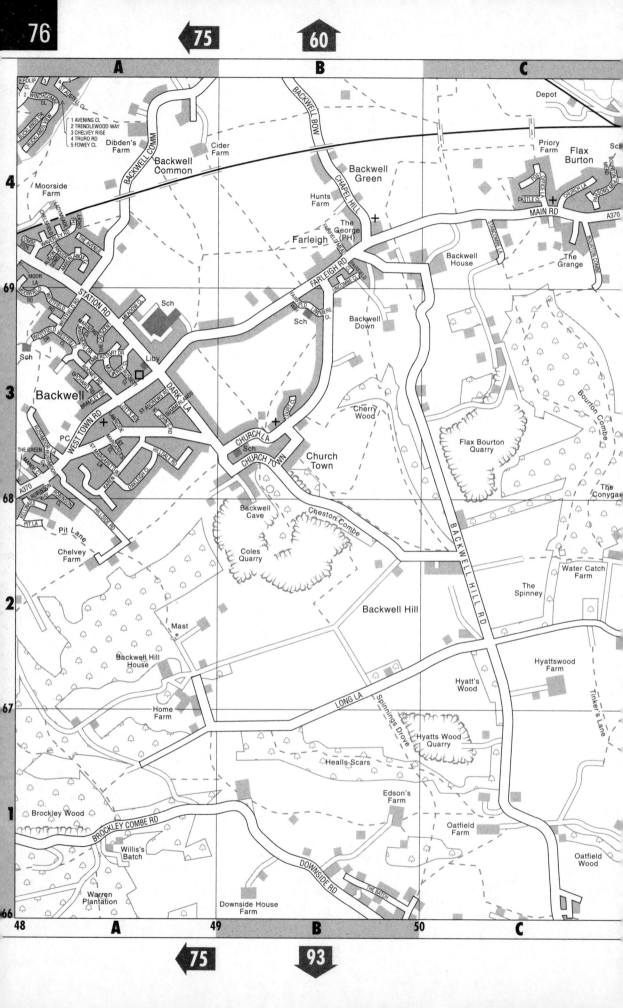

D E F

WARREN LA

Gatcombe Court
Ashton Watering
WESTON RD

CLEVEDON RD

Long Ashton Research Station

PAULTON FENSHURST GDNS
GDNS
BRADVILLE GDNS
RAYMORE RISE 2
HOLDERS WLK 3
ELMHURST GDNS 4

FARLEIGH HOSPITAL COTTS
FARLEIGH HOSPITAL COTTS

OLD WESTON RD
REDWOOD LA

Cambridge Batch

Hospl

4

A370

STATION RD
ORCHARD CL

B3129
Sch

MAIN RD
Jubilee Inn
Eastfield

B3130

REDWOOD LA
Redwood Farm

WILDCOUNTRY LA

69

Breach Hill Wood

VICARAGE LA
Hillside
The Vicarage
Barrow Mill

Crossgrove Wood

The Fillies

Hospl

Barrow Wood

BARROW COURT LA

Farleigh Hill

School Farm

Church Wood

3

Barrow Court
The Triangle

Home Farm

BARROW ST

Barrow Gurney

Water Works

HERN LA
Steps Farm

68

Park Cottages

Dead Hill Wood
SCHOOL LA

PH
BARNS CL

Water Catch

SLADE LA
Slade Wood

Batches Wood

HOBBS LA

B3130

A38

Stevens' Farm

Reservoirs

2

Barrow Hill

Hill Farm

Stevens' Wood

Mon

NAISH LA

67

Freeman's Farm

BRIDGWATER RD

Dial Farm

PH
Hall

Glenville House Farm

ELWELL BROOK

FREEMANS LA

BARROW LA

1

Yewtree Farm

DIAL LA

ROCKS LA

Quarry (dis)
Hartcliff Rocks

B3130

ELWELL LA

Waggon & Horses (PH)

NEWDITCH LA

Potters Hill

A38
CURRELLS LA

66

D 52 E 53 F

HOLLIS CL
FENSHURST GDNS
Sch

A370

Yanley Farm

Yanley

Resr

Hanging Hill Wood

Yewtree Farm

Crem

Mast Cemy Elm Farm

A38

BACKWELL WLK 1
FELTON GR 2
WRAXALL GR 3

4

Hospl

YANLEY LA

Ridings Wood

Hospl

The Wild Country

Barrow Big Wood

Castle Farm

Motel

Highridge Farm

KING'S HEAD LA

ROSE MEARE GDNS

PC's

Highridge

69

3

Colliter's Brook Farm

BRIDGWATER RD

PC

Highridge Common

Barrow Common

Colliter's Brook

Winford Arms (PH)

Resr

The Peart

Highridge RD

68

A38

Valley View Farm

The Peart

Greenditch Farm

Highridge

Highridge Farm

Four Acres

Sch

2

DUNDRY LA

Lower Grove Farm

Strawberry Lane

QUEEN'S RD

ROMAN ROAD

Grove Farm

Mast

Sch

HILL RD
BEECHCROFT

OXLEAZE LA

BROADOAK HILL

67

Castle Farm

Dundry Down

Mast

DOWNS RD

Dundry

THE MEAD
ANDRUSS

CHURCH RD

Dundry Inn (PH)

WEST DUNDRY LA

EAST DUNDRY LA

Maiden Head

1

ELWELL LA

CASTLE FARM LA

CRABTREE LA

WINFORD LA

Elwell Farm

CRABTREE CL

LITTLETON LA

WELLS RD

PH

UPTON LA

Watercress Farm

Mast

Upton Farm

66

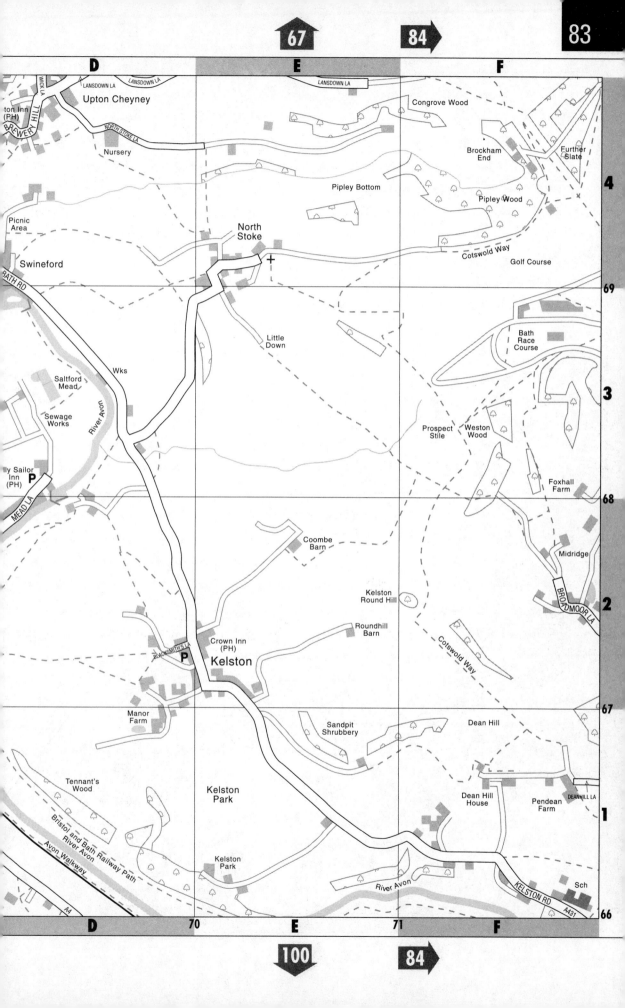

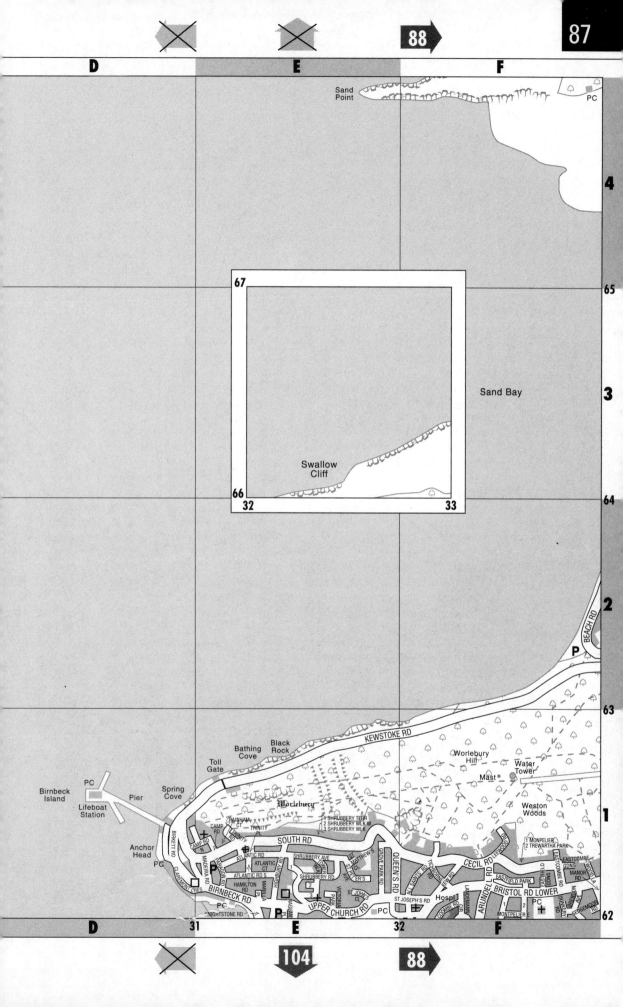

A B C

MEETINGHOUSE LA

BISHOPS RD
BISHOPS MEAD
BRATNEY CL
CLEEVE DR
WOODVIEW
MILLER RD
W WARNER CL
MAIN RD
Lord Nelson (PH)
CHAPEL LA
FALUNDER ST
P

Cleeve Combe
Cleeve Court
Walnut Tree Farm
Cleeve Toot

Saw Mill

Wrington Warren

Warren House

RHODYATE LA
RHODYATE HILL
A3370

Bickley

CLEEVE HILL RD

Goblin Combe

65

King's Wood

Nature Reserve

Woolmere

Wrington Hill

Wrington Hill Farm

3

Corporation Woods

Urchin Wood

Ball Wood

Oatlands

WRINGTON HILL

The Island

Bracken Hill

The Grove

64

Montreux Farm

Bullhouse Lane

Yeowood

Udley

Uplands

Simshill Wood

Littler Plantation

Prestow Wood

2

WRINGTON RD

WEST HAY RD

Iwood

West Hay

Piercahay

ROPER'S LA

Branches Cross

Barley Wood

Barle Far

Iwood Farm

IWOOD LA

Iwood Manor

CHAPEL HILL
YEOMANS CL
HIGH ST
Maines Batch
HOME CL
ORCHARD CL
Sch
OLD HILL
LONG LA

63

Two Rivers Way

ALBURYS
Plough Inn (PH)
SCHOOL RD
BELL WLK

Congresbury Yeo

LADYWELL
THE TRIANGLE
BROAD ST
PC
Court House
LAWRENCE RD
SOUTH MEADOWS
F Sta
CHURCH WLK
HANNAH MORE CL
RICKYARD RD

BAKER'S BLDGS 1
THE COTTS 2
STATION RD
MEMORIAL RD
SILVER ST
Wrington

Dismantled Railway

WILTONS CL
BROOKLYN
WESTWARD CL
THE GLEBE
KINGS RD
OLD STATION CL
GARSTONS ORCH
GARSTONS
GARSTONS CL

1

Stoneycroft House

Butt's Batch

BUTT'S BATCH

Burnett Ind Est

COX'S GN

Cox's Green

MILL LA

STOCK LA
B3133

Beam Bridge

HALF YD

HAVYAT RD

Oakdene Farm

NATES LA

62

D E F

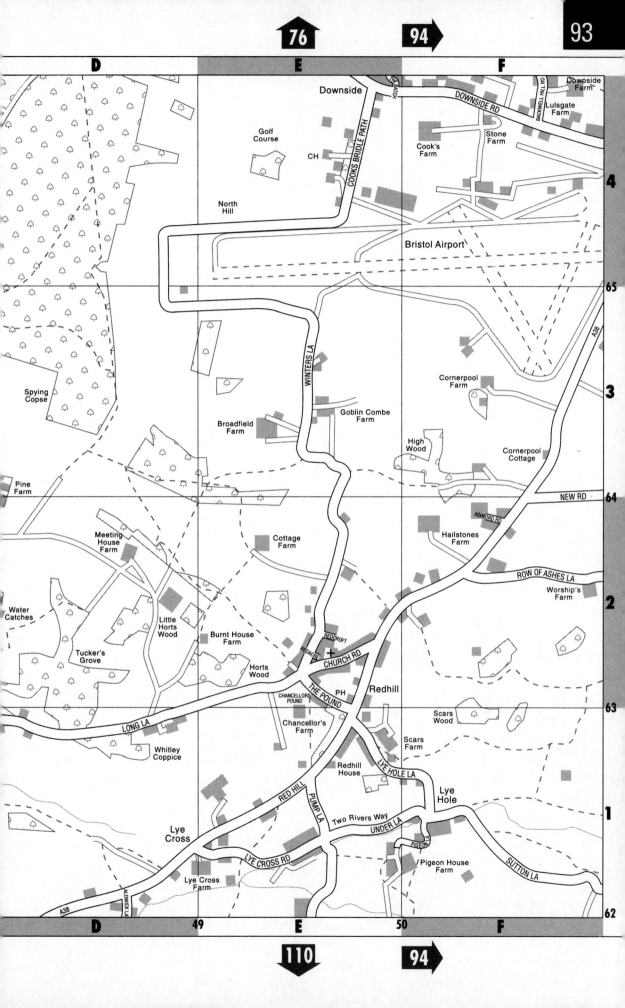

Downside

Downside Farm
Lulsgate Farm

DOWNSIDE RD

Golf Course

CH

Cook's Farm

Stone Farm

COOKS BRIDLE PATH

North Hill

4

Bristol Airport

65

WINTERS LA

Spying Copse

Cornerpool Farm

3

Broadfield Farm

Goblin Combe Farm

High Wood

Cornerpool Cottage

Pine Farm

NEW RD

64

Meeting House Farm

Cottage Farm

Hailstones Farm

ASHFORD RD

Water Catches

Little Horts Wood

Burnt House Farm

ROW OF ASHES LA

Worship's Farm

2

Tucker's Grove

Horts Wood

REDCROFT

REDACRE

CHURCH RD

Redhill

PH

THE POUND

Scars Wood

63

Long La

CHANCELLORS POUND

Chancellor's Farm

Scars Farm

Whitley Coppice

Redhill House

LYE HOLE LA

Lye Hole

RED HILL

PUMP LA

Two Rivers Way

UNDER LA

1

Lye Cross

PIGEON

SUTTON LA

LYE CROSS RD

Pigeon House Farm

A38

Lye Cross Farm

ALDWICK LA

62

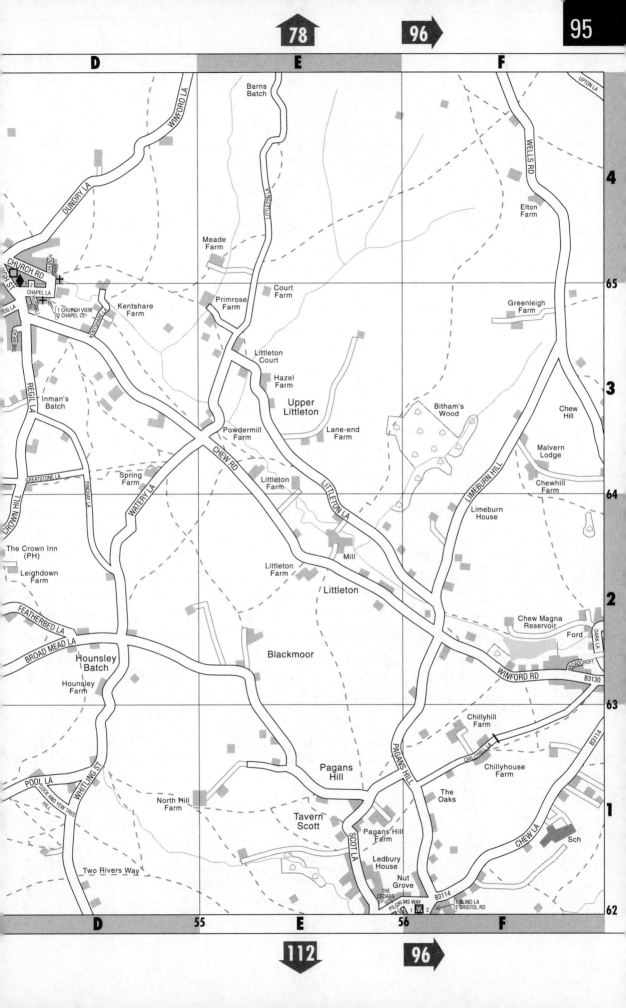

D E F

UPTON LA

WINFORD LA

DUNDRY LA

Barns Batch

LITTLETON LA

WELLS RD

4

Elton Farm

Meade Farm

CHURCH RD

CHURCH RD

CHAPEL LA

1 CHURCH VIEW
2 CHAPEL CL

Kentshare Farm

Primrose Farm

Court Farm

65

Greenleigh Farm

THE MEAD

REGIL LA

Inman's Batch

Littleton Court

Hazel Farm

Upper Littleton

Chew Hill

3

KENTSHARE LA

Bitham's Wood

Malvern Lodge

Powdermill Farm

Lane-end Farm

Greatstone La

Spring Farm

CHEW RD

Littleton Farm

LITTLETON LA

LIMEBURN HILL

Chewhill Farm

64

WATERY LA

PINGRAY LA

CROWN HILL

The Crown Inn (PH)

Leighdown Farm

Littleton Farm

Mill

Limeburn House

Chew Magna Reservoir

Ford

DARK LA

2

FEATHERBED LA

BROAD MEAD LA

Littleton

Littleton Farm

BROADCROFT

Hounsley Batch

Blackmoor

WINFORD RD

B3130

Hounsley Farm

63

Chillyhill Farm

B3114

POOL LA

WHITLING ST

COCK AND YEW TREE HILL

PAGANS HILL

CHILLYHILL LA

Chillyhouse Farm

North Hill Farm

Pagans Hill

The Oaks

1

Tavern Scott

SCOTT LA

Pagans Hill Farm

CHEW LA

Sch

Two Rivers Way

Ledbury House

Nut Grove

THE CEDARS

PILGRIMS WAY

B3114

1 BLIND LA
2 BRISTOL RD

62

D 55 E 56 F

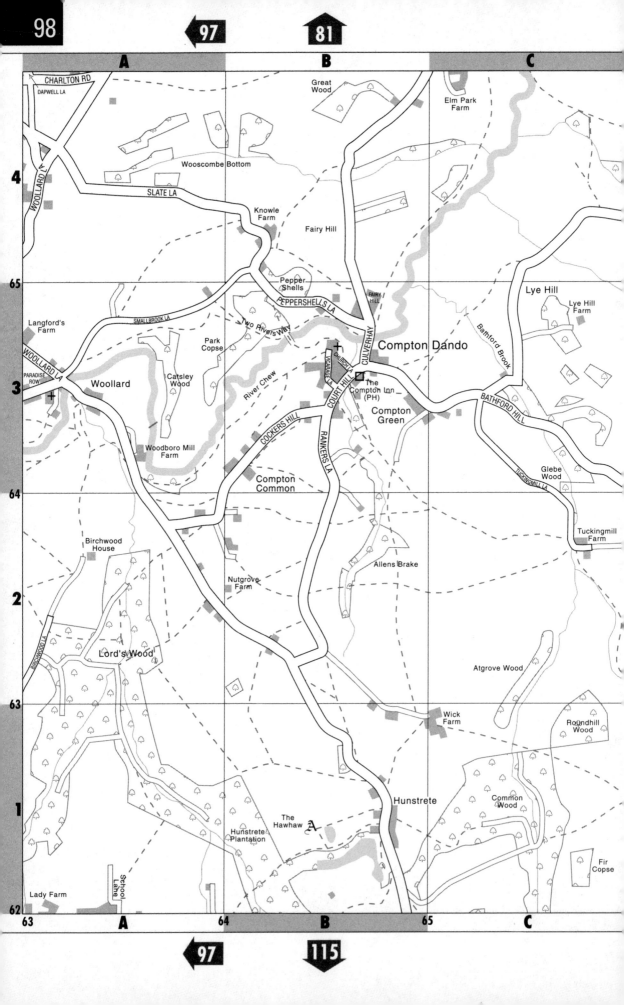

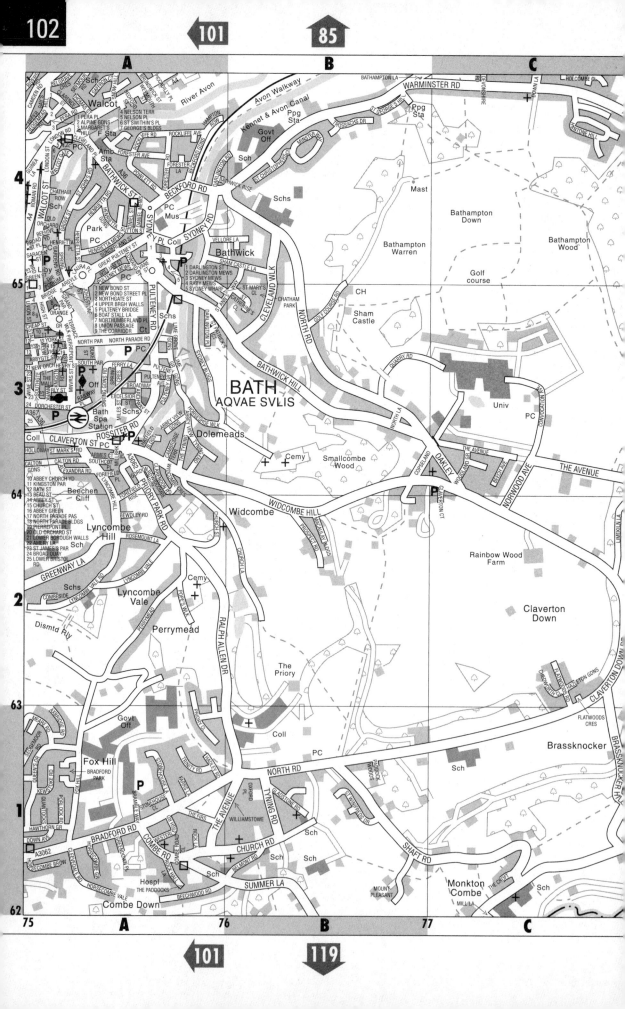

olcombe
arm

Warleigh Lodge
Farm

BRADFORD RD

Nature
Reserve

Bathford
Hill

King's Arms
Inn (PH)

**Monkton
Farleigh**

Manor House
and rems of
Priory

MONKTON
FARLEIGH

Sch

BROADSTONES

4

65

Limestone Link

WARMINSTER RD

SALLY IN THE WOOD RD

Coll

Home
Wood

Manor
Farm

Warleigh

WARLEIGH LA

Hengrove
Wood

PINCKNEY
GREEN

Willocks
Wood

3

Ppg
Sta

River Avon

Claverton

Claverton Manor
(The American
Museum)

Sheephouse
Farm

Warleigh
Hill

FARLEIGH
WICK

Hays Wood
Farm

P

Fox and Hounds
(PH)

A363

64

Vineyard
Farm

Avon Walkway

Inwoods

Challenge's
Grove

2

Claverton
Wood

Kennet and Avon Canal

**Warleigh
Wood**

Inwood

Sweeps
Coppice

63

Conkwell

RASSKNOCKER
HILL

Dundas
Aqueduct

BLACKBERRY LA

Haugh
Farm

Haugh Potticks
Farm

1

B3108

A36 LOWER STONE

Conkwell
Farm

Parsonage
Farm

Conkwell

62

D   79   E   80   F

WESTON-SUPER-MARE

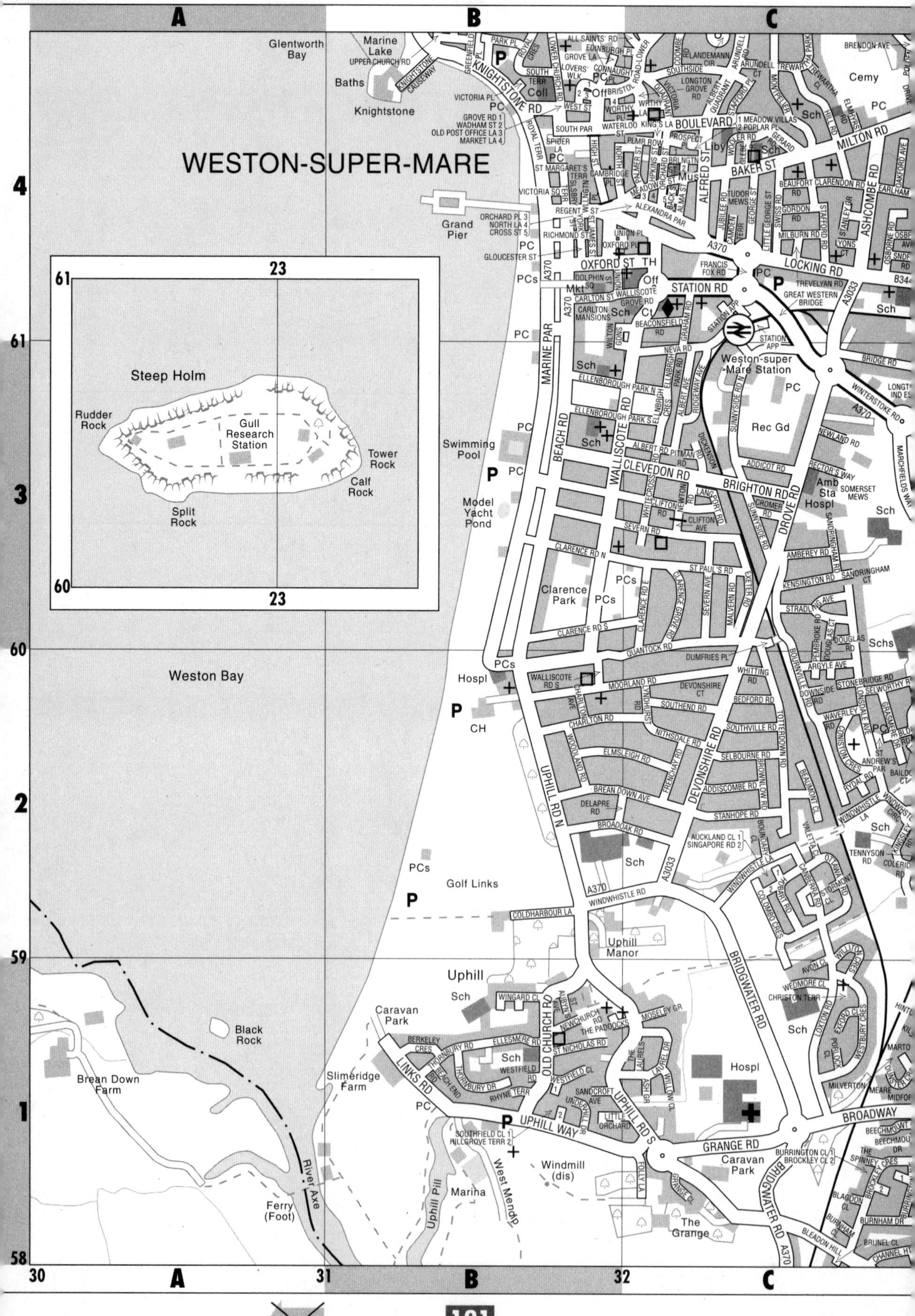

Glentworth Bay

Marine Lake

Upper Church Rd

Baths

Knightstone

Weston Bay

Grand Pier

Inset map:

23

61

Steep Holm

Rudder Rock

Gull Research Station

Tower Rock

Calf Rock

Split Rock

60

23

Swimming Pool

Model Yacht Pond

Clarence Park

Golf Links

Uphill

Caravan Park

Black Rock

Brean Down Farm

Slimeridge Farm

Links Rd

Uphill Way

West Mendip

Windmill (dis)

Marina

Ferry (Foot)

River Axe

The Grange

Bleadon Hill

Broadway

Caravan Park

Grange Rd

Bridgwater Rd

Uphill Manor

Uphill Rd

Marine Par

Beach Rd

Walliscote Rd

Clevedon Rd

Brighton Rd

Drove Rd

Locking Rd

Milton Rd

Ashcombe Rd

Oxford St

Station Rd

Weston-super-Mare Station

Rec Gd

Hospl

Uphill Rd S

Old Church Rd

90
108

D　E　F

4

61

3

60

2

59

1

58

124
108

The Homestead
The Poplars
WEST ROLSTONE RD
PUXTON RD
Laurel Farm
Gout House Farm
HAVAGE DRO
Rockers Rhyne
Nye Drove
Nye
Nye Farm
Rookery Farm
PUXTON LA
Liddy Yeo
DROVE WAY
Lower Gout Farm
Downend Farm
Moor Dairy
Middle Moor Rhyne
River Banwell Blind Ditch
Nye Drove
Hardmead Rhyne
Droveway Bridge
Droveway Farm
NYE RD
Court Farm
Moorland Farm
MOOR RD
RIVERSIDE
Towerhead Brook
West-Lea Farm
Mead Farm
MEAD LA
Railway Inn (PH)
STATION RD
A368
ROMAN RD
Stonebridge
WOLVERSHILL RD
WHITECROSS LA
COOKS LA
Elmcroft Farm
Golling
WOLVERSHILL PARK
THE PADDOCK
Towerhead
Dismantled Railway
HILL RD
KNIGHTCOTT RD
KNIGHTCOTT PARK
WEST GARSTON
ORCHARD CL
THE GABLES CL
WEST ST
ABBEY GATE
CHURCH ST
EAST ST
TOWERHEAD LA
TOWERHEAD RD
QUARRY RD
Quarry
SOUTH CROFT
GREENFIELDS CL
CHESTNUT CL
WESTFIELD RD THOMAS CL
THE ORCHARD
Sch
Liby
F Sta
THE SQUARE
A368
Banwell Plain
Sandford Batch
WIMBLESTONE RD
CORONATION RD
LITTLEFIELDS AVE
QUEENS RD
HIGH ST
HILL LA
Banwell
NORTH VIEW DR
DARK LA
Banwell Wood
1 SMALL DOWN END
2 COPSE END
BROADLEYS
BROADLEY WAY
LEX WAY
Works
CASTLE HILL
Banwell Castle
Nursery
Cemy
Sandford Batch
SHIPHAM LA
SANDFORD RD
WINT HILL
THE RHODYATE
Winthill House
Winthill Farm
Rhodyate Farm
CHRISTON RD
MAX MILL LA
BANWELL RD
A371
EVERGREEN CL
MOORHAM RD
THE GROVE

40　41

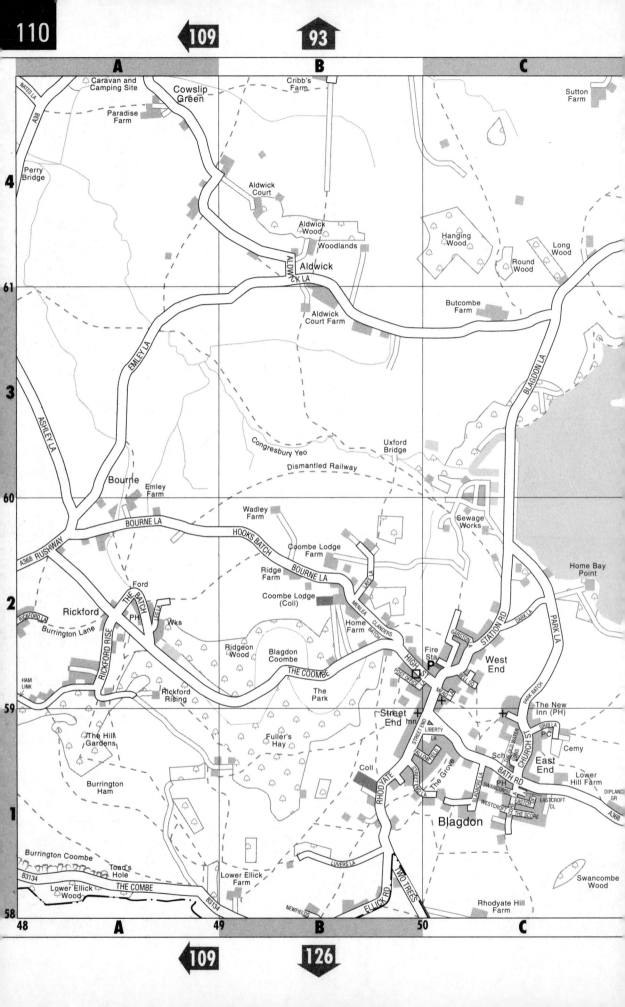

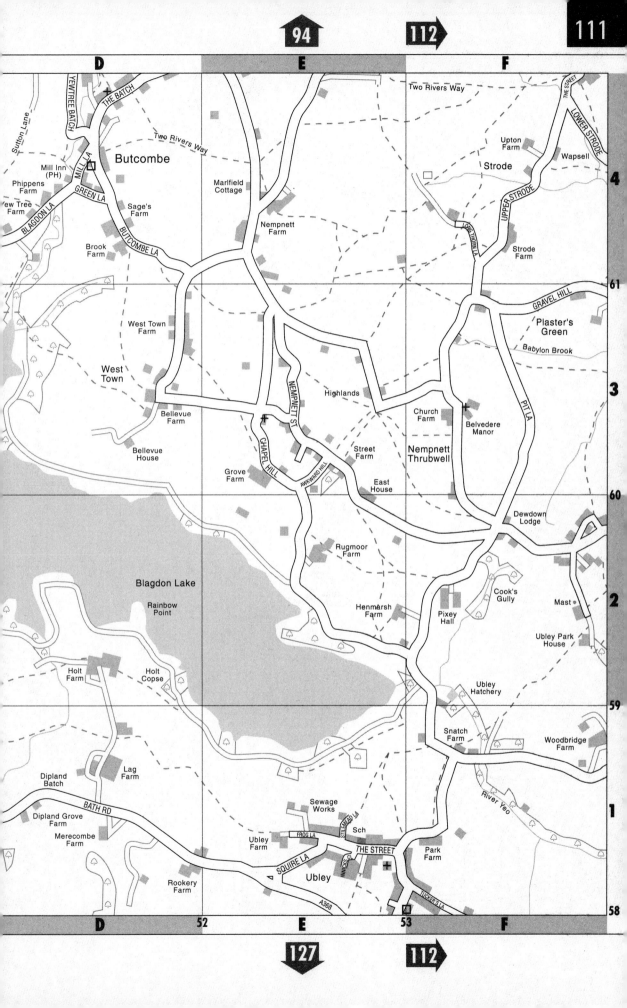

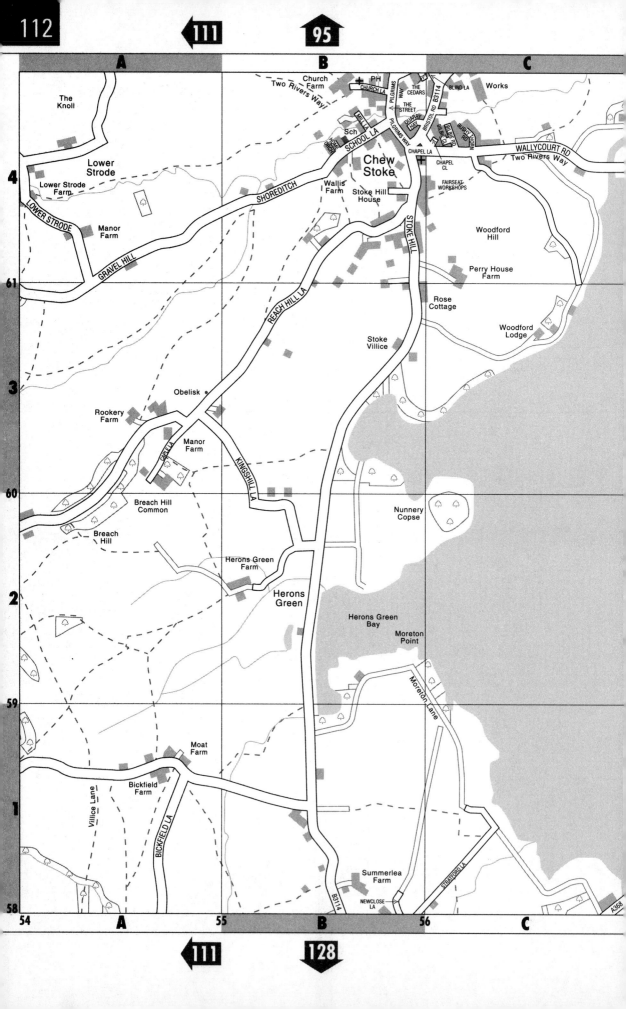

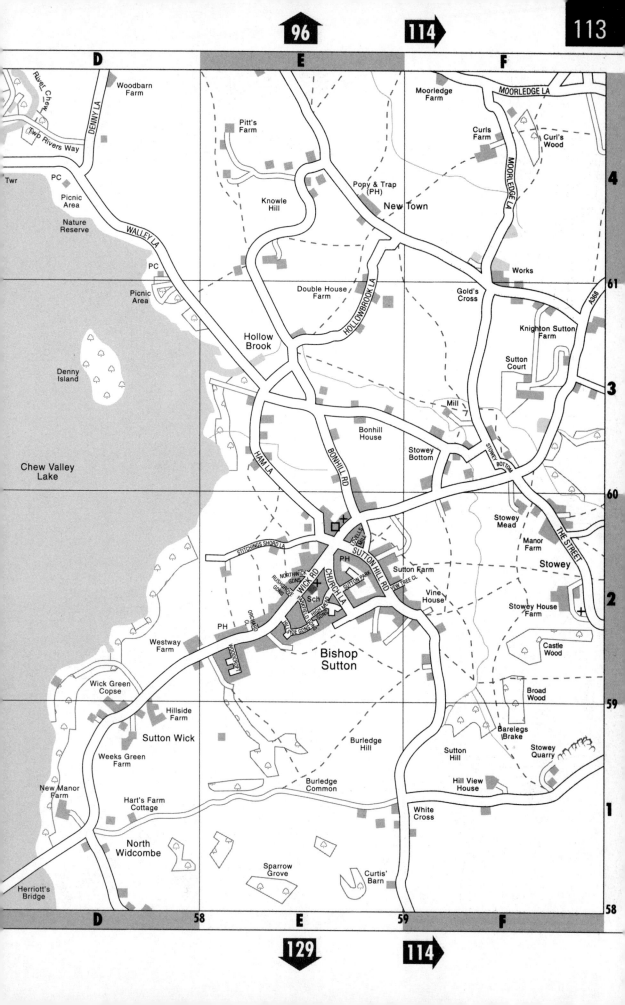

113
97

A B C

4

Bromley Farm

Curl's Farm

Utcombe Farm

STANTON WICK LA

Stanton Wick

Stanton Wick Farm

Chelwood Bridge

A37

A36

Chelwood House Hotel

Park Farm

Fry's Bottom

61

A368

Round Hill

Resr

Salter's Brook

FEATHERBED LA

Folly Wood

Honey Gaston

Red Hill

Breach

3

Folly Farm

Resr

North End Farm

Dowling's Wood

THE FLAT

North End

60

Hill Farm

Taylor's Farm

LOWER BRISTOL RD

KING LA

2

Cinderlands Brake

Tynemoor Wood

UPPER BRISTOL RD

Warwick Arms (PH)

Tynemore Farm

Warwick Gdns

TININGS WAY

BROOMHILL LA

FLINN LANE

ROGERS CL

THE MEAD

STATION RD

Sch

Clutton

MAYARD CL

GREENRIDGE

MOORSIDE

CLUTTON HILL

MAYNAR TERR

Church Farm

CHURCH LA

VENUS LA

VALLEY VIEW

KINGS OAK

CHURCH SQ

MEADOW

FAIR PLACE

Dismantled Railway

59

Sleight Farm

NANNY HURN'S LA

Cholwell Farm

Cholwell House (Off)

Bendalls Bridge

Willow Farm

MARSH LA

1

Cholwell

Cholwell Farm

Limestone Link

Temple Cloud

A37

Paul Wood

THE SQUARE

PAULWOOD RD

PAULMONT RISE

PH

JUNKLANES

ASHMEAD

OAKFIELD

MEADWAY

ELBROWN RD

CHURCH RD

FIELD GARDENS RD

BELLVIEW

GOLFNES

GREENFIELD

GREENFIELD VIEW

GOLDING

Sch

Sch

58

60 A 61 B 62 C

113
130

D
E
F

4
61
3
60
2
59
1
58

Priston Mill Farm
Inglesbatch
Wilmington Lane
Mill Lane
Inglesbatch Farm
Home Farm
STITCHINGS LA
MILL LA
KILKENNY LA
Ten Acre Cottages
Nailwell
Westvale
PRISTON RD
Hill Farm
PH
HILL VIEW
SUMMER LA
Village Farm
Duncorn Hill
Titfield Thunderbolt (PH)
B3115
A367
Manor House Farm
Westbury Farm
Priston
PRISTON LA
Longhouse
Severcombe Farm
North Hill Farm
TUNLEY RD
WITHYDITCH LA
Manor Farm
THE HOLLOW
Edelweiss Farm
King William IV Inn (PH)
ELIZABETH DR
BLUNDELL LA
Withyditch
Dismantled Railway
BROOKLANDS
Dunkerton
Dunkerton Bridge
Tunley
Lower Tunley Farm
Cam Brook
Home Farm
Hill Grove House
Limestone Link
Splott Farm
Bridge Farm
STONEAGE LA
Horse May
ROMAN ROAD
DUNKERTON HILL
Prince of Wales (PH)
Carlingcott Mill
Carlingcott
FIRGROVE LA
WHITE OX MEAD LA
ASHGROVE A367
Home Farm
White Ox Mead
The Beehive Inn (PH)

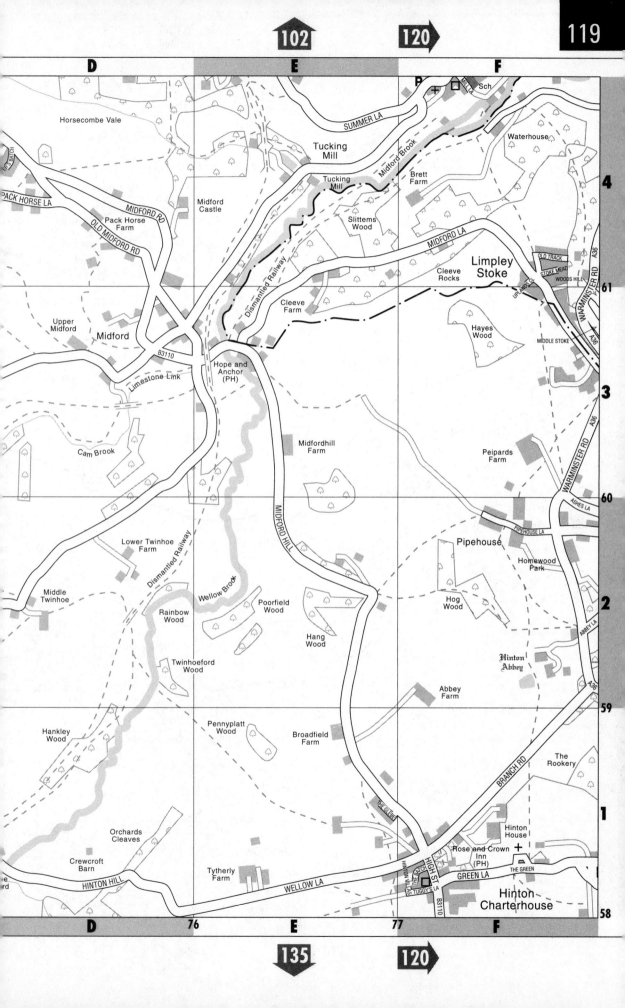

104   122

D   E   F

4

57

3

56

2

55

1

54

D   31   E   32   F

122

Walborough

West Mendip Way

West Mendip Way

West Mendip Way

West Mendip Way

BLEADON HILL

MENDIP EDGE

PURN RD

TOLL RD

BRIDGWATER RD A370

North Rhyne

North Rhyne

Hook Pill

Stroud Pill

WAYACRE DRO

Middle Rhyne

Summerways Bridge

River Axe

Bleadon Level

ACCOMMODATION RD

OLD WALL

Caravan Park

Turnbourne Farm

Diamond Farm

Caravan Park

WESTON RD

Southfield Farm

Caravan Park

Maitland Cottage

River Axe

Wharf Farm

Batch End Farm

Batch

56

Northam Farm (Caravan Park)

HAM RD

Ham Farm

WHARFSIDE

Leaze Farm

BATCH LA

West Rhyne

East Rhyne

Middle Rhyne

Yellowhayes

Tarr's Farm

RECTORY WAY

Poultry House

Martin's Hill Farmhouse

Animal Farm

RED RD

WICK RD

Wick Farm

Millfield Cottages

Golf Course

Berrow

Middle Rhyne

East Rhyne

Pitland Rhyne

Cripp's Bridge

Middle Rhyne

Hope Farm

BREAN RD

WICK LA

Caravan Park

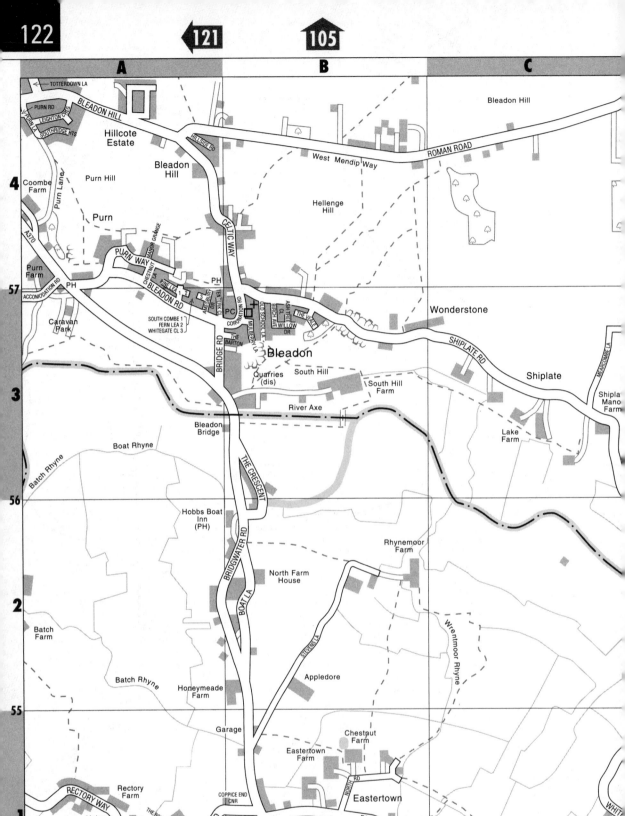

A B C

4

57

3

56

2

55

1

54

33 34 35

A B C

TOTTERDOWN LA
PURN RD
VIA PURN LA
LEIGHTON CRES
SOUTHRIDGE HTS
BLEADON HILL
Hillcote
Estate
Bleadon
Hill
Purn Hill
Coombe
Farm
Purn Lane
Purn
A370
Purn
Farm
PURN WAY
CHESTNUT MANOR GRANGE
PINE LEA 1
PH
AMESBURY DR
TENTERK CL
CELTIC WAY
BLEADON RD
ACCOMODATION RD
PH
Caravan
Park
SOUTH COMBE 1
FERN LEA 2
WHITEGATE CL 3
PC
OLD SCHOOL LA
CORONATION RD
ASH TREE CL
BIRCH AVE
THE VEALS
WILLOW DR
Wonderstone
SHIPLATE RD
Shiplate
BRIDGE RD
THE BARTON
MULBERRY LA
Bleadon
South Hill
Quarries
(dis)
River Axe
South Hill
Farm
Lake
Farm
Shiplate
Manor
Farm
MEARCOMBE LA
Bleadon Hill
West Mendip Way
ROMAN ROAD
HILLSIDE RD
Hellenge
Hill
Bleadon
Bridge
Boat Rhyne
Batch Rhyne
THE CRESCENT
Hobbs Boat
Inn
(PH)
BRIDGWATER RD
BOAT LA
North Farm
House
Rhynemoor
Farm
Wrentmoor Rhyne
Batch
Farm
Batch Rhyne
Honeymeade
Farm
STEVENS LA
Appledore
Garage
RECTORY WAY
Rectory
Farm
Holm
Farm
THE BOUNDARIES
Sch
LYMPSHAM RD
WORTHY RD
THE WORTHIES
SLADE LA
CHURCH LA
CHURCH RD
CHURCH CNR
Lympsham
WEST RD
SOUTH RD
COPPICE END
CNR
Chestnut
Farm
Eastertown
Farm
NORTH RD
Eastertown
EASTERTOWN
PURVING ROW
PURVING ROW LA
A370
Stonebow
Farm
Poplar
Farm
WHITLANDS LA

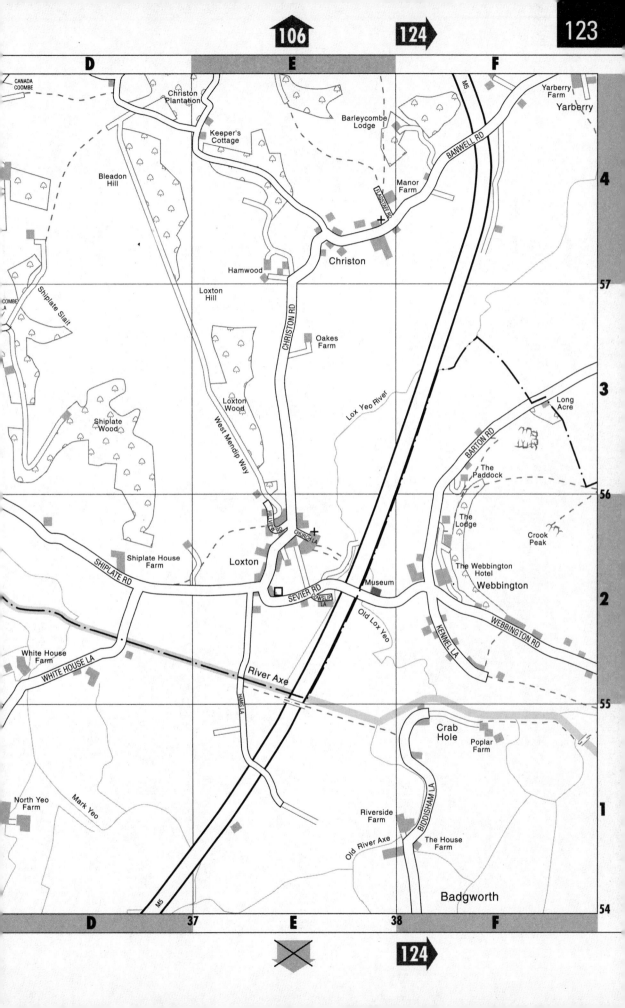

123
107

A **B** **C**

Lox Yeo River

Sewage Works

Water Works

BANWELL RD

A371

HOMEFIELD CL

BIGNE CL

Mooseheart

KNAPPS CL

Dismid Rhy

PO

KNAPPS DR

Nut Tree Farm

WOODBOROUGH RD A371

4

Max Mills Farm

MAX MILL LA

Max House Farm

Winscombe Brook

CHURCH RD

THE LYNCH

LYNCHMEAD

CH

57

Barton Farm

BARTON RD

Willow Farm

PARSONS WAY

THE SQUARE

Winscombe Brook

Laurel Farm

Barton

Winscombe Orchard

CHURCH LA

Eastwell Lane

3

Broad Knoll

Church Kndll

Old Quarry Farm

BARTON DRO

Saw Mill

WINSCOMBE HILL

Winscombe Hill

Barton Hill

Resr

Hill Farm

The Hall

56

Compton Hill

West Mendip Way

Coombe Cottage

King's Wood

Wavering Down

Cross Plain

2

COOMBE LA

Compton Bishop

Bourton Coombe

BUTTS BATCH

CHURCH LA

VICARAGE LA

VERNON LA

BIG TREE CL

Compton Farm

BOURTON LA

Bourton Farm

55

P

Caves

WEBBINGTON RD

New Town

Resr

RACKLEY LA

Dunnett Farm

Cross

White Hart (PH)

CF

Old River Axe

Rackley

OLD COACH RD

P

Cheddar Yeo

Bow Bridge

Stock's Rhyne

1

River Axe

Cross Culvert

Middle Rhyne

Compton Bishop Farm

Yeo Bridge

CROSS MOOR DRO

TURNPIKE RD

A38

54

39 **A** **40** **B** **41** **C**

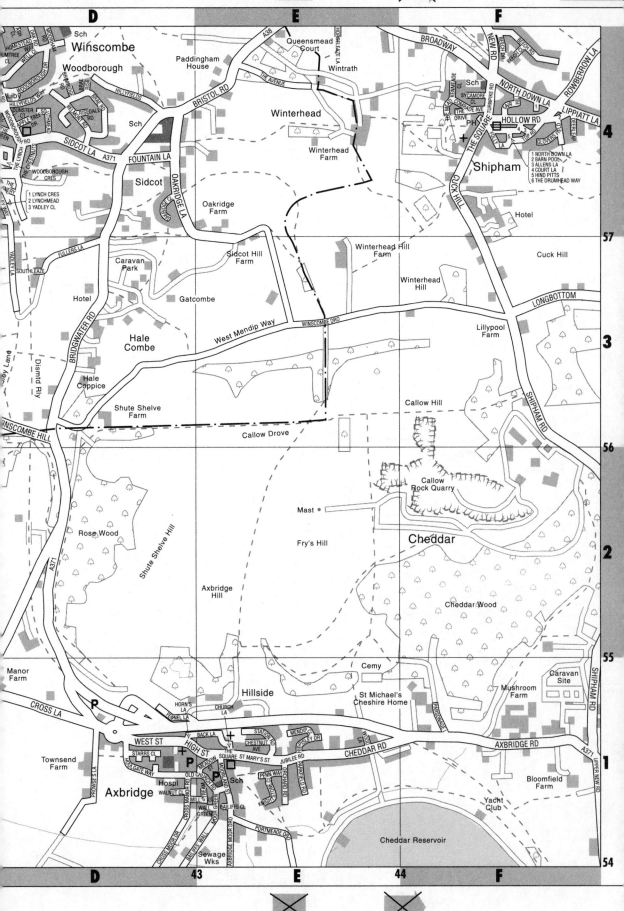

D **E** **F**

Sch

Winscombe

Woodborough

Paddingham
House

BROADWAY

NEW RD

BEECH LA

ROWBERROW LA

Lib'y

HOMESTEAD WAY

NUTREE WAY

WELL CL

MOORHAM RD

OAK LA

HILLYFIELDS

Sch

BRISTOL RD

A38

Queensmead
Court

HORSELEAZE LA

Sch

THE MEAD

KENNEADE
CL

SYCAMORE
CL

COMBE
HOE AVE

NORTH DOWN LA

LIPPIATT LA

BEERLEA

Winscombe
Woodborough
Way

DUNSTER
CT

APPLE TREE
CL

SOUTHMEAD

RISEDALE RD

HILLYFIELDS

THE AVENUE

Wintrath

THE DRIVE

P.H.

HOLLOW RD

BLOVERS RD

TOP RD

4

WOODBOROUGH
RD

BRAE RISE

BRIARMEAD

BRAE RD

Sch

Winterhead

THE SQUARE

TURNPIKE RD

COLES LA

CUCK HILL

Sch

1 NORTH DOWN LA
2 BARN POOL
3 ALLENS LA
4 COURT LA
5 HIND PITTS
6 THE DRUMHEAD WAY

THE LYNCH

SIDCOT LA

A371

FOUNTAIN LA

Winterhead
Farm

Shipham

THE LYNCH

WOODBOROUGH
CRES

Sidcot

OAKRIDGE LA

Hotel

1 LYNCH CRES
2 LYNCHMEAD
3 YADLEY CL

OAKRIDGE CL

Oakridge
Farm

57

YADLEY LA

FULLERS LA

SOUTHLEAZE

Caravan
Park

Sidcot Hill
Farm

Winterhead Hill
Farm

Cuck Hill

CUCK HILL

BRIDGWATER RD

Hotel

Gatcombe

Winterhead
Hill

LONGBOTTOM

Hale
Combe

West Mendip Way

WINSCOMBE DRO

Lillypool
Farm

3

Whitley Lane

Dismtd Rly

Hale
Coppice

SHIPHAM RD

Callow Hill

Shute Shelve
Farm

WINSCOMBE HILL

Callow Drove

56

Callow
Rock Quarry

Rose Wood

Mast

Cheddar

A371

Fry's Hill

2

Shute Shelve Hill

Cheddar Wood

Axbridge
Hill

55

Manor
Farm

Cemy

Caravan
Site

CROSS LA

Hillside

St Michael's
Cheshire Home

Mushroom
Farm

SHIPHAM RD

P

HORN'S
LA

CHURCH
LA

PARSONAGE LA

Townsend
Farm

FENNEL LA

WEST ST

HIGH ST

BACK LA

STATION
RD

MENDIP CL

MOXEY DR

POSLEY DR

CHEDDAR RD

AXBRIDGE RD

A371

UPPER NEW RD

1

PROWSE LA

STARRS CL

HOLMGATE WAY

THE SQUARE

ST MARY'S ST

JUBILEE RD

PARKFIELD RD

WOODCOTE RD

Bloomfield
Farm

Axbridge

Hospl

WALNUT CL

OLD CHURCH RD

MEADOW

CHESTNUT
AVE

PENN WAY

ORCHARD RD

KNIGHTCOTT RD

Yacht
Club

CROSS MOOR DR

MILL LA

WALL
GREEN

BAILIFFS CL

Sch

Sewage
Wks

CROSS MOOR DRO

BAILIFFS WALL

AXBRIDGE MOOR DRO

PORTMEADE DRO

Cheddar Reservoir

54

D 43 **E** 44 **F**

A

B

C

B3134

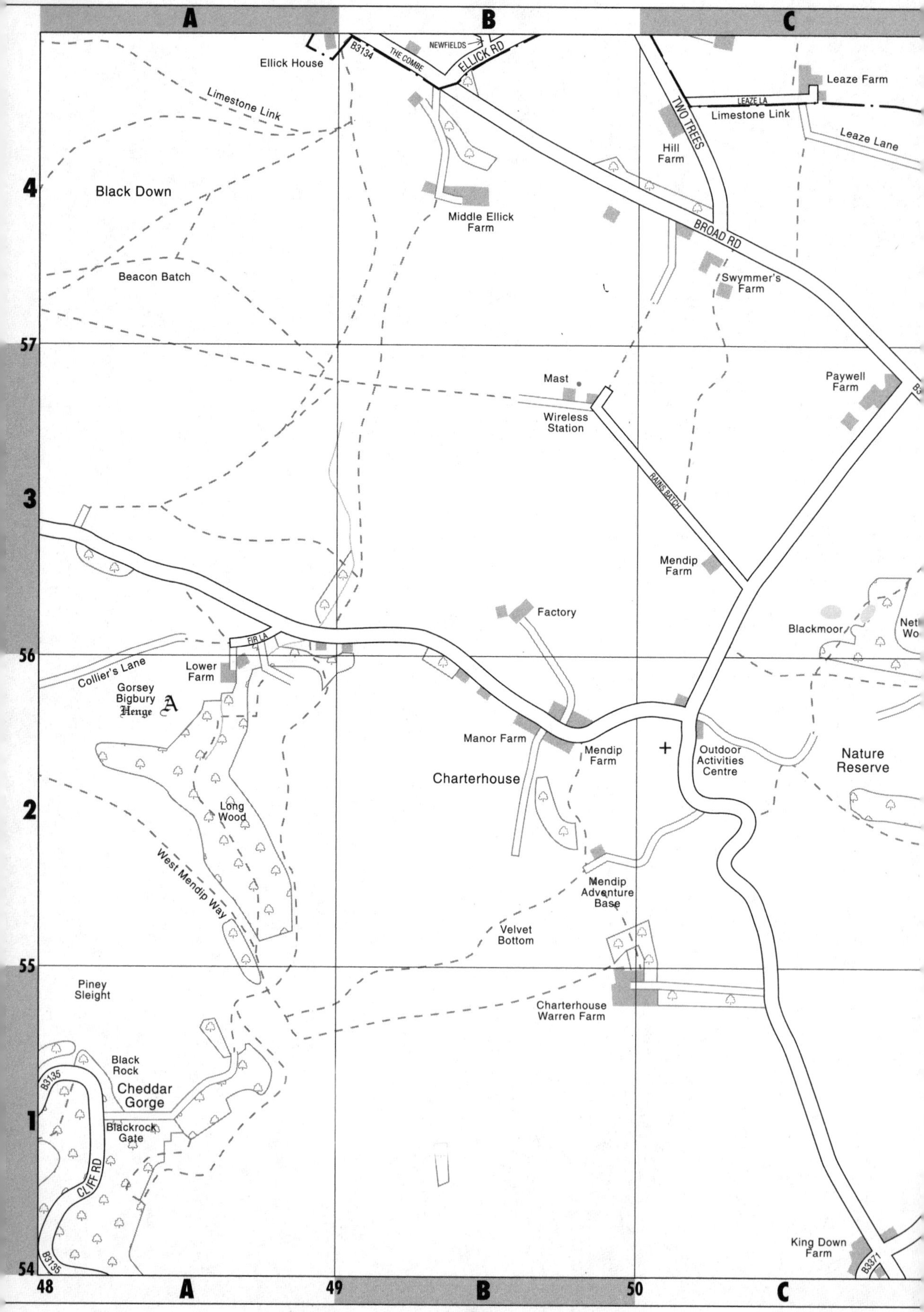

THE COMBE

NEWFIELDS

ELLICK RD

Ellick House

Limestone Link

LEAZE LA

Leaze Farm

Limestone Link

Leaze Lane

TWO TREES

Hill Farm

BROAD RD

4

Black Down

Middle Ellick Farm

Beacon Batch

Swymmer's Farm

Paywell Farm

B3

57

Mast

Wireless Station

RAINS BATCH

Mendip Farm

Blackmoor

Net Wo

3

Factory

FIR LA

56

Collier's Lane

Lower Farm

Gorsey Bigbury Henge

Manor Farm

Mendip Farm

Outdoor Activities Centre

Nature Reserve

Charterhouse

Long Wood

West Mendip Way

2

Mendip Adventure Base

Velvet Bottom

55

Piney Sleight

Charterhouse Warren Farm

Black Rock

B3135

Cheddar Gorge

Blackrock Gate

1

CLIFF RD

King Down Farm

B3371

B3135

54

48

A

49

B

50

C

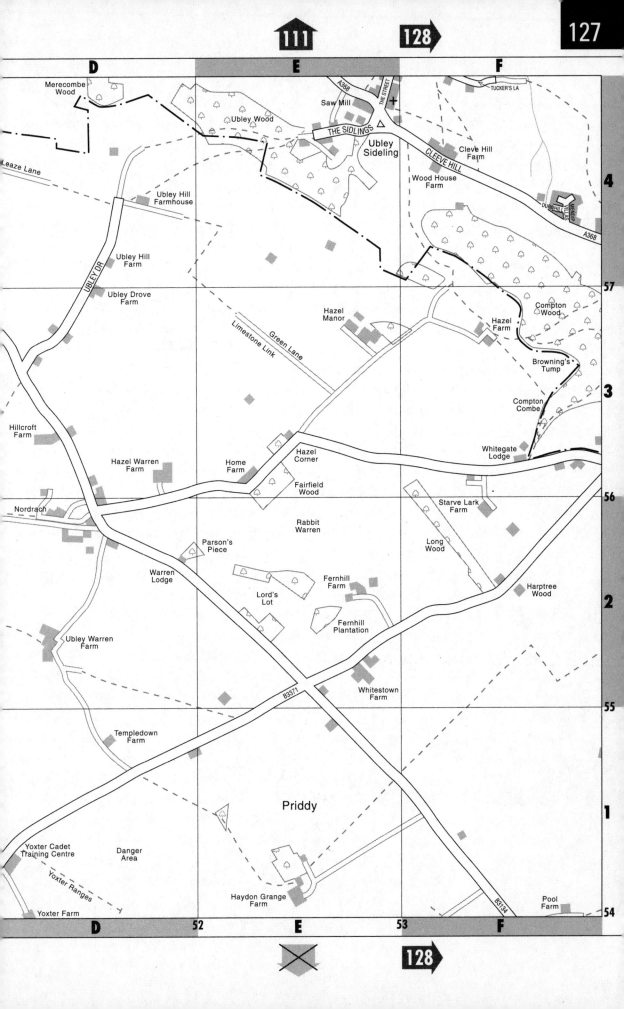

D   E   F

Merecombe Wood

Leaze Lane

Ubley Wood

Saw Mill

THE SIDLINGS

Ubley Sideling

CLEEVE HILL

Cleve Hill Farm

Wood House Farm

TUCKER'S LA

DURNHILL VILLAS

MENDIP

A368

4

Ubley Hill Farmhouse

UBLEY DR

Ubley Hill Farm

Ubley Drove Farm

57

Compton Wood

Hazel Manor

Hazel Farm

Limestone Link   Green Lane

Browning's Tump

Compton Combe

3

Hillcroft Farm

Hazel Warren Farm

Home Farm

Hazel Corner

Fairfield Wood

Whitegate Lodge

Nordrach

Starve Lark Farm

56

Rabbit Warren

Long Wood

Parson's Piece

Warren Lodge

Lord's Lot

Fernhill Farm

Harptree Wood

2

Ubley Warren Farm

Fernhill Plantation

B3371

Whitestown Farm

55

Templedown Farm

Priddy

1

Yoxter Cadet Training Centre

Danger Area

Yoxter Ranges

Haydon Grange Farm

B3134

Pool Farm

Yoxter Farm

54

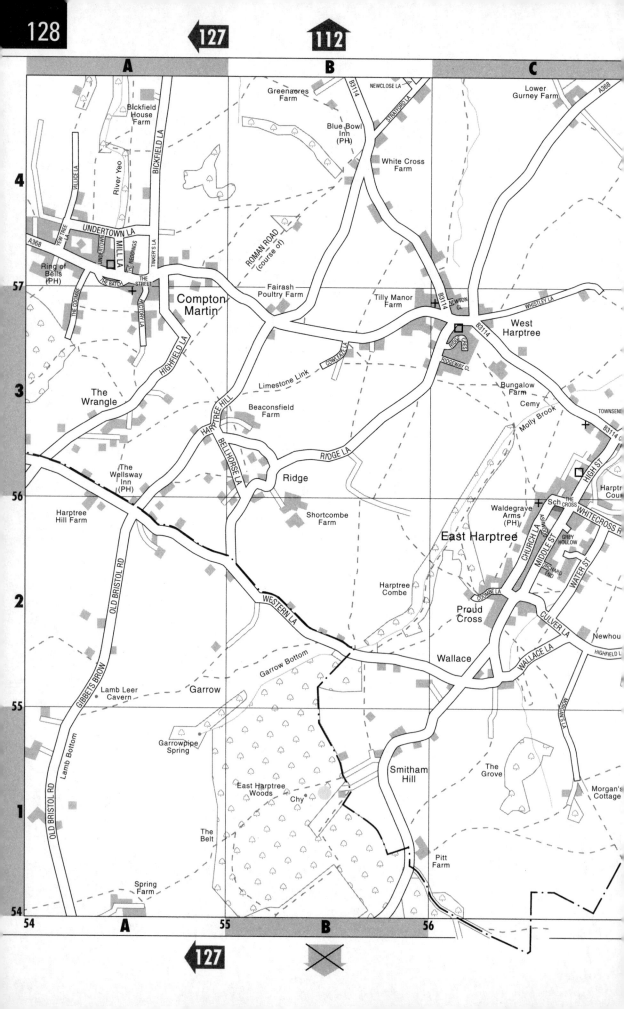

A   B   C

Greenacres Farm

NEWCLOSE LA

Lower Gurney Farm

A368

B3114

STRATFORD LA

Blue Bowl Inn (PH)

Bickfield House Farm

BICKFIELD LA

White Cross Farm

River Yeo

VILLICE LA

YEW TREE LA

UNDERTOWN LA

MILL LA

THE REDDINGS

TINKER'S LA

ROMAN ROAD (course of)

Fairash Poultry Farm

Tilly Manor Farm

B3114

NEWTON CL

West Harptree

WHISTLEY LA

A368

Ring of Bells (PH)

THE BATCH

THE STREET

RECTORY LA

THE COOMBE

Compton Martin

COWLEAZE LA

RIDGE CRES

RIDGEWAY CL

Bungalow Farm

TOWNSEND

B3114

The Wrangle

HIGHFIELD LA

HARPTREE HILL

Limestone Link

Beaconsfield Farm

RIDGE LA

Ridge

Molly Brook

Cemy

HIGH ST

Harptr Cou

BELLHORSE LA

The Wellsway Inn (PH)

Waldegrave Arms (PH)

Sch

THE CROSS

WHITECROSS R

Harptree Hill Farm

Shortcombe Farm

East Harptree

ASHWOOD

CHURCH LA

MIDDLE ST

GREY HOLLOW

ORCHARD END

WATER ST

Harpt

Harptree Combe

COOMBE LA

Newhou

OLD BRISTOL RD

WESTERN LA

Proud Cross

CULVER LA

HIGHFIELD L

WALLACE LA

Wallace

Garrow Bottom

Lamb Leer Cavern

Garrow

GIBBETS BROW

MORGAN'S LA

The Grove

Garrowpipe Spring

Smitham Hill

Morgan's Cottage

Lamb Bottom

East Harptree Woods

Chy

OLD BRISTOL RD

The Belt

Pitt Farm

Spring Farm

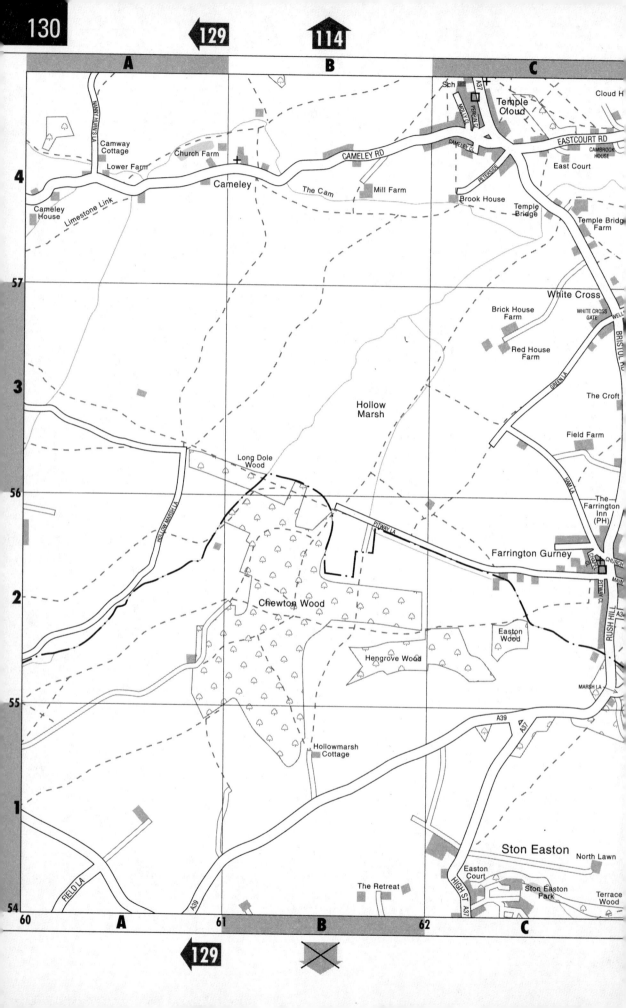

A · B · C

4

57

3

56

2

55

1

54

Dunford Farm
Dismtd Rly
Upper Radford
New Barn Farm
Withy Mills
Withymills Farm
Red House Farm
Radford
Radford Farm
WEEKESLEY LA
RADFORD HILL
Limestone Link
DURCOTT RD
Cam Brook
Cam Brook Cl
CAMERTON HILL
BRIDGE PLACE RD
Camerton
Camerton Court
Camerton Park
Abbey Farm
Sch
SKINNER'S HILL
Old Hayes
Parson's Brake
Glebe Cottage
Well Head Wood
PAULTON LA
Camerton Fram
PAULTO' HILL
Broadway Cottages
Clan Down
Starvelark Wood
BROADWAY LA
LOVERS LA
Clandown Bottom
POW'S HILL
NORTHDOWN RD
EASTDOWN RD
DUCHY RD
Clandown Farm
Clandown
SMALLCOMBE RD
OLD FOSSE WAY
Round Hill
WATER LA
CLANDOWN RD
Bowlditch Farm
CRAWL LA
Kitley Hill
KITLEY HILL
BOWLDITCH LA
MONGER LA
Sch
Chapel Rd
FOSSE GREEN
Springfield Hts
FOSSEWAY
OLD PIT TERR
BATH NEW RD
BRISTOL RD
COMBE END
Monger
BINCE'S LODGE LA
Welton Hill
OLD MILLARD'S HILL
FOSSE LA
ROMAN ROAD
MIDSOMER NORTON
Belle Vue
MONGER LA
GREENHILL PL
GREENHILL RD
WELTON GR
ST BARNABAS CL
Green Tree Rd
GLADSTONE ST
MILLARD'S HILL
Manor Farm
Dismtd Rly
Welton Hollow
WALDEGRAVE TERR
WATERLOO
WEST RD
A362
BARNABY
GELDOF DR
GRACE DR
ST CHARLES CL
ST ANTHONYS CL
EAST MEAD
LONG BARNS
ST PAULS PL
Works
STATION RD
VALLEY WLK
WELTON VALE
Wheeler's Hill
Sch
BURLINGTON ST
MIDSOMER ENTERPRISE PARK
Works
SOMERVALE RD
WELTON RD
FROME RD
FORTESCUE RD
THE STREET
Liby
Sch
PC
Hayes Park
VIVIEN AVE
HERBERTS RD
BERKELEY AVE
Stone's Cross
SOUTH VIEW
RADSTOCK RD
Florida Terr
WHEELER'S RD
FIVE ARCHES CL
F Sta
Coll
HAYES PARK RD
HAYES RD
CHRIS CRES
ST MARK'S RD
STANLEY CT
HOPE TERR
RAILWAY VIEW PL
LIAS TERR
River Somer
WHEELERS RD
Fosse Way Cotts
WELLS RD
WEST HILL
ACACIA RD
West Hill Gardens
RADSTOCK
NORTH RD
NORTH WAY
TYNING RD
CHURCH LA
Sch
Off
P
HIGH ST
POW'S ORCH
GUN HOLES
KYNING
Sports PC Centre
SHAKESP AVE
WESLEY AVE
RUSKIN
MILTON
WESTFIELD
Westfield
JUBILEE RD
OAK TERR
BRYANT AVE
WEST HILL
MAY TREE RD
ASH TREE
WATERSIDE
Waterside
REDFIELD RD
B3355
SILVER ST
PIT RD
Liby
Off
KINGS RD
LONGFELLOW RD
KIPLING RD
POETS CNR
SHELLEY RD
MILTON
WATERLOO
A367
ELM TREE RD
WALNUT
CHESTNUT RD
MAGNOLIA
KILMERSDON RD

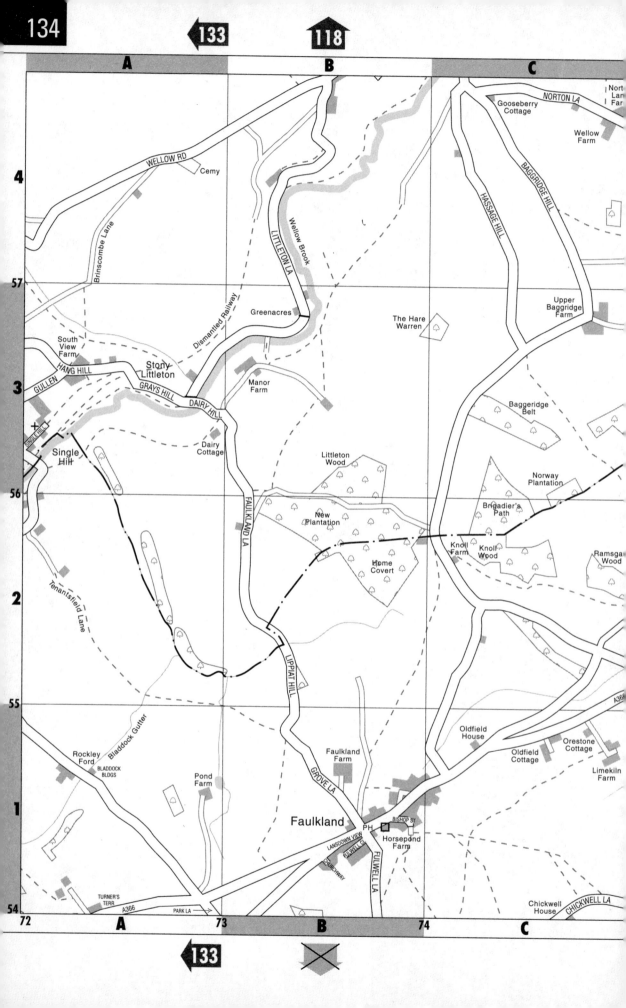

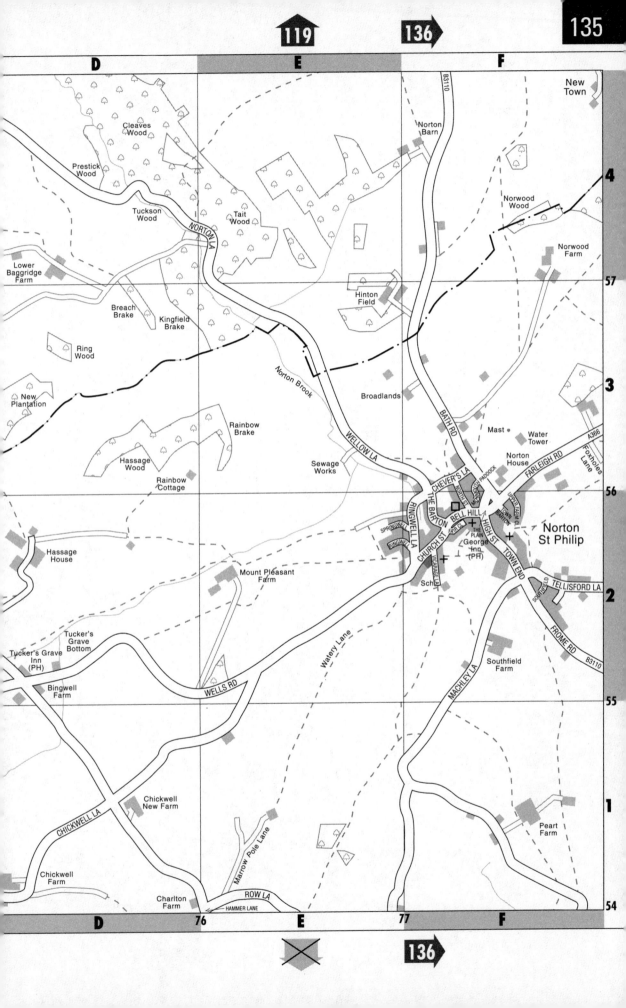

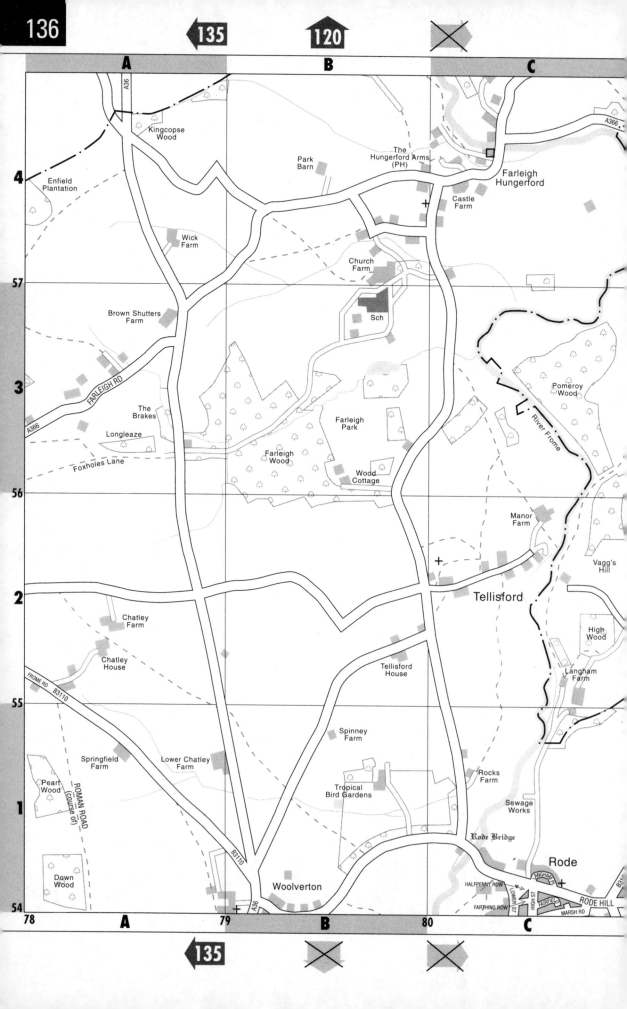

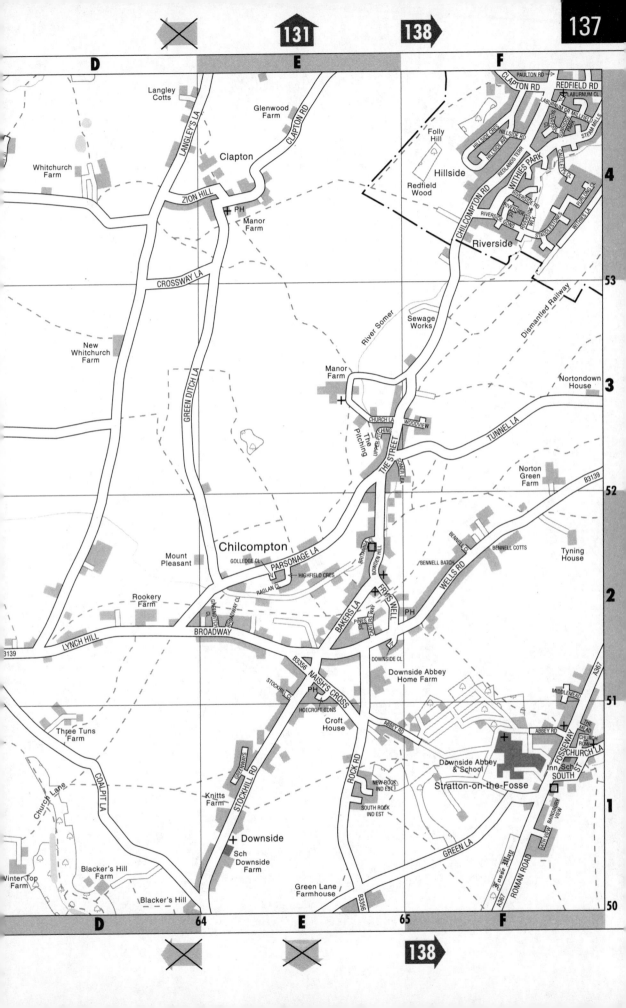

D E F

Haydon Farm

HAYDON HILL

Huish House

A362

GREEN PARLOUR RD

Peak's Wood

Haywood Farm

A366

TERRY HILL

FROME RD

KNOBSBURY LA

Upper Lentney Farm Cottage

Upper Knobsbury

AMMERDOWN TERR

A366

4

B3139

Lentney Farm

Upper Lentney Farm

Terry Hill Plantation

WATERSIDE LA

New Tyning Farm

Lower Knobsbury

KNOBSBURY LA

Nap Wood

53

Home Farm

Gagman Coppice

Ammerdown House

A362

Sch

Sewage Works

ANGELA

Ammerdown Park

3

KILMERSDON HILL

Ammerdown Bridge

Coldbath Plantation

Manor Farm

SILVER ST

The Column

Kilmersdon

Wedingham Coppice

Hatchet Hill Coppice

52

Walton Farm

Beatle's Wood

Babington Wood

Batch Farm

NEW RD

HATCHET HILL

Kingsdown Wood

HOARE'S LA

SOUTH VIEW

Upton's Piece

Mells Down Farm

2

Lowerfield Farm

CORNISH'S GRAVE

Works

Jericho Bridge

Babington Park

Babington House

51

Babington

Lodge

Cherry Garden Farm

Dismantled Railway

Edney's Farm

LUCKINGTON CROSS

Newbury House

CHARITY LA

White Cottage

1

DARK LA

TINKER'S LA

Newbury Farm

Newbury

POPLE'S LA

Luckington Manor Farm

Works

50

D 70 E 71 F

EXPLANATION OF THE STREET INDEX REFERENCE SYSTEM

Street names are listed alphabetically and show the locality, the page number and a reference to the square in which the name falls on the map page.

Example: Hill View Rd. Puck...53 E3

Hill View Rd   This is the full street name, which may have been abbreviated on the map.

Puck   This is the abbreviation for the town, village or locality in which the street falls.

53   This is the page number of the map on which the street name appears.

E3   The letter and figure indicate the square on the map in which the centre of the street falls. The square can be found at the junction of the vertical column carrying the appropriate letter and the horizontal row carrying the appropriate figure.

ABBREVIATIONS USED IN THE INDEX
Road Names

Approach	App	Grove	Gr
Arcade	Arc	Heights	Hts
Avenue	Ave	Industrial Estate	Ind Est
Boulevard	Bvd	Junction	Junc
Buildings	Bldgs	Lane	La
Business Park	Bsns Pk	North	N
Broadway	Bwy	Orchard	Orch
By-Pass	By-Ps	Parade	Par
Causeway	Cswy	Passage	Pas
Circle	Circ	Place	Pl
Circus	Cir	Pleasant	Plea
Close	Cl	Precinct	Prec
Common	Comm	Promenade	Prom
Corner	Cnr	Road	Rd
Cottages	Cotts	South	S
Court	Ct	Square	Sq
Courtyard	Ctyd	Stairs	Strs
Crescent	Cres	Steps	Stps
Drive	Dri	Street, Saint	St
Drove	Dro	Terrace	Terr
East	E	Walk	Wlk
Embankment	Emb	West	W
Esplanade	Espl	Yard	Yd
Gardens	Gdns		

Key to abbreviations of Town, Village and Rural locality names used in the index of street names.

Abbots Leigh .... Ab Lei	62	A4
Acton Turville .... A Tur	42	C3
Almondsbury .... Alm	24	A3
Alveston .... Alve	15	D2
Aust .... Aust	13	D3
Avonmouth .... Avon	33	E1
Axbridge .... Axb	125	D1
Backwell .... Back	76	A3
Badgworth .... Badg	123	F1
Banwell .... Ban	107	D1
Barrow Gurney .... Ba Gu	77	F3
Bath .... Bath	102	B3
Batheaston .... Bathe	85	F2
Bathford .... Bathf	86	B1
Berrow .... Berr	121	D1
Bishop Sutton .... Bi Sut	113	E2
Bitton .... Bitt	82	C4
Blagdon .... Blag	110	C1
Bleadon .... Blea	122	B3
Box .... Box	86	C2
Bristol .... Bris	63	E3
Brockley .... Brock	75	E1
Burton .... Burt	43	D2
Butcombe .... But	111	D4
Charfield .... Char	11	D3
Charlcombe .... Charl	84	C2
Cheddar .... Ched	125	F2
Chew Magna .... Ch Mag	96	B2
Chew Stoke .... Ch St	112	B4
Chilcompton .... Chil	137	E2
Chipping Sodbury ..... Ch Sod	28	B1
Churchill .... Chur	108	C2
Clevedon .... Cleve	57	D2

Clutton .... Clut	114	C2
Cold Ashton .... Co Ash	68	C3
Colerne .... Col	70	C2
Compton Bishop .... Co Bi	124	A2
Compton Dando ...... Co Dan	98	B3
Compton Martin .... Co Mar	128	A3
Congresbury .... Cong	91	F2
Corston .... Cor	100	A4
Cromhall .... Crom	10	A1
Didmarton .... Did	20	C3
Dodington .... Dod	41	D2
Doynton .... Doyn	54	A1
Dundry .... Dun	78	B1
Dyrham .... Dyrh	54	B2
East Harptree .... E Harp	128	C2
Easton in Gordano ..... E in G	47	D2
Englishcombe .... Engl	100	C1
Falfield .... Falf	9	F4
Farmborough .... Farm	116	A3
Faulkland .... Faulk	134	B1
Frampton Cotterell ...... Fr Cot	38	A4
Great Badminton ...... Gr Bad	30	C1
Grittleton .... Grit	43	F3
Hawkesbury Upton ...... H Up	20	A1
Hillesley .... Hill	19	E4
Hinton Blewett .... Hin Ble	129	F3
Hinton		
Charterhouse .... Hin Cha	119	F1
Holcombe .... Hol	138	B1
Horton .... Hort	29	E3
Iron Acton .... Ir Act	26	B2
Kelston .... Kel	83	E2
Keynsham .... Keyn	81	F2

Kilmersdon .... Kilm	139	D3
Kingston Seymour ...... K Sey	73	E1
Kingswood .... Kings	11	F2
Kingswood .... Kingsw	65	E4
Limpley Stoke .... Li St	119	F4
Litton .... Litt	129	F1
Locking .... Lock	106	A2
Long Ashton .... Lo Ash	62	A1
Luckington .... Luck	31	F2
Lympsham .... Lymp	122	A1
Mangotsfield .... Mang	51	F4
Marksbury .... Marks	99	D1
Marshfield .... Marsh	69	F4
Midsomer Norton ...... Mid No	132	A2
Monkton Farleigh .... Mon Far	103	F4
Nailsea .... Nail	59	E2
Newport .... Newp	4	A4
North Nibley .... N Nib	5	E2
North Wraxall .... N Wrax	56	C2
Norton St Philip .... N St P	135	F2
Oldbury-on-Severn ... O-on-S	7	E3
Olveston .... Olve	14	A2
Paulton .... Paul	131	F3
Peasedown St John .... P St J	133	E4
Pensford .... Pens	97	F2
Pilning .... Piln	22	B4
Portbury .... Portb	46	B2
Portishead .... Portis	45	D2
Priddy .... Priddy	127	E1
Priston .... Pris	117	D3
Pucklechurch .... Puck	53	D3
Puxton .... Pux	90	B2
Radstock .... Rad	132	C1

Rockhampton .... Rock	8	C4
Rode .... Rode	136	C1
Shipham .... Ship	125	F4
Siston .... Sist	52	C2
Southstoke .... Sosto	118	C4
Stinchcombe .... Stin	5	D4
Stoke Gifford .... St Gif	36	C2
Ston Easton .... Ston E	130	C1
Stone .... Stone	3	F2
Tellisford .... Tell	136	C2
Thornbury .... Thorn	8	C1
Timsbury .... Tims	116	A1
Tormarton .... Tor	41	F1
Tytherington .... Tyth	16	B3
Wellow .... Well	118	B1
Westerleigh .... West	39	D2
Weston in Gordano .... W in G	44	C1
Weston-Super-Mare .. W-S-M	104	B4
Westwood .... Westw	120	C2
Whitchurch .... Whit	80	B2
Wick .... Wick	67	E3
Wick St Lawrence ...... W St L	89	D4
Wickwar .... Wickw	18	A3
Winford .... Win	94	C4
Winscombe .... Winsc	125	D4
Winsley .... Winsl	120	C4
Winterbourne .... Wint	37	F3
Wotton-under-Edge .... W-u-E	11	F4
Wraxall .... Wrax	60	B2
Wrington .... Wring	92	C1
Yate .... Yate	27	E1
Yatton .... Yatt	91	E4

142

5c Bsns Centre. Cleve   **Back St. H Up**

Entry	Page	Grid
5c Bsns Centre. Cleve	57	D1
Abbey Church Yd. Bath	102	A3
Abbey Cl. Keyn	81	F3
Abbey Green. Bath	102	A3
Abbey La. Hi Cha	120	A2
Abbey Park. Keyn	81	F3
Abbey Rd. Bris	48	C4
Abbey Rd. Chil	137	D1
Abbey Rd. Chil	137	F1
Abbey St. Bath	102	A3
Abbey St. Kings	11	F3
Abbey View Gdns. Bath	102	A3
Abbey View. Bath	102	A3
Abbey View. Mid No	133	D2
Abbeydale. Wint	37	F3
Abbeygate St. Bath	102	A3
Abbeywood Dr. Bris	48	B3
Abbot's Cl. W-S-M	89	D2
Abbots Ave. Kingsw	65	E2
Abbots Cl. Bris	80	A2
Abbots Horn. Nail	59	E1
Abbots Leigh Rd. Ab Lei	62	B4
Abbots Leigh Rd. Lo Ash	62	B4
Abbots Rd. Kingsw	65	E1
Abbots Way. Bris	49	F3
Abbotsbury Rd. Nail	59	E1
Abbotsford Rd. Bris	49	D1
Abbotswood. Kingsw	65	E4
Abbotswood. Yate	39	E4
Abbott Rd. Piln	22	A3
Abbotts Farm Cl. Paul	131	E3
Aberdeen Rd. Bris	63	D4
Abingdon Gdns. Bath	118	B4
Abingdon Rd. Bris	51	D2
Ableton La. Avon	33	F4
Ableton La. Piln	22	A3
Ableton Wlk. Bris	48	B3
Abraham Cl. Bris	64	A4
Abson Rd. Wick	53	E2
Acacia Ave. Kingsw	51	E2
Acacia Ave. W-S-M	105	D4
Acacia Cl. Kingsw	51	E2
Acacia Ct. Keyn	81	E2
Acacia Gr. Bath	101	E2
Acacia Rd. Kingsw	51	E2
Acacia Rd. Rad	132	C1
Accommodation Rd. Blea	121	F3
Acid Rd. Avon	33	E2
Acorn Gr. Bris	78	C3
Acraman's Rd. Bris	63	E2
Acrebush Cl. Bris	79	D3
Acton Rd. Bris	51	D2
Adams Cl. P St J	133	E4
Addicot Rd. W-S-M	104	C3
Addiscombe Rd. Bris	80	A3
Addiscombe Rd. W-S-M	104	C2
Addison Rd. Bris	63	F2
Adelaide Pl. Bris	50	C2
Adelaide Pl. Bris	64	A4
Admiral's Wlk. Portis	45	D3
Agate St. Bris	63	D2
Aiken St. Bris	64	A3
Ainslie's Belvedere. Bath	101	F4
Aintree Dr. Bris	37	F1
Air Balloon Rd. Bris	65	D4
Airport Rd. Bris	80	A4
Aisecombe Way. W-S-M	105	E3
Akeman Way. Avon	47	E4
Alard Rd. Bris	79	F4
Albany Gate. St Gif	36	C3
Albany Rd. Bath	101	E3
Albany Rd. Bris	49	F1
Albany St. Bris	65	E2
Albany Way. Kingsw	66	B3
Albermarle Row. Bris	62	C3
Albert Ave. P St J	133	E4
Albert Ave. W-S-M	104	C3
Albert Cres. Bris	64	A3
Albert Gr. Bris	64	C4
Albert Par. Bris	64	B4
Albert Park Pl. Bris	49	F1
Albert Park. Bris	49	F1
Albert Pl. Bris	49	D4
Albert Pl. Bris	63	E2
Albert Quadrant. W-S-M	104	C4
Albert Rd. Bris	64	A2
Albert Rd. Cleve	57	E2
Albert Rd. Keyn	81	F3
Albert Rd. Kingsw	65	E3
Albert Rd. Mang	51	F2
Albert Rd. Piln	22	A3
Albert Rd. Portis	45	E3
Albert Rd. W-S-M	104	C3
Albert St. Bris	64	B4
Albert Terr. Bath	101	E4
Albert Terr. Bris	50	C2
Alberton Rd. Bris	50	C4
Albion Cl. Mang	51	F3
Albion Pl. Bris	50	A1
Albion St. Bris	64	B4
Alburys. Wring	92	B2
Alcove Rd. Bris	50	C2
Alder Dr. Bris	50	C1
Alder Terr. Rad	132	C1
Aldercombe Rd. Bris	48	B4
Alderdown Cl. Bris	48	A4
Alderley Rd. Bath	101	D2
Alderley Rd. Hill	19	E4
Aldermoor Way. Kingsw	65	F2
Aldernay Ave. Bris	64	C2
Alders The. Bris	37	D1
Alderton Rd. Grit	43	E3
Aldwick Ave. Bris	79	E2
Aldwick La. Blag	110	B4
Aldwick La. But	110	B4
Aldwick La. Wring	110	B4
Alex Ricketts Cl. Bath	100	C3
Alexander Way. Yatt	91	D4
Alexandra Cl. Kingsw	51	E2
Alexandra Gdns. Kingsw	51	E2
Alexandra Par. W-S-M	104	C4
Alexandra Park. Bris	49	E1
Alexandra Park. Bris	50	C2
Alexandra Park. Paul	131	F3
Alexandra Pl. Kingsw	51	E2
Alexandra Rd. Bath	102	A3
Alexandra Rd. Bris	49	E4
Alexandra Rd. Bris	63	D4
Alexandra Rd. Bris	78	C4
Alexandra Rd. Cleve	57	E2
Alexandra Rd. Fr Cot	38	B4
Alexandra Rd. Kingsw	65	E3
Alexandra Terr. Paul	131	F4
Alexandra Way. Thorn	8	A2
Alford Rd. Bris	64	B1
Alfred Hill. Bris	63	E4
Alfred Lovell Gdns. Kingsw	66	A2
Alfred Par. Bris	63	E4
Alfred Pl. Bris	63	E4
Alfred Rd. Bris	49	D2
Alfred Rd. Bris	63	E2
Alfred St. Bath	101	F4
Alfred St. Bris	64	A3
Alfred St. Bris	64	B4
Alfred St. W-S-M	104	C4
Algars Dr. Ir Act	26	C2
Algiers St. Bris	63	E2
Alison Gdns. Back	76	A4
All Hallows Rd. Bris	64	A4
All Saints La. Cleve	57	F2
All Saints' La. Bris	63	E3
All Saints' Rd. Bath	101	F4
All Saints' Rd. Bris	49	D1
All Saints' Rd. W-S-M	87	F1
All Saints' St. Bris	63	E4
Allanmead Rd. Bris	80	A4
Allengrove La. Luck	31	E2
Allens La. Wins	125	F4
Aller Par. W-S-M	105	D1
Aller. W-S-M	105	D1
Allerton Cres. Bris	80	A2
Allerton Gdns. Bris	80	A3
Allerton Rd. Bris	80	A2
Allfoxton Rd. Bris	50	A2
Allington Dr. Kingsw	65	F2
Allington Gdns. Nail	75	E4
Allington Rd. Bris	63	E3
Allison Ave. Bris	64	C2
Allison Rd. Bris	64	C2
Alma Cl. Kingsw	65	F4
Alma Pl. Well	118	B3
Alma Rd. Bris	63	D4
Alma Rd. Kingsw	51	F1
Alma Road Ave. Bris	63	D4
Alma St. Bris	49	D1
Alma St. W-S-M	104	C4
Alma Vale Rd. Bris	63	D4
Almeda Rd. Bris	65	D3
Almond Cl. W-S-M	89	D1
Almond Way. Mang	51	F3
Almondsbury Bsns Centre. St Gif	24	B2
Almorah Rd. Bris	63	F2
Alpha Centre The. Yate	27	E2
Alpha Rd. Bris	63	E2
Alpine Cl. Paul	131	F2
Alpine Gdns. Bath	102	A4
Alpine Rd. Bris	50	B1
Alpine Rd. Paul	131	F2
Alsop Rd. Kingsw	51	E1
Alton Rd. Bris	49	F3
Altringham Rd. Bris	64	B4
Alverstoke. Bris	79	F4
Alveston Hill. Thorn	15	D3
Alveston Rd. Olve	14	B2
Alveston Wlk. Bris	48	A4
Alwins Ct. Kingsw	65	F2
Amberd Rd. W-S-M	104	C3
Amberlands Cl. Back	76	A4
Amberley Cl. Keyn	81	F2
Amberley Gdns. Nail	59	E4
Amberley Rd. Mang	51	E4
Amberley Rd. St Gif	36	A4
Amberley Way. Wickw	18	A2
Amble Cl. Kingsw	65	F4
Ambleside Ave. Bris	35	D1
Ambleside Rd. Bath	101	E1
Ambra Vale E. Bris	63	D3
Ambra Vale S. Bris	63	D3
Ambra Vale W. Bris	63	D3
Ambra Vale. Bris	63	D3
Ambrose Rd. Bris	63	D3
Ambury. Bath	101	F3
Amercombe Wlk. Bris	80	B4
Amery La. Bath	102	A3
Ames La. Kilm	139	D3
Amesbury Dr. Blea	122	A3
Ammerdown Terr. Faulk	139	F4
Anchor La. Bris	63	E3
Anchor Rd. Bath	84	A1
Anchor Rd. Bris	63	E3
Anchor Rd. Kingsw	52	A1
Anchor Way. E in G	47	E2
Andereach Cl. Bris	80	A4
Andover Rd. Bris	63	F1
Andruss Dr. Dun	78	B1
Angers Rd. Bris	64	A2
Anglesea Pl. Bris	49	D1
Annandale Ave. W-S-M	88	C1
Anson Cl. Keyn	82	B1
Anstey St. Bris	50	B1
Anstey's Rd. Kingsw	65	E3
Anthea Rd. Bris	50	C1
Antona Ct. Bris	47	E4
Antona Dr. Bris	47	E4
Antrim Rd. Bris	49	D3
Anvil Rd. Yatt	74	C1
Anvil St. Bris	63	F3
Apex Ct. St Gif	24	B2
Apperley Cl. Yate	39	E4
Apple Tree Dr. Wins	125	D4
Appleby Wlk. Bris	79	E4
Applecroft. Well	133	F3
Appledore Cl. Bris	80	A4
Applegate. Bris	35	D2
Appletree Ct. W-S-M	89	D1
Apseleys Mead. St Gif	24	B1
Apsley Cl. W-S-M	88	B1
Apsley Cl. Bris	49	D1
Apsley St. Bris	50	B2
Arbutus Dr. Bris	48	B4
Arcade The. Bris	63	F4
Arch Cl. Lo Ash	61	F1
Archer Ct. Kingsw	65	F2
Archer Wlk. Bris	80	C3
Archfield Rd. Bris	49	E1
Archgrove. Lo Ash	61	F1
Archway St. Bath	102	A3
Arden Cl. St Gif	36	C3
Arden Cl. W-S-M	88	C2
Ardenton Wlk. Bris	35	D2
Ardern Cl. Bris	48	A4
Argus Rd. Bris	63	E2
Argyle Ave. Bris	50	B1
Argyle Ave. W-S-M	104	C2
Argyle Dr. Yate	27	F2
Argyle Pl. Bris	63	D3
Argyle Rd. Bris	51	D1
Argyle Rd. Bris	63	F4
Argyle Rd. Cleve	57	E3
Argyle St. Bath	102	A3
Argyle St. Bris	50	B1
Argyle St. Bris	63	E2
Argyle Terr. Bath	101	E3
Arley Cotts. Bris	49	E1
Arley Hill. Bris	49	E1
Arley Park. Bris	49	E1
Arley Terr. Bris	50	C1
Arlingham Way. Bris	23	F1
Arlington Rd. Bath	101	E3
Arlington Rd. Bris	64	B3
Arlington Villas. Bris	63	D4
Armada Pl. Bris	49	F1
Armes Ct. Bath	102	A3
Armidale Ave. Bris	49	F1
Armoury Sq. Bris	64	A4
Armstrong Ct. Yate	27	E2
Armstrong Way. Yate	27	D2
Arnall Dr. Bris	34	C1
Arneside Rd. Bris	35	E1
Arno's St. Bris	64	A2
Arnold Ct. Ch Sod	28	A1
Amor Cl. W-S-M	89	D2
Arrowfield Cl. Bris	80	A1
Arthur Skemp Cl. Bris	64	A4
Arthur St. Bris	64	A3
Arthur St. Bris	64	B4
Arthurswood Rd. Bris	79	D2
Arundel Cl. Bris	79	D3
Arundel Rd. Bath	85	D1
Arundel Rd. Bris	49	E2
Arundel Rd. Cleve	57	E2
Arundel Wlk. Keyn	81	E3
Arundell Ct. W-S-M	104	C4
Arundell Rd. W-S-M	87	F1
Ascot Cl. Bris	35	F1
Ascot Cl. Mang	37	F1
Ash Cl. St Gif	36	B4
Ash Cl. Wins	108	A1
Ash Cl. Yate	27	E2
Ash Gr. Bath	101	E2
Ash Gr. Bris	51	E2
Ash Gr. Cleve	57	F2
Ash Gr. W-S-M	104	C1
Ash Hayes Dr. Nail	59	F1
Ash Hayes Rd. Nail	59	F1
Ash La. Alm	23	E1
Ash Rd. Bris	49	E2
Ash Ridge Rd. St Gif	24	A2
Ash Tree Cl. Blea	122	B3
Ash Tree Ct. Rad	132	C1
Ash Wlk. Bris	35	D2
Ashbourne Cl. Kingsw	66	B3
Ashburton Rd. Bris	35	E1
Ashbury Dr. W-S-M	88	A1
Ashcombe Cres. Kingsw	66	B3
Ashcombe Gdns. W-S-M	105	D4
Ashcombe Park Rd. W-S-M	88	A1
Ashcombe Rd. W-S-M	104	C4
Ashcott. Bris	79	F4
Ashcroft Ave. Keyn	81	E3
Ashcroft Rd. Bris	48	B4
Ashcroft. W-S-M	105	D1
Ashdene Ave. Bris	50	B2
Ashdene Rd. W-S-M	105	D4
Ashdown Rd. Portis	45	D3
Ashel's Batch. Litt	129	E1
Asher La. Bris	63	F4
Ashes La. Hi Cha	120	A2
Ashfield Rd. Bris	63	D2
Ashford Dr. W-S-M	105	D1
Ashford Rd. Bath	101	E2
Ashford Rd. Bris	36	A4
Ashford Rd. Wring	93	F2
Ashford Way. Kingsw	66	A2
Ashgrove Ave. Ab Lei	62	A4
Ashgrove Ave. Bris	49	F2
Ashgrove Rd. Bris	49	D1
Ashgrove Rd. Bris	49	F2
Ashgrove Rd. Bris	63	D2
Ashgrove. P St J	133	E4
Ashgrove. Thorn	8	B1
Ashland Rd. Bris	79	D2
Ashleigh Cl. Paul	131	F3
Ashleigh Cl. W-S-M	105	D4
Ashleigh Cres. Yatt	91	D4
Ashleigh Rd. W-S-M	105	D4
Ashleigh Rd. Yatt	91	D4
Ashley Ave. Bath	101	E4
Ashley Cl. Bris	49	F2
Ashley Court Rd. Bris	49	F1
Ashley Down Rd. Bris	49	F2
Ashley Grove Rd. Bris	49	F1
Ashley Grove Rd. Bris	50	A1
Ashley Hill. Bris	49	F1
Ashley La. Blag	110	A3
Ashley La. Winsl	120	C4
Ashley La. Wring	110	A3
Ashley Par. Bris	49	F1
Ashley Park. Bris	49	F2
Ashley Rd. Bathf	86	B1
Ashley Rd. Bris	49	F1
Ashley Rd. Cleve	57	D1
Ashley St. Bris	50	A1
Ashley Trading Est. Bris	49	F1
Ashley. Kingsw	65	F4
Ashman Cl. Bris	64	A4
Ashmans Gate. Paul	131	F3
Ashmead Rd Ind Est. Keyn	82	A3
Ashmead Rd. Keyn	82	A3
Ashmead Way. Bris	62	C3
Ashmead. Clut	114	C1
Ashton Ave. Bris	63	D3
Ashton Cl. Cleve	57	D1
Ashton Cres. Nail	59	E1
Ashton Dr. Bris	62	C1
Ashton Gate Rd. Bris	63	D2
Ashton Gate Terr. Bris	63	D2
Ashton Rd. Bris	62	C2
Ashton Rd. Lo Ash	62	C2
Ashton Vale Rd. Bris	62	C2
Ashton Way. Keyn	81	F3
Ashton. Bris	37	E1
Ashvale Cl. Nail	60	A1
Ashville Rd. Bris	63	D2
Ashwell La. Marsh	70	A2
Ashwicke. Bris	80	A3
Ashwood. E Harp	128	C2
Aspen Cl. Col	70	C3
Aspley Cl. Bath	101	D4
Aspley Rd. Bath	101	D4
Assembly Rooms La. Bris	63	E3
Aston Gate Underpass. Bris	62	C2
Astry Cl. Bris	34	A1
Atchley St. Bris	64	A4
Atherston. Kingsw	66	B3
Athlone Wlk. Bris	63	F1
Atholl Cl. W-S-M	88	C2
Atkins Cl. Bris	80	C3
Atlantic Rd S. W-S-M	87	E1
Atlantic Rd. W-S-M	87	E1
Atlantic Rd. Avon	47	E4
Atlantic Rd. W-S-M	87	E1
Atlas Cl. Bris	51	D1
Atlas Rd. Bris	63	F2
Atlas St. Bris	64	A3
Atwell Dr. St Gif	24	A1
Atwood Dr. Bris	34	A1
Aubrey Meads. Bitt	82	C4
Aubrey Rd. Bris	63	D2
Auburn Ave. Kingsw	66	A2
Auburn Rd. Bris	49	D1
Auckland Cl. W-S-M	104	C2
Audley Ave. Bath	101	E4
Audley Cl. Bath	101	E4
Audley Gr. Bath	101	E4
Audley Park Rd. Bath	101	E4
Audrey Wlk. Bris	49	E4
Aust Rd. Aust	13	F3
Aust Rd. Olve	13	F3
Aust Rd. Piln	12	B2
Austen Dr. W-S-M	89	D2
Austen Gr. Bris	50	A4
Avalon Cl. Yatt	74	A1
Avalon House. Nail	59	E1
Avalon Rd. Bris	65	D3
Avebury Rd. Bris	62	C1
Avening Cl. Nail	75	F4
Avening Green. Char	10	B4
Avening Rd. Bris	65	D4
Avenue The. Back	76	A4
Avenue The. Bath	102	A3
Avenue The. Bath	102	C3
Avenue The. Bris	48	C2
Avenue The. Bris	49	D1
Avenue The. Bris	49	F2
Avenue The. Bris	64	C4
Avenue The. Cleve	57	F3
Avenue The. Keyn	81	F3
Avenue The. St Gif	24	A1
Avenue The. St Gif	36	B3
Avenue The. Tims	116	A1
Avenue The. Wins	125	E4
Avenue The. Yate	27	E1
Avenue The. Yatt	91	D4
Averay Rd. Bris	50	B2
Avon Bsns Pk. Bris	51	D2
Avon Cl. Keyn	81	F3
Avon Cl. W-S-M	104	C1
Avon Cres. Bris	63	D3
Avon Cres. Wickw	18	A3
Avon Ct. Bathe	86	A2
Avon Gorge Ind Est. Avon	47	E4
Avon Gr. Bris	48	B1
Avon La. Keyn	82	C2
Avon Mill La. Keyn	81	F3
Avon Park. Bath	101	D4
Avon Park. Bris	64	B4
Avon Rd. Char	11	D2
Avon Rd. E in G	47	E3
Avon Rd. Keyn	81	F3
Avon Rise. Luck	31	F2
Avon Riverside Est. Avon	47	E4
Avon St. Bath	101	F3
Avon St. Bris	63	F3
Avon Trading Est. Bris	64	A3
Avon Vale. Bris	48	B2
Avon Valley Bsns Pk. Bris	64	C3
Avon View. Kingsw	65	D2
Avon Way. Bris	48	B2
Avon Way. Portis	45	C3
Avon Way. Thorn	15	E4
Avon Wlk. Bris	79	D3
Avonbank Ind Centre. Avon	47	E4
Avonbridge Trading Est. Avon	33	E1
Avondale Bldgs. Bath	85	D1
Avondale Pl. Bathe	85	F2
Avondale Rd. Bath	101	D3
Avondale Rd. Bris	64	B4
Avondown Cl. Bris	35	E1
Avondown Ct. Bris	63	E1
Avonlea. Kingsw	65	E3
Avonleaze. Bris	48	A3
Avonleigh Ct. Bris	63	D1
Avonleigh Rd. Bris	63	D1
Avonmouth Rd. Avon	47	E4
Avonmouth Way. Avon	33	C2
Avonmouth Way. Avon	34	C2
Avonside Rd. Bris	64	B3
Avonside Way. Bris	64	C3
Avonsmere Residential Pk. Bris	36	B2
Avonwood Cl. Bris	47	F3
Awdelett Cl. Bris	34	A1
Awkley La. Olve	13	F1
Awkward Hill. But	111	E3
Axbridge Cl. Nail	75	F4
Axbridge Moor Dro. Axb	125	E1
Axbridge Rd. Bath	102	A1
Axbridge Rd. Bris	63	F1
Axbridge Rd. Ched	125	F1
Axe Cl. W-S-M	105	D3
Axford Way. P St J	133	E4
Axis. Bris	79	E3
Aycote Cl. W-S-M	88	B1
Ayford La. Marsh	69	F4
Aylesbury Cres. Bris	63	D1
Aylesbury Rd. Bris	63	D1
Aylmer Cres. Bris	80	A3
Aylminton Wlk. Bris	34	A1
Ayr St. Bath	101	E3
Aztec Centre The. St Gif	24	A1
Aztec West. St Gif	24	A1
Back La. Axb	125	E1
Back La. E in G	47	E3
Back La. K Sey	73	D3
Back La. Litt	129	D1
Back La. Litt	129	F1
Back La. Marsh	69	F4
Back La. Wickw	18	A3
Back Of Kingsdown Par. Bris	63	E4
Back Rd. Bris	63	D2
Back St. H Up	20	A2

Back St. W-S-M	104	C4
Back Stoke La. Bris	48	C3
Backfields La. Bris	63	F4
Backfields. Bris	63	F4
Backwell Bow. Back	60	B1
Backwell Comm. Back	76	A4
Backwell Hill Rd. Back	76	C2
Backwell Wlk. Bris	78	C4
Baden Hill Rd. Tyth	16	B3
Baden Rd. Bris	64	B4
Baden Rd. Kingsw	66	A4
Badenham Gr. Bris	47	F4
Bader Cl. Yate	27	E2
Badger's La. Alm	23	E1
Badgers Cl. St Gif	24	B2
Badgers Rise. Portis	44	C2
Badgers Wlk. Bris	64	B1
Badgeworth. Yate	39	E3
Badminton Centre The. Yate	27	E1
Badminton Ct. Yate	27	E1
Badminton Gdns. Bath	101	E4
Badminton Rd. Bris	49	F1
Badminton Rd. Ch Sod	40	C4
Badminton Rd. Fr Cot	38	B3
Badminton Rd. Mang	51	F4
Badminton Rd. West	38	B3
Badminton Rd. Yate	27	D1
Badminton Trading Est. Yate	27	D1
Badminton Wlk. Mang	51	F4
Badminton. Bris	37	E1
Baggridge Hill. Well	134	C4
Baglyn Ave. Kingsw	51	F2
Bagnell Cl. Bris	80	C3
Bagnell Rd. Bris	80	C3
Bagstone Rd. Wickw	16	C2
Bailbrook Gr. Bath	85	E2
Bailbrook La. Bath	85	E2
Baildon Cres. W-S-M	105	D2
Baildon Ct. W-S-M	104	C2
Baildon Rd. W-S-M	105	D2
Baileys Court Rd. St Gif	36	C3
Baileys Ct Rd. St Gif	37	D3
Baileys Ct. St Gif	36	C3
Bailiffs Cl. Axb	125	E1
Bailiffs' Wall. Axb	125	E1
Bainsbury View.	137	F1
Baker Cl. Cleve	73	D4
Baker St. W-S-M	104	C4
Baker's Bldgs. Wring	92	B1
Bakers Par. Tims	116	A1
Bakers La. Chil	137	E2
Bakers La. Wring	109	E4
Bakersfield. Kingsw	66	A2
Balaclava Rd. Bris	50	C2
Baldwin St. Bris	63	E3
Balfour Rd. Bris	63	D2
Ballance St. Bath	101	F4
Ballast La. Avon	33	F1
Balls Barn La. Ban	90	A1
Balmain St. Bris	64	A2
Balmoral Cl. St Gif	36	B2
Balmoral Ct. Mang	52	A3
Balmoral Rd. Bris	49	F1
Balmoral Rd. Keyn	81	F2
Balmoral Rd. Kingsw	65	F1
Balmoral Way. W-S-M	88	B1
Baltic Pl. E in G	47	E2
Bamfield. Bris	80	A3
Bampton Cl. Bris	79	D4
Bampton. W-S-M	88	C1
Banfield Cl. Bris	48	A4
Bangor Gr. Bris	64	C3
Bangrove Wlk. Bris	47	F4
Banister Gr. Bris	79	E4
Bank Pl. E in G	47	E2
Bank Rd. Avon	33	E4
Bank Rd. Kingsw	65	F4
Bank Rd. Piln	22	C3
Banks Cl. Cleve	73	E4
Bankside Rd. Bris	64	B2
Bankside. Mang	51	F2
Banner Rd. Bris	49	F1
Bannerdown Cl. Bathe	86	A2
Bannerdown Dr. Bathe	86	A2
Bannerdown Rd. Bathe	86	B3
Bannerleigh La. Lo Ash	62	C3
Bannerleigh Rd. Lo Ash	62	C3
Bannerman Rd. Bris	64	A4
Bannetts Tree Cres. Alve	15	D3
Bantock Cl. Bris	79	E3
Bantry Rd. Bris	79	D4
Banwell Cl. Bris	79	D4
Banwell Cl. Keyn	82	A1
Banwell Rd. Ban	123	F4
Banwell Rd. Bath	118	B4
Banwell Rd. Bris	63	D2
Banwell Rd. Lock	106	A2
Banwell Rd. Wins	123	F4
Banwell Rd. Wins	124	C4
Baptist St. Bris	50	A1
Barberry Farm Rd. Yatt	74	A1
Barbour Gdns. Bris	79	E2
Barbour Rd. Bris	79	E2
Barcroft Cl. Bris	65	E4
Barker Wlk. Bris	50	A1
Barley Cl. Fr Cot	38	A4
Barley Cl. Mang	52	A3
Barley Croft. Bris	48	C3
Barn End. Marsh	70	A4
Barn Hill. Well	133	F3
Barn La. Pens	115	D4
Barn Owl Way. St Gif	36	C3
Barn Pool. Ship	125	F4
Barnabas St. Bris	49	F1
Barnaby Cl. Mid No	132	A1
Barnack Trading Est. Bris	63	E1
Barnard Wlk. Keyn	81	E2
Barnard's Cl. Yatt	91	E4
Barnes St. Bris	64	B4
Barnfield Way. Bathe	86	A2
Barnhill Rd. Ch Sod	28	A1
Barns Cl. Ba Gu	77	F2
Barns Cl. Nail	59	F1
Barnstable House. Bris	63	F4
Barnstaple Rd. Bris	79	F4
Barnstaple Wlk. Bris	79	F4
Barnwood Rd. Yate	39	E4
Barossa Pl. Bris	63	E3
Barrack's La. Bris	47	E4
Barratt St. Bris	50	B1
Barrington Cl. Kingsw	51	F1
Barrington Ct. Bris	63	F2
Barrington Ct. Kingsw	51	F1
Barrow Court La. Kingsw	66	A3
Barrow Court La. Back	77	D3
Barrow Hill Cres. Bris	47	E4
Barrow Hill Rd. Bris	47	E3
Barrow Hill. Wick	67	D3
Barrow La. Ba Gu	77	F1
Barrow La. Win	94	C4
Barrow Rd. Bath	101	E1
Barrow Rd. Bris	64	A4
Barrow Rd. Lock	105	F1
Barrow St. Ba Gu	77	E3
Barrow St. Lo Ash	77	E3
Barrowmead Dr. Bris	47	F4
Barrows The. Bris	79	D2
Barrows The. W-S-M	105	E4
Barrs Court Ave. Kingsw	66	A3
Barrs Court Rd. Kingsw	66	A3
Barrs Court Rd. Kingsw	66	A3
Barrs La. N Nib	5	F2
Barry Cl. Kingsw	66	B3
Barry Cl. W-S-M	105	D1
Bartlett St. Bath	101	F4
Bartlett's Rd. Bris	63	E1
Bartley St. Bris	63	E2
Barton Cl. Alve	15	D3
Barton Cl. Bris	64	C3
Barton Cl. Wint	37	F3
Barton Dro. Wins	124	B3
Barton Green. Bris	64	A4
Barton Hill Rd. Bris	64	A4
Barton Manor. Bris	64	A3
Barton Rd.	124	""
Barton Rd. Bris	63	F3
Barton Rd. Co Bi	123	F3
Barton St. Bath	101	F3
Barton St. Bris	63	E4
Barton The. Blea	122	B3
Barton The. Cor	100	A4
Barton The. Kingsw	65	E2
Barton The. N St P	135	F2
Barton Vale. Bris	63	F3
Bartonia Gr. Bris	64	B1
Barwood Cl. Kingsw	65	F4
Batch La. Lymp	121	F2
Batch The. Blag	110	A2
Batch The. But	111	D4
Batch The. Ch Mag	96	A2
Batch The. Chur	108	C2
Batch The. Co Mar	128	A4
Batch The. Farm	116	A3
Batch The. Hin Cha	119	F1
Batch The. Wring	93	E4
Batch The. Yatt	91	D4
Batches The. Bris	63	D1
Batchfield La. West	53	E4
Bates Cl. Bris	64	A4
Bath Bldgs. Bris	49	F1
Bath Hill. Keyn	81	F3
Bath Hill. Well	118	B1
Bath New Rd. Mid No	132	C2
Bath Old Rd. Mid No	132	C2
Bath Rd. Bitt	82	B4
Bath Rd. Blag	109	E2
Bath Rd. Blag	110	C1
Bath Rd. Box	86	C3
Bath Rd. Bris	64	B2
Bath Rd. Ch Sod	41	D2
Bath Rd. Chur	109	E2
Bath Rd. Col	70	C1
Bath Rd. Doyn	67	F2
Bath Rd. Farm	115	F3
Bath Rd. Keyn	82	B2
Bath Rd. Kingsw	65	F2
Bath Rd. Kingsw	66	B3
Bath Rd. N St P	135	F3
Bath Rd. P St J	133	E4
Bath Rd. Paul	131	F3
Bath Rd. Sist	66	B3
Bath Rd. Thorn	15	D1
Bath Rd. Tor	41	E2
Bath Rd. Wick	67	E2
Bath Riverside Bsns Park.		
Bath	101	F3
Bath St. Bath	101	F3
Bath St. Bris	63	D2
Bath St. Bris	63	F3
Bath St. Kingsw	51	F2
Bath View. Chil	137	F1
Bathampton La. Bath	85	F1
Bathford Hill. Bathf	86	A1
Bathford Hill. Co Dan	98	C3
Bathurst Par. Bris	63	E3
Bathurst Rd. W-S-M	105	E4
Bathwell Rd. Bris	64	A2
Bathwick Hill. Bath	102	B3
Bathwick Rise. Bath	102	A4
Bathwick St. Bath	102	A4
Batley Ct. Kingsw	66	B2
Batstone Cl. Bath	85	D1
Batten Ct. Ch Sod	28	A1
Batten's La. Bris	65	D3
Battenburg Rd. Bris	65	D4
Battens Rd. Bris	65	D4
Battersby Way. Bris	34	C1
Battersea Rd. Bris	64	B4
Battery La. Portis	45	D4
Battery Rd. Portis	45	E3
Battle La. Ch Mag	96	A2
Battson Rd. Bris	80	C2
Baugh Gdns. Mang	37	F1
Baugh Rd. Mang	37	F1
Bay Gdns. Bris	50	B1
Bay Rd. Cleve	57	E3
Bay Tree Cl. Bris	35	F4
Bay Tree Rd. Bath	85	D1
Bay Tree Rd. Cleve	57	F1
Bayleys Dr. Kingsw	65	E3
Baynham Ct. Kingsw	65	D3
Baynton Rd. Bris	63	D2
Bayswater Ave. Bris	49	D2
Bayswater Rd. Bris	49	F4
Baytree Rd. W-S-M	88	B1
Baytree View. W-S-M	88	B1
Beach Ave. Cleve	57	E1
Beach Ave. Piln	22	A4
Beach End Rd. W-S-M	104	B1
Beach Hill. Bitt	66	C2
Beach Hill. Portis	45	E3
Beach La. Bitt	67	E1
Beach Rd E. Portis	45	E3
Beach Rd W. Portis	45	E3
Beach Rd. Piln	21	F4
Beach Rd. W St L	88	A3
Beach Rd. W-S-M	88	A2
Beach The. Cleve	57	E2
Beachgrove Gdns. Bris	51	E2
Beachgrove Rd. Bris	51	D2
Beachley Wlk. Bris	47	E4
Beacon La. Wint	37	E3
Beacon Rd. Bath	85	D1
Beaconlea. Kingsw	65	E3
Beaconsfield Rd. Bris	49	D1
Beaconsfield Rd. Bris	64	A2
Beaconsfield Rd. Cleve	57	F2
Beaconsfield Rd. W-S-M	104	C4
Beaconsfield St. Bris	64	A3
Beale Cl. Bris	80	C3
Beam St. Bris	64	B4
Bean Acre The. Bris	47	E4
Bean St. Bris	50	A1
Beanhill Cres. Alve	15	D3
Bearbridge Rd. Bris	78	C2
Beau St. Bath	101	F3
Beauchamp Rd. Bris	49	E2
Beauchamps Dr. Chil	138	A3
Beauford Sq. Bath	101	F3
Beaufort Ave. Mid No	132	A1
Beaufort Ave. Yate	27	E1
Beaufort Cl. Bris	64	B4
Beaufort Cres. St Gif	36	C2
Beaufort Ct. Mang	52	A4
Beaufort East. Bath	85	E1
Beaufort Gdns. Nail	59	E1
Beaufort Hts. Bris	64	C4
Beaufort Park. St Gif	24	B2
Beaufort Pl. Bath	85	E1
Beaufort Pl. Bris	37	D1
Beaufort Rd. Bris	37	D1
Beaufort Rd. Bris	49	D1
Beaufort Rd. Bris	49	F3
Beaufort Rd. Bris	51	E1
Beaufort Rd. Bris	64	C4
Beaufort Rd. Fr Cot	38	A4
Beaufort Rd. Mang	51	F3
Beaufort Rd. Mang	52	A4
Beaufort Rd. W-S-M	104	C4
Beaufort Rd. Yate	27	E1
Beaufort St. Bris	63	E1
Beaufort St. Bris	64	A4
Beaufort Terr. Bris	64	B1
Beaufort. Bris	37	E1
Beauley Rd. Bris	63	D2
Beaumont Cl. Kingsw	66	A2
Beaumont Cl. W-S-M	104	C2
Beaumont St. Bris	64	A4
Beaumont Terr. Bris	64	A4
Beaver Cl. Wint	37	F4
Beazer Cl. Kingsw	66	C4
Becket Ct. Puck	53	D3
Becket Dr. W-S-M	89	D2
Becket Rd. W-S-M	89	D2
Becket's La. Nail	75	F4
Beckford Gdns. Bath	102	A4
Beckford Gdns. Bris	80	A2
Beckford Rd. Bath	102	A4
Beckhampton Rd. Bath	101	E3
Beckington Rd. Bris	63	F1
Beckington Wlk. Bris	63	F1
Beckington. W-S-M	105	D1
Beckspool Rd. Bris	51	E4
Bedford Cres. Bris	49	F3
Bedford Rd. W-S-M	104	C2
Bedford St. Bath	102	A4
Bedminster Down Rd. Bris	63	D1
Bedminster Par. Bris	63	E2
Bedminster Pl. Bris	63	E2
Bedminster Rd. Bris	63	E1
Bedwin Cl. Portis	44	C2
Beech Ave. Bath	102	C3
Beech Cl. Alve	15	D3
Beech Cl. Kingsw	66	A3
Beech Cl. Ship	125	F4
Beech Dr. Nail	60	A2
Beech Dr. Ship	125	F4
Beech Gr. Bath	101	E2
Beech Leaze. Alve	15	D3
Beech Rd. Keyn	82	C2
Beech Rd. Ship	125	F4
Beech Rd. Yatt	91	E4
Beech Terr. Rad	132	B1
Beechcroft Wlk. Bris	50	A4
Beechcroft. Dun	78	B1
Beechen Cliff Rd. Bath	101	F3
Beechen Dr. Bris	51	D2
Beeches Gr. Bris	64	B1
Beeches Ind Est. Ir Act	27	D1
Beeches The. Bath	85	D1
Beeches The. Bris	101	E1
Beeches The. Kingsw	66	B1
Beeches The. Wins	108	A2
Beechfield Cl. Lo Ash	62	B1
Beechmont Cl. W-S-M	105	D1
Beechmont Dr. W-S-M	105	D1
Beechmount Gr. Bris	80	A4
Beechwood Ave. Kingsw	65	C3
Beechwood Ave. Lock	106	A2
Beechwood Cl. Bris	80	B4
Beechwood Dr. Portis	44	C3
Beechwood Rd. Bath	102	A1
Beechwood Rd. Bris	51	D2
Beechwood Rd. E in G	47	D2
Beechwood Rd. Nail	59	E1
Beechwood Rd. Portis	44	C3
Beehive Yd. Bath	102	A4
Beek's La. Marsh	69	E3
Beesmoor Rd. Fr Cot	38	A3
Begbrook Dr. Bris	50	C3
Begbrook La. Bris	50	C3
Begbrook Park. Bris	51	D4
Beggar Bush La. Lo Ash	61	F2
Beggar Bush La. Wrax	61	F2
Beggars Bush La. Ab Lei	61	F2
Beggarswell Cl. Bris	63	F4
Belfast Wlk. Bris	79	F4
Belfry Ave. Bris	65	D4
Belfry. Kingsw	66	A3
Belgrave Cres. Bath	85	D1
Belgrave Hill. Bris	49	D1
Belgrave Pl. Bris	63	D4
Belgrave Rd. Bath	85	D1
Belgrave Rd. Bris	63	D4
Belgrave Rd. W-S-M	105	D4
Bell Barn Rd. Bris	48	B3
Bell Cl. Farm	115	F3
Bell Hill Rd. Bris	65	D4
Bell Hill. Bris	50	B2
Bell Hill. N St P	135	F2
Bell La. Bris	63	E4
Bell Rd. Fr Cot	38	B3
Bell Sq. Blag	110	C2
Bell Sq. Marsh	70	A4
Bell Wlk. Wring	92	C1
Bella Vista Rd. Bath	101	F4
Bellamy Ave. Bris	79	E2
Bellamy Cl. Bris	65	D3
Belland Dr. Bris	79	F2
Belle Vue Rd. Bris	50	B1
Bellevue Cl. Kingsw	65	F4
Bellevue Cotts. Bris	63	D3
Bellevue Cres. Bris	63	D3
Bellevue Pk. Bris	64	B1
Bellevue Rd. Bris	63	F2
Bellevue Rd. Bris	65	D4
Bellevue Rd. Cleve	57	E2
Bellevue Rd. Kingsw	65	F4
Bellevue Terr. Bris	63	D4
Bellevue Terr. Bris	64	B1
Bellevue. Bris	63	D3
Bellhorse La. E Harp	128	B3
Bellhouse Wlk. Bris	34	A1
Bellifants. Farm	116	A3
Bellotts Rd. Bath	101	E3
Belluton La. Pens	97	E3
Belluton Rd. Bris	64	A2
Belmont Dr. St Gif	36	C3
Belmont Rd. Wrax	61	D2
Belmont Hill. Wrax	61	D1
Belmont Rd. Bath	102	B1
Belmont Rd. Bris	49	F2
Belmont Rd. Bris	64	B2
Belmont Rd. Wins	125	D4
Belmont St. Bris	50	A1
Belmore Gdns. Bath	101	D2
Beloe Rd. Bris	49	F3
Belroyal Ave. Bris	64	C2
Belstone Wlk. Bris	79	E4
Belton Ct. Bath	84	A1
Belton Rd. Bris	64	A4
Belton Rd. Portis	45	D3
Belvedere Cres. W-S-M	88	B1
Belvedere Rd. Bris	49	D2
Belvoir Rd. Bath	101	E3
Belvoir Rd. Bris	49	F1
Benches La. But	94	B2
Benford Cl. Bris	51	E3
Bennell Batch. Chil	137	F2
Bennell Cl. Chil	137	F2
Bennell Cotts. Chil	137	F2
Bennett La. Bath	85	D1
Bennett Rd. Bris	64	C4
Bennett St. Bath	101	F4
Bennett Way. Bris	62	C3
Bennett's Ct. Yate	28	A1
Bennett's Rd. Bath	85	E2
Bennetts Way. Cleve	57	F3
Bensaunt Gr. Bris	35	E2
Bentley Cl. Bris	79	F2
Bentley Rd. W-S-M	89	D2
Benville Ave. Bris	48	B4
Berenda Dr. Kingsw	66	A2
Beresford Cl. Keyn	82	C1
Beresford Gdns. Bath	84	A2
Berkeley Ave. Bris	49	E2
Berkeley Ave. Bris	63	E4
Berkeley Ave. Mid No	132	A1
Berkeley Cl. Char	11	D3
Berkeley Cl. Mang	52	A4
Berkeley Cres. W-S-M	104	B1
Berkeley Gdns. Keyn	81	F2
Berkeley Gr. Bris	50	B1
Berkeley Green Rd. Bris	50	B1
Berkeley Green. Bris	37	D1
Berkeley Mead. St Gif	37	D3
Berkeley Pl. Bris	63	D4
Berkeley Rd. Bris	49	D2
Berkeley Rd. Bris	51	D1
Berkeley Rd. Kingsw	65	D4
Berkeley Rd. Mang	51	E3
Berkeley Rd. Bris	63	E4
Berkeley St. Bris	50	B2
Berkshire Rd. Bris	49	E2
Berlington Ct. Bris	63	F3
Berners Cl. Bris	79	E4
Berrow Wlk. Bris	63	F1
Berrows Mead. Wickw	27	D4
Berry La. Bris	49	F3
Berwick La. Alm	34	B4
Berwick Rd. Bris	50	A1
Beryl Gr. Bris	80	B4
Beryl Rd. Bris	63	D2
Besom La. West	39	E3
Bethel Rd. Bris	64	C4
Betjeman Ct. Kingsw	66	A3
Bevan Ct. Bris	35	F1
Beverley Ave. Mang	37	F1
Beverley Cl. Bris	65	D3
Beverley Gdns. Bris	48	B4
Beverley Rd. Bris	49	F4
Beverston Gdns. Bris	34	A1
Beverstone. Kingsw	65	E4
Bevington Cl. Bris	23	F1
Bevington La. Stone	2	C4
Bevington Wlk. Bris	23	F1
Bewdley Rd. Bath	102	A2
Bexley Rd. Bris	51	D2
Bibstone. Kingsw	66	A4
Bibury Ave. St Gif	36	A4
Bibury Cl. Bris	49	E4
Bibury Cl. Nail	60	A1
Bibury Cres. Bris	49	E4
Bibury Cres. Kingsw	65	E3
Bickerton Cl. Bris	34	C2
Bickfield La. Co Mar	128	A4
Bickford Cl. Kingsw	66	A3
Bickley Cl. Kingsw	65	E1
Biddeston Rd. Bris	49	F4
Biddisham Cl. Nail	59	F1
Biddisham La. Badg	123	F1
Biddle St. Yatt	91	D4
Bideford Cres. Bris	79	F4
Bideford Rd. W-S-M	88	C1
Bidwell Cl. Bris	35	D2
Bifield Cl. Bris	80	C3
Bifield Gdns. Bris	80	C3
Bifield Rd. Bris	80	C3
Big Tree Cl. Co Bi	124	B2
Bignell Cl. Wins	124	C4
Bigwood La. Bris	63	D4
Bilberry Cl. Bris	48	B4
Bilbie Cl. Bris	49	F4
Bilbie Cl. Ch St	112	C4
Bilbie Rd. Ch St	112	C4
Bilbie Rd. W-S-M	89	D2
Bilbury La. Bath	101	F3

Billand Cl. Bris ... 78 C2
Bilsham La. Piln ... 12 C1
Bince's Lodge La. Mid No . 132 A2
Binces La. Marks ... 99 F2
Bindon Dr. Bris ... 35 E2
Binhay Rd. Yatt ... 91 E4
Binley Gr. Bris ... 80 B2
Binmead Gdns. Bris ... 79 D2
Birbeck Rd. Bris ... 48 C3
Birch Ave. Blea ... 122 B3
Birch Ave. Cleve ... 57 F2
Birch Cl. Bris ... 35 F4
Birch Cl. Lock ... 106 A2
Birch Croft. Bris ... 80 A2
Birch Ct. Keyn ... 81 E2
Birch Dr. Alve ... 14 C2
Birch Dr. Chur ... 109 D3
Birch Dr. Puck ... 53 D3
Birch Gr. Portis ... 45 E2
Birch Rd. Bris ... 63 D2
Birch Rd. Kingsw ... 51 F2
Birch Rd. Rad ... 132 C1
Birch Rd. Yate ... 27 E1
Birchall Rd. Bris ... 49 E2
Birchdale Rd. Bris ... 80 A4
Birches The. Nail ... 60 A1
Birchwood Ave. W-S-M ... 105 D4
Birchwood Dr. Wrax ... 61 D2
Birchwood La. Pens ... 97 F1
Birchwood Rd. Bris ... 64 C2
Birdale Cl. Bris ... 34 C2
Birdcombe Cl. Nail ... 59 F2
Birdlip Cl. Nail ... 76 A4
Birdwell La. Lo Ash ... 61 F1
Birdwell Rd. Lo Ash ... 61 F1
Birdwood. Kingsw ... 65 E3
Birgage Rd. H Up ... 19 F1
Birkdale. Kingsw ... 66 A3
Birkdale. Yate ... 39 F4
Birkett Rd. W-S-M ... 87 D1
Birkin St. Bris ... 64 A3
Birnbeck Rd. W-S-M ... 87 E1
Bisdee Rd. Lock ... 105 E1
Bishop Ave. W-S-M ... 89 D2
Bishop Manor Rd. Bris ... 49 E4
Bishop Rd. Bris ... 49 E2
Bishop St. Bris ... 63 F4
Bishop St. Faulk ... 134 B1
Bishop's Wood. Alm ... 24 B3
Bishops Cl. Bris ... 48 C2
Bishops Cove. Bris ... 78 C3
Bishops Mead. Brock ... 92 A4
Bishopsworth Rd. Bris ... 79 D4
Bishopthorpe Rd. Bris ... 49 F4
Bishport Ave. Bris ... 79 E2
Bishport Cl. Bris ... 79 D2
Bisley. Yate ... 39 E4
Bittern Cl. W-S-M ... 88 C1
Bitterwell Cl. West ... 38 B2
Bittlemead. Bris ... 79 F2
Black Boy Hill. Bris ... 49 D1
Blackacre. Whit ... 80 B2
Blackberry Ave. Bris ... 50 C3
Blackberry Dr. W-S-M ... 89 D1
Blackberry Hill. Bris ... 50 C3
Blackbird Cl. Rod ... 138 A4
Blackdown Ct. Bris ... 80 A3
Blackdown Rd. Portis ... 45 D3
Blackfriars Rd. Nail ... 59 D1
Blackfriars. Bris ... 63 E4
Blackhorse Hill. Alm ... 35 D4
Blackhorse La. Mang ... 52 A4
Blackhorse Pl. Mang ... 52 A3
Blackhorse Rd. Kingsw ... 65 E4
Blackhorse Rd. Mang ... 52 A4
Blackmoor Cl. Chur ... 109 E3
Blackmoor Rd. Ab Lei ... 47 F1
Blackmoor. Chur ... 109 E3
Blackmoor. Cleve ... 57 E1
Blackmoor. W-S-M ... 88 C1
Blackmoors La. Bris ... 62 C2
Blackmore Dr. Bath ... 101 E3
Blacksmith La. Bathe ... 85 D3
Blacksmith's La. Kel ... 83 D2
Blackthorn Cl. Bris ... 79 E3
Blackthorn Dr. St Gif ... 36 B4
Blackthorn Gdns. W-S-M ... 89 D1
Blackthorn Rd. Bris ... 79 E3
Blackthorn Sq. Cleve ... 57 E1
Blackthorn Terr. W-S-M ... 89 D1
Blackthorn Wlk. Nail ... 60 A1
Blackthorn Wlk. Kingsw ... 51 F1
Bladdock Bldgs. Faulk ... 134 A1
Bladen Cl. Portis ... 45 F2
Blagdon Cl. Bris ... 63 F1
Blagdon Cl. W-S-M ... 104 C1
Blagdon Cl. Blag ... 110 C3
Blagdon La. But ... 110 C3
Blagdon Park. Bath ... 101 D2
Blagrove Cl. Bris ... 79 E2
Blagrove Cres. Bris ... 79 E2
Blaisdon Cl. Bris ... 34 C1
Blaisdon. Yate ... 39 F4

Blaise Hamlet. Bris ... 34 B1
Blaise Wlk. Bris ... 48 B4
Blake End. W-S-M ... 88 C2
Blake Rd. Bris ... 50 A3
Blakeney Gr. Nail ... 75 E4
Blakeney Mills. Yate ... 27 E1
Blakeney Rd. Bris ... 23 F1
Blakeney Rd. Bris ... 50 A4
Blakes Rd. Thorn ... 8 A1
Blanchards. Ch Sod ... 40 B4
Blandford Cl. Bris ... 49 D3
Blandford Cl. Nail ... 59 F1
Bleadon Hill. W-S-M ... 122 A4
Bleadon Rd. Blea ... 122 A3
Blenheim Cl. P St J ... 133 E4
Blenheim Cl. W-S-M ... 89 D1
Blenheim Dr. Bris ... 36 A2
Blenheim Dr. Yate ... 27 E2
Blenheim Gdns. Bath ... 85 D1
Blenheim St. Bris ... 50 A1
Blenheim Way. Portis ... 45 F3
Blenheim Rd. Bris ... 49 D2
Blenman Cl. Bris ... 51 D4
Blind La. Bath ... 84 B1
Blind La. Ch St ... 112 C4
Blind La. Cong ... 91 F3
Blind La. Pris ... 117 D2
Bloomfield Ave. Bath ... 101 F2
Bloomfield Ave. Tims ... 116 A2
Bloomfield Cl. Tims ... 116 A2
Bloomfield Cres. Bath ... 101 E1
Bloomfield Dr. Bath ... 101 E1
Bloomfield Gr. Bath ... 101 F2
Bloomfield La. Paul ... 131 F3
Bloomfield Park Rd. Tims ... 116 A2
Bloomfield Park. Bath ... 101 F2
Bloomfield Rd. Bath ... 101 F2
Bloomfield Rd. Bris ... 64 B2
Bloomfield Rd. Tims ... 116 A2
Bloomfield Rise N. Bath ... 101 E1
Bloomfield Rise. Bath ... 101 E1
Bloomfield Terr. P St J ... 133 E4
Bloomfield. W-S-M ... 105 D1
Bloy St. Bris ... 50 B1
Bluebell Cl. Thorn ... 8 B1
Bluebells The. St Gif ... 36 C4
Blueberry Way. W-S-M ... 88 C1
Blythe Gdns. W-S-M ... 89 D2
Boat La. Lymp ... 122 B2
Boat Stall La. Bath ... 102 A3
Bobbin La. Westw ... 120 C2
Bobbin Parr. Westw ... 120 C2
Bockenem Cl. Thorn ... 15 E4
Bodey Cl. Kingsw ... 66 A3
Bodmin Wlk. Bris ... 79 F4
Bodyce Rd. Alve ... 15 D3
Boiling Wells La. Bris ... 50 A2
Bolton Rd. Bris ... 49 F2
Bond St. Bris ... 63 F4
Bond's La. Marsh ... 55 F1
Bonhill Rd. Bi Sut ... 113 E3
Bonnington Wlk. Bris ... 50 A4
Boot La. Bris ... 63 E2
Booth Rd. Bris ... 63 E2
Bordesley Rd. Bris ... 80 A2
Borgie Pl. W-S-M ... 88 C2
Borleyton Wlk. Bris ... 78 C2
Borver Gr. Bris ... 79 D2
Boscombe Cres. Mang ... 51 F4
Boston Rd. Bris ... 49 F4
Boswell Rd. Westw ... 120 C2
Boswell St. Bris ... 50 B1
Botham Cl. W-S-M ... 89 D2
Botham Dr. Bris ... 64 B1
Boucher Pl. Bris ... 50 A1
Boulevard. W-S-M ... 104 C4
Boulters Rd. Bris ... 79 E2
Boulton's La. Bris ... 65 E4
Boulton's Rd. Kingsw ... 65 E4
Boundaries The. Lymp ... 122 A1
Boundary Cl. Rod ... 138 A4
Boundary Cl. W-S-M ... 104 C2
Boundary Rd. Avon ... 33 E2
Boundary Rd. Fr Cot ... 38 B4
Bourchier Gdns. Bris ... 79 D2
Bourne Cl. Bris ... 65 D4
Bourne Cl. Wint ... 37 F4
Bourne La. Blag ... 110 A2
Bourne La. Bris ... 50 A1
Bourne Rd. Bris ... 65 D4
Bourneville Bsns Centre.
    Bris ... 64 C1
Bourneville Rd. Bris ... 64 B4
Bournville Rd. W-S-M ... 104 C2
Boursland Cl. St Gif ... 24 B1
Bourton Ave. St Gif ... 36 B4
Bourton Cl. St Gif ... 36 B4
Bourton Combe. Back ... 76 C4
Bourton La. Co Bi ... 124 C2
Bourton Mead. Back ... 76 C4
Bourton Mead. Lo Ash ... 62 A1
Bourton Wlk. Bris ... 79 D4
Bouverie St. Bris ... 64 A4
Boverton Rd. Bris ... 36 A2
Bowden Cl. Bris ... 48 B4
Bowden Hill. Chil ... 137 E2

Bowden Pl. Mang ... 51 F4
Bowden Rd. Bris ... 64 C4
Bowden Way. Wrax ... 61 D2
Bower Rd. Bris ... 63 D2
Bower Wlk. Bris ... 63 F2
Bowerleaze. Bris ... 48 B3
Bowditch La. Mid No ... 132 A2
Bowling Hill Bsns Pk.
    Ch Sod ... 28 A1
Bowling Hill. Ch Sod ... 28 A1
Bowling Rd. Ch Sod ... 40 A4
Bowood. Bris ... 37 E1
Bowring Cl. Bris ... 79 E2
Bowsland Way. St Gif ... 24 B1
Bowstreet La. Alm ... 35 D4
Box Bush La. Ban ... 90 B1
Box Rd. Bathe ... 86 B2
Box Rd. Bathf ... 86 B2
Box Wlk. Keyn ... 81 E2
Boxbury Hill. Paul ... 131 F2
Boxhedge Farm La. West ... 38 C2
Boyce Dr. Bris ... 50 A1
Boyce's Ave. Bris ... 63 D4
Boyd Cl. Wick ... 67 D4
Boyd Rd. Keyn ... 82 B2
Brabazon Rd. Bris ... 36 A1
Bracewell Gdns. Bris ... 35 E2
Bracey Dr. Bris ... 51 E3
Brackenbury Dr. St Gif ... 36 C3
Brackendean. St Gif ... 24 B1
Bracton Dr. Bris ... 80 A3
Bradeston Gr. Bris ... 51 D4
Bradford Cl. Cleve ... 57 E1
Bradford Park. Bath ... 102 A1
Bradford Rd. Bath ... 102 A1
Bradford Rd. Bathf ... 86 A1
Bradford Rd. Winsl ... 120 C4
Bradhurst St. Bris ... 64 A3
Bradley Ave. Wint ... 37 F3
Bradley Cres. Bris ... 47 F3
Bradley Rd. Bris ... 23 F1
Bradley Stoke Way. St Gif ... 24 B1
Bradley Stoke Way. St Gif ... 37 D3
Bradstone Rd. Wint ... 37 E3
Bradville Gdns. Lo Ash ... 77 F4
Bradwell Gr. Bris ... 49 E4
Brae Rd. Wins ... 125 D4
Brae Rise. Wins ... 125 D4
Braemar Ave. Bris ... 35 F1
Braemar Cres. Bris ... 35 F1
Bragg's La. Bris ... 63 F4
Braikenridge Cl. Cleve ... 57 E1
Braikenridge Rd. Bris ... 64 B2
Brainsfield. Bris ... 48 C3
Brake Cl. Kingsw ... 65 F4
Brake Cl. St Gif ... 36 C3
Brake The. Fr Cot ... 38 B3
Brake The. Yate ... 27 F3
Brakewell Gdns. Bris ... 80 A2
Bramble Dr. Bris ... 48 B2
Bramble La. Bris ... 48 B2
Bramble Rd. W-S-M ... 88 C2
Bramble Way. Bath ... 102 A1
Brambles The. Keyn ... 81 E2
Brambling Wlk. Bris ... 50 C3
Bramley Cl. E in G ... 47 E2
Bramley Cl. Kings ... 11 F2
Bramley Cl. Olve ... 14 A2
Bramley Cl. P St J ... 133 E4
Bramley Cl. Yatt ... 91 D4
Bramley Ct. Kingsw ... 65 F2
Bramley Dr. Back ... 76 A3
Bramley Sq. Cong ... 91 F2
Bramleys The. Nail ... 75 D4
Brampton Way. Portis ... 45 F2
Bramshill Dr. W-S-M ... 88 C2
Branch Rd. Hin Cha ... 119 F1
Branche Gr. Bris ... 79 E2
Brandash Rd. Ch Sod ... 28 A1
Brandon St. Bris ... 63 E3
Brandon Steep. Bris ... 63 E3
Brangwyn Gr. Bris ... 50 A3
Brangwyn Sq. W-S-M ... 88 C1
Branksome Cres. Bris ... 36 A2
Branksome Dr. Bris ... 36 A2
Branksome Dr. Wint ... 37 F3
Branksome Rd. Bris ... 49 D2
Branscombe Way. Portis ... 44 C2
Branscombe Wlk. Portis ... 44 C2
Branwhite Cl. Bris ... 50 A4
Brassknocker Hill. Bath ... 102 C1
Brassmill La. Bath ... 101 D4
Bratton Rd. Bris ... 79 E4
Braunton Rd. Bris ... 63 E2
Braydon Ave. St Gif ... 36 B4
Brayne Ct. Kingsw ... 65 F2
Braysdown Cl. P St J ... 133 D3
Braysdown La. P St J ... 133 D4
Braysdown La. P St J ... 133 E4
Breach La. Nail ... 74 C4
Breach Rd. Bris ... 63 D2
Breaches Gate. St Gif ... 36 C3
Breaches La. Keyn ... 82 A2
Breaches The. E in G ... 47 D3
Brean Down Ave. Bris ... 49 D2
Brean Down Ave. Bris ... 49 D3

Brean Down Ave. W-S-M .. 104 B2
Brean Rd. Lymp ... 121 F1
Brecknock Rd. Bris ... 64 A2
Brecon Rd. Bris ... 49 D3
Brecon View. W-S-M ... 105 D1
Bredon Cl. Kingsw ... 65 F4
Bredon Nook Rd. Bris ... 49 E4
Bredon. Yate ... 39 E4
Bree Cl. W-S-M ... 89 D2
Brendon Ave. W-S-M ... 104 C4
Brendon Cl. Kingsw ... 66 B2
Brendon Gdns. Nail ... 59 F1
Brendon Rd. Bris ... 63 E2
Brendon Rd. Portis ... 45 D3
Brenner St. Bris ... 50 A1
Brent Cl. W-S-M ... 105 D1
Brent Rd. Bris ... 49 F3
Brentry Ave. Bris ... 64 A4
Brentry Hill. Bris ... 35 D1
Brentry La. Bris ... 35 D2
Brentry Rd. Bris ... 50 C2
Brereton Way. Kingsw ... 66 A2
Brewerton Cl. Bris ... 35 E2
Brewery Hill. Bitt ... 82 C4
Brewery La. Hol ... 138 B1
Briar Cl. Nail ... 60 A1
Briar Cl. Rod ... 138 B4
Briar Mead. Yatt ... 74 A1
Briar Rd. Lock ... 105 F2
Briar Way. Bris ... 51 E2
Briar Wlk. Bris ... 51 E2
Briarfield Ave. Kingsw ... 65 E3
Briarleaze. Alve ... 14 C1
Briars The. Back ... 75 F4
Briarside Rd. Bris ... 35 E2
Briarwood. Bris ... 48 C3
Briary Rd. Portis ... 45 E3
Briavels Gr. Bris ... 49 F1
Brick St. Bris ... 63 F4
Bridewell La. Bath ... 101 F3
Bridewell La. Lock ... 106 B1
Bridewell St. Bris ... 63 E4
Bridge Cl. Whit ... 80 B2
Bridge Farm Cl. Bris ... 80 A2
Bridge Farm Sq. Cong ... 91 E2
Bridge Gdns. Farm ... 116 A3
Bridge Place Rd. Tims ... 132 C4
Bridge Rd. Bath ... 101 E3
Bridge Rd. Blea ... 122 A3
Bridge Rd. Bris ... 50 A2
Bridge Rd. Ir Act ... 27 D1
Bridge Rd. Kingsw ... 52 A2
Bridge Rd. Lo Ash ... 62 C3
Bridge Rd. Sist ... 52 B2
Bridge St. Bath ... 102 A3
Bridge St. Bris ... 50 B1
Bridge St. Bris ... 63 E3
Bridge Valley Rd. Bris ... 62 C4
Bridge Way. Fr Cot ... 38 A4
Bridge Wlk. Bris ... 50 A4
Bridgeleap Rd. Mang ... 51 F4
Bridges Dr. Bris ... 51 E3
Bridgman Gr. Bris ... 36 A2
Bridgwater Ct. W-S-M ... 105 D2
Bridgwater Rd. Ba Gu ... 77 F1
Bridgwater Rd. Blea ... 122 B2
Bridgwater Rd. Bris ... 78 B3
Bridgwater Rd. Dun ... 78 B3
Bridgwater Rd. Lymp ... 122 B2
Bridgwater Rd. W-S-M ... 104 C1
Bridgwater Rd. Wins ... 125 D3
Bridle Way. Alve ... 14 C2
Briercliffe Rd. Bris ... 48 B4
Brierly Furlong. St Gif ... 36 C2
Briery Leaze Rd. Bris ... 80 A3
Bright St. Bris ... 64 A4
Bright St. Kingsw ... 65 E4
Brighton Cres. Bris ... 63 E1
Brighton Mews. Bris ... 63 D4
Brighton Pl. Kingsw ... 51 E1
Brighton Rd. Bris ... 35 F4
Brighton Rd. Bris ... 49 E1
Brighton Rd. W-S-M ... 104 C3
Brighton St. Bris ... 63 F4
Brighton Terr. Bris ... 63 D1
Brigstocke Rd. Bris ... 63 F4
Brimbles. Bris ... 36 A1
Brimbleworth La. Lock ... 89 E2
Brimridge Rd. Wins ... 125 D4
Brinkmarsh La. Fall ... 9 E1
Brinkworthy Rd. Bris ... 50 C3
Brinmead Wlk. Bris ... 78 C2
Brins Cl. St Gif ... 36 C2
Brinsea Batch. Cong ... 108 C4
Brinsea La. Cong ... 108 C4
Brinsea Rd. Cong ... 91 F1
Brinsham La. Yate ... 28 A3
Briscoes Ave. Bris ... 79 E2
Brislington Hill. Bris ... 64 C1
Brislington Trading Est. Bris ... 64 C1
Bristol And Exeter Mews.
    Bris ... 63 F3
Bristol Gate. Bris ... 62 C3
Bristol Hill. Bris ... 64 B1
Bristol Phoenix. Bris ... 63 D1
Bristol Rd Lower. W-S-M ... 87 F1
Bristol Rd. Bris ... 37 D1
Bristol Rd. Ch St ... 112 C4

Bristol Rd. Chur ... 109 D3
Bristol Rd. Co Dan ... 81 F3
Bristol Rd. Cong ... 91 E3
Bristol Rd. Cor ... 100 B4
Bristol Rd. Crom ... 17 D4
Bristol Rd. Fr Cot ... 26 A2
Bristol Rd. Ir Act ... 26 A2
Bristol Rd. Lock ... 89 E1
Bristol Rd. Luck ... 31 F2
Bristol Rd. Mid No ... 132 C2
Bristol Rd. Paul ... 130 C3
Bristol Rd. Paul ... 131 F4
Bristol Rd. Pens ... 97 E4
Bristol Rd. Portis ... 45 F2
Bristol Rd. Ship ... 108 B1
Bristol Rd. Thorn ... 15 D4
Bristol Rd. Whit ... 80 B2
Bristol Rd. Wins ... 125 E4
Bristol Rd. Wint ... 37 E2
Bristol Vale Centre For Industry.
    Bris ... 63 D1
Bristol View. Bath ... 118 B4
Bristowe House. Bris ... 51 D4
Britannia Cl. Chil ... 137 E2
Britannia Cres. St Gif ... 36 B3
Britannia Rd. Bris ... 35 F4
Britannia Rd. Bris ... 50 B1
Britannia Rd. Bris ... 65 E4
Britannia Rd. Kingsw ... 65 E4
Britannia Way. Cleve ... 57 E1
British Rd. Bris ... 63 E2
Brittan Pl. Portb ... 46 C2
Britten Ct. Kingsw ... 65 F2
Britten's Cl. Paul ... 131 F3
Britten's Hill. Paul ... 131 F3
Brixham Rd. Bris ... 63 E1
Brixton Rd. Bris ... 64 A4
Broad Croft. St Gif ... 24 B1
Broad La. West ... 38 D2
Broad La. West ... 39 D2
Broad La. Yate ... 27 E2
Broad Mead La. Win ... 95 D2
Broad Oak Rd. Bris ... 78 C2
Broad Oaks. Lo Ash ... 62 C3
Broad Plain. Bris ... 63 F3
Broad Quay. Bath ... 101 F3
Broad Quay. Bris ... 63 E3
Broad Rd. Bris ... 51 E1
Broad Rd. Priddy ... 126 C4
Broad St. Bath ... 102 A4
Broad St. Bris ... 63 E4
Broad St. Cong ... 91 E2
Broad St. Kingsw ... 51 F2
Broad St. Mang ... 51 F4
Broad St. Wring ... 92 B1
Broad Street Pl. Bath ... 102 A4
Broad Weir. Bris ... 63 F4
Broad Wlk. Bris ... 64 A1
Broadbury Rd. Bris ... 79 F4
Broadcroft Ave. Yatt ... 74 C1
Broadcroft. Ch Mag ... 95 F2
Broadfield Ave. Bris ... 51 E1
Broadfield Rd. Bris ... 64 A1
Broadlands Ave. Keyn ... 81 E3
Broadlands Dr. Bris ... 34 A1
Broadlands. Cleve ... 57 F2
Broadleas. Bris ... 79 E4
Broadleaze Way. Winsc ... 107 F1
Broadleys Ave. Bris ... 49 E4
Broadmead La. Keyn ... 82 A3
Broadmead. Bris ... 63 F4
Broadmoor La. Bath ... 84 A2
Broadmoor La. Charl ... 83 F2
Broadmoor Park. Bath ... 84 A1
Broadmoor Vale. Bath ... 84 A2
Broadoak Hill. Bris ... 78 C2
Broadoak Rd. Chur ... 109 D3
Broadoak Rd. W-S-M ... 104 B2
Broadoak Wlk. Bris ... 51 D2
Broadstone La. K Sey ... 72 C2
Broadstone Wlk. Bris ... 79 E3
Broadstones. Mon Far ... 103 F4
Broadway Ave. Bris ... 49 E3
Broadway Cl. Chil ... 137 E2
Broadway La. Paul ... 132 A3
Broadway Rd. Bris ... 49 E2
Broadway Rd. Bris ... 78 C3
Broadway. Bath ... 102 A3
Broadway. Chil ... 137 E2
Broadway. Keyn ... 82 B2
Broadway. Ship ... 125 F4
Broadway. W-S-M ... 105 D1
Broadway. Yate ... 27 F1
Broadways Dr. Bris ... 50 C4
Brock End. Portis ... 44 C2
Brock St. Bath ... 101 F4
Brockhurst Gdns. Bris ... 65 D4
Brockhurst Rd. Bris ... 65 D4
Brockley Cl. Nail ... 59 E1
Brockley Cl. St Gif ... 36 B4
Brockley Cl. W-S-M ... 104 C1
Brockley Combe Rd. Brock . 76 A1
Brockley Combe Rd. Wring . 76 A1
Brockley Cres. W-S-M ... 104 C1
Brockley La. Brock ... 75 D2
Brockley Rd. Keyn ... 82 B2

145

rockley Way. Brock

Chapel Row. Bathf

ckley Way. Brock 75 D2
ckley Way. Yatt 75 D2
ckley Wlk. Bris 79 D4
ckridge La. Fr Cot 38 B4
cks La. Lo Ash 61 F1
cks Rd. Bris 79 E2
ckway. Nail 59 F1
ckwood. Winsl 120 C4
ckworth Cres. Bris 50 C3
ckworth. Yate 39 E3
mley Dr. Mang 51 E4
mley Heath Ave. Mang 51 E4
mley Heath Rd. Mang 37 E1
mley Heath Rd. Mang 51 E4
mley Rd. Bris 49 F3
mley Rd. Pens 96 C1
mpton Cl. Kingsw 66 A4
mpton Rd. W-S-M 105 D1
ncksea Rd. Bris 35 F1
ok Cl. Lo Ash 62 A1
ok Gate. Bris 62 C1
ok Hill. Bris 49 F1
ok La. Bris 49 F1
ok La. Bris 50 C3
ok Lintons. Bris 64 B2
ok Rd. Bath 101 E3
ok Rd. Bris 49 F1
ok Rd. Bris 50 C1
ok Rd. Bris 51 D2
ok Rd. Bris 63 E2
ok Rd. Kingsw 66 A4
ok Rd. Mang 51 F3
ok St. Bris 64 B4
ok St. Ch Sod 28 A1
ok Way. St Gif 36 B4
okcote Dr. St Gif 36 B3
okdale Rd. Bris 79 D3
okfield Ave. Bris 49 E2
okfield Cl. Ch Sod 28 A1
okfield La. Bris 49 E1
okfield Park. Bath 84 A1
okfield Rd. Bris 49 E1
okfield Rd. St Gif 36 A4
okfield Wlk. Cleve 57 F2
okfield Wlk. Kingsw 66 B2
okland Rd. Bris 49 E3
okland Rd. W-S-M 105 D4
oklands. Pris 117 E2
oklea. Kingsw 66 A2
okleaze Bldgs. Bath 85 D1
okleaze. Bris 48 B3
oklyn Rd. Bath 85 E1
oklyn Rd. Bris 79 D4
oklyn. Wring 92 B1
okmead. Thorn 15 E4
okside Cl. Bathe 85 F3
okside Cl. Paul 131 F3
okside Dr. Farm 115 F3
okside Dr. Fr Cot 38 A4
okside House. Bath 84 A1
okside Rd. Bris 64 C1
okside. E in G 47 E2
okside. Paul 131 F3
okside. Win 94 C4
okthorpe Ave. Bris 34 A1
okthorpe. Yate 39 E4
okview Wlk. Bris 79 D4
om Farm Cl. Nail 75 F4
om Hill La. Paul 131 F4
om Hill. Bris 50 C3
omground. Winsl 120 C4
omhill La. Clut 114 C2
therswood Ct. St Gif 24 B2
ugham Hayes. Bath 101 E3
w Hill. Bathe 85 F2
w The. Bath 101 D3
wning Ct. Bris 50 A4
wnlow Rd. W-S-M 104 C2
ce Ave. Bris 50 B1
ce Rd. Bris 50 B1
ummel Way. Paul 131 E3
nel Cl. W-S-M 104 C1
nel Ct. Yate 27 E1
nel Lock Rd. Bris 62 C3
nel Rd. Bris 79 D4
nel Rd. Nail 59 D1
nel Way. Bris 62 C2
nel Way. Thorn 15 D4
nswick Pl. Bris 62 C3
nswick Sq. Bris 63 F4
nswick St. Bath 102 A4
nswick St. Bris 63 F4
nswick St. Bris 64 B4
ton Ave. Bath 101 F2
ton Ave. Portis 45 D3
ton Cl. Nail 75 F4
ton. W-S-M 105 D1
ansons Cl. Bris 50 B3
ant Ave. Rad 132 B1
ant Gdns. Cleve 57 E1
ant's Hill. Bris 65 D3
ants Cl. Bris 37 E1
nland Ave. Bris 49 F2
ns Pk The. Bris 79 F2
ckingham Dr. St Gif 36 B3
ckingham Gdns. Mang 51 F3
ckingham Pl. Bris 63 D4
ckingham Pl. Mang 51 F3
Buckingham Rd. Bris 64 B3
Buckingham Rd. W-S-M 105 D1
Buckingham St. Bris 63 E1
Buckingham Vale. Bris 63 D4
Buckland Green. W-S-M 89 D3
Bucklands Batch. Nail 75 F4
Bucklands Dr. Nail 76 A4
Bucklands End. Nail 75 F4
Bucklands Gr. Nail 75 F4
Bucklands La. Nail 75 F4
Bucklands View. Nail 76 A4
Bude Ave. Bris 65 D4
Bude Cl. Nail 60 A1
Bude Rd. Bris 36 A2
Bull La. Bris 64 C3
Bull La. E in G 47 E2
Bull's Hill. Well 118 C1
Bullens Cl. St Gif 24 B1
Buller Rd. Bris 64 B1
Bullocks La. K Sey 73 E2
Bully La. Yate 17 E1
Bumper's Batch. Sosto 119 D4
Bungay's Hill. Paul 115 F1
Bunting Ct. W-S-M 88 C1
Burbank Cl. Kingsw 66 A2
Burchells Ave. Bris 51 D1
Burchells Green Cl. Bris 51 D1
Burchells Green Rd. Bris 51 D1
Burcott Rd. Avon 33 E3
Burden Cl. St Gif 36 C3
Burfoot Gdns. Bris 80 C2
Burfoot Rd. Bris 80 C2
Burford Cl. Bath 101 D2
Burford Cl. Portis 45 F2
Burford Gr. Bris 47 F3
Burgage Cl. Ch Sod 40 A4
Burgess Green Cl. Bris 64 C4
Burghill Rd. Bris 35 D1
Burghley Rd. Bris 49 F1
Burgis Rd. Bris 80 B3
Burleigh Gdns. Bath 101 D4
Burleigh Way. Wickw 18 A3
Burley Ave. Mang 51 F3
Burley Crest. Mang 51 F3
Burley Gr. Mang 51 F2
Burlington Rd. Bris 49 D1
Burlington Rd. Mid No 132 B1
Burlington St. Bath 101 F4
Burlington St. W-S-M 104 C4
Burnbush Cl. Bris 80 C3
Burnell Dr. Bris 63 F4
Burneside Cl. Bris 35 E1
Burney Way. Kingsw 66 A2
Burnham Cl. Kingsw 51 F1
Burnham Cl. W-S-M 104 C1
Burnham Dr. Kingsw 51 F1
Burnham Dr. W-S-M 104 C1
Burnham Rd. Bath 101 E3
Burnham Rd. Bris 47 E3
Burrington Ave. W-S-M 104 C1
Burrington Cl. Nail 59 F1
Burrington Cl. W-S-M 104 C1
Burrington Wlk. Bris 79 D4
Burrough Way. Wint 37 F3
Burrows La. Hol 138 A1
Burton Cl. Bris 63 F3
Burton Cl. Bris 64 C4
Burton Ct. Bris 63 D4
Burton Rd. A Tur 42 C3
Burton St. Bath 101 F3
Burwalls Rd. Lo Ash 62 C3
Bury Hill La. Yate 28 A4
Bury Hill. Wint 37 F2
Bury La. Doyn 67 F4
Bury The. Lock 106 A2
Burycourt Cl. Bris 34 A1
Bush Ave. St Gif 36 B3
Bushes La. Hort 29 D3
Bushy Park. Bris 63 F2
Bushy Thorn Rd. Ch St 112 C4
Butcombe La. But 111 D4
Butcombe Wlk. Bris 80 A3
Butcombe. W-S-M 105 D1
Butham La. Ch Mag 96 A2
Butlass Cl. Paul 115 E1
Butt's Batch. Wring 92 B1
Butt's La. Mon Far 103 F4
Butt's La. Tor 55 D2
Butterfield Cl. Bris 49 F4
Butterfield Park. Cleve 57 E1
Butterfield Rd. Bris 49 F4
Buttermere Rd. W-S-M 105 D3
Butterworth Ct. Bris 79 E4
Button Cl. Bris 80 A3
Butts Batch. Co Bi 124 A2
Buxton Wlk. Bris 50 A4
Byfields. Cleve 73 E4
Byron Pl. Bris 63 D4
Byron Pl. Kingsw 51 F2
Byron Rd. Bath 101 F2
Byron Rd. Lock 106 A2
Byron Rd. W-S-M 105 D2
Byron St. Bris 50 A1
Byron St. Bris 64 B4

Cabot Cl. Keyn 82 B1
Cabot Cl. Yate 27 F1
Cabot Green. Bris 64 A4
Cabot Rise. Portis 45 D3
Cabot Way. Bris 62 C3
Cabot Way. E in G 47 E2
Cabot Way. W-S-M 89 D2
Cabstand. Portis 45 E3
Cadbury Camp La W. Nail 58 B3
Cadbury Camp La. Nail 59 E3
Cadbury Farm Rd. Yatt 91 E4
Cadbury Halt. W in G 44 C1
Cadbury Heath Rd. Kingsw 66 A3
Cadbury La. W in G 44 C1
Cadbury Rd. Keyn 82 A1
Cadbury Rd. Portis 45 F2
Cadbury Sq. Cong 91 E2
Caddick Cl. Kingsw 51 F1
Cade Cl. Kingsw 65 F3
Cade Cl. St Gif 36 C3
Cadogan Rd. Bris 80 A4
Caen Rd. Bris 63 E2
Caernarvon Rd. Keyn 81 E2
Caine Rd. Bris 49 F4
Cains Cl. Kingsw 65 F3
Cairn Cl. Nail 60 A1
Cairns Rd. Bris 49 E2
Cairns' Cres. Bris 49 F1
Cakenhill Rd. Bris 64 C1
Calcott Rd. Bris 64 A2
Caldbeck Cl. Bris 35 E1
Calder Cl. Keyn 82 A2
Caldicot Cl. Bris 34 B1
Caldicot Cl. Kingsw 66 A1
Caledonia Mews. Bris 62 C3
Caledonia Pl. Bris 62 C4
Caledonian Rd. Bath 101 E3
California Rd. Kingsw 66 A2
Callicroft Rd. Bris 36 A4
Callington Rd. Bris 64 B1
Callowhill Ct. Bris 63 F4
Calton Gdns. Bath 101 F3
Calton Rd. Bath 102 A3
Cam Brook Cl. Tims 132 C4
Camberley Dr. Fr Cot 37 F4
Camberley Rd. Bris 79 E4
Camborne Rd. Bris 50 A4
Cambrian Dr. Yate 27 F2
Cambridge Cres. Bris 49 D4
Cambridge Gr. Cleve 57 E3
Cambridge Park. Bris 49 D2
Cambridge Rd. Bris 49 F2
Cambridge Rd. Cleve 57 F3
Cambridge St. Bris 63 F2
Cambridge st. Bris 64 B4
Cambridge Terr. Bath 102 A3
Cambrook House. Clut 130 C4
Camden Rd. Bath 85 D1
Camden Rd. Bris 63 D3
Camden Row. Bath 101 F4
Camden Terr. Bris 63 D3
Camden Terr. W-S-M 104 C4
Cameley Cl. Clut 130 C4
Cameley Green. Bath 100 C3
Cameley Rd. Clut 130 B4
Camelford Rd. Bris 50 B1
Cameron Wlk. Bris 50 B3
Cameroons Cl. Keyn 81 F2
Camerton Cl. Keyn 82 C2
Camerton Hill. Tims 132 C4
Camerton Rd. Bris 50 B1
Camerton Rd. Tims 116 C1
Camp La. Tor 55 E2
Camp Rd N. W-S-M 87 D1
Camp Rd. Bris 62 C4
Camp Rd. O-on-S 7 D3
Camp Rd. W-S-M 87 E1
Camp View. Nail 59 E1
Campbell Farm Dr. Bris 33 F1
Campbell St. Bris 49 F1
Campion Cl. Thorn 8 B1
Campion Cl. W-S-M 105 E4
Campion Dr. St Gif 24 B1
Campion Wlk. Bris 79 E3
Camplins. Cleve 57 E1
Camvale. P St J 133 D4
Camview. Paul 131 E3
Camwal Rd. Bris 64 A3
Canada Coombe. Blea 106 A1
Canada Coombe. Lock 106 A1
Canada Way. Bris 63 D3
Canberra Gr. Bris 36 A2
Canberra Rd. W-S-M 104 C2
Canford La. Bris 48 C4
Canford La. Bris 49 D4
Canford Rd. Bris 48 C4
Cann La. Bitt 66 C3
Cann La. Sist 66 C3
Cannans Cl. Wint 37 F4
Cannon St. Bris 63 E2
Cannon St. Bris 63 E4
Cannon St. Bris 64 B4
Cannons Gate. Cleve 73 E4
Canon's Rd. Bris 63 E3
Canon's Wlk. Kingsw 51 F1
Canons Wlk. W-S-M 88 B1
Canowie Rd. Bris 49 D2
Cantell Gr. Bris 80 C3
Canterbury Cl. W-S-M 89 D2
Canterbury Cl. Yate 27 F2
Canterbury Rd. Bath 101 E3
Canterbury St. Bris 64 A3
Canters Leaze. Wickw 18 A2
Cantock's Cl. Bris 63 E4
Canvey Cl. Bris 49 F4
Canynge Rd. Bris 62 C4
Canynge Sq. Bris 62 C4
Canynge St. Bris 63 F3
Capel Cl. Kingsw 66 A4
Capel Rd. Bris 34 A1
Capenor Cl. Portis 45 E2
Capgrave Cl. Bris 65 D2
Capgrave Cres. Bris 65 D2
Caple La. Ch St 112 A3
Caraway Gdns. Bris 50 B1
Cardigan Cres. W-S-M 105 E4
Cardigan Rd. Bris 49 D3
Cardill Cl. Bris 79 D4
Carditch Dro. Cong 108 A4
Carey's Cl. Cleve 57 F2
Carice Gdns. Cleve 73 E4
Carisbrooke Rd. Bris 79 E4
Carlingford Terr Rd. Rad 133 D1
Carlingford Terr. Rad 133 D1
Carlisle Rd. Bris 50 B1
Carlow Rd. Bris 79 F4
Carlton Cl. Clut 114 C2
Carlton Ct. Bris 49 D4
Carlton Mansions. W-S-M 104 B4
Carlton Pk. Bris 64 B4
Carlton St. W-S-M 104 B4
Carmarthen Cl. Yate 27 F2
Carmarthen Gr. Kingsw 66 A1
Carmarthen Rd. Bris 49 D3
Carnarvon Rd. Bris 49 E1
Caroline Cl. Keyn 81 E2
Caroline Pl. Bath 101 F4
Carpenters La. Keyn 81 F3
Carre Gdns. W-S-M 88 C2
Carrington Rd. Bris 63 D2
Carroll Ct. Bris 36 C1
Carsons Rd. Sist 52 A1
Carter Rd. Paul 131 E3
Carter's Bldgs. Bris 62 C4
Carters Way. Chil 137 E2
Cartledge Rd. Bris 50 B1
Cashmore Ho. Bris 64 A4
Cassell Rd. Bris 51 E3
Cassey Bottom La. Bris 65 D4
Castle Cl. Back 76 C4
Castle Cl. Bris 34 C1
Castle Ct. Thorn 8 A1
Castle Farm La. Dun 78 A1
Castle Farm Rd. Kingsw 65 E1
Castle Gdns. Bath 101 F2
Castle Hill. Ban 107 E1
Castle La. Marsh 55 F1
Castle Rd. Cleve 57 F3
Castle Rd. Kingsw 51 E1
Castle Rd. Kingsw 66 B2
Castle Rd. Puck 53 E3
Castle Rd. W-S-M 88 C2
Castle St. Bris 63 F4
Castle St. Thorn 8 A1
Castle View Rd. Cleve 57 E3
Castlewood Cl. Cleve 57 E3
Caswell Hill. Portb 46 A1
Caswell La. Portb 46 B1
Catbrain Hill. Bris 35 D3
Catbrain La. Bris 35 D3
Catchpot La. Ch Sod 41 D3
Catemead. Cleve 73 E4
Cater Rd. Bris 79 D3
Catherine Hill. Olve 13 F1
Catherine Mead St. Bris 63 E2
Catherine Pl. Bath 101 F4
Catherine St. Avon 47 E4
Catherine Way. Bathe 86 A3
Catley Gr. Lo Ash 62 A1
Cato St. Bris 50 A1
Catsley Pl. Bath 85 E1
Cattistock Dr. Bris 65 D3
Cattle Market Rd. Bris 63 F3
Cattybrook Rd. Puck 52 B3
Cattybrook St. Bris 64 A4
Caulfield Rd. W-S-M 89 D2
Causeway The. Cong 91 E2
Causeway The. Fr Cot 38 B4
Causeway The. W in G 45 F1
Causeway The. Yatt 91 E4
Causeway View. Nail 59 E1
Causeway. Nail 59 D2
Causley Dr. Kingsw 66 A3
Cautletts Cl. Mid No 137 F4
Cavan Wlk. Bris 63 E1
Cave Ct. Bris 63 F4
Cave Dr. Bris 51 E3
Cave St. Bris 63 F4
Cavell Ct. Cleve 57 E1
Cavendish Cl. Keyn 82 B1
Cavendish Cres. Bath 101 F4
Cavendish Gdns. Bris 48 B2
Cavendish Rd. Bath 101 F4
Cavendish Rd. Bris 35 F4
Cavendish Rd. Bris 49 D3
Caveners Ct. W-S-M 88 A1
Caversham Dr. Nail 60 A1
Cecil Ave. Bris 50 C1
Cecil Rd. Bris 62 C4
Cecil Rd. Kingsw 65 E4
Cecil Rd. W-S-M 87 F1
Cedar Ave. W-S-M 88 B1
Cedar Cl. Bris 35 F4
Cedar Cl. Kingsw 66 A2
Cedar Cl. Lo Ash 61 F1
Cedar Dr. Keyn 81 E2
Cedar Gr. Bath 101 E2
Cedar Gr. Bris 48 B3
Cedar Hall. Bris 51 E4
Cedar Park. Bris 48 B3
Cedar Row. Bris 47 F3
Cedar Terr. Rad 132 B1
Cedar Way. Bath 101 F3
Cedar Way. Nail 60 A1
Cedar Way. Portis 45 E2
Cedar Way. Puck 53 E3
Cedar Way. Wint 37 E3
Cedarhurst Rd. Portis 44 C2
Cedars The. Ch St 95 E1
Cedric Rd. Bath 101 E4
Celandine Cl. Thorn 8 B1
Celestine Rd. Yate 27 E2
Celtic Way. Blea 122 B4
Cemetery Rd. Bris 64 A2
Cennick Ave. Kingsw 51 F1
Centaurus Rd. Bris 35 E4
Central Ave. Avon 22 A2
Central Ave. Kingsw 65 E3
Central Way. Cleve 57 F1
Ceres Cl. Kingsw 65 F1
Cerimon Gate. St Gif 36 C3
Cerney Gdns. Nail 60 A1
Cerney La. Bris 47 F3
Cesson Cl. Ch Sod 40 B4
Chadleigh Gr. Bris 79 E4
Chaffinch Dr. Rod 138 A4
Chaffins The. Cleve 57 F1
Chaingate La. Ir Act 27 D3
Chakeshill Cl. Bris 35 E2
Chakeshill Dr. Bris 35 E2
Chalcombe Cl. St Gif 36 B4
Chalcroft Wlk. Bris 78 C2
Chalfont Rd. W-S-M 105 E4
Chalford Cl. Yate 39 E4
Chalks Rd. Bris 64 B4
Chalks The. Ch Mag 96 A2
Challender Ave. Bris 34 C1
Challoner Ct. Bris 63 E3
Challow Dr. W-S-M 88 A1
Champion Rd. Kingsw 52 A1
Champneys Ave. Bris 34 C2
Chancel Cl. Nail 59 E1
Chancellors Pound. Wring 93 E2
Chancery St. Bris 64 A4
Chandag Rd. Keyn 82 A2
Chandler Cl. Bath 84 A1
Chandos Rd. Bris 49 E1
Chandos Rd. Keyn 81 F4
Chandos Trading Est. Bris 64 A3
Channel Hts. W-S-M 104 C1
Channel Rd. Cleve 57 F3
Channel View Cres. Portis 45 D3
Channel View Rd. Portis 45 D3
Channel's Hill. Bris 49 D4
Channon's Hill. Bris 50 C2
Chantry Cl. Nail 59 E1
Chantry Dr. W-S-M 89 D2
Chantry Gr. Bris 34 B1
Chantry La. Mang 37 F1
Chantry Mead Rd. Bath 101 F2
Chantry Rd. Bris 49 D1
Chantry Rd. Thorn 8 A1
Chapel Barton. Bris 63 D1
Chapel Barton. Nail 59 E1
Chapel Cl. Ch St 112 C4
Chapel Cl. Kingsw 66 A4
Chapel Cl. Nail 59 F1
Chapel Cl. Paul 130 C2
Chapel Cl. Win 95 D3
Chapel Gdns. Bris 35 D1
Chapel Green La. Bris 49 D1
Chapel Hill. Back 76 B4
Chapel Hill. But 111 E3
Chapel Hill. Cleve 57 E2
Chapel Hill. Newp 4 A4
Chapel Hill. Wring 92 B2
Chapel La. A Tur 43 D3
Chapel La. Bris 34 B1
Chapel La. Bris 50 C1
Chapel La. Bris 51 D2
Chapel La. Bris 51 E4
Chapel La. Brock 92 A4
Chapel La. Ch Sod 41 D4
Chapel La. Ch St 112 B4
Chapel La. Dyrh 54 B3
Chapel La. Hill 19 E4
Chapel La. Kingsw 66 A4
Chapel La. Thorn 9 D1
Chapel La. Win 95 D3
Chapel La. Yatt 91 F4
Chapel Rd. Bris 50 A1
Chapel Rd. Bris 79 D3
Chapel Rd. Kingsw 65 E3
Chapel Rd. Mid No 132 C2
Chapel Rd. O-on-S 7 E3
Chapel Row. Bath 101 F3
Chapel Row. Bathf 86 B1

Name	Page	Grid
Chapel Row. E in G	47	E2
Chapel Row. Luck	31	F2
Chapel St. Bris	64	A3
Chapel St. Thorn	15	D4
Chaplin Rd. Bris	50	A1
Chapter St. Bris	63	F4
Charbon Gate. St Gif	36	C3
Charborough Rd. Bris	35	F1
Charbury Wlk. Bris	47	F3
Chard Cl. Nail	75	F4
Chard Rd. Cleve	57	E2
Chardstock Ave. Bris	48	B4
Chardyke Dr. Clut	114	C1
Charfield Rd. Bris	35	E1
Charfield Rd. Kings	11	F3
Charfield. Kingsw	66	A4
Chargrove. Kingsw	66	B3
Chargrove. Yate	39	E4
Charis Ave. Bris	49	E4
Charity La. Hol	139	E1
Charity La. Kilm	139	E1
Charlcombe La. Bath	84	C2
Charlcombe La. Charl	84	C2
Charlcombe Rise. Bath	84	C1
Charlcombe View Rd. Bath	85	C1
Charlcombe Way. Bath	84	C1
Charlecombe Ct. Bris	48	C3
Charlecombe Rd. Bris	48	C3
Charles Ave. St Gif	36	C2
Charles Cl. Thorn	8	B2
Charles Pl. Bris	63	D3
Charles Rd. Bris	36	A2
Charles St. Bath	101	F3
Charles St. Bris	63	E4
Charlotte St S. Bris	63	E3
Charlotte St. Bath	101	F3
Charlotte St. Bris	63	E4
Charlotte St. Bris	63	F4
Charlton Ave. Bris	35	F1
Charlton Ave. W-S-M	104	B2
Charlton Dr. Wrax	60	B4
Charlton Gdns. Bris	35	E2
Charlton La. Bris	35	D2
Charlton La. Kilm	138	B4
Charlton Mead Ct. Bris	35	E2
Charlton Mead Dr. Bris	35	E2
Charlton Park. Keyn	81	E3
Charlton Park. Rod	138	A4
Charlton Pl. Bris	35	E2
Charlton Rd. Bris	35	E2
Charlton Rd. Bris	51	D1
Charlton Rd. Co Dan	81	E2
Charlton Rd. Hol	138	B2
Charlton Rd. Keyn	81	E2
Charlton Rd. Kilm	138	B2
Charlton Rd. Rod	138	A4
Charlton Rd. W-S-M	104	B2
Charlton St. Bris	64	A4
Charlton View. Portis	45	E3
Charminster Rd. Bris	51	D2
Charmouth Rd. Bath	101	D4
Charnell Rd. Kingsw	51	F2
Charnhill Brow. Kingsw	52	A2
Charnhill Cres. Kingsw	51	F2
Charnhill Dr. Kingsw	51	F2
Charnhill Ridge. Kingsw	52	A2
Charnhill Vale. Kingsw	51	F2
Charnwood. Kingsw	52	A2
Charter Rd. W-S-M	105	D2
Charter Wlk. Bris	80	A3
Charterhouse Cl. Nail	59	F1
Charterhouse Rd. Bris	64	B4
Chase La. Kings	18	B3
Chase La. Wickw	18	B3
Chase Rd. Kingsw	51	E1
Chase The. Bris	51	E2
Chatcombe. Yate	39	F4
Chatham Park. Bath	102	B3
Chatham Row. Bath	102	A4
Chatsworth Pk. Thorn	8	B1
Chatsworth Rd. Bris	51	D2
Chatsworth Rd. Bris	64	B2
Chatterton Green. Bris	79	F2
Chatterton Rd. Yate	27	E1
Chatterton Sq. Bris	63	F3
Chatterton St. Bris	63	F3
Chaucer Rd. Bath	101	F2
Chaucer Rd. Rod	138	A4
Chaucer Rd. W-S-M	105	D2
Chaucer Wlk. Bris	50	A4
Chaundey Gr. Bris	79	D3
Chavenage. Kingsw	66	A4
Cheap St. Bath	102	A3
Cheapside St. Bris	63	F2
Cheapside. Bris	63	F4
Cheddar Cl. Nail	75	F4
Cheddar Gr. Bris	79	D4
Cheddar Rd. Axb	125	E1
Chedworth Cl. Bath	102	C2
Chedworth Rd. Bris	50	A3
Chedworth. Kingsw	51	F2
Chedworth. Yate	39	D4
Cheese La. Bris	63	F3
Chelford St Gif	34	A4
Chelmer Gr. Keyn	81	F2
Chelmsford Wlk. Bris	64	C3
Chelscombe. Bath	84	B1
Chelsea Cl. Keyn	82	A3
Chelsea Rd. Bath	101	E4
Chelsea Rd. Bris	50	A1
Chelsea Rd. Bris	64	A4
Chelsfield. Back	76	A4
Chelston Rd. Bris	79	E4
Chelswood Ave. W-S-M	105	E4
Chelswood Gdns. W-S-M	105	E4
Cheltenham La. Bris	49	F1
Cheltenham Rd. Bris	49	F1
Cheltenham St. Bath	101	F3
Chelvey Batch. Brock	75	F2
Chelvey La. Brock	75	F2
Chelvey Rd. Nail	75	E3
Chelvey Rise. Nail	60	A1
Chelvy Cl. Bris	79	E2
Chelwood Dr. Bath	101	E1
Chelwood Rd. Bris	47	E4
Chelwood Rd. Keyn	82	C2
Chepstow Rd. Bris	79	E4
Chepstow Park. Mang	37	F1
Chepstow Wlk. Keyn	81	E3
Chequers Cl. Kingsw	66	B2
Cherington Rd. Bris	49	E4
Cherington Rd. Nail	60	A1
Cherington. Kingsw	65	D3
Cherington. Yate	39	E3
Cheriton Pl. Bris	49	D4
Cheriton Pl. Kingsw	66	B3
Cherry Ave. Cleve	57	F1
Cherry Cl. Yatt	91	D4
Cherry Garden La. Kingsw	66	A1
Cherry Garden Rd. Kingsw	66	B1
Cherry Gdns. Kingsw	66	B1
Cherry Gr. Mang	52	A3
Cherry Gr. Yatt	91	D4
Cherry Hay. Cleve	57	E1
Cherry La. Bris	63	F4
Cherry Orchard La. Bris	64	C4
Cherry Orchard La. Luck	31	E3
Cherry Rd. Ch Sod	28	A1
Cherry Rd. Lo Ash	61	F1
Cherry Rd. Nail	59	E1
Cherry Tree Cl. Bris	51	E1
Cherry Tree Cl. Keyn	81	E2
Cherry Tree Cl. Rad	132	C1
Cherry Tree Cres. Bris	51	E1
Cherry Wood. Kingsw	66	A1
Cherrytree Rd. Bris	51	E1
Cherrywood Rd. W-S-M	88	C1
Cherrywood Rise. W-S-M	88	C1
Chertsey Rd. Bris	49	D1
Cherwell Cl. Thorn	15	E4
Cherwell Rd. Keyn	82	A2
Chescombe Rd. Yatt	91	D4
Chesham Road N. W-S-M	105	D4
Chesham Road S. W-S-M	105	D4
Chesham Way. Kingsw	51	F2
Cheshire Cl. Yate	27	F2
Chesle Cl. Portis	44	C2
Chesle Way. Portis	44	C2
Cheslefield. Portis	44	C2
Chesley Hill. Wick	66	C4
Chessel Cl. St Gif	24	B1
Chessel St. Bris	63	D2
Chessington Ave. Bris	80	A3
Chester Park Rd. Bris	51	D1
Chester Rd. Bris	64	C4
Chester St. Bris	50	A1
Chesterfield Ave. Bris	49	F1
Chesterfield Cl. Ban	106	C2
Chesterfield Rd. Bris	49	F1
Chesterfield Rd. Mang	51	F3
Chestermaster Cl. Alm	24	A3
Chesters. Kingsw	66	A2
Chesterton Dr. Nail	60	A1
Chestnut Ave. Axb	125	E1
Chestnut Ave. W-S-M	89	D1
Chestnut Cl. Ban	107	D2
Chestnut Cl. Bris	80	C3
Chestnut Cl. Cong	91	E2
Chestnut Cl. Paul	131	F3
Chestnut Cl. Rad	132	C1
Chestnut Ct. Mang	52	A3
Chestnut Dr. Ch Sod	28	A1
Chestnut Dr. Thorn	8	B1
Chestnut Gr. Yatt	74	C1
Chestnut Gr. Bath	101	E2
Chestnut Gr. Cleve	57	F2
Chestnut Gr. Westw	120	C2
Chestnut La. Blea	122	A4
Chestnut Park Est. Kings	11	F2
Chestnut Rd. Kingsw	51	E2
Chestnut Rd. Lo Ash	62	A1
Chestnut Rd. Mang	51	E3
Chestnut Way. Kingsw	51	F2
Chestnut Wlk. Bris	79	D3
Chestnut Wlk. Keyn	82	C2
Chestnuts The. Wins	125	D4
Chetwoode Cl. Bris	35	E2
Chevening Cl. St Gif	36	B2
Chever's La. N St P	135	F3
Cheviot Dr. Thorn	15	F4
Cheviot Way. Kingsw	66	B3
Chew Hill. Ch Mag	95	F2
Chew La. Ch Mag	95	F1
Chew La. Ch St	95	F1
Chew Rd. Ch Mag	95	E3
Chew Rd. Win	95	E3
Chew St. Ch Mag	96	A2
Chewton Cl. Bris	51	D2
Chewton Rd. Co Dan	81	F1
Chewton Rd. Keyn	81	F1
Cheyne Rd. Bris	48	B3
Che Ivey Rd. Brock	75	E3
Chichester Pl. Rad	133	D1
Chichester Way. Yate	27	E2
Chickwell La. Faulk	135	D1
Chilcompton Rd. Chil	137	F4
Chilcompton Rd. Mid No	137	F4
Chillington Ct. Bris	23	F1
Chillyhill La. Ch Mag	95	F1
Chillyhill La. Ch St	95	F1
Chiltern Cl. Bris	80	A2
Chiltern Cl. Kingsw	66	B3
Chiltern Park. Thorn	15	F4
Chilton Rd. Bath	85	D1
Chilton Rd. Bris	80	A4
Chilwood Cl. Ir Act	26	C2
Chimes The. Nail	75	E4
Chine View. Mang	51	F4
Chiphouse Rd. Kingsw	51	F2
Chippenham Rd. Marsh	70	A4
Chipperfield Dr. Kingsw	51	F1
Chipping Cross. Cleve	73	E4
Chipping The. Kings	11	F2
Chippings The. Bris	50	B3
Chisbury St. Bris	50	B2
Chittening Rd. Avon	33	F4
Chock La. Bris	49	D4
Christchurch Ave. Mang	51	E3
Christchurch Cl. Nail	59	F1
Christchurch La. Mang	51	E3
Christchurch Rd. Bris	63	D4
Christian Cl. W-S-M	89	D2
Christmas St. Bris	63	E4
Christmas Steps. Bris	63	E4
Christon Rd. Ban	107	D1
Christon Rd. Blea	123	E3
Christon Terr. W-S-M	104	C1
Chubb Cl. Kingsw	65	F3
Church Ave. Bris	48	C2
Church Ave. Bris	50	A1
Church Ave. Falf	9	F4
Church Ave. Sist	66	B4
Church Cl. Bathf	86	A1
Church Cl. Bris	34	C1
Church Cl. Cleve	57	D1
Church Cl. Fr Cot	38	A4
Church Cl. Portis	45	E3
Church Cl. Yatt	91	E4
Church Cnr. Lymp	122	A1
Church Ct. Mid No	132	A1
Church Dr. Bris	64	C4
Church Dr. Cong	91	E2
Church Farm Cl. Marks	99	D1
Church Hayes Cl. Nail	75	F4
Church Hayes Dr. Nail	75	F4
Church Hill. Bris	64	C1
Church Hill. Hi Cha	120	A3
Church Hill. Kilm	133	E2
Church Hill. O-on-S	7	D3
Church Hill. Olve	14	A2
Church Hill. Tims	116	A1
Church La. Axb	125	E1
Church La. Back	76	B3
Church La. Back	76	C4
Church La. Bath	102	B2
Church La. Bathe	85	F2
Church La. Bi Sut	113	E2
Church La. Bitt	82	C4
Church La. Blea	123	E2
Church La. Bris	34	C1
Church La. Bris	63	D2
Church La. Bris	63	E2
Church La. Bris	63	F3
Church La. Ch Sod	41	D4
Church La. Ch St	112	B4
Church La. Chil	137	E3
Church La. Chil	137	F1
Church La. Chur	108	B3
Church La. Clut	114	C2
Church La. Co Bi	124	A2
Church La. Co Dan	98	B3
Church La. Crom	10	A1
Church La. E Harp	128	C2
Church La. Farm	116	A3
Church La. Fr Cot	38	B3
Church La. Li St	120	A3
Church La. Lo Ash	62	B1
Church La. Lock	105	F1
Church La. Lymp	122	A1
Church La. Mang	37	F1
Church La. Marsh	70	A4
Church La. Mid No	132	A1
Church La. Nail	59	E1
Church La. Nail	59	E2
Church La. Paul	131	D2
Church La. Paul	131	F3
Church La. Portb	46	C2
Church La. Tims	116	A1
Church La. Wickw	16	C1
Church La. Wickw	18	A3
Church La. Wins	124	C3
Church La. Wint	37	E3
Church La. Yatt	91	E4
Church Leaze. Bris	47	E3
Church Par. Bris	64	C1
Church Pl. E in G	47	E2
Church Rd N. Portis	45	E3
Church Rd S. Portis	45	E3
Church Rd. Ab Lei	62	A4
Church Rd. Alm	23	D1
Church Rd. Alm	24	A3
Church Rd. Alve	15	D1
Church Rd. Bath	84	B1
Church Rd. Bath	102	B1
Church Rd. Bitt	82	C4
Church Rd. Bris	36	A2
Church Rd. Bris	48	B2
Church Rd. Bris	49	D4
Church Rd. Bris	49	F3
Church Rd. Bris	51	D1
Church Rd. Bris	63	E2
Church Rd. Bris	64	B4
Church Rd. Bris	79	D3
Church Rd. Bris	80	A2
Church Rd. Doyn	54	A1
Church Rd. Dun	78	B1
Church Rd. E in G	47	D2
Church Rd. Fr Cot	38	B4
Church Rd. Kingsw	51	F1
Church Rd. Kingsw	51	F1
Church Rd. Lo Ash	62	B3
Church Rd. Luck	31	F2
Church Rd. Lymp	122	A1
Church Rd. O-on-S	7	D2
Church Rd. O-on-S	7	D3
Church Rd. P St J	133	D4
Church Rd. Piln	22	A3
Church Rd. St Gif	36	C2
Church Rd. Thorn	8	A1
Church Rd. W-S-M	88	C1
Church Rd. Whit	80	A2
Church Rd. Whit	97	D4
Church Rd. Wick	67	D3
Church Rd. Win	95	D4
Church Rd. Wins	124	C4
Church Rd. Wint	37	F2
Church Rd. Yate	27	F1
Church Rise. Win	95	D4
Church Row. Chil	137	F1
Church Sq. Clut	114	C2
Church Sq. Mid No	132	A1
Church St. Ban	107	D2
Church St. Bath	84	A1
Church St. Bath	102	A2
Church St. Bath	102	A3
Church St. Bathf	86	A1
Church St. Blag	110	C1
Church St. Bris	50	A1
Church St. Bris	63	F3
Church St. Bris	64	A3
Church St. Charl	84	C3
Church St. N St P	135	F2
Church St. Paul	131	E3
Church St. Pens	97	E3
Church St. Rad	132	C1
Church Town. Back	76	B3
Church View. Bris	36	A2
Church View. Mang	51	E3
Church View. Newp	4	B4
Church View. Win	95	D3
Church Wlk. E in G	47	E2
Church Wlk. Wring	92	B1
Churchdown Wlk. Bris	47	F3
Churchend La. Char	10	C2
Churchfarm Cl. Yate	27	F2
Churchill Rd. Bris	64	B2
Churchill Ave. Cleve	57	E1
Churchill Cl. Cleve	57	E1
Churchill Cl. Kingsw	66	A3
Churchill Dr. Bris	48	B4
Churchill Gate. Chur	108	C2
Churchill Green. Chur	108	A3
Churchill Rd. W-S-M	105	D4
Churchlands Rd. Bris	63	D1
Churchpath Rd. E in G	47	E2
Churchside. Bris	51	D4
Churchward Cl. Kingsw	65	D3
Churchward Rd. W-S-M	89	D2
Churchward Rd. Yate	27	D2
Churchway. Faulk	134	B1
Churchways Ave. Bris	49	F3
Churchways Cres. Bris	49	F3
Churchways. Whit	80	B2
Churston Cl. Bris	80	A2
Circle The. Bath	101	D2
Circular Rd. Bris	48	C1
Circus Mews. Bath	101	F4
Circus Pl. Bath	101	F4
Circus The. Bath	101	F4
City Bsns Pk. Bris	64	A4
City Rd. Bris	49	F1
Clamp The. Kingsw	66	B2
Clanage Rd. Bris	62	C2
Clandown Rd. Paul	131	F2
Clapton Dro. W in G	45	E1
Clapton Rd. Mid No	131	E1
Clapton Rd. Ston E	131	E1
Clare Ave. Bris	49	E
Clare Gdns. Bath	101	E
Clare Rd. Bris	49	E
Clare Rd. Bris	50	A
Clare Rd. Bris	51	E
Clare St. Bris	63	E
Clare St. Bris	64	B
Clare Wlk. Thorn	8	A
Claremont Ave. Bris	49	E
Claremont Bldgs. Bath	85	D
Claremont Cres. W-S-M	87	D
Claremont Gdns. Cleve	57	F
Claremont Gdns. Nail	59	E
Claremont Gdns. Paul	131	C
Claremont Rd. Bath	85	D
Claremont Rd. Bris	49	E
Claremont St. Bris	50	A
Claremont Terr. Bris	64	B
Claremont Wlk. Bath	85	D
Clarence Ave. Mang	51	F
Clarence Gdns. Mang	51	F
Clarence Grove Rd. W-S-M	104	C
Clarence Pl. Bath	101	D
Clarence Pl. Bris	63	E
Clarence Rd E. W-S-M	104	B
Clarence Rd N. W-S-M	104	B
Clarence Rd S. W-S-M	104	B
Clarence Rd. Bris	51	D
Clarence Rd. Bris	63	F
Clarence Rd. Bris	64	A
Clarence Rd. Mang	51	F
Clarence St. Bath	102	A
Clarendon Rd. Bath	102	A
Clarendon Rd. Bris	49	E
Clarendon Rd. W-S-M	104	C
Clark Dr. Bris	50	C
Clark St. Bris	64	A
Clarke St. Bris	63	E
Clarken Cl. Nail	59	E
Clarken Coombe. Lo Ash	62	A
Clarkson Ave. W-S-M	88	B
Clatworthy Dr. Bris	80	A
Claude Ave. Bath	101	E
Clavell Rd. Bris	34	C
Claverham Cl. Yatt	91	E
Claverham Dro. Yatt	74	B
Claverham Park. Yatt	91	F
Claverham Rd. Bris	51	E
Claverham Rd. Yatt	91	F
Claverton Ct. Bath	102	C
Claverton Down Rd. Bath	102	C
Claverton Rd W. Keyn	82	B
Claverton Rd. Keyn	82	B
Claverton St. Bath	102	A
Clay Bottom. Bris	50	C
Clay Hill. Bris	50	C
Clay La. Bitt	66	B
Clay La. St Gif	36	B
Clay La. Thorn	8	C
Clay Pit Rd. Bris	49	D
Claydon Green. Bris	79	F
Clayfield Rd. Bris	64	C
Clayfield. Yate	27	F
Claymore Cres. Bris	51	E
Claypiece Rd. Bris	79	D
Claypit Hill. Ch Sod	40	A
Claypool Rd. Kingsw	65	F
Clayton Cl. Portis	45	E
Clayton St. Avon	33	D
Clayton St. Bris	64	A
Cleave St. Bris	50	A
Cleeve Ave. Mang	51	F
Cleeve Dr. Brock	92	A
Cleeve Gdns. Mang	51	E
Cleeve Gr. Keyn	81	E
Cleeve Green. Bath	100	C
Cleeve Hill Extension. Mang	51	F
Cleeve Hill Rd. Brock	92	B
Cleeve Hill. Co Mar	127	F
Cleeve Hill. Mang	51	E
Cleeve La. Wick	53	E
Cleeve Lawns. Mang	51	E
Cleeve Lodge Cl. Mang	51	F
Cleeve Lodge Rd. Mang	51	F
Cleeve Park Rd. Mang	51	F
Cleeve Pl. Nail	60	A
Cleeve Rd. Bris	51	E
Cleeve Rd. Bris	64	B
Cleeve Rd. Mang	51	F
Cleeve Rd. Yate	27	F
Cleeve Wood Rd. Mang	51	F
Cleevedale Rd. Bath	102	A
Clement St. Bris	63	F
Cleve Rd. Bris	36	A
Clevedale. Mang	51	E
Clevedon La. W in G	59	F
Clevedon Rd. Bris	49	E
Clevedon Rd. Lo Ash	61	E
Clevedon Rd. Lo Ash	77	D
Clevedon Rd. Mid No	132	A
Clevedon Rd. Nail	59	E
Clevedon Rd. Portis	45	E
Clevedon Rd. W-S-M	104	C
Clevedon Rd. Wrax	60	B
Clevedon Rd. Wrax	60	B
Clevedon Terr. Bris	63	E
Cleveland Cl. Thorn	15	D
Cleveland Pl. Bath	102	A

Cleveland Wlk. Bath 102 B3
Cliff Court Dr. Bris 51 D4
Cliff Rd. Priddy 126 A1
Cliff Rd. W-S-M 88 A1
Cliffe Dr. Li St 120 A3
Clifford Gdns. Bris 47 F3
Clifford Rd. Bris 51 E2
Clift House Rd. Bris 63 D2
Clift House Spur. Bris 62 C2
Clift Pl. Bris 63 E3
Clift Rd. Bris 63 D2
Clifton Ave. W-S-M 104 C3
Clifton Cl. Bris 62 C4
Clifton Down Rd. Bris 63 D4
Clifton Down. Bris 62 C4
Clifton Hill. Bris 63 D3
Clifton Park Rd. Bris 62 C4
Clifton Park. Bris 63 D4
Clifton Pl. Bris 64 A4
Clifton Rd. Bris 63 D4
Clifton Rd. W-S-M 104 C3
Clifton St. Bris 63 E2
Clifton St. Bris 64 A4
Clifton St. Portis 45 E1
Clifton Vale Cl. Bris 63 D3
Clifton Vale. Bris 63 D3
Clifton View. Bris 63 F2
Clifton Wood Rd. Bris 63 D3
Cliftonwood Cres. Bris 63 D3
Cliftonwood Terr. Bris 63 D3
Clinton Rd. Bris 63 E1
Clive Rd. Bris 80 B4
Cloisters Rd. Wint 37 F3
Clonmel Rd. Bris 63 E1
Close The. Bris 35 D3
Close The. Fr Cot 38 B3
Close The. Kingsw 51 E2
Close The. St Gif 24 B1
Close The. St Gif 36 B3
Close The. W in G 44 C1
Closemead. Cleve 57 F2
Clothier Rd. Bris 64 C1
Clouds Hill Ave. Bris 64 C4
Clouds Hill Rd. Bris 64 C4
Clovelly Cl. Bris 64 C4
Clovelly Rd. Bris 64 C4
Clovelly Rd. W-S-M 89 D1
Clover Cl. Cleve 57 F2
Clover Ground. Bris 49 D4
Clover Leaze. St Gif 36 B3
Cloverdale Dr. Kingsw 66 A2
Cloverlea Rd. Kingsw 66 B3
Clutton Hill. Clut 115 D2
Clyde Ave. Keyn 81 F2
Clyde Gdns. Bath 101 D3
Clyde Gdns. Bris 65 D3
Clyde Gr. Bris 35 F1
Clyde La. Bris 49 E1
Clyde Park. Bris 49 D1
Clyde Rd. Bris 49 D1
Clyde Rd. Bris 64 A2
Clyde Rd. Fr Cot 38 A4
Clyde Terr. Bris 63 E2
Clyde Terr. Bris 64 A2
Clydesdale Cl. Bris 80 A3
Clynder Gr. Cleve 57 F3
Co-operation Rd. Bris 50 B1
Coalbridge Cl. W-S-M 88 C1
Coaley Rd. Bris 47 E3
Coalpit La. Chil 137 D1
Coalpit Rd. Bathe 86 A2
Coalsack La. West 38 A2
Coalville Rd. Fr Cot 38 B4
Coape Rd. Bris 80 C3
Coates Wlk. Bris 79 E3
Cobblestone Mews. Bris 63 D4
Cobhorn Dr. Bris 78 C2
Cobley Croft. Cleve 73 E4
Cobourg Rd. Bris 49 F1
Cobthorn Way. Cong 91 F3
Cock And Yew Tree Hill. Win 95 D1
Cock La. Dyrh 54 B3
Cock Rd. Kingsw 65 F3
Cockers Hill. Co Dan 98 B3
Codben St. Bris 64 B4
Codrington Rd. Bris 49 E2
Cody Ct. Kingsw 65 D3
Cogan Rd. Kingsw 51 F2
Cogsall Rd. Bris 80 C3
Coker Rd. W-S-M 89 D1
Colbourne Rd. Bath 101 E1
Colchester Cres. Bris 79 E4
Coldharbour La. Bris 36 C1
Coldharbour La. W-S-M 104 B2
Coldharbour Rd. Bris 49 D2
Coldpark Gdns. Bris 78 C3
Coldpark Rd. Bris 78 C3
Coldrick Cl. Bris 79 F2
Cole Rd. Bris 64 A3
Colebrook Rd. Bris 65 E4
Coleford Rd. Bris 35 E1
Colehouse La. Cleve 73 E4
Coleridge Rd. Bris 50 B2
Coleridge Rd. Cleve 57 E2
Coleridge Rd. W-S-M 105 D2
Coleridge Vale Rd E. Cleve ... 57 E1
Coleridge Vale Rd N. Cleve ... 57 E1

Coleridge Vale Rd S. Cleve ... 57 E1
Coleridge Vale Rd W. Cleve ... 57 E1
Coles Gdns. Kilm 139 D3
Colesborne Cl. Yate 39 E4
Coleshill Dr. Bris 79 D3
Coley Rd. E Harp 129 D2
Colin Rd. Thorn 8 B1
College Ave. Bris 51 D3
College Ct. Bris 51 D3
College Fields. Bris 62 C4
College Green. Bris 63 E3
College Park Dr. Bris 34 C1
College Rd. Bath 84 C1
College Rd. Bris 49 D4
College Rd. Bris 51 D3
College Rd. Bris 62 C4
College Sq. Bris 63 E3
College St. Bris 63 E3
Collet Cl Lock 89 E2
Collett Cl. Kingsw 65 D3
Collier Cl. Tims 132 B4
Colliers La. Charl 84 C2
Collin Rd. Bris 64 B2
Collingwood Ave. Kingsw 51 F1
Collingwood Cl. Keyn 82 C1
Collingwood Cl. W-S-M 88 C2
Collingwood Rd. Bris 49 D1
Collins Ave. St Gif 36 B3
Collins St. Avon 47 D4
Collinson Rd. Bris 79 D3
Colliter Cres. Bris 63 D1
Collum La. W St L 88 C3
Collum La. W-S-M 88 C3
Coln Sq. Thorn 15 E4
Colne Green. Keyn 82 A2
Colombo Cres. W-S-M 104 C2
Colonnades The. Bath 101 F3
Colston Ave. Bris 63 E4
Colston Cl. Kingsw 51 E2
Colston Cl. Wint 37 F2
Colston Ct. Bris 49 E2
Colston Dale. Bris 50 C2
Colston Hill. Bris 50 B1
Colston Par. Bris 63 F3
Colston Rd. Bris 50 B1
Colston St. Bris 63 E4
Colston St. Kingsw 51 E2
Colthurst Dr. Kingsw 65 F3
Colts Green. Ch Sod 40 C4
Colwyn Rd. Bris 50 B1
Colyton. W-S-M 89 D1
Comb Paddock. Bris 49 D4
Combe Ave. Portis 45 E3
Combe End. Mid No 132 C2
Combe Fields. Portis 45 E3
Combe Hay La. Bath 118 A3
Combe Hay La. Sosto 118 A3
Combe La. Paul 131 D3
Combe Rd. Bath 101 E4
Combe Rd. Portis 45 E3
Combe Road Cl. Bath 102 A1
Combe Side. Back 76 A4
Combe The. Blag 109 F1
Combermere. Thorn 15 E4
Combeside. Bath 102 A2
Combfactory La. Bris 64 A4
Commercial Rd. Bris 63 E3
Common (E) The. St Gif 24 B1
Common La. Chur 108 A3
Common La. E in G 47 D1
Common Mead La. Bris 37 D1
Common Rd. Kingsw 65 D2
Common Rd. Wint 37 F4
Common The. Bris 51 D4
Common The. St Gif 24 B1
Commonfield Rd. Bris 34 A1
Commonmead La. Ch Sod .. 29 D1
Compton Dr. Bris 48 B4
Compton Green. Keyn 81 F2
Compton St. Bris 64 B4
Comrade Ave. Ship 125 F4
Comyn Wlk. Bris 51 D3
Concorde Dr. Bris 35 D1
Concorde Rd. Bris 35 F4
Condor Cl. W-S-M 105 E4
Condover Rd. Bris 65 D2
Conduit Pl. Bris 50 A1
Conduit Rd. Bris 50 A1
Congleton Rd. Bris 64 B4
Conham Hill. Kingsw 65 D3
Conham Rd. Bris 64 C3
Conham Vale. Bris 65 D3
Conham Vale. Kingsw 65 D3
Conifer Cl. Bris 51 E3
Conifer Cl. Fr Cot 26 A1
Conifer Way. Lock 105 F3
Coniston Ave. Bris 48 C3
Coniston Cl. Kingsw 66 B3
Coniston Cres. W-S-M 104 C2
Coniston Rd. Bris 23 F1
Conkwell. Winsl 103 E1
Connaught Rd. Bris 79 F4
Connection Rd. Bath 101 D3
Constable Dr. W-S-M 88 C2
Constable Rd. Bris 50 A3
Constantine Ave. St Gif 36 C3
Constitution Hill. Bris 63 D3

Convent Cl. Bris 34 B2
Convocation Ave. Bath 102 C3
Conway Green. Keyn 82 A2
Conway Rd. Bris 64 B2
Conygar Cl. Cleve 57 F3
Conygre Gr. Bris 36 B2
Conygre Rd. Bris 36 A2
Conygre Rise. Farm 115 F3
Cook Cl. Kingsw 66 B2
Cook St. Avon 47 E4
Cook's Folly Rd. Bris 48 B2
Cook's La. Ban 107 D2
Cook's La. Cleve 58 A1
Cook's La. Cleve 58 B1
Cooke's Dr. Alm 23 D1
Cooks Bridle Path. Wring ... 93 F1
Cooks Cl. St Gif 24 B2
Cooks La. West 38 B2
Cooksley Rd. Bris 64 B4
Cookworthy Cl. Bris 64 A3
Coombe Ave. Thorn 8 A1
Coombe Bridge Ave. Bris ... 48 B3
Coombe Cl. Bris 34 B2
Coombe Dale. Bris 48 B3
Coombe Dale. Wring 94 A4
Coombe Gdns. Bris 48 C3
Coombe La. Bris 48 C3
Coombe La. Co Bi 124 A2
Coombe La. E Harp 128 C2
Coombe La. E n G 47 D1
Coombe Park. Bath 101 E4
Coombe Rd. Bris 50 B1
Coombe Rd. Nail 59 F1
Coombe Rd. W-S-M 104 C4
Coombe The. Blag 110 B2
Coombe The. Co Mar 128 A3
Coombe Way. Kingsw 66 B2
Coombes Way. Kingsw 66 B2
Cooper Rd. Thorn 15 D4
Cooper Rd. Bris 48 C4
Cooperage La. Bris 63 D3
Cooperage Rd. Bris 64 B4
Coots The. Bris 80 C3
Cope Park. Alm 24 B3
Copeland Dr. Bris 80 A3
Copford La. Lo Ash 62 A1
Copley Ct. Kingsw 65 F3
Copley Gdns. Bris 50 A3
Copley Gdns. W-S-M 88 C1
Copperfield Dr. W-S-M 88 C2
Coppice The. Bris 78 C2
Coppice The. St Gif 36 C4
Copse Cl. W-S-M 105 D1
Copse End. Winsc 107 F1
Copse Rd. Bris 64 A2
Copse Rd. Cleve 57 E2
Copse Rd. Keyn 82 B2
Copseland. Bath 102 B3
Copythorne Rd. Bris 50 A4
Coralberry Dr. W-S-M 88 C1
Corbet Cl. Bris 34 B1
Cordington Pl. Bris 63 D4
Cordwell Wlk. Bris 49 E4
Corey Cl. Bris 49 F1
Corfe Cl. Nail 59 E1
Corfe Cres. Keyn 81 F2
Corfe Pl. Kingsw 66 A1
Corfe Rd. Bris 79 E4
Coriander Wlk. Bris 50 B1
Corinthian Ct. Bris 63 F3
Cork St. Bath 101 E4
Corker's Hill. Bris 64 C3
Cormorant Cl. W-S-M 88 C1
Corn St. Bath 101 F3
Corn St. Bris 63 E3
Corner Croft. Cleve 57 E1
Cornhill Dr. Bris 80 A4
Cornish Gr. Bris 80 C3
Cornish Rd. Bris 80 C3
Cornish Wlk. Bris 80 C3
Cornish's Grave. Kilm 139 F2
Cornleaze. Bris 79 D3
Cornwall Cres. Yate 27 F2
Cornwall Rd. Bris 49 E2
Cornwallis Ave. Bris 63 D3
Cornwallis Ave. W-S-M 88 C2
Cornwallis Cres. Bris 62 C3
Cornwallis Gr. Bris 63 D3
Coronation Ave. Bath 101 E2
Coronation Ave. Bris 51 D2
Coronation Ave. Keyn 81 E2
Coronation Cl. Kingsw 66 A3
Coronation Pl. Bris 63 E3
Coronation Rd. Ban 107 D2
Coronation Rd. Bath 101 E4
Coronation Rd. Blea 122 B3
Coronation Rd. Bris 63 E3
Coronation Rd. Kingsw 66 A3
Coronation Rd. Kingsw 66 A4
Coronation Rd. Mang 51 F3
Coronation Rd. W-S-M 88 C1
Corondale Rd. W-S-M 105 D4
Corridor The. Bath 102 A3
Corsley Wlk. Bris 79 F4
Corston View. Bath 101 E1
Corston Wlk. Bris 47 E4

Corston. W-S-M 105 D1
Cossham Cl. Thorn 8 B1
Cossham Rd. Bris 64 B4
Cossham Rd. Puck 53 E2
Cossham St. Mang 52 A3
Cossham Wlk. Bris 51 D1
Cossington Rd. Bris 79 F4
Cossins Rd. Bris 49 D2
Costers Cl. Alve 15 D3
Costiland Dr. Bris 78 C3
Cote Dr. Bris 49 D2
Cote House La. Bris 49 D3
Cote La. Bris 49 D3
Cote Lea Park. Bris 49 D4
Cote Paddock. Bris 48 C2
Cote Rd. Bris 49 D2
Cotham Brow. Bris 49 E1
Cotham Gdns. Bris 49 D1
Cotham Gr. Bris 49 E1
Cotham Hill. Bris 63 E4
Cotham Lawn Rd. Bris 49 E1
Cotham Park N. Bris 49 E1
Cotham Park. Bris 49 E1
Cotham Rd S. Bris 63 E4
Cotham Rd. Bris 63 E4
Cotham Side. Bris 49 E1
Cotham Vale. Bris 49 E1
Cotman Wlk. Bris 50 A3
Cotman Wlk. W-S-M 88 C1
Cotrith Gr. Bris 34 C2
Cotswold Cl. Portis 45 F2
Cotswold La. Ch Sod 41 D4
Cotswold Rd. Bath 101 E2
Cotswold Rd. Bris 63 E2
Cotswold Rd. Ch Sod 40 A4
Cotswold View. Bris 36 A2
Cotswold View. Char 11 D3
Cotswold View. Kingsw 51 E1
Cotswold View. Wickww 18 A3
Cottage Pl. Bris 63 E4
Cottington Ct. Kingsw 65 F3
Cottisford Rd. Bris 50 A2
Cottle Gdns. Bris 80 C3
Cottle Rd. Bris 80 C3
Cottles La. Winsl 120 C3
Cotton Mead. Cor 100 A4
Cottonwood Dr. Kingsw 66 A2
Cottrell Ave. Bris 51 E1
Cottrell Rd. Bris 50 B2
Cotts The. Wring 92 B1
Coulson Dr. W-S-M 89 D2
Coulson Wlk. Bris 51 E1
Coulson's Cl. Bris 80 A2
Coulson's Rd. Bris 80 A2
Counterpool Rd. Kingsw 65 E4
Counterslip Gdns. Bris 80 B3
Counterslip. Bris 63 F3
Countess Wlk. Bris 50 B3
County St. Bris 64 A2
Court Ave. St Gif 36 C3
Court Ave. Yatt 91 E4
Court Cl. Back 76 B3
Court Cl. Bris 49 F4
Court Cl. Portis 45 E2
Court Dr. Wins 108 A2
Court Farm Rd. Bris 79 F2
Court Farm Rd. Kingsw 65 F1
Court Gdns. Bathe 86 A2
Court Hay. E in G 47 D2
Court Hill. Co Dan 98 B3
Court La. Bathf 86 A1
Court La. Cleve 58 A2
Court La. Wick 67 D3
Court La. Wins 125 F4
Court Mead. Stone 3 F2
Court Meadow. Stone 3 F2
Court Pl. W-S-M 88 C1
Court Rd. Bris 49 F3
Court Rd. Fr Cot 37 F4
Court Rd. Kingsw 65 E4
Court Rd. Kingsw 66 B2
Court Rd. W St L 88 A3
Court View Cl. Alm 24 A3
Court View. Wick 67 E3
Courtenay Rd. Keyn 82 A1
Courtenay Wlk. W-S-M 89 D2
Courteney Cres. Bris 79 E4
Courtfield Gr. Bris 51 D1
Courtlands La. Bris 62 C2
Courtlands. Keyn 81 F3
Courtlands. St Gif 24 B1
Courtmead. Sosto 118 C4
Courtney Rd. Kingsw 65 F4
Courtney Way. Kingsw 66 A4
Courtside Mews. Bris 49 E1
Courtville Cl. Alve 15 D2
Courtyard The. Nail 59 F1
Cousins Cl. Bris 34 B2
Cousins La. Bris 64 C4
Couzens Cl. Yate 28 A1
Couzens Pl. St Gif 36 C3
Coventry Wlk. Bris 64 C3
Cowdray Rd. Bris 79 E4
Cowleaze La. E Harp 128 B3
Cowler Wlk. Bris 78 C2
Cowling Dr. Bris 80 B3
Cowling Rd. Bris 80 B3
Cowper Rd. Bris 49 E1

Cowper St. Bris 64 B4
Cowship La. Crom 17 E3
Cowship La. Wickw 17 E3
Cowslip La. Blea 123 E2
Cox Ct. Kingsw 65 F2
Cox's Green. Wring 92 C1
Coxley Dr. Bath 85 D1
Coxway. Cleve 57 F1
Crabtree Cl. Dun 78 B1
Crabtree La. Dun 78 B1
Crabtree Wlk. Bris 50 B1
Craddock Cl. Kingsw 66 A2
Cranberry Wlk. Bris 48 B4
Cranbourne Chase. W-S-M . 88 A1
Cranbourne Rd. Bris 35 F4
Cranbrook Rd. Bris 49 E2
Crandale Rd. Bath 101 E3
Crandell Cl. Bris 34 C2
Crane Cl. Kingsw 66 A4
Cranford Cl. W-S-M 88 B1
Cranham Cl. Kingsw 51 F1
Cranham Dr. St Gif 24 B1
Cranham Rd. Bris 49 E4
Cranham. Yate 39 E4
Cranhill Rd. Bath 101 E4
Cranleigh Court Rd. Yate ... 27 E1
Cranleigh Gdns. Bris 48 C2
Cranleigh Rd. Bris 80 A3
Cranleigh. Sosto 118 C4
Cranmore Ave. Keyn 81 F3
Cranmore Cres. Bris 35 E1
Cranmore Pl. Bath 118 C4
Cranmore. W-S-M 105 D1
Cranside Ave. Bris 49 E2
Cransley Cres. Bris 49 E4
Crantock Ave. Bris 79 D4
Crantock Dr. Alm 24 B3
Crantock Rd. Yate 27 E1
Cranwell Gr. Bris 80 A3
Cranwells Park. Bath 101 E4
Crates Cl. Kingsw 65 F4
Craven Way. Kingsw 65 E3
Crawford Cl. Cleve 57 D1
Crawl La. Mid No 132 B2
Craydon Gr. Bris 80 B2
Craydon Rd. Bris 80 B3
Craydon Wlk. Bris 80 B3
Crediton Cres. Bris 63 F1
Crediton. W-S-M 89 D1
Crescent La. Bath 101 F4
Crescent Rd. Bris 51 E3
Crescent The. Back 76 A3
Crescent The. Bris 48 B3
Crescent The. Bris 49 E3
Crescent The. Kingsw 51 E2
Crescent The. Lymp 122 B3
Crescent The. Olve 14 B2
Crescent The. Paul 131 D2
Crescent The. Pens 96 C1
Crescent The. W-S-M 88 A1
Crescent The. Wick 67 E4
Crescent View. Bath 101 F3
Cresswell Cl. W-S-M 89 D1
Crest The. Bris 64 B1
Creswicke Ave. Kingsw 65 E3
Creswicke Rd. Bris 79 F4
Crew's Hole Rd. Bris 64 C4
Crewkerne Cl. Nail 60 A1
Cribbs Causeway Centre.
  Bris 35 D3
Cribbs Causeway. Bris 35 D3
Crickback La. Ch Mag 96 A2
Cricket Field Green. Nail ... 59 E1
Cricklade Ct. Nail 60 A1
Cricklade Rd. Bris 49 F2
Cripps Rd. Bris 63 E2
Crispin La. Thorn 8 A1
Crispin Way. Kingsw 51 F1
Crockerne Dr. E in G 47 E2
Crocombe La. Tims 116 B2
Crocombe. Tims 116 B2
Croft Ave. Bris 50 B2
Croft Cl. Bitt 82 B4
Croft Rd. Bath 85 D1
Croft The. Back 76 A4
Croft The. Bath 102 C1
Croft The. Cleve 57 F2
Croft The. Kingsw 66 B2
Croft The. Lock 105 F2
Croft The. Mang 51 F3
Croft The. Westw 120 C2
Croft View. Bris 49 E3
Crofton Ave. Bris 49 F3
Crofts End Rd. Bris 50 C1
Crokeswood Wlk. Bris 34 A1
Crome Rd. Bris 50 A4
Cromer Rd. Bris 50 B1
Cromer Rd. W-S-M 104 C3
Cromhall La. Crom 9 F1
Cromwell Ct. Kingsw 65 F3
Cromwell Dr. W-S-M 89 D2
Cromwell Rd. Bris 49 F1
Cromwell Rd. Bris 51 D1
Cromwell St. Bris 63 E2
Cromwells Hide. Mang 51 E3
Cropthorne Rd. Bris 36 A1

Crosby Row. Bris	63	D3
Cross Combe Dr. Bris	79	E2
Cross Combez Wlk. Bris	79	D2
Cross Elms La. Bris	48	C3
Cross Hands Rd. Piln	22	B4
Cross La. Co Bi	125	D1
Cross Lanes. E in G	47	E2
Cross Manor Rd. Axb	125	D1
Cross Moor Dr. Axb	125	D1
Cross Moor Dro. Co Bi	124	C2
Cross St. Bris	51	E1
Cross St. Keyn	81	F1
Cross St. W-S-M	104	C4
Cross The. E Harp	128	C2
Cross Tree Gr. St Gif	36	B4
Cross Wlk. Bris	80	A3
Crossfield Rd. Kingsw	51	F2
Crossleaze Rd. Kingsw	65	E2
Crossley Cl. Wint	37	F4
Crossman Ave. Wint	37	F3
Crossman Wlk. Cleve	57	F1
Crosspost La. Co Dan	99	D2
Crossway La. Ston E	137	D4
Crossways Rd. Bris	64	A1
Crossways Rd. Thorn	8	A1
Crossways. Newp	4	C4
Crow La. Bris	34	C1
Crow La. Bris	63	E3
Crow Meadow. Kings	11	F2
Crowe Hill. Li St	120	A3
Crowe La. Hi Cha	120	A3
Crown Gdns. Kingsw	66	A4
Crown Glass Pl. Nail	59	F1
Crown Hill Wlk. Bris	50	C1
Crown Hill. Bath	84	B1
Crown Hill. Bris	64	C4
Crown Hill. Kingsw	66	B2
Crown Hill. Win	95	D2
Crown House. Nail	59	E1
Crown La. Kingsw	51	E2
Crown Rd. Bath	84	A1
Crown Rd. Kingsw	51	E1
Crown Rd. Kingsw	66	B3
Crowndale Rd. Bris	64	A2
Crownleaze. Kingsw	51	E2
Crows Gr. St Gif	24	B2
Crowther Park. Bris	50	A2
Crowther Rd. Bris	50	A2
Crowther St. Bris	63	D2
Crowthers Ave. Yate	27	F2
Croydon St. Bris	64	A4
Crunnis The. St Gif	36	C3
Cuck Hill. Ship	125	F4
Cuckoo La. Clut	115	D2
Cuckoo La. Wint	37	F2
Cuckoo La. Wrax	60	A3
Cuffington Ave. Bris	64	B2
Culleysgate La. Wick	67	F3
Culver La. E Harp	128	C2
Culver St. Bris	63	E3
Culverhay. Co Dan	98	B3
Culverhill Rd. Ch Sod	28	A1
Culvers Rd. Keyn	81	F3
Culverwell Rd. Bris	79	D2
Cumberland Basin Rd. Bris	62	C3
Cumberland Cl. Bris	63	D3
Cumberland Gr. Bris	49	F1
Cumberland Pl. Bris	62	C3
Cumberland Rd. Bris	63	D3
Cumberland Row. Bath	101	F3
Cumberland St. Bris	63	F4
Cumbria Cl. Thorn	8	C1
Cunningham Gdns. Bris	51	D3
Curland Gr. Bris	80	A3
Curlew Cl. Bris	50	C3
Curlew Gdns. W-S-M	88	C1
Currells La. Win	77	D1
Curtis La. St Gif	37	D2
Custom Cl. Bris	80	A4
Cutler Rd. Bris	78	C3
Cutsheath Rd. Tyth	16	B4
Cutsheath Rd. Thorn	16	B4
Cygnet Cres. W-S-M	88	C1
Cynthia Rd. Bath	101	E3
Cypress Ct. Bris	48	B2
Cypress Gdns. Lo Ash	62	C3
Cypress Gr. Bris	49	E3
Cypress Terr. Rad	132	B1
Cypress Wlk. Col	70	C3
Dafford St. Bath	85	E1
Dafford's Bldgs. Bath	85	E1
Daglands The. Tims	132	C4
Dairy Hill. Well	134	A3
Daisy Green La. N Nib	5	E1
Daisy Rd. Bris	50	B1
Dakota Dr. Bris	80	A2
Dalby Ave. Bris	63	E2
Daldry Gdns. Olve	14	A2
Dale St. Bris	63	F4
Dale St. Bris	64	C4
Daley Cl. W-S-M	89	D2
Dalkeith Ave. Bris	51	E1
Dalrymple Rd. Bris	49	F1
Dalston Rd. Bris	63	D2
Dalton Sq. Bris	63	F4
Dalwood. W-S-M	89	D1
Dame Court Cl. W-S-M	88	C2
Damery La. N Nib	4	A1
Damery La. Stone	4	A1
Dampier Rd. Bris	63	D2
Danbury Cres. Bris	35	E1
Danbury Wlk. Bris	35	E1
Dancey Mead. Bris	78	C4
Dane Cl. Winsl	120	C4
Dane Rise. Winsl	120	C4
Daneacre Rd. Mid No	133	D2
Dangerfield Ave. Bris	78	C3
Daniel Cl. Cleve	57	F2
Daniel Mews. Bath	102	A4
Daniel St. Bath	102	A4
Dapps Hill. Keyn	81	F3
Dapwell La. Co Dan	81	D1
Dark La. Back	76	A3
Dark La. Ban	107	E1
Dark La. Blag	110	C2
Dark La. Ch Mag	95	F2
Dark La. Hi Cha	120	A3
Dark La. Hol	138	B1
Dark La. Hol	139	D1
Darley Cl. Bris	34	B2
Darlington Mews. Bath	102	A4
Darlington Pl. Bath	102	A3
Darlington Rd. Bath	102	A4
Darlington St. Bath	102	A4
Darmead. W-S-M	89	D1
Darnley Ave. Bris	49	F3
Dart Cl. Thorn	15	D4
Dart Rd. Cleve	57	E1
Dartmoor St. Bris	63	D2
Dartmouth Ave. Bath	101	E3
Dartmouth Cl. W-S-M	89	D1
Dartmouth Wlk. Keyn	81	E2
Daubeny Cl. Bris	51	D3
Daventry Rd. Bris	63	F1
Davey St. Bris	49	F1
David St. Bris	63	F4
David's La. Alve	15	D2
David's Rd. Bris	80	B3
David's Rd. Thorn	8	B1
Davids Cl. Alve	15	D2
Davin Cres. E in G	47	E2
Davis Cl. Kingsw	65	F3
Davis St. Thorn	8	B1
Davis St. Avon	47	D4
Dawes Cl. Cleve	57	E1
Dawley Cl. Wint	37	F4
Dawlish Rd. Bris	63	E1
Dawn Rise. Kingsw	52	A1
Day Cres. Bath	100	C3
Day House La. Hill	19	E4
Day's Rd. Bris	64	A3
De Clifford Rd. Bris	34	B1
De Verose Ct. Kingsw	65	F2
Deacon Cl. Wint	37	F3
Deacons Cl. W-S-M	88	C1
Deadmill La. Bath	85	E2
Dean Ave. Thorn	8	B1
Dean Cl. Kingsw	65	D2
Dean Cl. W-S-M	89	D2
Dean Cres. Bris	63	E2
Dean La. Bris	63	E2
Dean Rd. Avon	33	E3
Dean Rd. Yate	27	E2
Dean St. Bris	63	E2
Dean St. Bris	63	F4
Dean's Dr. Bris	51	D1
Deanery Cl. Kingsw	66	A4
Deanery Rd. Bris	63	E3
Deanery Rd. Kingsw	66	A4
Deanhill La. Charl	84	A1
Deans Mead. Bris	48	A4
Deans The. Portis	45	D2
Debecca's La. E in G	47	D2
Deep Coombe Rd. Bris	63	D1
Deep Pit Rd. Bris	50	C1
Deer Mead. Cleve	57	D1
Deerhurst. Kingsw	51	F2
Deerhurst. Yate	39	E4
Deering Cl. Bris	34	A1
Deerleap. Ship	125	F4
Deerswood. Kingsw	52	A1
Delabere Ave. Bris	51	D3
Delapre Rd. W-S-M	104	B2
Delius Gr. Bris	79	E4
Dell The. Bris	48	C3
Dell The. Kingsw	66	B3
Dell The. Nail	59	E1
Dell The. St Gif	36	C4
Dell The. W-S-M	88	C2
Delvin Rd. Bris	49	E4
Denbigh St. Bris	49	F1
Dene Cl. Keyn	81	F2
Dene Rd. Whit	80	B2
Denham House. Bris	79	E2
Denleigh Cl. Bris	80	A2
Denmark Ave. Bris	63	E3
Denmark Pl. Bris	49	F2
Denmark Rd. Bath	101	E3
Denmark St. Bris	63	E3
Denning Ct. W-S-M	89	D2
Dennisworth. Puck	53	D3
Dennor Park. Bris	80	A4
Denny Cl. Portis	45	D3
Denny Isle Dr. Piln	22	A3
Denny La. Ch Mag	96	A1
Denny View. Portis	45	D3
Dennyview Rd. Ab Lei	61	F4
Denston Dr. Portis	45	F2
Denston Wlk. Bris	79	D4
Dentwood Gr. Bris	48	A4
Denys Ct. Olve	14	A2
Derby Rd. Bris	49	F2
Derby St. Bris	64	B4
Derham Cl. Yatt	91	D4
Derham Park. Yatt	91	D4
Derham Rd. Bris	79	D3
Dermot St. Bris	50	A1
Derrick Rd. Kingsw	65	E4
Derricke Rd. Bris	80	C3
Derry Rd. Bris	63	D1
Derwent Cl. Bris	36	A4
Derwent Ct. Thorn	15	E4
Derwent Gr. Keyn	82	A3
Derwent Rd. Bris	50	C1
Derwent Rd. W-S-M	105	D2
Desmond Rd. Lock	89	E2
Deveron Gr. Keyn	82	A2
Devil's La. Char	11	D1
Devon Gr. Bris	64	B4
Devon Rd. Bris	50	B1
Devonshire Bldgs. Bath	101	F2
Devonshire Dr. Portis	44	C3
Devonshire Pl. Bath	101	F2
Devonshire Rd. Bath	85	F1
Devonshire Rd. Bris	49	D2
Devonshire Rd. W-S-M	104	C2
Dial Hill Rd. Cleve	57	E2
Dial Cl. Ba Gu	77	E1
Dial La. Mang	51	E3
Dial La. Win	77	E1
Diamond St. Bris	63	E2
Dibden Cl. Mang	52	A4
Dibden La. Mang	52	A4
Dibden Rd. Mang	52	A4
Dickens Cl. Bris	50	A4
Dickenson Rd. W-S-M	104	C3
Dickenson's Gr. Cong	91	F2
Didsbury Cl. Bris	34	C1
Dighton Gate. St Gif	36	C3
Dighton St. Bris	63	E4
Dillon Ct. Bris	64	B4
Dimond Rd. Bris	64	C4
Dinder Cl. Nail	75	F4
Dinghurst Rd. Chur	108	C2
Dingle Cl. Bris	48	B3
Dingle Rd. Bris	48	B4
Dingle The. Bris	48	B4
Dingle The. Wint	37	F2
Dingle View. Bris	48	B4
Dinglewood Cl. Bris	48	B4
Dings Wlk. Bris	64	A3
Dipland Gr. Blag	110	C1
Dixon Gdns. Bath	84	C1
Dixon Rd. Bris	64	C1
Dock Gate La. Bris	63	D3
Dodington La. Dod	40	B3
Dodington Rd. Ch Sod	40	A4
Dodisham Wlk. Bris	51	D3
Doleberrow. Chur	108	C2
Dolemoor La. Cong	91	D2
Dolemoor La. Cong	91	E2
Dolman Cl. Bris	34	C2
Dolphin Sq. W-S-M	104	B4
Dominion Rd. Bath	101	D3
Dominion Rd. Bris	50	C2
Donald Rd. Bris	78	C4
Doncaster Rd. Bris	49	E4
Doncombe Hill. Col	70	C4
Doncombe La. Col	70	C4
Donegal Rd. Bris	63	E1
Dongola Ave. Bris	49	F2
Dongola Rd. Bris	49	F2
Donnington Wlk. Keyn	81	E2
Doone Rd. Bris	49	F4
Dorcas Ave. St Gif	36	C3
Dorchester Cl. Nail	59	E1
Dorchester Rd. Bris	50	A4
Dorchester St. Bath	102	A3
Dorester Cl. Bris	35	E2
Dorian Cl. Bris	49	F4
Dorian Rd. Bris	49	F4
Dormer Cl. Fr Cot	38	B3
Dormer Rd. Bris	50	A2
Dorset Cl. Bath	101	E3
Dorset Gr. Bris	50	A1
Dorset Rd. Bris	49	D3
Dorset Rd. Kingsw	51	E1
Dorset St. Bath	101	E3
Dorset St. Bris	63	D2
Dorset Way. Yate	28	A2
Douglas Ct. W-S-M	104	C3
Douglas Rd. Bris	49	F4
Douglas Rd. Kingsw	65	E4
Douglas Rd. W-S-M	104	C3
Doulton Way. Bris	80	A3
Dove La. Bris	63	F4
Dove St S. Bris	63	E4
Dove St. Bris	63	E4
Dovecote. Yate	39	F4
Dovedale. Thorn	15	E4
Dover Pl. Bath	85	D1
Dovercourt Rd. Bris	50	A3
Dovers La. Bathf	86	B1
Dovers Park. Bathf	86	B1
Dovey Ct. Kingsw	66	B3
Dowdeswell Cl. Bris	34	C2
Dowding Rd. Bath	85	D1
Dowland. W-S-M	89	D1
Dowling Rd. Bris	79	E2
Down Ave. Bath	102	A1
Down Cl. Portis	44	C3
Down Hill. Olve	14	B2
Down La. Bath	85	F1
Down Leaze. Alve	15	D3
Down Rd. Alve	15	D3
Down Rd. Marsh	56	B1
Down Rd. Portis	45	D2
Down Rd. Wint	37	F2
Down The. Alve	14	C3
Down The. Olve	14	B2
Down View. Bris	49	F2
Downend Park Rd. Mang	51	E3
Downend Park. Bris	49	F3
Downend Rd. Bris	49	F3
Downend Rd. Bris	51	E3
Downend Rd. Kingsw	51	E1
Downend Rd. Mang	51	E3
Downfield Cl. Alve	15	D3
Downfield Dr. Fr Cot	38	A4
Downfield Rd. Bris	49	D1
Downland Cl. Bris	79	E3
Downleaze Dr. Ch Sod	40	A4
Downleaze. Bris	48	C2
Downleaze. Mang	51	E4
Downleaze. Portis	45	D3
Downman Rd. Bris	50	A3
Downs Cl. Alve	15	D3
Downs Cl. W-S-M	88	C1
Downs Cote Ave. Bris	48	C3
Downs Cote Dr. Bris	49	D3
Downs Cote Gdns. Bris	49	D3
Downs Cote Park. Bris	49	D3
Downs Cote View. Bris	49	D3
Downs Park E. Bris	49	D2
Downs Park W. Bris	49	D2
Downs Rd. Bris	49	D3
Downs Rd. Dun	78	B1
Downs The. Portis	45	D2
Downs The. Wickw	17	F4
Downside Cl. Bath	85	F1
Downside Cl. Chil	137	E2
Downside Cl. Kingsw	65	F3
Downside Rd. Bris	49	D1
Downside Rd. W-S-M	104	C2
Downside Rd. Wring	93	F4
Downside. Portis	45	E3
Downsway. Paul	131	E3
Downton Rd. Bris	79	E4
Dowry Rd. Bris	63	D3
Dowry Sq. Bris	63	D3
Doynton La. Doyn	54	A2
Doynton La. Dyrh	54	A2
Dr White's Cl. Bris	63	F3
Dragon Rd. Wint	37	E3
Dragon Wlk. Bris	50	C1
Dragons Hill Cl. Keyn	81	F3
Dragons Hill Ct. Keyn	81	F3
Dragons Hill Gdns. Keyn	81	F3
Dragonswell Rd. Bris	35	D1
Drake Ave. Bath	101	F1
Drake Cl. Keyn	82	B1
Drake Cl. W-S-M	88	C2
Drake Rd. Bris	63	D2
Drakes Way. Portis	45	D3
Draycot Pl. Bris	63	E3
Draycott Rd. Bris	49	F3
Draydon Rd. Bris	79	E4
Drayton Cl. Bris	80	A4
Drayton Rd. Bris	48	B4
Drayton. W-S-M	105	D1
Dring The. Rad	132	C1
Drive The. Bris	49	D3
Drive The. Bris	80	B3
Drive The. Chur	108	C2
Drive The. Pens	96	C1
Drive The. Ship	125	F4
Drive The. W-S-M	104	C4
Drove Ct. Nail	59	F2
Drove Rd. W-S-M	104	C4
Drove The. Portb	46	B3
Drove Way. Winsc	107	F4
Druetts Cl. Bris	49	F3
Druid Hill. Bris	48	C3
Druid Rd. Bris	48	C2
Druid Stoke Ave. Bris	48	B3
Druid Woods. Bris	48	B3
Drumhead Way The. Ship	125	F4
Drummond Ct. Kingsw	65	F2
Drummond Rd. Bris	50	C2
Drummond Rd. Bris	49	F1
Dryleaze Rd. Bris	50	C3
Dryleaze. Keyn	81	F3
Drysdale Cl. W-S-M	88	B1
Dubbers La. Bris	50	C1
Dublin Cres. Bris	49	D3
Duchess Rd. Bris	49	D3
Duchess Way. Bris	50	B3
Duchy Cl. Mid No	132	C3
Duchy Rd. Mid No	132	C3
Ducie Rd. Bris	64	A4
Ducie Rd. Mang	51	F3
Duck La. Chur	109	D4
Duck La. Yatt	74	A3
Duck St. Chur	108	B3
Duck St. Tyth	16	B3
Duckmoor Rd. Bris	63	D2
Dudley Cl. Keyn	81	F2
Dudley Ct. Kingsw	65	F2
Dudley Gr. Bris	50	A4
Dugar Wlk. Bris	49	E2
Duke St. Bath	102	A3
Dulverton Rd. Bris	49	E2
Dumaine Ave. St Gif	36	C3
Dumfries Pl. W-S-M	104	C3
Dumpers La. Ch Mag	96	A1
Duncan Gdns. Bath	84	A2
Duncombe La. Bris	51	D1
Duncombe Rd. Bris	51	D1
Dundas Cl. Bris	34	C1
Dundonald Rd. Bris	49	D2
Dundridge Gdns. Bris	65	D3
Dundridge La. Bris	65	D3
Dundry Cl. Kingsw	65	E3
Dundry La. Dun	78	B2
Dundry La. Win	95	D4
Dundry View. Bris	64	A1
Dunkeld Ave. Bris	35	F1
Dunkerry Rd. Bris	63	E2
Dunkerton Hill. P St J	117	F1
Dunkerton Hill. Pris	117	F1
Dunkery Cl. Nail	59	F1
Dunkery Rd. W-S-M	87	F1
Dunkirk Rd. Bris	50	C2
Dunkite La. W-S-M	88	C2
Dunmail Rd. Bris	35	E1
Dunmore St. Bris	63	F2
Dunsdown La. Tor	55	D3
Dunster Cres. W-S-M	105	D1
Dunster Ct. Wins	125	D4
Dunster Gdns. Kingsw	66	A1
Dunster Gdns. Nail	59	F1
Dunster Rd. Bris	79	F4
Dunster Rd. Keyn	81	F2
Dunsters Rd. Yatt	74	C1
Durban Rd. Bris	35	F4
Durban Way. Yatt	74	A1
Durbin Park Rd. Cleve	57	E3
Durbin Wlk. Bris	64	A4
Durcott Rd. Tims	132	B4
Durham Gr. Keyn	81	E2
Durham Park. Bris	49	D2
Durham Rd. Bris	50	A1
Durham Rd. Char	11	D3
Durleigh Cl. Bris	79	D4
Durley Hill. Keyn	81	E4
Durley Park. Bath	101	F2
Durnford Ave. Bris	63	D2
Durnford Rd. Bris	63	E2
Durnford St. Bris	63	D2
Durnhill. Co Mar	127	F4
Dursley Cl. Yate	27	F1
Dursley Rd. Bris	47	F3
Durston. W-S-M	105	D1
Durville Rd. Bris	79	D3
Durweston Wlk. Bris	80	B4
Dutton Cl. Bris	80	B3
Dutton Rd. Bris	80	B3
Dyer's La. Yate	27	D2
Dyers Cl. Bris	79	E2
Dylan Thomas Ct. Kingsw	66	A3
Dymboro Ave. Mid No	131	F1
Dymboro Cl. Mid No	131	F1
Dymboro Gdns. Mid No	131	F1
Dymboro The. Mid No	131	F1
Dyrham Cl. Bris	49	E3
Dyrham Cl. Kingsw	65	F4
Dyrham Cl. Thorn	8	B2
Dyrham Par. St Gif	36	B4
Dyrham Rd. Kingsw	65	F4
Dyrham. Bris	37	E1
Dyson Cl. Yatt	91	D4
Eagle Cl. W-S-M	105	E4
Eagle Cres. Puck	53	E2
Eagle Dr. Bris	35	F4
Eagle Park. Bathe	85	F3
Eagle Rd. Bathe	85	F3
Eagle Rd. Bris	64	C4
Eagles The. Yatt	91	D4
Eagles Wood Bsns Pk. St Gif	24	B2
Earl Russell Way. Bris	64	A4
Earl St. Bris	63	E4
Earlesfield. Nail	59	E1
Earlham Gr. W-S-M	105	D4
Earlsmead. Bris	50	C2
Earlstone Cl. Kingsw	66	A2
Earlstone Cres. Kingsw	66	A2
Easedale Cl. Bris	35	E1
East Cl. Bath	101	D3
East Clevedon Triangle. Cleve	57	F2
East Croft. Bris	49	E4
East Dundry La. Dun	79	D1

ast Dundry Rd. Bris

Firgrove Cres. Yate

t Dundry Rd. Bris 79 F1
t Dundry Rd. Whit 79 F1
t Gr. Bris 49 F1
t Hill. Bris 49 D4
st Mead. Mid No 132 A1
st Par. Bris 48 B3
st Park Dr. Bris 50 B1
st Park. Bris 50 B1
st Priory Cl. Bris 49 D4
st Ridge Dr. Bris 78 C3
st Shrubbery. Bris 49 D1
st St. Avon 33 D1
st St. Ban 107 E2
st St. Bris 63 E2
st St. Bris 63 F4
st View. Mang 51 F3
st Way. Bath 101 D3
st Wlk. Yate 27 F1
st Wood Pl. Portis 45 F4
stbury Cl. Thorn 8 B1
stbury Rd. Bris 51 D2
stbury Rd. Thorn 8 B1
stcombe Gdns. W-S-M 87 F1
stcombe Rd. W-S-M 87 F1
stcote Pk. Bris 80 A3
stcourt Gdns. Bris 50 B3
stcourt Rd. Clut 130 D2
stcroft Cl. Blag 110 C1
stcroft. Blag 110 C1
stdown Rd. Mid No 132 C3
stertown. Lymp 122 B1
stfield Ave. Bath 84 A1
stfield Gdns. W-S-M 87 F1
stfield Park. Bath 84 A1
stfield Park. W-S-M 87 F1
stfield Rd. Bris 49 D4
stfield Rd. Bris 49 E1
stfield Rd. Lock 105 F1
stfield Terr. Bris 49 D3
stfield. Bris 49 D4
stgate Office Centre. Bris 50 A2
stlake Cl. Bris 50 A4
stland Ave. Thorn 8 B1
stland Rd. Thorn 8 B1
stlea. Cleve 57 D1
stleigh Cl. Kingsw 51 F2
stleigh Rd. Bris 35 E1
stleigh Rd. Kingsw 51 F2
stley Cl. Falf 9 F4
stlyn Rd. Bris 79 D4
stmead La. Ban 107 E2
stmead La. Bris 48 C2
stnor Rd. Bris 80 A2
ston Hill Rd. Thorn 8 B1
ston Rd. Bris 64 A4
ston Rd. E in G 47 E2
ston Way. Bris 64 A4
stover Cl. Bris 49 D4
stover Gr. Bath 101 E1
stover Rd. Paul 115 E1
stville. Bath 85 D1
stway Cl. Nail 59 F1
stway Sq. Nail 59 F2
stway. Nail 59 F2
stwood Cl. Paul 115 E1
stwood Cres. Bris 64 C2
stwood Rd. Bris 64 C2
stwoods. Bathe 86 A2
ton Cl. Bris 51 D2
ton Cl. Bris 80 C3
ton Cres. Bris 63 D4
ton St. Bris 63 E2
don Rd. W ST L 89 D3
don Rd. W-S-M 88 C2
enezer La. Bris 48 C3
enezer St. Bris 64 B4
kweek Gdns. P St J 133 E4
kweek La. P St J 133 F4
kweek Rd. P St J 133 E4
lipse Office Pk. Kingsw ... 51 E2
en Gr. Bris 36 A1
en Park Cl. Bathe 86 A2
en Park Dr. Bathe 86 A2
garley Ct. Cleve 57 E3
gecombe Ave. W-S-M 88 B1
gecombe Cl. Kingsw 51 F1
gecorner La. Burt 43 D2
gecumbe Rd. Bris 49 E1
gefield Cl. Bris 79 F2
gefield Rd. Bris 79 F2
gehill Rd. Cleve 57 E3
geware Rd. Bris 63 E2
geware Rd. Kingsw 51 E2
gewood Cl. Bris 80 A4
gewood Cl. Kingsw 66 A2
geworth Rd. Bath 101 E1
geworth. Yate 39 E3
inburgh Pl. W-S-M 104 C4
inburgh Rd. Keyn 81 F2
ington Gr. Bris 35 D1
mund Cl. Mang 51 E2
mund Ct. Puck 53 D3
na Ward R S. Cleve 57 F3
ward Rd W. Cleve 57 F3
ward Rd. Bris 64 C2
ward Rd. Cleve 57 F3

Edward Rd. Kingsw 65 F4
Edward St. Bath 101 E4
Edward St. Bath 102 A4
Edward St. Bris 50 B1
Edward St. Bris 64 B4
Edwin Short Cl. Bitt 82 C4
Effingham Rd. Bris 49 F2
Egerton Brow. Bris 49 E2
Egerton Rd. Bath 101 F2
Egerton Rd. Bris 49 E2
Eggshill La. Yate 27 E1
Eighth Ave. Bris 36 A1
Eirene Terr. E in G 47 E2
Elberton Rd. Aust 14 A2
Elberton Rd. Bris 48 A4
Elberton Rd. Olve 14 A4
Elberton. Kingsw 66 A4
Elbury Ave. Bris 51 E1
Elderberry Wlk. W-S-M 89 D1
Elderbury Wlk. Bris 35 E2
Elderwood Dr. Kingsw 66 A2
Elderwood Rd. Bris 80 A4
Eldon Pl. Bath 85 D1
Eldon Terr. Bris 63 E2
Eldon Way. Bris 64 B3
Eleanor Cl. Bath 101 D3
Eleventh Ave. Bris 36 A1
Elfin Rd. Bris 51 D3
Elgar Cl. Bris 79 E3
Elgar Cl. Cleve 57 F1
Elgin Ave. Bris 35 F1
Elgin Croft. Bris 79 D2
Elgin Park. Bris 49 D1
Elgin Rd. Bris 51 D1
Eliot Cl. W-S-M 105 D2
Elizabeth Cl. Lock 105 E2
Elizabeth Cl. Thorn 15 E4
Elizabeth Cres. St Gif 36 C2
Elizabeth House. E in G 47 E2
Ellacombe Rd. Kingsw 65 F1
Ellan Hay Rd. St Gif 37 D3
Ellbridge Cl. Bris 48 B3
Ellenborough Park N.
    W-S-M 104 B3
Ellenborough Park Rd.
    W-S-M 104 C3
Ellenborough Park S.
    W-S-M 104 B3
Ellerncroft Rd. W-u-E 11 F4
Ellesmere Rd. Bris 64 B1
Ellesmere Rd. Kingsw 65 E4
Ellesmere Rd. W-S-M 104 B1
Ellesmere. Thorn 15 E4
Ellfield Cl. Bris 78 C3
Ellick Rd. Blag 126 B4
Ellicks Cl. St Gif 24 C1
Ellinghurst Cl. Bris 35 D1
Elliot Rd. Bris 49 F3
Elliott Ave. Bris 37 E1
Ellis Ave. Bris 79 D4
Elliston Dr. Bath 101 D2
Elliston La. Bris 49 E1
Elliston Rd. Bris 49 E1
Ellsbridge Cl. Keyn 82 A3
Ellsworth Rd. Bris 34 C3
Elm Cl. Ch Sod 28 A1
Elm Cl. Nail 59 E1
Elm Cl. Ship 108 B1
Elm Cl. St Gif 36 B4
Elm Cl. Yatt 91 D4
Elm Ct. Keyn 81 E2
Elm Gr. Bath 85 E1
Elm Gr. Bath 101 E2
Elm Gr. Lock 105 F2
Elm La. Bris 49 D1
Elm Park. Bris 36 A1
Elm Rd. Bris 49 F3
Elm Rd. Kingsw 65 F3
Elm Rd. Paul 131 F3
Elm Terr. Rad 132 B1
Elm Terr. Rod 138 B4
Elm Tree Ave. Mang 52 A4
Elm Tree Ave. Rad 132 B1
Elm Tree Rd. Cleve 57 E1
Elm Tree Rd. Lock 106 A2
Elm View. Mid No 132 A1
Elm Wlk. Portis 45 E2
Elm Wlk. Yatt 91 D4
Elm Wood. Yate 39 F4
Elmcroft Cres. Bris 50 A2
Elmdale Cres. Thorn 8 B2
Elmdale Gdns. Bris 51 D2
Elmdale Rd. Bris 63 D1
Elmdale Rd. Bris 63 D4
Elmfield Cl. Kingsw 65 F3
Elmfield Rd. Bris 49 D4
Elmfield. Kingsw 65 F3
Elmgrove Ave. Bris 64 A4
Elmgrove Dr. Yate 27 F1
Elmgrove Park. Bris 51 E1
Elmgrove Rd. Bris 49 E1
Elmgrove Rd. Bris 50 C2
Elmhurst Ave. Bris 50 B2
Elmhurst Est. Bathe 86 A2
Elmhurst Gdns. Lo Ash 77 D1
Elmhurst Rd. Lock 105 F1

Elmhyrst Rd. W-S-M 104 C4
Elming Down Cl. St Gif 36 B3
Elmlea Ave. Bris 48 C3
Elmleigh Ave. Mang 52 A3
Elmleigh Cl. Mang 52 A3
Elmleigh Rd. Mang 52 A3
Elmore Rd. Bris 23 F1
Elmore Rd. Bris 50 A3
Elmore. Kingsw 51 F1
Elmore. Yate 39 E4
Elms Gr. St Gif 24 A1
Elms The. Bris 37 E1
Elmsleigh Rd. W-S-M 104 B2
Elmsley La. W St L 88 B3
Elmtree Cl. Kingsw 51 E1
Elmtree Dr. Bris 78 C3
Elmtree Way. Kingsw 51 E1
Elmvale Dr. Lock 105 F2
Elsbert Dr. Bris 78 C3
Elstree Rd. Bris 50 C1
Elton La. Bris 49 E1
Elton Rd. Bris 49 E1
Elton Rd. Bris 51 E1
Elton Rd. Bris 63 E4
Elton Rd. Bris 63 E3
Elton Rd. Cleve 57 E2
Elton Rd. W-S-M 89 D2
Elton St. Bris 63 F4
Elvard Cl. Bris 79 D2
Elvard Rd. Bris 79 D2
Elvaston Rd. Bris 63 F2
Elwell Cl. Dun 77 F1
Elwell La. Win 77 F1
Ely Gr. Bris 48 A4
Embassy Rd. Bris 50 C1
Embassy Wlk. Bris 50 C1
Embercourt Dr. Back 76 A3
Embleton Rd. Bris 35 E1
Emerson Sq. Bris 50 A4
Emery Gate. Ban 107 D2
Emery Rd. Bris 64 C1
Emlyn Cl. W-S-M 89 D2
Emlyn Rd. Bris 50 B1
Emmett Wood. Bris 80 A2
Emra Cl. Bris 50 C1
Enderleigh Gdns. Chur 108 C2
Enfield Rd. Bris 51 D2
Engine Common La. Yate 27 E3
Engine La. Nail 75 D4
England's Cres. Wint 37 F4
Englishcombe La. Bath 101 E2
Englishcombe Rd. Bris 79 E2
Englishcombe Way. Bath .. 101 F2
Enmore. W-S-M 105 D1
Ennerdale Cl. W-S-M 105 D3
Ennerdale Rd. Bris 35 E1
Entry Hill Dr. Bath 101 F2
Entry Hill Gdns. Bath 101 F2
Entry Hill Park. Bath 101 F1
Entry Hill. Bath 101 F2
Entry Rise. Bath 101 F1
Epney Cl. Bris 23 F1
Epsom Cl. Mang 37 F1
Epworth Rd. Bris 35 D2
Equinox. St Gif 24 B2
Erin Wlk. Bris 79 E4
Ermine Way. Bris 47 E4
Ermleet Rd. Bris 49 E1
Ernestville Rd. Bris 50 C2
Ernist Barker Cl. Bris 64 A4
Ervine Terr. Bris 63 F4
Esgar Rise. W-S-M 88 C2
Eskdale Cl. W-S-M 105 E4
Eskdale. Thorn 15 E4
Esmond Gr. Cleve 57 E2
Esplanade Rd. Portis 45 D4
Essery Rd. Bris 50 B1
Essex St. Bris 63 E2
Esson Rd. Bris 51 D1
Estoril. Yate 27 F1
Estune Wlk. Lo Ash 62 A1
Etloe Rd. Bris 49 D2
Eton La. Ban 106 C4
Eton Rd. Bris 64 B2
Ettlingen Way. Cleve 57 F1
Ettricke Dr. Bris 80 A2
Eugene St. Bris 63 E4
Eugene St. Bris 63 F3
Evans Rd. Bris 49 D1
Eve Rd. Bris 50 A1
Evelyn Rd. Bath 101 D4
Evelyn Rd. Bris 49 E4
Evenlode Gdns. Bris 47 F3
Evenlode Way. Keyn 82 A2
Evercreech Rd. Bris 80 A2
Everest Ave. Bris 50 C2
Everest Rd. Bris 50 C2
Evergreen Cl. Winsc 107 F1
Ewart Rd. W-S-M 105 E4
Exbourne. W-S-M 89 D1
Excelsior St. Bath 102 A3
Excelsior Terr. Mid No 132 A1
Exchange Ave. Bris 63 E3
Exeter Bldgs. Bris 49 D1
Exeter Rd. Portis 45 F2
Exeter Rd. W-S-M 104 C3
Exford Cl. W-S-M 104 C1

Exley Cl. Kingsw 66 B3
Exmoor Rd. Bath 101 F1
Exmoor St. Bris 63 D2
Exmouth Rd. Bris 63 F1
Exton Cl. Bris 80 A3
Exton. W-S-M 105 D1
Eyer's La. Bris 63 F4

Faber Gr. Bris 79 E2
Fabian Dr. St Gif 36 C3
Factory Rd. Wint 37 F4
Failand Cres. Bris 48 B3
Failand La. Portb 46 C1
Failand La. Wrax 61 D4
Failand Wlk. Bris 48 B3
Fair Cl. N St P 135 F2
Fair Furlong. Bris 79 D2
Fair Hill. Ship 125 F4
Fair Lawn. Kingsw 66 A2
Fair View Dr. Bris 49 E1
Fairacre Cl. Bris 50 A3
Fairacre Cl. Lock 106 A2
Fairacres Cl. Keyn 81 F3
Fairfax St. Bris 63 E4
Fairfield Ave. Bath 85 D1
Fairfield Cl. Back 76 B4
Fairfield Cl. Marsh 69 F4
Fairfield Cl. W-S-M 88 A1
Fairfield Mead. Back 76 B4
Fairfield Park Rd. Bath 85 D1
Fairfield Pl. Bris 63 D2
Fairfield Rd. Bath 85 D1
Fairfield Rd. Bris 49 F1
Fairfield Rd. Bris 63 E2
Fairfield St. Bris 64 A2
Fairfield Terr. P St J 133 E4
Fairfield Way. Back 76 B3
Fairfield. Rode 136 C1
Fairfoot Rd. Bris 64 A2
Fairford Cl. Kingsw 51 F1
Fairford Cres. St Gif 36 B4
Fairford Rd. Bris 47 E4
Fairhaven Rd. Bris 49 E2
Fairhaven. Yate 27 F1
Fairlawn Ave. Bris 36 A2
Fairlawn Rd. Bris 49 F1
Fairlyn Dr. Kingsw 51 F2
Fairoaks. Kingsw 66 A2
Fairseat Workshops. Ch St 112 C4
Fairview Rd. Kingsw 65 F4
Fairview. W-S-M 88 C2
Fairway Cl. Kingsw 66 A2
Fairway Cl. W-S-M 88 A1
Fairway Ind Centre. Bris .. 35 F2
Fairway. Bris 64 B1
Fairways. Keyn 82 C1
Fairy Hill. Co Dan 98 B3
Falcon Cl. Bris 35 F4
Falcon Cl. Bris 48 C4
Falcon Cl. Portis 45 E2
Falcon Cres. W-S-M 105 E4
Falcon Dr. Bris 35 F4
Falcon Way. Thorn 8 B1
Falcon Wlk. Bris 23 F1
Falcondale Rd. Bris 48 C4
Falcondale Wlk. Bris 49 D4
Falconer Rd. Bath 84 A2
Falfield Rd. Bris 64 B2
Falfield Wlk. Bris 49 E4
Falkland Rd. Bris 49 F1
Fallodon Ct. Bris 49 D3
Fallodon Way. Bris 49 D3
Fallowfield. Kingsw 66 B3
Fallowfield. W-S-M 88 C2
Falmouth Cl. Nail 60 A1
Falmouth Rd. Bris 49 F1
Fane Cl. Bris 35 D2
Fanshawe Rd. Bris 80 A4
Far Handstones. Kingsw .. 66 A2
Faraday Rd. Bris 62 C3
Farington Rd. Bris 49 E4
Farleigh Hospital Cotts.
    Back 77 D4
Farleigh La. Crom 10 B1
Farleigh Rd. Back 76 B4
Farleigh Rd. Cleve 57 D1
Farleigh Rd. Keyn 81 E2
Farleigh Rd. N St P 136 A3
Farleigh Rise. Mon Far 86 C1
Farleigh View. Westw 120 C2
Farleigh Wick. Mon Far 103 F3
Farleigh Wlk. Bris 79 D4
Farler's End. Nail 75 F4
Farley Cl. St Gif 36 B4
Farm Ct. Mang 51 F4
Farm La. Alm 22 C1
Farm La. Piln 22 C1
Farm La. Well 118 C1
Farm Lees. Char 11 D3
Farm Rd. Lock 105 F1
Farm Rd. Mang 51 F4
Farmer Rd. Bris 78 C2
Farmhouse Cl. Nail 59 F1
Farmhouse Ct. Nail 59 F1
Farmwell Cl. Bris 79 D3
Farndale Rd. W-S-M 105 E4
Farndale. Bris 65 D3
Farne Cl. Bris 49 D3

Farr St. Avon 47 D4
Farr's La. Bris 63 E3
Farrant Cl. Bris 79 E3
Farrington Fields. Paul 131 E2
Farrington Rd. Paul 131 E3
Farrington Way. Paul 131 D2
Farrs La. Bath 102 A1
Farthing Row. Rode 136 C1
Faukland View. P St J 133 F4
Faulkland La. Well 134 B2
Faulkland Rd. Bath 101 E3
Faversham Dr. W-S-M 105 D1
Fawkes Cl. Kingsw 66 A4
Fearnville Est. Cleve 57 E1
Featherbed La. Clut 114 B3
Featherbed La. O-on-S 7 D3
Featherbed La. Pens 114 B3
Featherbed La. Win 95 D2
Featherstone Rd. Bris 50 C2
Fedden Village. Portis 44 C3
Feeder Rd. Bris 64 A3
Felix Rd. Bris 64 A4
Felstead Rd. Bris 35 F1
Feltham Rd. Puck 53 E3
Felton Gr. Bris 79 D4
Felton La. Win 94 C4
Felton St. Win 94 B4
Fenbrook Cl. Bris 37 D1
Feniton. W-S-M 89 D1
Fennel La. Axb 125 D1
Fennel Gr. Bris 35 D1
Fenners. W-S-M 89 D2
Fenshurst Gdns. Lo Ash .. 77 F4
Fenswood Mead. Lo Ash . 61 F1
Fenswood Rd. Lo Ash 61 F1
Fenton Cl. Keyn 82 B2
Fenton Rd. Bris 49 E2
Ferenberge Cl. Farm 116 A3
Fermaine Ave. Bris 64 C2
Fern Cl. Bris 35 D2
Fern Gr. Nail 75 E4
Fern Lea. Blea 122 A3
Fern Rd. Mang 51 E3
Fernbank Rd. Bris 49 E1
Ferndale Ave. Bris 65 D1
Ferndale Ave. Kingsw 66 A2
Ferndale Rd. Bath 85 E2
Ferndale Rd. Bris 36 A1
Ferndale Rd. Portis 45 E3
Ferndean. St Gif 24 B1
Ferndown Cl. Bris 48 A4
Ferndown. Yate 27 F1
Fernhill La. Bris 34 A1
Fernhill. Alve 24 B4
Fernhill. Olve 24 B4
Fernhurst Rd. Bris 50 C1
Fernlea Gdns. E in G 47 D2
Fernlea Rd. W-S-M 105 E4
Fernleaze. Fr Cot 38 B3
Fernside. Back 76 A4
Fernsteed Rd. Bris 78 C3
Ferry La. Bath 102 A3
Ferry Rd. Kingsw 65 E1
Ferry St. Bris 63 F3
Ferry Steps Ind Est. Bris .. 64 A2
Fiddes Rd. Bris 49 E2
Field La. Aust 14 A4
Field La. Dyrh 54 C3
Field La. Kingsw 65 F2
Field La. Ston E 130 A1
Field La. Tyth 15 F2
Field Rd. Bris 51 E1
Field View Dr. Bris 51 E3
Fielders The. W-S-M 89 D2
Fieldgardens Rd. Clut 114 C1
Fielding's Rd. Bath 101 E3
Fieldings. Winsl 120 C4
Fieldway. Wins 108 A2
Fiennes Cl. Kingsw 51 F2
Fifth Ave. Bris 36 A1
Fifth Way. Avon 33 F1
Filby Dr. St Gif 36 B4
Filer Cl. P St J 133 E4
Filton Ave. Bris 36 A1
Filton Ave. Bris 36 A2
Filton Gr. Bris 49 F3
Filton La. Bris 36 B1
Filton Rd. Bris 36 B1
Filton Rd. Bris 37 D1
Filwood Broadway. Bris 79 F4
Filwood Dr. Kingsw 65 F4
Filwood Rd. Bris 51 D2
Finch Cl. Thorn 8 B1
Finch Cl. W-S-M 105 F4
Finch Rd. Ch Sod 40 A4
Finmere Gdns. W-S-M 89 D2
Fir La. Priddy 126 A3
Fir Leaze. Nail 59 D1
Fir Rd. Col 70 C3
Fir Tree Ave. Lock 105 F2
Fir Tree Ave. Paul 131 F2
Fir Tree Cl. Bris 35 F4
Fir Tree La. Bris 65 D4
Fircliff Park. Portis 45 D4
Fire Engine La. Fr Cot 38 B4
Fireclay Rd. Bris 64 B3
Firework Cl. Kingsw 66 A4
Firgrove Cres. Yate 28 A1

Firgrove La. P St J 117 D1
Firs Ct. Keyn 81 E2
Firs The. Bath 102 A1
Firs The. Li St 120 A3
Firs The. Mang 51 F3
First Ave. Bath 101 E2
First Ave. Bris 64 C3
First Ave. Portb 46 C3
First Ave. Rod 138 B4
First Way. Avon 33 E1
Fisher Ave. Kingsw 52 A1
Fisher Rd. Kingsw 52 A1
Fishponds Rd. Bris 50 C2
Fishpool Hill. Bris 35 D2
Fitchett Wlk. Bris 34 C2
Fitzgerald Rd. Bath 63 F2
Fitzroy Rd. Bris 51 D1
Fitzroy St. Bris 64 A2
Fitzroy Terr. Bris 49 D1
Five Acre Dr. Bris 50 C4
Five Arches Cl. Mid No 132 B1
Flagstaff Rd. Blea 123 E4
Flamingo Cres. W-S-M 105 F4
Flat The. Clut 114 B3
Flatwoods Cres. Bath 102 C2
Flatwoods Rd. Bath 102 C2
Flax Bourton Rd. Wrax 61 D2
Flaxman Cl. Bris 50 A3
Flaxpits La. Wint 37 F3
Florence Gr. W-S-M 105 D4
Florence Park. Alm 24 B3
Florence Park. Bris 49 D2
Florence Rd. Kingsw 51 F2
Florida Terr. Mid No 132 B1
Flowers Hill Cl. Bris 64 C1
Flowers Hill. Bris 64 C1
Flowerwell Rd. Bris 79 D3
Folleigh Cl. Lo Ash 62 A1
Folleigh Dr. Lo Ash 62 A1
Folleigh La. Lo Ash 62 A1
Folliot Cl. Bris 51 D4
Folly Bridge Cl. Yate 27 E1
Folly La. Bris 64 A3
Folly La. Ship 125 F4
Folly La. W-S-M 104 C1
Folly Rd. Ir Act 25 F2
Folly The. Keyn 82 C1
Folly The. Mang 51 F4
Fontana Cl. Kingsw 66 A2
Fonthill Rd. Bath 84 C1
Fonthill Rd. Bris 35 E1
Fonthill Way. Kingsw 66 B1
Fontmell Cl. Bris 80 B4
Fontwell Dr. Mang 37 F1
Footes La. Fr Cot 38 A4
Footshill Cl. Kingsw 65 E3
Footshill Dr. Kingsw 65 E3
Footshill Rd. Kingsw 65 E3
Ford Rd. P St J 133 E4
Ford La. Litt 129 E1
Ford Rd. Well 118 C1
Ford St. Bris 64 B3
Forde Cl. Kingsw 65 F3
Fordell Pl. Bris 64 A2
Forefield Pl. Bath 102 A3
Forefield Rise. Bath 102 A3
Forest Ave. Bris 51 D2
Forest Dr. Bris 35 E2
Forest Edge. Kingsw 65 E2
Forest Hills. Alm 24 A3
Forest Rd. Bris 51 D2
Forest Rd. Kingsw 65 E4
Forest Wlk. Bris 51 D1
Forest Wlk. Kingsw 65 E4
Forester Ave. Bath 102 A4
Forester La. Bath 102 A4
Forester Rd. Bath 102 A4
Forester Rd. Portis 45 E2
Forge End. Portb 46 C2
Fortescue Rd. Rad 132 C1
Fortfield Rd. Bris 80 A3
Forty Acre La. Alve 15 D2
Foss La. O-on-S 7 F3
Fosse Barton. Nail 59 E1
Fosse Cl. Nail 59 E1
Fosse Gdns. Bath 118 B4
Fosse Green. Mid No 132 C2
Fosse La. Bathe 86 A2
Fosse La. Mid No 132 B2
Fosse La. Nail 59 E1
Fossedale Ave. Bris 80 B3
Fossefield Rd. Kilm 138 A4
Fosseway Gdns. Rad 132 B1
Fosseway S. Kilm 138 A4
Fosseway The. Bris 63 D4
Fosseway. Chil 137 F1
Fosseway. Chil 138 A2
Fosseway. Cleve 57 E1
Fosseway. Mid No 132 C2
Fosseway. Rod 138 B4
Foster St. Bris 50 A1
Foundry La. Bris 50 C1
Fountain Ct. St Gif 24 B2
Fountain La. Wins 125 D4
Fountaine Ct. Bris 50 B1
Fountains Dr. Kingsw 65 F3

Four Acre Ave. Mang 51 F4
Four Acre Cres. Mang 37 F1
Four Acre Rd. Mang 51 F4
Four Acres Cl. Bris 78 C2
Four Acres Cl. Nail 75 F4
Four Acres. Bris 78 C2
Fourth Ave. Bris 36 A1
Fourth Ave. Rod 138 B4
Fourth Way. Avon 33 F1
Fowey Cl. Nail 76 A4
Fowey Rd. W-S-M 89 D2
Fox And Hounds La. Keyn .. 81 F3
Fox Ave. Yate 27 E1
Fox Ct. Kingsw 65 F2
Fox Den Rd. St Gif 36 B2
Fox Hill. Bath 102 A1
Fox House. Bris 64 C2
Fox Rd. Bris 50 A1
Foxborough Gdns. St Gif 24 B1
Foxcombe Rd. Bath 101 D4
Foxcombe Rd. Bris 80 A2
Foxcote. Kingsw 65 F4
Foxcote. Kingsw 65 F4
Foxcroft Cl. St Gif 36 C3
Foxcroft Rd. Bris 64 B4
Foxe Rd. Fr Cot 38 A4
Foxfield Ave. St Gif 24 B2
Foxglove Cl. Bris 50 C2
Foxglove Cl. Thorn 8 B1
Foxholes La. Olve 14 B2
Foye House. Lo Ash 62 B3
Fraley Rd. Bris 49 D4
Frampton Cres. Bris 51 E2
Frampton Ct. Kingsw 65 F2
Frampton End Rd. Fr Cot 38 B4
Frampton End Rd. Ir Act 26 B2
France La. H Up 20 A1
Francis Fox Rd. W-S-M 104 C4
Francis Pl. Kingsw 65 F2
Francis Rd. Bris 49 E4
Francis Rd. Bris 63 E1
Francombe Gr. Bris 49 F3
Frankland Cl. Bath 84 A1
Frankley Bldgs. Bath 85 D1
Franklin Ct. Bris 63 F3
Franklin's Way. Yatt 74 C1
Franklyn La. Bris 49 F1
Franklyn St. Bris 49 F1
Fraser Cl. W-S-M 88 C2
Fraser St. Bris 63 E2
Frayne Rd. Bris 63 D2
Frederick Ave. P St J 133 E4
Frederick Pl. Bris 63 D4
Fredrick St. Bris 64 A2
Free Tank. Bris 64 A3
Freeland Bldgs. Bris 50 B1
Freeland Pl. Bris 62 C3
Freelands. Cleve 73 E4
Freemans La. Ba Gu 77 D1
Freemantle Gdns. Bris 50 B2
Freemantle Rd. Bris 49 E1
Freemantle Rd. Bris 49 E1
Freemantle Rd. Bris 50 B2
Freemantle Sq. Bris 49 E1
Freestone Rd. Bris 64 A3
Freeview Rd. Bath 101 D3
Freezinghill La. Co Ash 68 A2
French Cl. Nail 59 E2
French Cl. P St J 133 E4
Frenchay Cl. Bris 51 E4
Frenchay Hill. Bris 51 E4
Frenchay Park Rd. Bris 50 C3
Frenchay Rd. Bris 51 E3
Frenchay Rd. W-S-M 104 C2
Frenchfield Rd. P St J 133 E4
Freshford La. Hi Cha 120 A3
Freshland Way. Bris 65 D4
Freshmoor. Cleve 57 F2
Friar Ave. W-S-M 88 C2
Friary Cl. Cleve 57 E3
Friary Cl. Westw 120 C2
Friary Grange Park. Wint 37 F3
Friary Rd. Bris 49 E2
Friary Rd. Portis 45 D3
Friendly Row. E in G 47 E3
Friendship Gr. Nail 59 F1
Friendship Rd. Bris 64 A1
Friendship Rd. Nail 59 F2
Friezewood Rd. Bris 63 D2
Fripp Cl. Bris 64 A3
Frith La. Yate 17 F2
Frobisher Ave. Portis 45 D3
Frobisher Cl. W-S-M 88 C2
Frobisher Rd. Bris 63 D2
Frog La. Bris 63 E3
Frog La. Co Mar 111 E1
Frog La. N Nib 5 E3
Frog La. Win 94 A4
Frog La. Win 94 C3
Frog La. Yate 38 C4
Frogmore St. Bris 63 E3
Frome Ct. Thorn 15 E4
Frome Glen. Wint 37 F2
Frome Old Rd. Rad 133 D1
Frome Pl. Bris 50 C2
Frome Rd. Bath 101 E1
Frome Rd. Ch Sod 28 A1
Frome Rd. Kilm 139 E4

Frome Rd. N St P 135 F2
Frome Rd. Rad 133 D1
Frome St. Bris 63 F4
Frome Terr. Bris 50 C3
Frome Valley Rd. Bris 50 C3
Frome View. Fr Cot 38 A4
Frome Way. Wint 37 F3
Fromeside Park. Bris 51 D4
Front St. Chur 108 C2
Froomshaw Rd. Bris 51 D4
Frost Hill. Yatt 91 E4
Fry's Cl. Bris 50 B2
Fry's La. Blag 109 F2
Fry's Well. Chil 137 E2
Frys Hill. Kingsw 51 F1
Fryth House. Wrax 60 B2
Fryth Way. Nail 59 E1
Fulford Rd. Bris 79 E3
Fulford Wlk. Bris 79 D3
Fullens Cl. W-S-M 105 E4
Fuller Rd. Bath 85 E1
Fullers La. Wins 125 D3
Fullers Way. Bath 118 B4
Fulmar Cl. Thorn 8 B1
Fulmar Rd. W-S-M 88 C1
Fulwell Cl. Faulk 134 B1
Fulwell La. Faulk 134 B1
Furber Ct. Bris 65 D3
Furber Rd. Bris 65 D3
Furber Ridge. Bris 65 D3
Furber Vale. Bris 65 D3
Furland Rd. W-S-M 88 B1
Furlong Cl. Mid No 137 F4
Furnleaze. Clut 114 C2
Furnwood. Bris 65 D3
Furze Cl. W-S-M 88 A1
Furze Rd. Bris 51 E2
Furze Rd. W-S-M 88 A2
Furzewood Rd. Kingsw 65 F2
Fussell Ct. Kingsw 65 F4
Fylton Croft. Bris 80 A2

Gable Cl. Alm 23 D1
Gable Rd. Bris 50 A1
Gables Cl. Ban 107 D2
Gadshill Dr. St Gif 36 C3
Gadshill Rd. Bris 50 B1
Gages Cl. Kingsw 65 F4
Gages Rd. Kingsw 65 F4
Gainsborough Dr. W-S-M 88 C2
Gainsborough Gdns. Bath .. 101 E4
Gainsborough Rd. Keyn 81 F3
Gainsborough Sq. Bris 50 A4
Gallivan Cl. St Gif 36 A4
Galway Rd. Bris 63 F1
Gambril La. Crom 9 F3
Gander Cl. Bris 79 D3
Garden Cl. Bris 48 B3
Gardeners Wlk. Lo Ash 62 A1
Gardens Rd. Cleve 57 E2
Gardens The. Kingsw 51 E2
Gardner Ave. Bris 78 C4
Gardner Rd. Portis 45 E3
Garfield Rd. Bris 65 D4
Garner Ct. W-S-M 89 D2
Garnet St. Bris 63 D2
Garnett Pl. Mang 51 F1
Garonor Way. E in G 46 C3
Garrett Dr. St Gif 36 B4
Garrick Rd. Bath 100 C3
Garsdale Rd. W-S-M 105 E4
Garston La. Blag 110 C2
Garstons Cl. Wring 92 C1
Garstons Orch. Wring 92 B1
Garstons The. Portis 45 E2
Garstons. Bathf 86 B1
Garstons. Cleve 73 E4
Garstons. Wring 92 C1
Garth Rd. Bris 79 D4
Gas La. Bris 64 A3
Gasferry Rd. Bris 63 F3
Gaskins The. Bris 50 A3
Gaston Ave. Keyn 81 F4
Gastons The. Bris 48 A4
Gatcombe Dr. St Gif 36 C2
Gatcombe Rd. Bris 79 D3
Gatehouse Ave. Bris 79 D3
Gatehouse Cl. Bris 79 D3
Gatesby Mead. St Gif 36 C3
Gathorne Rd. Bris 63 D2
Gatton Rd. Bris 50 A1
Gaunt's Earthcott La. Alve .. 25 D3
Gaunt's La. Bris 63 E3
Gaunts Cl. Portis 44 C2
Gaunts Rd. Ch Sod 40 A4
Gay Elms Rd. Bris 79 D2
Gay St. Bath 101 F4
Gay's Hill. Bath 102 A4
Gayner Rd. Bris 36 A1
Gays Rd. Kingsw 65 D2
Gaythorne Cres. Yate 27 E1
Gazelle Rd. W-S-M 105 D2
Gazzard Cl. Wint 37 F4
Gazzard Rd. Wint 37 F4
Gee Moors. Kingsw 65 F3
Geldof Dr. Mid No 132 A1
Gelfe Cl. Bris 63 D3
Geoffrey Cl. Bris 78 C3

George & Dragon La. Bris ... 64 B4
George La. Marsh 55 F1
George St. Bath 101 F4
George St. Bris 64 B4
George St. Portis 45 E1
George St. W-S-M 104 C4
George Whitefield Ct. Bris ... 63 F4
George's Bldgs. Bath 102 A4
George's Rd. Bath 85 D1
Georgian View. Bath 101 E1
Gerald Rd. Bris 63 D2
Gerard Rd. W-S-M 104 C4
Gerrish Ave. Bris 64 B4
Gerrish Ave. Mang 51 F3
Gibbet La. Whit 80 B1
Gibbets Brow. Priddy 128 A2
Gibbsfold Rd. Bris 79 E2
Gibson Rd. Bris 49 E1
Gifford Cl. Wickw 27 D4
Gifford Cres. St Gif 36 B3
Gifford Rd. Bris 34 C2
Gilbeck Rd. Nail 59 E1
Gilbert Rd. Bris 64 B4
Gilbert Rd. Kingsw 51 E1
Gilberyn Dr. W-S-M 89 D2
Gilda Cl. Bris 80 B3
Gilda Cres. Bris 80 B3
Gilda Par. Bris 80 B3
Gilda Sq W. Bris 80 A3
Gill Ave. Bris 51 D3
Gill Mews. W-S-M 89 D2
Gillard Cl. Bris 65 D4
Gillard Rd. Bris 65 D4
Gillebank Cl. Bris 80 B2
Gillingham Hill. Bris 65 D3
Gillingham Terr. Bath 85 D1
Gillingstool. Thorn 15 E4
Gillmore Cl. W-S-M 88 B1
Gillmore Rd. W-S-M 88 B1
Gillray Cl. Bris 50 A3
Gillson Cl. Lock 105 E1
Gilpin Cl. Kingsw 51 F1
Gilroy Cl. Kingsw 66 A2
Gilslake Ave. Bris 35 D2
Gimblet Rd. W-S-M 89 D2
Gingell's Green. Bris 65 D4
Gipsy Patch La. St Gif 36 B3
Glades The. Bris 50 C1
Gladstone Dr. Kingsw 51 F2
Gladstone La. Fr Cot 38 B4
Gladstone Rd. Bath 102 B1
Gladstone Rd. Bris 80 A3
Gladstone Rd. Kingsw 51 E1
Gladstone St. Bris 63 D2
Gladstone St. Bris 64 B4
Gladstone St. Kingsw 51 E2
Glaisdale Rd. Bris 51 D3
Glanville Dr. Hin Ble 129 F3
Glanville Gdns. Kingsw 65 F4
Glass House La. Bris 64 A3
Glastonbury Cl. Kingsw 65 F3
Glastonbury Cl. Nail 60 A1
Glastonbury Way. W-S-M 89 D1
Glebe Ave. Portis 45 F2
Glebe Field. Alm 24 A3
Glebe Rd. Bath 101 D2
Glebe Rd. Bris 64 C4
Glebe Rd. Cleve 57 E1
Glebe Rd. Lo Ash 62 B1
Glebe Rd. Portis 45 F2
Glebe Rd. W-S-M 104 C4
Glebe The. Hi Cha 120 A2
Glebe The. Hin Cha 119 E1
Glebe The. Piln 22 B4
Glebe The. Tims 116 A2
Glebe The. Wring 92 B1
Glebe Wlk. Keyn 81 E2
Glebelands Rd. Bris 36 A2
Glebelands. Rad 132 B1
Gledemoor Dr. Fr Cot 38 B4
Glen Ave. Ab Lei 61 F4
Glen Dr. Bris 48 B3
Glen La. Bris 64 B1
Glen Park Gdns. Bris 65 D4
Glen Park. Bris 50 B1
Glen Park. Bris 65 D4
Glen The. Bris 49 D2
Glen The. Keyn 82 C1
Glen The. Kingsw 65 D2
Glen The. W-S-M 88 A1
Glen The. Yate 27 F1
Glen Yeo Terr. Cong 91 E2
Glena Ave. Bris 64 A1
Glenarm Rd. Bris 64 C1
Glenarm Wlk. Bris 64 C1
Glenavon Park. Bris 48 B2
Glenburn Rd. Bris 51 D1
Glencoyne Sq. Bris 35 E1
Glendale. Bris 51 E2
Glendale. Bris 62 C3
Glendale. Mang 51 E4
Glendare St. Bris 64 B3
Glendevon Rd. Bris 80 A2
Gleneagles Cl. Nail 60 A1
Gleneagles Cl. W-S-M 88 C2
Gleneagles Dr. Bris 34 B2
Gleneagles Rd. Kingsw 66 A3

Gleneagles. Yate .... 27 F
Glenfall. Yate .... 39 E
Glenfrome Rd. Bris .... 50 A
Glenroy Ave. Bris .... 51 D
Glenside Cl. Bris .... 51 E
Glenside Park. Bris .... 50 C
Glentworth Ct. Bris .... 49 E
Glentworth Rd. Bris .... 63 D
Glenview Rd. Bris .... 64 B
Glenwood Dr. Kingsw .... 66 A
Glenwood Rd. Bris .... 49 E
Glenwood Rise. Portis .... 44 C
Glenwood. Bris .... 51 E
Gloster Ave. Bris .... 50 B
Gloucester Cl. St Gif .... 36 B
Gloucester La. Bris .... 63 F
Gloucester Rd N. Bris .... 36 A
Gloucester Rd. Alm .... 24 A
Gloucester Rd. Alve .... 14 C
Gloucester Rd. Avon .... 33 D
Gloucester Rd. Bath .... 85 E
Gloucester Rd. Bathe .... 85 E
Gloucester Rd. Bris .... 36 A
Gloucester Rd. Bris .... 49 F
Gloucester Rd. Kingsw .... 51 F
Gloucester Rd. St Gif .... 24 A
Gloucester Rd. Thorn .... 8 D
Gloucester Row. W-u-E .... 11 F
Gloucester St. Bath .... 101 F
Gloucester St. Bris .... 50 B
Gloucester St. Bris .... 62 C
Gloucester St. Bris .... 63 F
Gloucester St. W-S-M .... 104 B
Glovers Field. Ship .... 125 F
Glyn Vale. Bris .... 63 F
Goddard Dr. W-S-M .... 89 D
Godfrey Ct. Kingsw .... 65 F
Goffenton Dr. Bris .... 51 D
Goldcrest Rd. Ch Sod .... 39 F
Golden La. Kings .... 11 F
Golden Valley La. Bitt .... 66 C
Goldfinch Way. Puck .... 53 E
Goldney Ave. Bris .... 63 D
Goldney Ave. Sist .... 66 B
Goldney Cl. Clut .... 114 C
Goldney Rd. Bris .... 63 D
Goldney Way. Clut .... 114 C
Goldsbury Wlk. Bris .... 34 A
Golf Club La. Keyn .... 82 C
Golf Course La. Bris .... 35 F
Golf Course Rd. Bath .... 102 B
Golledge Cl. Chil .... 137 E
Gooch Way. W-S-M .... 89 D
Good Shepherd Cl. Bris .... 49 F
Goodeve Park. Bris .... 48 B
Goodeve Rd. Bris .... 48 B
Goodhind St. Bris .... 64 A
Goodneston Rd. Bris .... 51 D
Goodring Hill. Bris .... 34 A
Goodwin Dr. Bris .... 79 F
Goodwin Dr. Nail .... 59 F
Goodwood Gdns. Mang .... 37 F
Goold Cl. Cor .... 100 A
Goolden St. Bris .... 64 A
Goosard La. Paul .... 131 E
Goose Acre. St Gif .... 36 C
Goose Green Way. Yate .... 27 F
Goose Green. Fr Cot .... 38 B
Goose Green. Yate .... 27 F
Gooseland Cl. Bris .... 79 F
Goosy La. Lock .... 89 E
Gordano Gdns. E in G .... 47 D
Gordano Rd. E in G .... 46 B
Gordano View. Portis .... 45 E
Gordano Way. E in G .... 46 C
Gordon Ave. Bris .... 50 C
Gordon Cl. Bris .... 50 C
Gordon Rd. Bath .... 102 A
Gordon Rd. Bris .... 49 F
Gordon Rd. Bris .... 50 B
Gordon Rd. Bris .... 63 D
Gordon Rd. P St J .... 133 E
Gordon Rd. W-S-M .... 104 C
Gore Rd. Bris .... 63 D
Gore's Marsh Rd. Bris .... 63 D
Gorham Cl. Bris .... 34 B
Gorlands Rd. Ch Sod .... 28 A
Gorlangton Cl. Bris .... 80 A
Gorse Cover Rd. Piln .... 22 A
Gorse Hill. Bris .... 51 E
Gorse La. Bris .... 63 D
Gorse La. Co Ash .... 68 B
Gorse La. Marsh .... 54 C
Gosforth Rd. Bris .... 35 D
Goslet Rd. Bris .... 80 C
Goss Barton. Nail .... 59 E
Goss Cl. Nail .... 59 E
Goss La. Nail .... 59 E
Goss View. Nail .... 59 E
Gotley Rd. Bris .... 64 B
Gott Dr. Bris .... 64 B
Goulston Rd. Bris .... 79 D
Goulston Wlk. Bris .... 79 D
Goulter St. Bris .... 64 A
Gournay Ct. Paul .... 131 D
Gourney Cl. Bris .... 34 A
Grace Cl. Ch Sod .... 28 A
Grace Cl. Yatt .... 91 D

Grace Ct. Mang 51 E3
Grace Dr. Kingsw 66 A4
Grace Dr. Mid No 132 A1
Grace Park Rd. Bris 64 B1
Grace Rd. Mang 51 E3
Grace Rd. W-S-M 89 D2
Gradwell Cl. W-S-M 89 D2
Graeme Cl. Bris 51 D2
Graham Rd. Bris 50 A1
Graham Rd. Bris 63 E2
Graham Rd. Mang 51 F3
Graham Rd. W-S-M 104 C4
Grainger Ct. Bris 47 F4
Graitney Cl. Brock 92 A4
Grampian Cl. Kingsw 66 B2
Granby Hill. Bris 62 C3
Grandmother's Rock La.
   Bitt 67 E1
Grange Ave. Kingsw 65 E3
Grange Ave. St Gif 36 B3
Grange Cl N. Bris 49 D3
Grange Cl. St Gif 24 B1
Grange Cl. W-S-M 104 C1
Grange Court Rd. Bris 49 D3
Grange Ct. Kingsw 65 E3
Grange Dr. Bris 51 E3
Grange End. Rod 138 A4
Grange Park. Bris 49 D3
Grange Park. Bris 51 E4
Grange Rd. Bris 63 D4
Grange Rd. Bris 79 D3
Grange Rd. Keyn 82 B2
Grange Rd. W-S-M 104 C1
Grange The. Bris 48 B4
Grangeville Cl. Kingsw 66 A2
Grangewood Cl. Bris 51 E3
Grantham La. Bris 65 E4
Grantham Rd. Bris 51 E1
Grantson Cl. Bris 64 C1
Granville Cl. Kingsw 65 D2
Granville Rd. Bath 84 C2
Granville St. Bris 64 B3
Grasmere Cl. Bris 49 D4
Grasmere Dr. W-S-M 104 C2
Grass Meers Dr. Bris 80 A2
Grassington. Ch Sod 40 A4
Grassmere Gdns. Kingsw 66 B3
Grassmere Rd. Yatt 91 D4
Gratitude Rd. Bris 50 B1
Gravel Hill Rd. Yate 28 A3
Gravel Hill. Ch St 112 A4
Gravel Hill. Win 112 A4
Gray's Cl. Bris 64 B1
Grayle Rd. Bris 35 D1
Grays Hill. Well 134 A3
Great Ann St. Bris 63 F4
Great Bedford St. Bath 101 F4
Great Brockeridge. Bris 48 C3
Great Dowles. Kingsw 66 A2
Great George St. Bris 63 E4
Great George St. Bris 63 F4
Great Hayles Rd. Bris 80 A4
Great Leaze. Kingsw 66 A2
Great Meadow Rd. St Gif 36 C3
Great Meadow. St Gif 37 D3
Great Park Rd. St Gif 24 B2
Great Pulteney St. Bath 102 A4
Great Stanhope St. Bath 101 F3
Great Stoke Way. St Gif 36 B2
Great Stoke. St Gif 37 D3
Great Western Bridge.
   W-S-M 104 C4
Great Western La. Bris 64 A3
Great Western Rd. Cleve 57 E1
Great Western Way. Bris 63 F3
Greatstone La. Win 94 C3
Greatstone La. Win 94 C3
Green Cl. Bris 50 A4
Green Croft. Bris 51 D1
Green Dell Cl. Bris 34 B2
Green Ditch La. Chil 137 D3
Green Ditch La. Ston E 137 D3
Green Dragon Rd. Wint 37 E3
Green Hayes. Ch Sod 40 B4
Green La. Avon 33 D1
Green La. But 94 B2
Green La. But 111 D4
Green La. Chil 137 F1
Green La. Hin Cha 119 F1
Green La. Marsh 69 F4
Green La. Paul 130 C3
Green La. Thorn 16 A4
Green La. Win 94 B2
Green La. Wrax 61 E2
Green Park Rd. Bath 101 F3
Green Park. Bath 101 F3
Green Parlour Rd. Kilm 133 E1
Green Side. Mang 52 A3
Green St. Bath 102 A4
Green St. Bris 63 F2
Green St. Well 133 F3
Green The. Back 75 F3
Green The. Bath 101 E1
Green The. Crom 17 D4
Green The. E in G 47 E2
Green The. Hin Cha 119 F1

Green The. Kingsw 51 F1
Green The. Lock 106 A2
Green The. Olve 14 A1
Green The. St Gif 36 C2
Green The. Wins 125 D4
Green Tree Rd. Mid No 132 A2
Green Wlk. Bris 64 A1
Greenacre Rd. Bris 80 A2
Greenacre. W-S-M 88 A1
Greenacres. Bris 48 C4
Greenacres. Mid No 131 F1
Greenbank Ave W. Bris 50 B1
Greenbank Ave. Bris 50 B1
Greenbank Gdns. Bath 84 A1
Greenbank Rd. Bris 50 B1
Greenbank Rd. Bris 63 D2
Greenbank Rd. Kingsw 65 E3
Greenbank View. Bris 50 B1
Greendale Rd. Bris 49 D2
Greendale Rd. Bris 63 F1
Greenditch Ave. Bris 79 E3
Greenditch Cl. Chil 137 E2
Greenditch St. Piln 13 E1
Greendown Pl. Bath 102 A1
Greendown. Bris 65 D4
Greenfield Ave. Bris 49 E4
Greenfield Cres. Nail 59 F2
Greenfield Park. Portis 45 E2
Greenfield Pl. W-S-M 104 B4
Greenfield Rd. Bris 35 E1
Greenfields Ave. Ban 107 D2
Greenfinch Lodge. Bris 50 C3
Greenhaven. Bris 50 B1
Greenhill Cl. W-S-M 89 D2
Greenhill Down. Alve 15 D2
Greenhill Gdns. Alve 15 D2
Greenhill Gr. Bris 63 D1
Greenhill La. Alve 14 C2
Greenhill La. Bris 34 B1
Greenhill Par. Alve 15 D3
Greenhill Pl. Mid No 132 A2
Greenhill Rd. Alve 15 D3
Greenhill Rd. Mid No 132 A2
Greenhill Rd. Wins 108 A2
Greenhill. Alve 15 D2
Greenland Rd. W-S-M 88 B1
Greenlands Rd. P St J 133 E4
Greenlands Way. Bris 34 C2
Greenleaze Ave. Mang 37 F1
Greenleaze Cl. Mang 37 E1
Greenleaze. Bris 64 A1
Greenmore Rd. Bris 64 A1
Greenore. Kingsw 65 E4
Greenpark Rd. Bris 35 F1
Greenridge Cl. Bris 78 C2
Greenridge. Clut 114 C2
Greenside Cl. Bris 34 B2
Greenslade Gdns. Nail 59 E2
Greensplott Rd. Avon 33 F4
Greenvale Cl. Tims 116 A1
Greenvale Dr. Tims 116 A1
Greenvale Rd. Paul 131 E3
Greenvale. Tims 116 A1
Greenview. Kingsw 66 A1
Greenway Bush La. Bris 63 D2
Greenway Ct. Bath 101 F2
Greenway Dr. Bris 49 E4
Greenway La. Bath 102 A2
Greenway La. Co Ash 68 C3
Greenway Park. Bris 49 E4
Greenway Park. Cleve 57 F2
Greenway Rd. Bris 49 D1
Greenway The. Bris 51 E2
Greenways Rd. Yate 27 F2
Greenways. Chil 137 E1
Greenways. Kingsw 52 A1
Greenwell La. Chur 109 E4
Greenwood Cl. Bris 49 F4
Greenwood Dr. Alve 14 C2
Greenwood Rd. Bris 64 A1
Greenwood Rd. W-S-M 88 C1
Gregory Ct. Kingsw 66 A3
Gregorys Tyning. Paul 131 F3
Greinton. W-S-M 105 D1
Grenville Ave. Lock 106 A2
Grenville Cl. Bris 64 C4
Grenville Pl. Bris 62 C3
Grenville Rd. Bris 49 F2
Greve Ct. Kingsw 65 F2
Greville Rd. Bris 63 D2
Greville St. Bris 63 E2
Grey Hollow. E Harp 128 C2
Greyfield Comm. Paul 115 E1
Greyfield Rd. Paul 115 E1
Greyfield View. Clut 114 C1
Greylands Rd. Bris 78 C4
Greystoke Ave. Bris 35 E1
Greystoke Gdns. Bris 49 D4
Greystones. Mang 37 F1
Grib La. Blag 110 C1
Griffin Cl. W-S-M 89 D1
Griffin Rd. Cleve 57 F2
Griggfield Wlk. Bris 80 A4
Grimsbury Rd. Kingsw 66 A4
Grindell Rd. Bris 64 B4

Grinfield Ave. Bris 79 E2
Grinfield Cl. Bris 79 E2
Grinfield Ct. Bris 79 E2
Grittleton Rd. Bris 49 F4
Grosvenor Bridge Rd. Bath 85 E1
Grosvenor Park. Bath 85 E1
Grosvenor Pl. Bath 85 E1
Grosvenor Rd. Bris 49 F1
Grove Ave. Bris 48 B4
Grove Ave. Bris 50 C2
Grove Ave. Bris 63 E3
Grove Bank. Bris 37 E1
Grove Ind Est The. Bris 36 A4
Grove La. Dyrh 54 B3
Grove La. Faulk 134 B1
Grove La. W-S-M 104 B4
Grove Leaze. Bris 47 E3
Grove Park Ave. Bris 64 B1
Grove Park Rd. Bris 64 B1
Grove Park Rd. W-S-M 87 E1
Grove Park Terr. Bris 50 C2
Grove Park. Bris 49 E1
Grove Pk. Bris 64 B1
Grove Rd. Bris 48 B4
Grove Rd. Bris 49 D1
Grove Rd. Bris 50 C2
Grove Rd. W-S-M 88 B1
Grove Rd. W-S-M 104 B4
Grove St. Bath 102 A4
Grove The. Bris 63 E3
Grove The. Kingsw 66 A2
Grove The. Wickw 27 D4
Grove The. Winsc 107 F1
Grove The. Wrax 60 B2
Grove View. Bris 50 C3
Grove Wood Rd. Rod 138 C4
Grovesend Rd. Thorn 15 E4
Guernsey Ave. Bris 64 C2
Gug The. Paul 115 E1
Guildford Rd. Bris 64 C3
Guinea La. Bath 101 F4
Guinea La. Bris 51 D2
Guinea St. Bris 63 E3
Gullen. Well 134 A3
Gulliford's Bank. Cleve 57 F1
Gullimores Gdns. Bris 79 D2
Gullivers Pl. Ch Sod 40 A4
Gullon Wlk. Bris 78 C3
Gullons Cl. Bris 79 D3
Gully La. Rock 8 C4
Gully The. Wint 37 F4
Gullybrook La. Bris 64 A3
Gunter's Hill. Bris 65 D3
Guthrie Rd. Bris 48 C3
Gwilliam St. Bris 63 E2
Gwyn St. Bris 49 F1
Gypsy La. Keyn 99 D4

Haberfield Hill. Ab Lei 47 F1
Hacket Hill. Thorn 15 F4
Hacket La. Thorn 15 F4
Hadley Cl. Kingsw 66 A3
Hadley Rd. Bath 102 A1
Hadrian Cl. Bris 48 B2
Hagg Hill. Tims 116 A1
Haggs La. Bris 50 C1
Haig Cl. Bris 48 A4
Halbrow Cres. Bris 51 E3
Haldon Cl. Bris 63 E1
Hales Horn Cl. St Gif 36 B3
Half Yd. Wring 109 E4
Halfacre Cl. Bris 80 A2
Halfacre La. Bris 80 A2
Halfpenny Row. Rode 136 C1
Halifax Rd. Yate 27 E2
Hall End La. Yate 17 E1
Hall La. Co Ash 68 A2
Hall La. Co Ash 68 C2
Hall La. Hort 29 F3
Hall St. Bris 63 D1
Hallam Rd. Cleve 57 E2
Hallards Cl. Bris 47 F4
Hallatrow Rd. Paul 131 E3
Hallen Cl. Bris 34 B2
Hallen Dr. Bris 48 B4
Hallen Rd. Bris 34 B2
Halletts Way. Portis 45 E3
Halliwell Rd. Portis 44 B2
Halls Rd. Kingsw 65 E4
Halsbury Rd. Bris 49 D2
Halstock Ave. Bris 50 C2
Halston Dr. Bris 63 F4
Halswell Gdns. Bris 79 D2
Halswell Rd. Cleve 57 E1
Halt End. Whit 80 B2
Ham Cl. Clut 114 C1
Ham Gr. Paul 131 F4
Ham Green. E in G 47 E2
Ham La. Bi Sut 113 D3
Ham La. Bris 50 C3
Ham La. Dun 78 B2
Ham La. K Sey 72 C1
Ham La. O-on-S 7 E3
Ham La. Paul 130 C3
Ham La. Paul 131 F3
Ham La. Wick 53 F1
Ham La. Wrax 60 A2
Ham La. Yatt 74 A2

Ham Link. Blag 109 F2
Ham Rd. Berr 121 D2
Ham Wood Cl. W-S-M 105 D1
Hamble Cl. Thorn 15 E4
Hambledon Rd. Lock 89 E2
Hambrook La. Bris 37 D2
Hambrook La. St Gif 37 D2
Hamersmith Rd. Bris 64 B4
Hamilton Rd. Bath 84 C1
Hamilton Rd. Bris 63 D2
Hamilton Rd. Bris 64 A4
Hamilton Rd. W-S-M 87 E1
Hamlet The. Nail 60 A2
Hammer La. Faulk 135 E1
Hammond Cl. Bris 64 B1
Hammond Gdns. Bris 48 C4
Hampden Cl. Yate 27 E2
Hampden Rd. Bris 64 A2
Hampden Rd. W-S-M 88 C1
Hampshire Way. Yate 27 F2
Hampstead Rd. Bris 64 B2
Hampton Cl. Kingsw 66 A3
Hampton Cnr. Bris 47 F3
Hampton La. Bris 49 D1
Hampton Park. Bris 49 D1
Hampton Rd. Bris 49 D1
Hampton Row. Bath 102 A4
Hampton St. Kingsw 51 E1
Hampton View. Bath 85 D1
Hams La. Badg 123 E1
Hams Rd. Keyn 81 F4
Hanbury Cl. Kingsw 65 E3
Hanbury Rd. Bris 63 D4
Handel Ave. Bris 64 B4
Handel Rd. Keyn 81 F3
Handford Way. Kingsw 66 A2
Hanford Ct. Bris 80 B4
Hang Hill. Well 134 A3
Hanham Bsns Pk. Kingsw 65 D3
Hanham La. Paul 131 F4
Hanham Rd. Kingsw 65 E4
Hanham Way. Nail 59 E1
Hannah More Cl. Wring 92 C1
Hannah More Rd. Nail 75 E4
Hanny's La. Ch Mag 96 A2
Hanover Cl. W-S-M 89 D2
Hanover Ct. Bris 63 F4
Hanover Ct. Rad 133 E1
Hanover Pl. Bris 63 D3
Hanover St. Bath 85 D1
Hanover St. Bris 63 E3
Hanover St. Bris 64 B4
Hansford Cl. Bath 101 F1
Hansford Sq. Bath 101 F1
Hanson's Way. Cleve 57 E1
Hantone Hill. Bath 102 C4
Happerton La. E in G 47 E1
Hapsburg Cl. W-S-M 89 D2
Harbour Rd. Portis 45 E3
Harbour Wall. Bris 48 B2
Harbour Way. Bris 63 E3
Harbury Rd. Bris 49 E4
Harbutts. Bath 85 F1
Harcombe Hill. Wint 37 F2
Harcombe Rd. Wint 37 E3
Harcourt Ave. Bris 65 D3
Harcourt Cl. Keyn 82 C1
Harcourt Gdns. Bath 84 A1
Harcourt Hill. Bris 49 E2
Harcourt Rd. Bris 49 D2
Harden Rd. Bris 80 C3
Hardenhuish Rd. Bris 64 B3
Harding Pl. Keyn 82 A3
Hardwick Cl. Bris 64 C2
Hardwick Cl. Kingsw 66 B3
Hardwick Rd. E in G 47 E3
Hardwicke. Yate 39 E4
Hardy Ave. Bris 63 D2
Hardy Ct. Kingsw 65 F3
Hardy La. Olve 14 A1
Hardy La. Piln 23 F4
Hardy Rd. Bris 63 D1
Hareclive Rd. Bris 79 E2
Harefield Cl. Kingsw 65 E1
Harescombe. Yate 39 F4
Harewood Rd. Bris 51 D1
Harford Cl. Bris 48 B4
Harford Dr. Bris 37 E1
Harford Sq. Ch Mag 96 A2
Harington Pl. Bath 101 F3
Harlech Way. Kingsw 66 A1
Harleston St. Bris 64 A4
Harley La. Cleve 58 B3
Harley St. Bath 101 F4
Harmer Cl. Bris 34 C2
Harmony Dr. Portis 44 C2
Harnhill Cl. Bris 79 D2
Harolds Way. Kingsw 65 E3
Harptree Ct. Kingsw 66 A2
Harptree Gr. Bris 63 D1
Harptree Hill. E Harp 128 A3
Harptree. W-S-M 105 D1
Harrier Path. W-S-M 105 F4
Harrington Ave. Bris 80 C3
Harrington Gr. Bris 80 C3
Harrington Rd. Bris 80 C3
Harrington Wlk. Bris 80 C3
Harris Barton. Fr Cot 38 A4

Harris Ct. Kingsw 65 F2
Harris La. Ab Lei 61 F4
Harrow Rd. Bris 64 B2
Harrowdene Rd. Bris 64 A2
Harry Stoke Rd. St Gif 36 C1
Hart's La. Paul 131 D4
Hartcliffe Rd. Bris 79 F4
Hartcliffe Way. Bris 79 E4
Hartcliffe Wlk. Bris 79 F4
Hartcombe Rd. E in G 47 D1
Hartfield Ave. Bris 49 E1
Hartgill Cl. Bris 79 D2
Hartington Park. Bris 49 E1
Hartland. W-S-M 89 D1
Hartley Cl. Ch Sod 28 A1
Harts Paddock. Mid No 131 F2
Harvey Cl. W-S-M 89 D2
Harveys La. Bris 64 C4
Harwood Gdns. W-S-M 88 C2
Haselbury Gr. Keyn 82 C1
Haskins Ct. Kingsw 66 A2
Haslands. Nail 75 E4
Haslemere Ind Est. Avon 33 E4
Hassage Hill. Well 134 C4
Hassell Dr. Bris 64 A4
Hastings Cl. Bris 63 E1
Hastings Rd. Bris 63 E1
Hatchet Hill. Kilm 139 F2
Hatchet La. St Gif 36 C2
Hatchet Rd. St Gif 36 C3
Hatchmere. Thorn 15 E4
Hatfield Bldgs. Bath 102 A3
Hatfield Rd. Bath 101 F2
Hatfield Rd. W-S-M 105 D3
Hatherley Rd. Bris 49 F2
Hatherley. Yate 39 F4
Hathway Wlk. Bris 64 A4
Hatters' La. Ch Sod 28 A1
Havage Dro. Ban 107 E4
Haven The. Kingsw 51 F1
Haversham Cl. W-S-M 88 B1
Haverstock Rd. Bris 64 A2
Haviland Gr. Bath 84 A1
Haviland Park. Bath 84 A1
Havory. Bath 85 E1
Havyat Rd. Wring 109 F4
Haw La. Olve 14 A2
Hawarden Terr. Bath 85 D1
Hawburn Cl. Bris 64 B1
Haweswater Cl. Kingsw 66 B2
Hawke Rd. W-S-M 88 C2
Hawkesbury Rd. Bris 50 C2
Hawkesbury Rd. Hill 19 E4
Hawkesley Dr. St Gif 36 B3
Hawkfield Cl. Bris 79 E3
Hawkfield Rd. Bris 79 E3
Hawkfield Way. Bris 79 E3
Hawkins Cl. Kingsw 66 B3
Hawkins St. Bris 63 F4
Hawkley Dr. St Gif 24 B2
Hawkridge Dr. Puck 53 E3
Hawksmoor Cl. Bris 80 A3
Hawksworth Dr. Kingsw 65 D3
Hawksworth Dr. W-S-M 89 D2
Hawlyn Cl. Bris 48 B3
Hawthorn Ave. Kingsw 65 D3
Hawthorn Cl. Bris 35 F4
Hawthorn Cl. Char 11 D2
Hawthorn Cl. Portis 44 C1
Hawthorn Coombe. W-S-M 88 C2
Hawthorn Cres. Thorn 8 B1
Hawthorn Cres. Yatt 74 A1
Hawthorn Gdns. W-S-M 88 B1
Hawthorn Gr. Bath 101 F1
Hawthorn Hill. W-S-M 88 C1
Hawthorn Hts. W-S-M 88 C1
Hawthorn Park. W-S-M 88 C2
Hawthorn Rd. Rad 133 D1
Hawthorn Way. Nail 60 A1
Hawthorn Way. St Gif 36 C3
Hawthorne Cl. Puck 53 E3
Hawthorne Gdns. Kingsw 51 F2
Hawthorne St. Bris 64 A2
Hawthornes The. Kingsw 51 F2
Hawthorns La. Keyn 81 F3
Hay Hill. Bath 101 F4
Hay La. Win 94 B3
Hay Leaze. Yate 27 E2
Hay St. Marsh 70 A4
Hay St. Ston E 137 D4
Haycombe Dr. Bath 101 D2
Haycombe La. Engl 100 C2
Haycombe. Bris 79 F3
Haycroft La. Newp 4 B3
Haycroft Rd. Bris 36 A2
Hayden Cl. Bath 101 F3
Haydock Cl. Mang 37 F1
Haydon Gate. Rod 138 C4
Haydon Gdns. Bris 50 A3
Haydon Hill. Rod 138 C4
Haydon Ind Est. Rod 138 C4
Hayeley Dr. St Gif 36 C3
Hayes Cl. Bris 64 A4
Hayes La. Gr Bad 30 C1
Hayes Park Rd. Mid No 131 F1
Hayes Rd. Mid No 131 F1
Hayesfield Park. Bath 101 F3
Hayeswood Rd. Farm 115 F2

Hayeswood Rd. Tims 116 A1
Hayfield. Marsh 70 A4
Hayleigh House. Bris 79 E2
Haymarket The. Bris 63 E4
Haymarket Wlk. Bris 63 E4
Haynes La. Mang 51 E3
Haythorn Ct. Mang 51 F3
Haytor Park. Bris 48 B3
Hayward Ct. Cleve 57 E1
Hayward Rd. Bris 64 B4
Hayward Rd. Kingsw 51 E2
Haywood Cl. W-S-M 105 D1
Haywood Gdns. W-S-M 105 D1
Hazel Ave. Bris 49 D1
Hazel Cres. Thorn 8 B1
Hazel Gdns. Alve 14 C2
Hazel Gr. Bath 101 E2
Hazel Gr. Bris 50 A4
Hazel La. Olve 14 C2
Hazel Terr. Rod 138 B4
Hazelbury Dr. Kingsw 66 B3
Hazelbury Rd. Nail 59 E1
Hazelcote Rd. Bris 80 A2
Hazeldene Rd. Bris 36 A4
Hazeldene Rd. W-S-M 105 D4
Hazell Cl. Cleve 57 F1
Hazelton Rd. Bris 49 E2
Hazelwood Ct. Bris 48 B2
Hazelwood Rd. Bris 48 B2
Hazleton Gdns. Bath 102 C2
Headford Ave. Bris 65 D4
Headford Rd. Bris 63 E1
Headley La. Bris 79 D3
Headley Park Ave. Bris 79 D4
Headley Park Rd. Bris 79 D4
Headley Rd. Bris 79 D3
Headley Wlk. Bris 79 D4
Healey Dr. Dyrh 54 B3
Heart Meers. Bris 80 A3
Heath Cl. Wint 37 F3
Heath Ct. Mang 51 E4
Heath Gdns. Fr Cot 38 B3
Heath Gdns. Mang 51 E4
Heath Rd. Bris 50 A2
Heath Rd. Kingsw 65 D2
Heath Rd. Mang 51 E4
Heath Rd. Nail 59 F2
Heath Ridge. Lo Ash 62 A1
Heath Rise. Kingsw 66 A3
Heath St. Bris 50 B2
Heath Wlk. Mang 51 E4
Heathcote Dr. Fr Cot 38 B4
Heathcote La. Fr Cot 38 B4
Heathcote Rd. Bris 51 D1
Heathcote Rd. Mang 51 F3
Heathcote Wlk. Bris 51 E1
Heather Ave. Fr Cot 38 A3
Heather Cl. Bris 65 D4
Heatherdene. Bris 79 F4
Heathfield Cl. Bath 84 A2
Heathfield Cl. Keyn 81 E3
Heathfield Cres. Bris 80 A2
Heathfield Rd. Nail 59 F2
Heathfield Way. Nail 59 F1
Heathgate. Yatt 91 D4
Hebden Rd. Westw 120 C2
Heber St. Bris 64 B4
Hebron Rd. Bris 63 E2
Hedgemead Cl. Bris 50 B3
Hedgemead View. Bris 50 C3
Hedges Cl. Cleve 57 D1
Hedges The. Lock 89 E1
Hedwick Ave. Bris 64 C4
Hedwick St. Bris 64 C4
Heggard Cl. Bris 79 D3
Helens Rd. Wins 108 A2
Hellier Wlk. Bris 79 E2
Helston Rd. Nail 60 A1
Hemming Way. Lock 105 F2
Hemmings Par. Bris 64 A4
Hemplow Cl. Bris 80 B4
Hempton La. St Gif 24 A1
Hen La. Win 94 C2
Henacre Rd. Bris 47 F4
Henbury Gdns. Bris 34 C1
Henbury Hill. Bris 34 C1
Henbury Rd. Bris 34 C1
Henbury Rd. Kingsw 65 D3
Hencliffe Rd. Bris 80 B4
Hencliffe Way. Kingsw 65 D2
Henderson Rd. Kingsw 65 D3
Hendre Rd. Bris 63 D1
Heneage La. Falf 9 F4
Henfield Cres. Kingsw 66 A2
Henfield Rd. Fr Cot 38 B2
Henfield Rd. West 38 B2
Hengaston St. Bris 63 D1
Hengrove Ave. Bris 80 A4
Hengrove La. Bris 80 A4
Hengrove Rd. Bris 64 A1
Hengrove Way. Bris 79 E3
Henleaze Ave. Bris 49 D3
Henleaze Gdns. Bris 49 D3
Henleaze Park. Bris 49 E3
Henleaze Park Dr. Bris 49 E3
Henleaze Rd. Bris 49 D3
Henleaze Terr. Bris 49 D4
Henley Gr. Bris 49 D3

Henley La. Yatt 91 E4
Henley Lodge. Yatt 91 E4
Henley Park. Yatt 91 E4
Henley View. Well 118 B1
Hennessy Cl. Bris 79 F2
Henrietta Gdns. Bath 102 A4
Henrietta Mews. Bath 102 A4
Henrietta Pl. Bath 102 A4
Henrietta Rd. Bath 102 A4
Henrietta St. Bath 102 A4
Henrietta St. Bris 50 A1
Henrietta St. Bris 63 E4
Henry St. Bath 102 A3
Henry St. Bris 63 F2
Henry Williamson Ct.
  Kingsw 66 A3
Henshaw Cl. Bris 51 E1
Henshaw Rd. Bris 51 E1
Henshaw Wlk. Bris 51 E1
Hensley Gdns. Bath 101 F2
Hensley Rd. Bath 101 F2
Hensman's Hill. Bris 63 D3
Hepburn Rd. Bris 49 F1
Herald Cl. Bris 48 B3
Herapath St. Bris 64 B3
Herbert Cres. Bris 50 B2
Herbert Rd. Bath 101 E3
Herbert Rd. Cleve 57 E2
Herbert St. Bris 63 E2
Herbert St. Bris 64 B4
Hercules Cl. St Gif 36 B3
Hereford Rd. Bris 50 A1
Hereford St. Bris 63 E2
Heritage Cl. P St J 133 E4
Herkomer Cl. Bris 50 A4
Herluin Way. W-S-M 105 D3
Hermes Cl. Keyn 82 B1
Hermitage Cl. Bris 47 F4
Hermitage Rd. Bath 84 C1
Hermitage Rd. Mang 51 F3
Hern La. Ba Gu 77 F3
Heron Cl. W-S-M 105 F4
Heron Rd. Bris 50 A1
Heron Way. Ch Sod 40 A4
Herridge Cl. Bris 79 D2
Herridge Rd. Bris 79 D2
Hersey Gdns. Bris 78 C2
Hesding Cl. Kingsw 65 E2
Hestercombe Rd. Bris 79 D3
Heyford Ave. Bris 50 A2
Heyron Wlk. Bris 79 D2
Heywood Rd. E in G 47 E2
Heywood Terr. E in G 47 E2
Hibbs Cl. Marsh 69 F4
Hicks Common Rd. Wint 37 F3
Hicks Cl. Kingsw 65 F2
High Acre. Paul 131 F2
High Bannerdown. Bathe 86 A2
High Elm. Kingsw 65 F3
High Gr. Bris 48 A4
High Mead Gdns. Bi Sut 113 E2
High Meadows. Mid No 131 F1
High Park. Bris 64 A1
High Park. Paul 131 E3
High St. Axb 125 D1
High St. Ban 107 D1
High St. Bath 84 A1
High St. Bath 85 F1
High St. Bath 101 D3
High St. Bath 102 A3
High St. Bathe 85 F2
High St. Bathf 86 B1
High St. Bitt 82 C4
High St. Blag 110 B2
High St. Bris 47 E4
High St. Bris 49 D1
High St. Bris 49 D4
High St. Bris 50 A1
High St. Bris 63 E3
High St. Ch Mag 96 A2
High St. Ch Sod 28 A1
High St. Charl 84 C3
High St. Cong 91 E2
High St. Doyn 53 F1
High St. Dyrh 54 B2
High St. E Harp 128 C3
High St. Gr Bad 30 C1
High St. H Up 19 F1
High St. Hi Cha 120 A3
High St. Hill 19 E4
High St. Hin Cha 119 F1
High St. Ir Act 26 B2
High St. Keyn 81 F3
High St. Keyn 82 C2
High St. Kings 11 F2
High St. Kingsw 51 E2
High St. Kingsw 65 E3
High St. Kingsw 65 F4
High St. Kingsw 66 A4
High St. Kingsw 66 B2
High St. Mang 51 E4
High St. Marsh 69 F4
High St. Mid No 132 A1
High St. N St P 135 F2
High St. Nail 59 F1
High St. Paul 115 E1
High St. Paul 131 F3
High St. Pens 97 F2

High St. Portb 46 B2
High St. Portis 45 E3
High St. Rode 136 C1
High St. Ston E 130 C1
High St. Thorn 15 D4
High St. Tims 116 A1
High St. W-S-M 88 C1
High St. W-S-M 104 B4
High St. Well 118 B1
High St. Wick 67 E3
High St. Wickw 18 A3
High St. Win 95 D4
High St. Wint 37 E3
High St. Wring 92 B2
High St. Yatt 74 C1
High St. Yatt 91 D4
High View. Portis 45 D2
Higham St. Bris 63 F2
Highbury Pl. Bath 85 D1
Highbury Rd. Bris 49 F4
Highbury Rd. Bris 63 E1
Highbury Rd. Paul 131 D4
Highbury Rd. W-S-M 87 E1
Highbury Terr. Bath 85 D1
Highbury Villas. Bris 63 E4
Highcroft. Kingsw 66 B3
Highdale Ave. Cleve 57 F2
Highdale Cl. Bris 80 A2
Highdale Pl. Cleve 57 F2
Highdale Rd. Cleve 57 F2
Highett Dr. Bris 50 A1
Highfield Ave. Kingsw 65 E3
Highfield Cl. Bath 101 D3
Highfield Cl. St Gif 36 C2
Highfield Cres. Chil 137 E2
Highfield Dr. Portis 44 C2
Highfield Gdns. Kingsw 66 B1
Highfield Gr. Bris 49 E3
Highfield La. Co Mar 128 A3
Highfield La. E Harp 129 D2
Highfield La. H Up 29 F4
Highfield La. Hort 29 F4
Highfield Rd. Ch Sod 28 A1
Highfield Rd. Keyn 81 F1
Highfield Rd. P St J 133 E4
Highfield Rd. W-S-M 105 D1
Highfields. H Up 19 F1
Highfields. Pens 96 C1
Highfields. Rad 132 B1
Highgrove St. Bris 64 A2
Highland Cl. W-S-M 88 A1
Highland Cres. Bris 49 D1
Highland Rd. Bath 101 D3
Highland Sq. Bris 49 D1
Highland Terr. Bath 101 E3
Highlands Dr. N Nib 5 F2
Highlands Rd. Lo Ash 62 A1
Highlands Rd. Portis 45 D3
Highleaze Rd. Kingsw 66 B2
Highmore Ct. Bris 50 A4
Highmore Gdns. Bris 50 B4
Highnam Cl. St Gif 24 A1
Highridge Cres. Bris 78 C3
Highridge Green. Bris 78 C3
Highridge Park. Bris 78 C3
Highridge Rd. Bris 63 D1
Highridge Rd. Bris 78 C2
Highridge Rd. Dun 78 C2
Highridge Wlk. Bris 78 C4
Highview Rd. Kingsw 51 F1
Highwall La. Co Dan 80 C1
Highway. Yate 27 F1
Highwood La. Bris 35 E4
Highwood Rd. Bris 35 F4
Highworth Cres. Yate 39 E4
Highworth Rd. Bris 64 B3
Hill Ave. Bath 101 F1
Hill Ave. Bris 63 F2
Hill Burn. Bris 49 E3
Hill Crest. Bris 64 A1
Hill Dr. Wrax 61 E2
Hill End Dr. Bris 34 B2
Hill Gay Cl. Portis 44 C2
Hill Gr. Bris 49 E3
Hill House Rd. Mang 51 F3
Hill La. Ch Sod 41 D4
Hill La. Nail 58 B2
Hill La. O-On-S 1 C1
Hill La. Rock 2 A2
Hill La. Ship 109 D1
Hill Lawn. Bris 64 B2
Hill Moor. Cleve 57 F1
Hill Park. Cong 91 F3
Hill Rd E. W-S-M 88 C1
Hill Rd. Cleve 57 E2
Hill Rd. Dun 78 B1
Hill Rd. W-S-M 88 C1
Hill Rd. W-S-M 104 C4
Hill Rd. Wins 108 A2
Hill St. Bris 63 E3
Hill St. Bris 63 F2
Hill St. Bris 64 C4
Hill St. Kingsw 65 F4
Hill The. Alm 24 A2
Hill The. Hi Cha 120 B3
Hill Top. Portis 45 D2
Hill View Cl. Kingsw 66 B2

Hill View Ct. W-S-M 105 E4
Hill View Rd. Bath 85 D1
Hill View Rd. Bris 79 D4
Hill View Rd. Puck 53 E3
Hill View Rd. W-S-M 105 D4
Hill View. Bris 36 A2
Hill View. Bris 49 E3
Hill View. Bris 63 D3
Hill View. Kingsw 51 E1
Hill View. Marks 99 D1
Hill View. Paul 131 D2
Hill View. Pris 117 D3
Hillbrook Rd. Thorn 15 E4
Hillburn Rd. Bris 65 D4
Hillcrest Cl. Nail 59 F1
Hillcrest Dr. Bath 101 E2
Hillcrest Rd. Nail 59 F1
Hillcrest Rd. Portis 44 C3
Hillcrest. P St J 133 E4
Hillcrest. Pens 97 F2
Hillcrest. Thorn 8 A1
Hillcroft Cl. W-S-M 88 A1
Hilldale Rd. Back 76 A3
Hillesley Rd. Kings 11 F2
Hillfields Ave. Bris 51 E2
Hillgrove St N. Bris 63 E4
Hillgrove Terr. W-S-M 104 B1
Hillier's La. Chur 108 B2
Hillmead. Chur 109 D3
Hillmer Rise. Ban 106 C2
Hillpath. Ban 107 D1
Hills Cl. Keyn 82 A3
Hillsborough Rd. Bris 64 B2
Hillsborough. Bris 63 D3
Hillsdon Rd. Bris 48 C4
Hillside Ave. Bris 65 E4
Hillside Ave. Mid No 137 F4
Hillside Cl. Fr Cot 38 B4
Hillside Cl. Paul 131 F3
Hillside Cres. Mid No 137 F4
Hillside Gdns. Bi Sut 113 E2
Hillside Gdns. W-S-M 88 A1
Hillside La. Fr Cot 38 B4
Hillside Rd. Back 76 A2
Hillside Rd. Bath 101 E2
Hillside Rd. Blea 122 A4
Hillside Rd. Bris 65 D4
Hillside Rd. Cleve 57 E2
Hillside Rd. Lo Ash 62 A1
Hillside Rd. Mid No 137 F4
Hillside Rd. Portis 44 B2
Hillside St. Bris 64 A3
Hillside View. P St J 133 E4
Hillside W. Lock 105 F1
Hillside. Bris 63 E4
Hillside. Mang 52 A3
Hillside. Portb 46 C2
Hilltop Gdns. Bris 65 D4
Hilltop Gdns. Kingsw 51 E1
Hilltop Rd. Kingsw 51 E1
Hilltop View. Bris 65 D4
Hillview Ave. Cleve 57 E1
Hillview Gdns. Win 94 B4
Hillview Rd. Blea 123 E2
Hillview. Tims 116 A1
Hillyfield Rd. Bris 79 D3
Hillyfields Way. Wins 125 D4
Hillyfields. Wins 125 D4
Hilverton Gdns. Bris 49 F1
Hind Pitts. Wins 125 F4
Hinton Cl. Bath 100 C3
Hinton Cl. Keyn 82 C2
Hinton Dr. Kingsw 66 B3
Hinton Hill. Hin Cha 119 D1
Hinton La. Bris 62 C3
Hinton Rd. Bris 50 B1
Hinton Rd. Bris 51 D2
Hinton Villas. Hin Cha 119 F1
Hinton. W-S-M 104 C1
Hippisley Dr. Axb 125 E1
Hiscocks Dr. Bath 101 F2
Hitchen Cl. Marsh 69 F4
Hither Green. Cleve 57 F1
Hoare's La. Kilm 139 D2
Hobart Rd. W-S-M 104 C2
Hobb's La. Bris 63 E3
Hobbiton Rd. W-S-M 89 D3
Hobbs Ct. Nail 59 F1
Hobbs La. Ba Gu 77 F2
Hobbs La. Sist 52 A1
Hobhouse Cl. Bris 49 E4
Hobwell La. Lo Ash 62 B1
Hockey's La. Bris 51 D2
Hoddon La. Puck 53 E3
Hodshill. Sosto 118 C3
Hoecroft Gdns. Chil 137 E2
Hogarth Mews. W-S-M 89 D2
Hogarth Wlk. Bris 50 B4
Hogarth Wlk. W-S-M 89 D2
Hogues Wlk. Bris 79 D2
Holbeach Way. Bris 80 A2
Holbrook Cres. Bris 79 E2
Holbrook La. Wick 67 D4
Holcombe Cl. Bath 85 F1
Holcombe Gn. Keyn 81 E3
Holcombe Gr. Keyn 81 E3
Holcombe La. Bath 85 F1
Holcombe Vale. Bath 85 F1

Holcombe. Bris 80
Holdenhurst Rd. Bris 51
Holders Wlk. Lo Ash 61
Holford Cl. Nail 59
Holford Ct. Bris 80
Holland Rd. Bath 85
Holland Rd. Cleve 57
Holland St. Bris 63
Holland St. W-S-M 105
Hollidge Gdns. Bris 63
Hollies La. Bathe 86
Hollis Ave. Portis 45
Hollis Cl. Lo Ash 78
Hollis Cres. Portis 45
Hollis Gdns. Luck 31
Hollister's Dr. Bris 79
Hollow La. W-S-M 88
Hollow Marsh La. Hin Ble .. 130
Hollow Rd. Alm 24
Hollow Rd. Kingsw 65
Hollow Rd. Wins 125
Hollow The. Bath 101
Hollow The. Pris 117
Holloway. Bath 101
Hollowbrook La. Ch Mag .. 113
Hollowmead Cl. Yatt 91
Hollows The. West 38
Hollway Cl. Bris 80
Hollway Rd. Bris 80
Holly Cl. Alve 14
Holly Cl. Bris 51
Holly Cl. Nail 60
Holly Cl. Puck 53
Holly Cl. W-S-M 88
Holly Cres. Kingsw 51
Holly Dr. Col 70
Holly Gr. Bris 51
Holly Green. Kingsw 52
Holly Hill Rd. Kingsw 66
Holly Hill. Ir Act 26
Holly La. Cleve 57
Holly Lodge Rd. Bris 50
Holly Ridge. Portis 45
Holly Wlk. Keyn 81
Holly Wlk. Rad 132
Hollybush Cl. A Tur 43
Hollybush Cl. Winsl 120
Hollybush La. Bris 48
Hollybush La. Bris 48
Hollyguest Rd. Kingsw 65
Hollyleigh Ave. Bris 35
Hollyman Wlk. Cleve 57
Hollymead La. Bris 35
Hollyridge. Bris 80
Hollywood La. Alm 35
Hollywood Rd. Bris 64
Holm La. Piln 13
Holm Rd. Lock 105
Holmdale Rd. Bris 36
Holmes Gr. Bris 49
Holmes Hill Rd. Bris 64
Holmes St. Bris 64
Holmesdale Rd. Bris 63
Holmoak Rd. Keyn 81
Holms Rd. W-S-M 105
Holmwood Cl. Wint 37
Holmwood. Kingsw 65
Holsom Cl. Bris 80
Holsom Rd. Bris 80
Holst Gdns. Bris 79
Holton Rd. Bris 64
Holy Well Cl. Bris 64
Holyrood Cl. St Gif 36
Home Cl. Bris 35
Home Cl. Wring 92
Home Farm Cl. P St J 133
Home Farm Rd. Ab Lei 62
Home Farm Way. Alm 23
Home Ground. Bris 49
Home Orch. Ch St 112
Home Orch. Yate 27
Homeapple Hill. Sist 66
Homefield Cl. Keyn 82
Homefield Cl. Lock 106
Homefield Cl. Winsc 125
Homefield Dr. Bris 51
Homefield Rd. Keyn 82
Homefield Rd. Puck 53
Homefield. Cong 91
Homefield. Lock 106
Homefield. Thorn 15
Homefield. Yate 27
Homeground. Cleve 57
Homelea Park E. Bath 101
Homelea Park W. Bath 101
Homeleaze Rd. Bris 35
Homemead Dr. Bris 80
Homestead Gdns. Bris 51
Homestead Rd. Bris 51
Homestead The. Cleve 57
Homestead The. Keyn 81
Homestead Way. Wins 125
Homestead. Portis 44
Honey Garston Cl. Bris 79
Honey Garston Rd. Bris 79
Honey Hill Rd. Kingsw 66
Honey Way. Kingsw 65
Honeyborne Way. Wickw 18

153

Honeyhall La. Cong

Kinsale Wlk. Bris

Honeyhall La. Cong 108 B4
Honeylands. Portis 45 E2
Honeymead. Bris 80 B3
Honeysuckle Cl. St Gif 24 C1
Honeysuckle La. Bris 50 C2
Honiton Rd. Bris 51 D2
Honiton Rd. Cleve 57 F1
Honiton. W-S-M 89 D1
Hook La. Hin Ble 129 F2
Hooks Batch. Blag 110 B2
Hooper Rd. Bris 80 B3
Hope Ct. Bris 63 D3
Hope Rd. Bris 63 E2
Hope Rd. Ir Act 27 D1
Hope Sq. Bris 62 C3
Hope Terr. Mid No 132 A1
Hopechapel Hill. Bris 62 C3
Hopetoun Rd. Bris 49 F2
Hopewell Gdns. Bris 47 F4
Hopkins Ct. Bris 49 D1
Hopkins St. W-S-M 104 C4
Hopland Cl. Kingsw 66 A2
Hopp's Rd. Kingsw 65 E4
Horesham Gr. Bris 79 E3
Horfield Rd. Bris 63 E4
Horley Rd. Bris 50 A1
Horn's La. Axb 125 D1
Hornbeam Wlk. Keyn 81 E2
Hornbeams The. Bris 37 D1
Horse La. Thorn 8 B3
Horse Race La. Wrax 61 D3
Horse St. Ch Sod 28 A1
Horsecastle Cl. Yatt 74 A1
Horsecastle Farm Rd. Yatt .. 74 A1
Horsecombe Brow. Bath ... 102 A1
Horsecombe Gr. Bath 102 A1
Horsecombe Vale. Bath 102 A1
Horsecroft Gdns. Kingsw 66 A3
Horsefair The. Bris 63 F4
Horsefield Rd. Char 11 D3
Horseleaze La. Ship 108 B1
Horsepool La. Doyn 67 F4
Horsepool Rd. Bris 78 C2
Horseshoe Dr. Bris 48 B2
Horseshoe La. Ch Sod 28 A1
Horseshoe La. Thorn 15 D4
Horseshoe Wlk. Bath 102 A3
Hortham La. Alve 24 C3
Horton Hill. Hort 29 E3
Horton Rd. Ch Sod 28 B2
Horton St. Bris 63 F4
Horwood Ct. Kingsw 66 A2
Horwood La. Wickw 18 A2
Horwood Rd. Nail 59 F1
Hosey Wlk. Bris 79 D3
Host St. Bris 63 E4
Hot Bath St. Bath 101 F3
Hot Water La. Kingsw 52 A2
Hottom Gdns. Bris 50 A4
Hotwell Rd. Bris 62 C3
Houlgate Way. Axb 125 D1
Houlton St. Bris 63 F4
Hounds Cl. Ch Sod 28 A1
Hounds Rd. Ch Sod 28 A1
Hover's La. Fr Cot 26 A2
How Hill. Bath 101 D3
Howard Ave. Bris 64 C4
Howard Cl. Keyn 82 B2
Howard Rd. Bris 49 D2
Howard Rd. Bris 63 E2
Howard Rd. Kingsw 51 E2
Howard Rd. Thorn 8 B1
Howard St. Bris 50 C1
Howecroft Gdns. Bris 48 C2
Howes Cl. Kingsw 66 A3
Howett Rd. Bris 64 B4
Howsmoor La. Mang 52 B4
Hoylake Dr. Kingsw 66 A3
Hoylake. Yate 39 F4
Huckford La. West 38 A2
Huckford Rd. Wint 37 F3
Huckley Way. St Gif 36 C3
Hudd's Hill Gdns. Bris 64 C4
Hudd's Hill Rd. Bris 64 C4
Hudd's Vale Rd. Bris 64 C4
Hudson Cl. Ch Sod 39 F4
Hughenden Rd. Bris 49 D1
Hughenden Rd. Bris 49 F3
Hughenden Rd. W-S-M 105 D4
Huish Ct. Rad 133 D1
Hulbert Cl. Bris 65 D1
Hulse Rd. Bris 64 B1
Humber Way. Avon 33 E3
Humberstan Wlk. Bris 47 F4
Humphry Davy Way. Bris 62 C3
Hung Rd. Bris 47 F3
Hungerford Cl. Bris 80 C4
Hungerford Cres. Bris 64 C1
Hungerford Gdns. Bris 80 C4
Hungerford Rd. Bath 101 E4
Hungerford Rd. Bris 80 C4
Hungerford Terr. Well 118 B1
Hungerford Wlk. Bris 64 C1
Hunstrete Rd. Farm 115 F3
Hunt's La. Yatt 91 F4
Hunter's La. A Tur 42 C3
Hunter's Way. Bris 36 A2
Hunters Cl. Kingsw 65 E3
Hunters Dr. Kingsw 51 F1
Hunters Mead. H Up 20 A1
Hunters Rd. Kingsw 65 E3
Huntingham Rd. Bris 78 C2
Huntley Gr. Nail 60 A1
Hunts La. Bris 49 F3
Hurle Cres. Bris 49 D1
Hurle Rd. Bris 49 D1
Hurlingham Rd. Bris 49 F1
Hurn La. Keyn 82 A2
Hurn Rd. Cleve 57 F1
Hursley Hill. Pens 97 E4
Hursley La. Pens 80 C1
Hurst Rd. Bris 79 F4
Hurst Rd. W-S-M 105 D3
Hurst Wlk. Bris 79 F4
Hurston Rd. Bris 79 E4
Hurstwood Rd. Mang 51 E3
Hutton Cl. Bris 48 C4
Hutton Cl. Keyn 82 A1
Hutton Hill. Lock 105 F1
Hutton Moor Rd. W-S-M 105 E4
Huyton Rd. Bris 50 C2
Hyde Ave. Thorn 8 A2
Hyde The. Cleve 73 E4
Hyde's La. Co Ash 69 D3
Hyland Gr. Bris 48 C4

I.S.F Rd. Avon 33 E2
Ida Rd. Bris 64 B4
Iddesleigh Rd. Bris 49 D2
Idstone Rd. Bris 51 D2
Idwal Cl. P St J 133 E4
Iford Cl. Keyn 82 C2
Iford Hill. Westw 120 C1
Iford Rd. Hi Cha 120 B2
Ilchester Cres. Bris 63 D1
Ilchester Rd. Bris 79 D4
Ilex Ave. Cleve 57 F1
Ilex Cl. Bris 78 C3
Ilex La. Winsc 107 F1
Ilminster Ave. Bris 79 F4
Ilminster Cl. Cleve 57 F1
Ilminster Cl. Nail 75 E4
Ilminster. W-S-M 105 D1
Ilsyn Gr. Bris 80 B4
Imber Court Cl. Bris 80 A4
Imperial Rd. Bris 49 D1
Imperial Rd. Bris 80 B4
Imperial Wlk. Bris 64 A1
Ingleside Rd. Bris 51 E1
Inglestone Rd. Wickw 18 A3
Ingleton Dr. W-S-M 89 D2
Ingmire Rd. Bris 50 A2
Ingst Hill. Aust 13 E2
Ingst Rd. Aust 13 F2
Inkerman Cl. Bris 49 F4
Inner Down The. Olve 14 B2
Inner Elm Terr. Rad 132 B1
Innicks Cl. Co Mar 111 E1
Innocks Est. N Nib 5 E2
Innox Gdns. Bris 79 D3
Innox Gr. Engl 100 C1
Innox La. Bathe 85 D3
Innox Rd. Bath 101 D3
Inns Court Ave. Bris 79 E4
Inns Court Dr. Bris 79 E3
Instow Rd. Bris 79 F4
Instow Wlk. Bris 79 F4
Instow. W-S-M 89 D1
Inverness Rd. Bath 101 E3
Ipswich Dr. Bris 64 C3
Irby Rd. Bris 63 D2
Irena Rd. Bris 50 C1
Ireton Rd. Bris 63 D2
Iron Hogg La. Falf 9 E2
Ironchurch Rd. Avon 33 E3
Ironmould La. Bris 65 D1
Irving Cl. Cleve 57 F2
Irving Cl. Kingsw 51 F2
Island Gdns. Bris 50 B2
Island The. Mid No 132 A1
Isleys Ct. Kingsw 65 F2
Islington Rd. Bris 63 D2
Ison Hill Rd. Bris 34 B2
Itchington Rd. Alve 15 F2
Itchington Rd. Tyth 15 F2
Itchington Rd. Tyth 16 A2
Ivo Peters Rd. Bath 101 F3
Ivor Rd. Bris 64 B4
Ivy Ave. Bath 101 E2
Ivy Bank Park. Bath 101 F1
Ivy Ct. Portis 44 C3
Ivy Gr. Bath 101 E2
Ivy La. Bris 51 D2
Ivy Pl. Bath 101 E2
Ivybridge. W-S-M 89 D1
Ivywell Rd. Bris 48 C2
Iwood La. Cong 92 A1

Jackson Cl. Piln 22 B4
Jacob St. Bris 63 F4
Jacob's Wells Rd. Bris 63 D3
Jamaica St. Bris 63 F4
James Cl. Kingsw 51 F2
James Pl. Bris 62 C4
James Rd. Kingsw 51 F2
James St W. Bath 101 F3
James St. Bris 50 A1
James St. Bris 63 F4
Jane St. Bris 64 A4
Jarvis St. Bris 64 A3
Jasmine Cl. W-S-M 89 D1
Jasmine Gr. Bris 34 B1
Jasmine La. Yatt 74 C1
Jasper St. Bris 63 D2
Jays The. Tyth 16 A3
Jean Rd. Bris 64 C1
Jefferies Hill Bottom. Bris 65 D3
Jeffery Ct. Kingsw 66 A3
Jellicoe Ct. W-S-M 88 C2
Jena Ct. Keyn 82 B2
Jenner Cl. Ch Sod 40 B4
Jersey Ave. Bris 64 C2
Jesmond Rd. Cleve 57 E2
Jesse Hughes Ct. Bath 85 E1
Jessop Underpass. Bris 62 C2
Jews La. Bath 101 E3
Jews La. Chur 108 C2
Jocelin Dr. W-S-M 88 C2
Jocelyn Rd. Bris 49 F4
Jockey La. Bris 65 D4
John Cabot Ct. Bris 63 D3
John Carr's Terr. Bris 63 D3
John James Ct. Bris 50 A4
John St. Bath 101 F4
John St. Bris 50 A1
John St. Bris 63 E4
John St. Bris 65 E4
John Wesley Rd. Bris 65 D3
Johnson Dr. Kingsw 65 F3
Johnsons La. Bris 50 B1
Johnsons Rd. Bris 50 B1
Johnstone St. Bath 102 A3
Jones Cl. Yatt 73 F1
Joy Hill. Bris 62 C3
Jubilee Cres. Mang 52 A3
Jubilee Dr. Thorn 8 B1
Jubilee Dr. Wrax 61 D2
Jubilee La. Chur 109 D3
Jubilee La. Crom 17 D4
Jubilee Pl. Bris 63 E3
Jubilee Pl. Cleve 57 E1
Jubilee Rd. Axb 125 E1
Jubilee Rd. Bris 50 A1
Jubilee Rd. Bris 64 B1
Jubilee Rd. Bris 64 C4
Jubilee Rd. Kingsw 51 F2
Jubilee Rd. Rad 132 B1
Jubilee Rd. W-S-M 104 C4
Jubilee St. Bris 63 F3
Jubilee Terr. Paul 131 F3
Jubilee Way. Avon 33 D1
Julian Cl. Bris 48 C2
Julian Rd. Bath 101 F4
Julian Rd. Bris 48 C2
Julius Rd. Bris 49 E2
Junction Ave. Bath 101 F3
Junction Rd. Bath 101 F3
Junction Rd. Bris 64 B2
Juniper Ct. Bris 50 B1
Jupiter Rd. Bris 35 F4
Justice Ave. Keyn 82 C2
Justice Rd. Bris 51 D2
Jutland Rd. Avon 33 D1

Karen Dr. Back 76 A3
Kathdene Gdns. Bris 49 F2
Kathrine Dr. Char 11 D3
Keats Rd. Rod 138 B4
Keble Ave. Bris 78 C3
Keeds La. Lo Ash 61 F1
Keedwell Hill. Lo Ash 61 F1
Keedwell House. Bris 79 E2
Keel's Hill. P St J 133 E4
Keen's Gr. Piln 22 B4
Keene's Way. Cleve 57 E1
Keep The. Kingsw 66 B3
Keep The. W-S-M 89 D2
Keinton Wlk. Bris 35 D1
Kellaway Ave. Bris 49 E3
Kellaway Cres. Bris 49 E3
Kellways. Back 76 A2
Kelston Cl. Keyn 82 B2
Kelston Cl. Yate 39 E4
Kelston Gdns. Bris 49 E4
Kelston Gdns. W-S-M 89 D3
Kelston Gr. Kingsw 65 F3
Kelston Rd. Bath 101 D4
Kelston Rd. Bris 49 E4
Kelston Rd. Keyn 81 E3
Kelston Rd. W-S-M 89 D3
Kelston View. Bath 101 D3
Kelston Wlk. Bris 51 E2
Kelting Gr. Cleve 57 F1
Kemble Cl. Kingsw 65 F3
Kemble Cl. Nail 60 A1
Kemble Gdns. Bris 47 F3
Kempe's Cl. Lo Ash 62 A1
Kemperleye Way. St Gif 36 B4
Kempton Cl. Mang 37 F1
Kempton Cl. Thorn 8 A2
Kencot Wlk. Bris 79 D2
Kendal Rd. Bris 50 A4
Kendall Gdns. Kingsw 51 E2
Kendall Rd. Kingsw 51 E2
Kendon Dr. Bris 49 E4
Kenilworth Cl. Keyn 81 E2
Kenilworth Dr. Kingsw 66 A1
Kenilworth Rd. Bris 49 E1
Kenilworth. Yate 27 F1
Kenmare Rd. Bris 63 F1
Kenmeade Cl. Ship 125 F4
Kenmore Cres. Bris 35 F1
Kenmore Dr. Bris 35 F1
Kenmore Gr. Bris 35 F1
Kenn Cl. W-S-M 105 D3
Kenn Est. Yatt 73 F3
Kenn Moor Dr. Cleve 57 F1
Kenn Rd. Bris 65 D4
Kenn Rd. Yatt 73 F4
Kenn St. Yatt 73 F4
Kennard Cl. Bris 65 E4
Kennard Rd. Bris 65 E4
Kennard Rise. Bris 65 E4
Kennaway Rd. Cleve 57 E1
Kennedy Way. Ch Sod 40 A4
Kennedy Way. Yate 27 F1
Kennel Dr. Gr Bad 30 C1
Kennel La. Co Bi 123 F2
Kennel Lodge Rd. Bris 62 C2
Kennet Park. Bath 85 F1
Kennet Rd. Keyn 82 A2
Kennet Way. Thorn 15 E4
Kenneth Rd. Bris 64 B1
Kennford. W-S-M 89 D1
Kennington Ave. Bris 49 F2
Kennington Ave. Kingsw 51 E1
Kennington Rd. Bath 101 D4
Kennion Rd. Bris 65 D4
Kennmoor Cl. Kingsw 66 A3
Kennmoor Rd. Yatt 74 A3
Kensal Ave. Bris 63 F2
Kensal Rd. Bris 63 F2
Kensington Cl. Thorn 8 A1
Kensington Ct. Bath 85 D1
Kensington Gdns. Bath 85 D1
Kensington Park Rd. Bris 64 B1
Kensington Park. Bris 50 A1
Kensington Pl. Bris 63 D4
Kensington Rd. Bris 49 E1
Kensington Rd. Bris 65 D4
Kensington Rd. Kingsw 51 E2
Kensington Rd. W-S-M 104 C3
Kent Ave. Yate 27 F2
Kent Cl. St Gif 36 B2
Kent Rd. Bris 49 F2
Kent Rd. Cong 91 E3
Kent St. Bris 63 E2
Kent Way. W-S-M 89 D2
Kenton Mews. Bris 49 E3
Kents Green. Kingsw 51 F1
Kentshare La. Win 95 D3
Keppel Cl. Keyn 82 B1
Kerry Rd. Bris 63 F1
Kersteman Rd. Bris 49 E2
Kestrel Cl. Bris 35 F4
Kestrel Cl. Ch Sod 39 F4
Kestrel Cl. Thorn 8 B1
Kestrel Dr. Puck 53 E2
Kestrel Dr. W-S-M 88 C1
Kestrel Pl. Rod 138 A4
Keswick Wlk. Bris 35 E1
Ketch Rd. Bris 63 F2
Ketley Hill. Mid No 132 B2
Kew Rd. W-S-M 87 F1
Kew Wlk. Bris 80 B4
Kewside. W-S-M 88 A2
Kewstoke Rd. Bath 102 A1
Kewstoke Rd. Bris 48 C2
Kewstoke Rd. W-S-M 88 B2
Keyes Path. W-S-M 88 C2
Keynsham By-pass. Keyn 81 F4
Keynsham Rd. Bitt 82 A4
Keys Ave. Bris 49 F4
Kielder Dr. W-S-M 88 C2
Kilbirnie Rd. Bris 80 A2
Kilburn St. Bris 64 A4
Kildare Rd. Bris 63 E1
Kilkenny La. Engl 118 A4
Kilkenny St. Bris 63 F3
Killcott Rd. Hill 19 F4
Kilmersdon Hill. Kilm 139 D3
Kilmersdon Rd. Bris 79 D2
Kilmersdon Rd. Rod 138 C4
Kilminster Rd. Bris 47 E4
Kiln Cl. Bris 51 D1
Kiln Park. W-S-M 105 D3
Kilnhurst Cl. Kingsw 65 F1
Kilve. W-S-M 104 C1
Kilvert Cl. Bris 64 B3
Kimberley Ave. Bris 51 E3
Kimberley Cl. Mang 51 F4
Kimberley Cres. Bris 51 E3
Kimberley Rd. Bris 51 E3
Kimberley Rd. Cleve 57 E1
Kimberley Rd. Kingsw 51 E1
Kinber Cl. Bath 84 A2
King Alfred Way. Winsl 120 B4
King Dick's La. Bris 64 C4
King Edward Cl. Bris 80 A3
King Edward Rd. Bath 101 E3
King George V Pl. Bris 63 E3
King George's Rd. Bath 101 E3
King George's Rd. Bris 78 C3
King John's Rd. Bris 51 D1
King La. Clut 114 C2
King La. Hort 29 D4
King Rd. Bris 64 B1
King Rd. Chur 108 C3
King Road Ave. Avon 33 D1
King Sq. Bris 63 E4
King Square Ave. Bris 63 E4
King St. Avon 33 D1
King St. Bris 50 B1
King St. Bris 63 E3
King St. Bris 65 D4
King William Ave. Bris 63 E3
King William St. Bris 63 D2
King's Ave. Bris 49 E2
King's Dr. Bris 49 E2
King's Head La. Bris 78 C4
King's La. W-S-M 104 C4
King's Parade Ave. Bris 49 D1
King's Parade Mews. Bris ... 49 D1
King's Rd. Bris 63 D4
King's Rd. Bris 64 B2
King's Rd. Cleve 57 E3
King's Rd. Portis 44 C2
Kingfisher Cl. Thorn 8 B1
Kingfisher Dr. Bris 50 C3
Kingfisher Dr. Rod 138 A4
Kingfisher Rd. Ch Sod 40 A4
Kingfisher Rd. W-S-M 105 F4
Kingrove Cres. Ch Sod 40 B4
Kingrove La. Ch Sod 40 B4
Kings Ave. Kingsw 65 D2
Kings Chase. Kingsw 65 E4
Kings Dr. Kingsw 65 D2
Kings Oak Meadow. Clut ... 114 C1
Kings Park Ave. Bris 64 B3
Kings Rd. Wring 92 B1
Kings Weston Ave. Bris 47 E4
Kings Weston La. Avon 33 F2
Kings Weston La. Bris 48 A4
Kings Weston Rd. Bris 34 B1
Kings Wlk. Bris 78 C4
Kingscote Park. Bris 65 D3
Kingscote. Yate 39 E3
Kingscourt Cl. Bris 80 A2
Kingsdown Gr. Box 86 C2
Kingsdown Par. Bris 63 E4
Kingsdown View. Bath 85 D1
Kingsfield La. Kingsw 65 F2
Kingsfield La. Kingsw 65 F3
Kingsfield. Bath 101 E2
Kingshill Gdns. Nail 59 E1
Kingshill House. Bris 64 A1
Kingshill La. Ch St 112 B3
Kingshill Rd. Bris 64 A1
Kingshill. Nail 59 E1
Kingsholm Rd. Bris 49 E4
Kingsholme Rd. Kingsw 51 E1
Kingsland Cl. Bris 64 A3
Kingsland Rd Br. Bris 64 A3
Kingsland Rd. Bris 64 A3
Kingsland Trading Est. Bris . 64 A4
Kingsleigh Ct. Kingsw 65 F4
Kingsleigh Gdns. Kingsw 65 F4
Kingsleigh Park. Kingsw 65 F4
Kingsley Rd. Bris 49 E1
Kingsley Rd. Bris 50 B1
Kingsley Rd. Cleve 57 E1
Kingsley Rd. Rad 132 B1
Kingsley Rd. W-S-M 104 C2
Kingsmead N. Bath 101 F3
Kingsmead Rd. Bris 51 D1
Kingsmead Sq. Bath 101 F3
Kingsmead St. Bath 101 F3
Kingsmead W. Bath 101 F3
Kingsmead Wlk. Bris 51 D1
Kingsmead. Nail 59 E1
Kingsmill. Bris 48 B3
Kingston Ave. Cleve 57 F2
Kingston Ave. Keyn 82 B2
Kingston Cl. Mang 52 A4
Kingston Dr. Mang 52 A4
Kingston Dr. Nail 75 E4
Kingston La. Win 94 C4
Kingston Mead. Win 94 C4
Kingston Par. Bath 102 A3
Kingston Rd. Bath 102 A3
Kingston Rd. Bris 63 E2
Kingston Rd. Nail 75 E4
Kingston Way. Nail 75 E4
Kingstree St. Bris 64 A2
Kingsway Ave. Bris 65 D4
Kingsway Cres. Bris 65 E4
Kingsway. Bath 101 E2
Kingsway. Bris 65 D4
Kingsway. St Gif 36 B3
Kingswear Rd. Bris 63 E1
Kingswear. W-S-M 89 D1
Kingswood Rd. Hill 19 E4
Kingswood Trading Est.
Kingsw 51 E1
Kington La. Thorn 7 F1
Kington Rd. O-on-S 7 F2
Kington Rd. Thorn 7 F2
Kingwell View. Paul 115 E1
Kinsale Rd. Bris 80 B4
Kinsale Wlk. Bris 63 F1

Kinvara Rd. Bris	79	F4
Kipling Rd. Bris	36	A1
Kipling Rd. Rad	132	B1
Kipling Rd. W-S-M	105	D2
Kiplingave. Bath	101	F2
Kirkby Rd. Bris	34	A1
Kirkstone Gdns. Bris	35	E1
Kirtlington Rd. Bris	50	A2
Kite Hay Cl. Bris	50	C3
Kite Wlk. W-S-M	105	F4
Kites Cl. St Gif	24	B1
Kitland La. Chur	109	E4
Knapp La. Crom	10	A2
Knapp Rd. Thorn	8	C1
Knapps Cl. Wins	124	C4
Knapps Dr. Wins	124	C4
Knapps La. Bris	50	C1
Knightcott Gdns. Ban	106	C2
Knightcott Ind Est Ban	106	C2
Knightcott Park. Ban	107	D2
Knightcott Rd. Ab Lei	61	F4
Knightcott Rd. Ban	107	D2
Knighton Rd. Bris	35	F1
Knights Cl. W-S-M	89	D3
Knightstone Ave. Axb	125	E1
Knightstone Cl. P St J	133	D4
Knightstone Cswy. W-S-M	104	B4
Knightstone Ct. Bris	50	B1
Knightstone Pl. Bath	84	A1
Knightstone Pl. Kingsw	65	D2
Knightstone Rd. W-S-M	104	B4
Knightstone Sq. Bris	80	B3
Knightwood Rd. St Gif	36	C3
Knobsbury Hill. Kilm	139	E3
Knobsbury La. Kilm	139	E4
Knobsbury La. Rad	133	E1
Knole Cl. Alm	23	F2
Knole La. Bris	35	D2
Knole Park. Alm	23	F2
Knoll Hill. Bris	48	B2
Knoll The. Portis	45	D4
Knovill Cl. Bris	34	A1
Knowle Rd. Bris	63	F2
Knowles Rd. Cleve	57	E1
Knowsley Rd. Bris	50	C2
Kylross Ave. Bris	80	A3
Kynges Mill Cl. Bris	51	D4
Kyrle Gdns. Bathe	85	F2
Labbott The. Keyn	81	F3
Laburnham Wlk. Keyn	81	E2
Laburnum Cl. Mid No	137	F4
Laburnum Ct. W-S-M	105	D4
Laburnum Gr. Bris	51	D2
Laburnum Gr. Mid No	137	F4
Laburnum Rd. Kingsw	65	E3
Laburnum Rd. W-S-M	105	D4
Lacey Rd. Bris	80	C3
Lacock Dr. Kingsw	65	F3
Ladd Cl. Kingsw	65	F4
Ladden Ct. Thorn	15	E4
Ladies Mile. Bris	48	C1
Ladman Gr. Bris	80	C3
Ladman Rd. Bris	80	C3
Ladycroft. Cleve	57	D1
Ladye Bay. Cleve	57	E4
Ladye Wake. W-S-M	88	C2
Ladymead. Back	76	A4
Ladymead La. Chur	108	C3
Ladysmith Rd. Bris	49	D4
Ladywell. Wring	92	B1
Laggan Gdns. Bath	84	C1
Lake Rd. Bris	49	D4
Lake Rd. Portis	45	D4
Lake View Rd. Bris	64	B4
Lakemead Gdns. Bris	78	C2
Lakemead Gr. Bris	78	C3
Lakeside. Bris	50	C2
Lakewood Cres. Bris	49	D4
Lakewood Rd. Bris	49	D4
Lamb St. Bris	63	F4
Lambert Pl. Bris	79	E3
Lambley Rd. Bris	64	C4
Lambourn Cl. Bris	63	E2
Lambourn Rd. Keyn	82	A2
Lambridge Mews. Bath	85	E1
Lambridge Pl. Bath	85	E1
Lambridge St. Bath	85	E1
Lambrook Rd. Bris	51	D2
Lamford Gate. St Gif	36	C3
Lampard's Bldgs. Bath	101	F4
Lampeter Rd. Bris	49	D4
Lampley Rd. K Sey	73	E1
Lampley Rd. Yatt	73	E1
Lampton Ave. Bris	79	F2
Lampton Gr. Bris	79	F2
Lampton Rd. Lo Ash	61	F1
Lanaway Rd. Bris	51	D3
Lancashire Rd. Bris	49	F2
Lancaster Cl. St Gif	36	B2
Lancaster Rd. Bris	50	A1
Lancaster Rd. Yate	27	F2
Lancaster St. Bris	64	B4
Land The. Fr Cot	38	B4
Landemann Cir. W-S-M	87	E1
Landsdown View. Kingsw	65	F4
Landseer Ave. Bris	50	A4
Landseer Cl. W-S-M	88	C2
Landseer Rd. Bath	101	D3
Lane The. Alm	22	C1
Lanercost Rd. Bris	35	E1
Lanesborough Rise. Bris	80	B4
Laneys Dro. Lock	105	F3
Langdale Rd. Bris	50	C2
Langdon Rd. Bath	101	D2
Langdown Ct. Bris	80	C3
Langfield Cl. Bris	34	C2
Langford La. Blag	109	F3
Langford Rd. Bris	78	C4
Langford Rd. Chur	109	D3
Langford Way. Kingsw	65	F4
Langfords La. Paul	131	E4
Langham Pl. Rode	136	C1
Langham Rd. Bris	64	A1
Langhill Ave. Bris	79	E4
Langley Cres. Bris	62	C1
Langley's La. Ston E	131	E1
Langport Gdns. Nail	75	F4
Langport Rd. W-S-M	104	C3
Langridge La. Charl	84	B4
Langthorn Cl. Fr Cot	38	B4
Langton Court Rd. Bris	64	B3
Langton Park. Bris	63	E2
Langton Rd. Bris	64	B3
Langton Way. Bris	64	C3
Lansdown Cl. Kingsw	51	E1
Lansdown Cres. Bath	101	F4
Lansdown Cres. Tims	116	B1
Lansdown Gdns. W-S-M	89	D3
Lansdown Gr. Bath	101	F4
Lansdown La. Bath	84	A2
Lansdown La. Bitt	67	E1
Lansdown La. Charl	84	A2
Lansdown Park. Bath	84	C2
Lansdown Pl. Bris	63	D4
Lansdown Pl. Paul	115	E1
Lansdown Place W. Bath	84	C1
Lansdown Rd. Bath	84	C2
Lansdown Rd. Bris	49	E1
Lansdown Rd. Bris	63	D4
Lansdown Rd. Bris	64	A4
Lansdown Rd. Keyn	82	C2
Lansdown Rd. Kingsw	51	E1
Lansdown Rd. Puck	53	E3
Lansdown Terr. Bath	84	B1
Lansdown Terr. Bris	49	E3
Lansdown View. Bath	84	A1
Lansdown View. Bath	101	E3
Lansdown View. Faulk	134	B1
Lansdown View. Tims	116	B1
Lansdown. Yate	39	F4
Lansdowne. Bris	37	E1
Lapdown La. Tor	41	E1
Laphams Ct. Kingsw	65	F2
Lapwing Cl. St Gif	24	B1
Lapwing Gdns. Bris	50	C3
Lapwing Gdns. W-S-M	88	C1
Larch Cl. Chur	109	D3
Larch Cl. Nail	60	A1
Larch Ct. Rod	138	B4
Larch Rd. Col	70	C3
Larch Rd. Kingsw	51	F2
Larch Way. Bris	35	F4
Larches The. W-S-M	89	D2
Larchgrove Cres. W-S-M	88	C1
Larchgrove Wlk. W-S-M	89	D1
Lark Cl. Rod	138	A4
Lark Rd. W-S-M	88	C1
Lark's Field. Bris	50	C3
Larkfield. Fr Cot	38	B4
Larkhall Pl. Bath	85	E1
Larksleaze Rd. Kingsw	65	F1
Larkspur Cl. Thorn	8	B1
Lasbury Gr. Bris	79	E3
Latchmoor House. Bris	79	D4
Late Broads. Winsl	120	B4
Latimer Cl. Bris	64	C2
Latteridge La. Ir Act	26	A4
Latteridge La. Tyth	26	A4
Latteridge Rd. Ir Act	26	B2
Latton Rd. Bris	49	F4
Launceston Ave. Kingsw	65	D3
Launceston Rd. Bris	51	D1
Laura Pl. Bath	102	A4
Laurel Dr. Col	70	C3
Laurel Dr. Nail	59	F1
Laurel Dr. Paul	131	F1
Laurel Dr. W-S-M	104	C1
Laurel Gdns. Yatt	74	A1
Laurel St. Kingsw	65	E4
Laurel Terr. Yatt	74	A1
Laurels The. Mang	52	A3
Laurels The. W-S-M	104	C1
Laurie Cres. Bris	49	E3
Laurie Lee Ct. Kingsw	66	A3
Lavender Cl. Thorn	8	B1
Lavers Cl. Kingsw	65	F3
Lavington Cl. Cleve	57	D1
Lavington Rd. Bris	65	D3
Lawford Ave. St Gif	36	B3
Lawford St. Bris	63	F4
Lawfords Gate. Bris	63	F4
Lawn Ave. Bris	51	D3
Lawn Rd. Bris	51	D3
Lawns Rd. Yate	27	F1
Lawns The. Bris	47	F4
Lawns The. W-S-M	89	D2
Lawns The. Yatt	74	A1
Lawnside. Back	76	A3
Lawnwood Rd. Bris	64	A4
Lawrence Ave. Bris	50	A1
Lawrence Cl. W-S-M	88	C1
Lawrence Dr. Yate	27	D1
Lawrence Gr. Bris	49	D3
Lawrence Hill Ind Pk. Bris	64	A4
Lawrence Hill Roundabout. Bris	64	A4
Lawrence Hill. Bris	64	A4
Lawrence Mews. W-S-M	88	C1
Lawrence Rd. W-S-M	88	C1
Lawrence Rd. Wring	92	C1
Lawrence Weston Rd. Avon	33	F3
Lawrence Weston Rd. Bris	34	A1
Lawrence Weston Rd. Bris	34	B3
Lawson Cl. Keyn	82	B1
Laxey Rd. Bris	49	F4
Laxton Cl. Olve	14	A2
Laxton Dr. Kings	11	F2
Laxton Way. P St J	133	E4
Lays Dr. Keyn	81	E3
Lays La. Blag	110	B2
Lea Croft. Bris	79	D2
Lea Grove Rd. Cleve	57	E2
Leach Cl. Cleve	57	E1
Leafy Way. Lock	106	A2
Leaholme Gdns. Bris	80	A2
Leaman Cl. Ch Sod	28	A1
Leap Vale. Mang	52	A4
Leap Valley Cres. Mang	52	A4
Leaze La. Priddy	126	C4
Leaze The. Rod	138	B4
Leaze The. Yate	27	E1
Leda Ave. Bris	80	A4
Ledbury Rd. Bris	51	E2
Lee Cl. Bris	35	F4
Leechpool Way. Yate	27	F3
Leeming Way. Avon	47	E4
Lees Hill. Kingsw	51	F1
Lees La. Kingsw	66	B3
Lees The. Cong	91	E2
Leeside. Portis	45	E3
Leewood Rd. W-S-M	87	F1
Leg La. Blag	110	A2
Leicester Sq. Kingsw	51	E1
Leicester St. Bris	63	E2
Leicester Wlk. Bris	64	C3
Leigh Cl. Bath	85	D1
Leigh La. Co Ash	69	D2
Leigh La. West	39	E1
Leigh Rd. Bris	63	D4
Leigh St. Bris	63	D2
Leigh View Rd. Portis	45	F4
Leighton Cres. W-S-M	122	A4
Leighton Rd. Bath	84	A2
Leighton Rd. Bris	63	D2
Leighton Rd. Bris	64	A1
Leighwood Dr. Nail	59	D1
Leighwood House. Lo Ash	62	B3
Leinster Ave. Bris	79	E4
Lemon La. Bris	63	F4
Lena Ave. Bris	50	B1
Lena St. Bris	50	B1
Lenover Gdns. Bris	79	D2
Leonard La. Bris	63	E4
Leonard Rd. Bris	64	B4
Leonards Ave. Bris	50	B1
Leopold Rd. Bris	49	F1
Lescren Way. Avon	33	E1
Leslie Rise. Westw	120	C2
Lester Dr. W-S-M	89	D2
Lewin St. Bris	64	B4
Lewington Rd. Bris	51	E2
Lewins Mead. Bris	63	E4
Lewis Cl. Kingsw	66	B3
Lewis Rd. Bris	79	D4
Lewis St. Bris	64	A3
Lewisham Gr. W-S-M	105	D4
Lewton La. Wint	37	F4
Ley La. Olve	13	F2
Leyland Rd. Bris	78	C2
Leys The. Cleve	57	D1
Leyton Villas. Bris	49	D1
Liberty Ind Park. Bris	63	D1
Liberty La. Blag	110	C1
Lichfield Rd. Bris	64	C3
Lilac Cl. Bris	35	E1
Lilac Cl. Keyn	81	E2
Lilac Terr. Mid No	132	B1
Lilian Terr. Paul	131	F3
Lillian St. Bris	64	B4
Lillington Cl. Rad	133	D1
Lillington Rd. Rad	133	D1
Lilliput Ave. Ch Sod	40	A4
Lilliput Ct. Ch Sod	40	A4
Lilstock Ave. Bris	49	F2
Lilton Wlk. Bris	63	D1
Lilymead Ave. Bris	64	A2
Lime Cl. Bris	35	D2
Lime Cl. Col	70	C3
Lime Cl. Lock	106	A2
Lime Cl. W-S-M	89	D1
Lime Croft. Yate	27	F2
Lime Ct. Keyn	81	E2
Lime Gr. Alve	14	C3
Lime Gr. Bath	102	A3
Lime Grove Gdns. Bath	102	A3
Lime Kiln Gdns. St Gif	24	B2
Lime Rd. Bris	63	D2
Lime Rd. Kingsw	65	D3
Lime Terr. Rad	132	B1
Lime Tree Gr. E in G	47	E2
Limeburn Hill. Ch Mag	95	F3
Limekiln La. Bath	102	C2
Limekiln Rd. Yate	27	E4
Limerick Rd. Bris	49	E1
Limes The. Bris	37	D1
Limes The. Gr Bad	30	C1
Limpley Stoke Rd. Winsl	120	B3
Lincoln Cl. Keyn	81	E2
Lincoln St. Bris	64	A4
Lincombe Ave. Mang	51	E3
Lincombe Rd. Mang	51	E3
Lincombe Rd. Rod	138	B4
Lincott View. P St J	133	E4
Linden Ave. W-S-M	105	D4
Linden Cl. Bris	51	D1
Linden Cl. Bris	80	C3
Linden Cl. Col	70	C3
Linden Cl. Wint	37	F3
Linden Dr. St Gif	36	C4
Linden Gdns. Bath	101	E4
Linden Rd. Bris	49	D2
Linden Rd. Cleve	57	E2
Lindens The. W-S-M	88	C2
Lindrea St. Bris	63	D2
Lindsay Rd. Bris	50	A2
Lindsey Cl. Portis	44	C2
Linemere Cl. Back	76	B3
Lines Way. Whit	80	B2
Lingfield Park. Mang	37	F1
Link La. Blag	109	F2
Link Rd. Bris	35	F2
Link Rd. Bris	36	A1
Link Rd. Nail	59	F1
Link Rd. Portis	45	E3
Link Rd. Yate	27	F1
Links Rd. W-S-M	104	B1
Linkside. Cleve	57	F3
Linley Cl. Bath	101	D3
Linleys The. Bath	101	E4
Linnell Cl. Bris	50	A3
Linnet Cl. Bris	35	F4
Linnet Cl. W-S-M	88	C1
Linnet Way. Rod	138	A4
Lintern Cres. Kingsw	66	A3
Lintham Dr. Kingsw	65	F3
Linton Rd. Bris	63	E1
Lion Cl. Nail	59	E1
Lippiat Hill. Faulk	134	B2
Lippiatt La. Ship	125	F4
Lippiatt La. Tims	116	A2
Lisburn Rd. Bris	63	F1
Lisle Rd. W-S-M	89	D2
Lister Gr. Westw	120	C2
Litfield Rd. Bris	62	C4
Litt Hill. Litt	129	F1
Little Ann St. Bris	63	F4
Little Birch Croft. Bris	80	A2
Little Bishop St. Bris	63	F4
Little Bristol La. Char	11	D2
Little Caroline Pl. Bris	62	C3
Little Dowles. Kingsw	66	A2
Little George St. Bris	63	F4
Little George St. W-S-M	104	C4
Little Green La. Piln	22	A4
Little Halt. Portis	44	C2
Little Ham. Cleve	73	E4
Little Headley Cl. Bris	79	E4
Little King St. Bris	63	E3
Little La. Farm	116	A3
Little Mead Cl. Lock	105	F2
Little Mead. Bris	34	A1
Little Mead. Bris	34	A1
Little Meadow End. Nail	75	F4
Little Meadow. St Gif	37	D3
Little Orch. W-S-M	104	B1
Little Paradise. Bris	63	E2
Little Paul St. Bris	63	E4
Little Solsbury La. Bathe	85	F2
Little Stoke La. St Gif	36	B4
Little Stoke Rd. Bris	48	C2
Little Withey Mead. Bris	48	C3
Littlebrook. Paul	131	F3
Littledean. Yate	39	F4
Littlefields Ave. Ban	107	D2
Littlefields La. Ban	107	D2
Littleton Ct. Bris	23	F1
Littleton La. Ch Mag	95	E2
Littleton La. Dun	95	E2
Littleton La. Well	134	B4
Littleton La. Win	95	E4
Littleton Rd. Bris	63	D2
Littleton St. Bris	50	B1
Littlewood Cl. Bris	80	A2
Littlewood La. Brock	75	E1
Litton. W-S-M	105	D1
Livingstone Rd. Bath	101	E3
Llewellyn Ct. Bris	49	D4
Llewellyn Way. W-S-M	89	D2
Lock Gdns. Bris	78	C4
Lockemor Rd. Bris	79	F2
Locking Head Dro. Lock	106	A4
Locking Moor Rd. W-S-M	105	E4
Locking Rd. W-S-M	105	D4
Lockingwell Rd. Keyn	81	E3
Lockleaze Rd. Bris	50	A3
Locksbrook Rd. Bath	101	E3
Locksbrook Rd. W-S-M	89	D3
Lodge Causeway. Bris	51	D2
Lodge Cl. Yatt	91	D4
Lodge Dr. Kingsw	66	B1
Lodge Dr. Lo Ash	62	A1
Lodge Dr. W-S-M	88	A1
Lodge Gdns. Bath	101	E4
Lodge Hill. Bris	51	E1
Lodge La. Wrax	60	A1
Lodge Pl. Bris	63	E4
Lodge Rd. Bris	51	E1
Lodge Rd. Wick	53	D4
Lodge Rd. Yate	27	D2
Lodge St. Bris	63	E4
Lodge Wlk. Mang	51	E4
Lodgeside Ave. Bris	51	E1
Lodgeside Gdns. Bris	51	E1
Lodore Rd. Bris	50	C2
Lodway Cl. E in G	47	E1
Lodway Gdns. E in G	47	E2
Lodway Rd. Bris	64	B1
Lodway. E in G	47	E1
Logan Rd. Bris	49	E2
Logus Ct. Kingsw	65	F2
Lombard St. Bris	63	E2
Lomond Rd. Bris	35	F1
London Rd E. Bathe	86	A2
London Rd W. Bath	85	F1
London Rd. Bath	102	A3
London Rd. Bris	49	F1
London Rd. Sist	66	B4
London Rd. Wick	67	F3
London St. Bath	102	A4
London St. Kingsw	65	E4
Long Acres Cl. Bris	48	B4
Long Ashton Rd. Lo Ash	62	B3
Long Ave. Cleve	57	D1
Long Barnaby. Mid No	132	A1
Long Beach Rd. Kingsw	66	A2
Long Cl. Bris	51	E3
Long Cl. St Gif	36	C3
Long Croft. Yate	27	E2
Long Cross. Bris	34	A1
Long Cross. Win	94	B4
Long Eaton Dr. Bris	80	A4
Long Handstones. Kingsw	66	A2
Long Hay Cl. Bath	101	D3
Long La. Back	76	B2
Long La. But	94	A3
Long La. Wring	93	D1
Long Leaze. Burt	43	D1
Long Mead. Yate	27	F3
Long Meadow. Bris	50	B3
Long Rd. Mang	52	A3
Long Row. Bris	63	F3
Long Thorn La. Win	111	F4
Longacre Rd. Bris	80	A2
Longacre. Cleve	73	D4
Longbottom. Ched	125	F3
Longcross. Crom	10	A1
Longden Rd. Mang	51	F3
Longdown Dr. W-S-M	89	D2
Longfellow Ave. Bath	101	F2
Longfellow Rd. Rad	132	B1
Longfellow Rd. Rod	138	B4
Longfield Rd. Bris	49	F2
Longford Ave. Bris	49	E4
Longford. Yate	39	E4
Longleat Cl. Bris	49	E3
Longleaze Gdns. Lock	105	F2
Longmead Ave. Bris	49	E3
Longmead Croft. Bris	78	C2
Longmeadow Rd. Keyn	81	E2
Longmoor Rd. Bris	63	D1
Longney Pl. Bris	51	E3
Longreach Gr. Bris	80	B3
Longs Dr. Yate	27	E1
Longs View. Char	11	D3
Longton Grove Rd. W-S-M	104	C4
Longton Ind Est. W-S-M	104	C3
Longway Ave. Bris	79	F2
Longwell House. Kingsw	65	F2
Longwood La. Lo Ash	61	F2
Longwood. Bris	65	D1
Lonsdale Ave. W-S-M	105	D1
Lorain Wlk. Bris	34	C1
Lorne Rd. Bath	101	E3
Lorton Rd. Bris	35	D1
Lott's Ave. Back	76	A3
Louisa St. Bris	63	F3
Louise Ave. Kingsw	52	A3
Love La. Ch Sod	40	A4
Love La. Yate	28	A2
Love's La. Farm	115	F3
Lovelinch Gdns. Lo Ash	61	F1
Lovell Ave. Kingsw	66	B2
Lovells Mill. Bi Sut	113	D2
Loveringe Cl. Bris	34	C2
Lovers La. Paul	132	A3

Lovers' Wlk. W-S-M 104 B4
Loves Hill. Tims 116 A1
Lowbourne. Bris 79 F3
Lower Ashley Rd. Bris 49 F1
Lower Ashley Rd. Bris 50 A1
Lower Batch. Ch Mag 96 A2
Lower Borough Walls. Bath 101 F3
Lower Bristol Rd. Bath 101 E3
Lower Bristol Rd. Clut 114 C4
Lower Castle St. Bris 63 F4
Lower Chapel La. Fr Cot 38 B4
Lower Chapel Rd. Kingsw 65 E3
Lower Cheltenham Pl. Bris .. 49 F1
Lower Church La. Bris 63 E4
Lower Church Rd. W-S-M . 104 B4
Lower Claverham. Yatt 74 C2
Lower Clifton Hill. Bris 63 D3
Lower Cock Rd. Kingsw 65 F4
Lower College St. Bris 63 E3
Lower Court Rd. Alm 24 A3
Lower Down Rd. Portis 45 E1
Lower Fallow Cl. Bris 79 F2
Lower Gay St. Bris 63 E4
Lower Grove Rd. Bris 50 C2
Lower Hanham Rd. Kingsw .. 65 E3
Lower High St. Bris 47 E4
Lower House Cres. Bris 36 A2
Lower Kingsdown Rd. Box .. 86 C2
Lower Knole La. Bris 35 D2
Lower Knowles Rd. Cleve ... 57 E1
Lower Lamb St. Bris 63 E3
Lower Linden Rd. Cleve 57 E2
Lower Maudlin St. Bris 63 E4
Lower Moor Rd. Yate 27 F2
Lower Northend Est. Bathe . 85 F3
Lower Norton La. W St L 88 B2
Lower Norton La. W-S-M 88 C2
Lower Oldfield Park. Bath .. 101 F3
Lower Park Row. Bris 63 E4
Lower Queen's Rd. Cleve ... 57 E2
Lower Rd. Hin Ble 129 F3
Lower Redland Rd. Bris 49 D1
Lower Sidney St. Bris 63 D2
Lower St. Rode 136 C1
Lower Station Rd. Bris 51 D2
Lower Station Rd. Kingsw ... 51 E2
Lower Stoke. Bath 103 D1
Lower Stoke. Li St 120 A4
Lower Stone Cl. Fr Cot 38 B4
Lower Strode Rd. Cleve 73 D4
Lower Strode. Win 112 A4
Lower Thirlmere Rd. Bris ... 36 A4
Lower Tockington Rd. Olve . 14 A1
Lower Whitelands. Mid No 133 D2
Lowlis Cl. Bris 34 C2
Lowther Rd. Bris 35 E1
Loxley Gdns. Bath 101 E2
Loxton Dr. Bath 101 D3
Loxton Rd. W-S-M 104 C1
Loxton Sq. Bris 80 A3
Lucas Cl. Bris 64 B1
Luccombe Hill. Bris 49 D1
Luckington Cross. Hol 139 D1
Luckington Rd. Bris 49 F4
Lucklands Rd. Bath 84 B1
Luckley Ave. Bris 79 E3
Luckwell Rd. Bris 63 D2
Lucky La. Bris 63 E2
Ludlow Cl. Bris 49 F1
Ludlow Cl. Keyn 81 E3
Ludlow Cl. Kingsw 66 A1
Ludlow Rd. Bris 50 A4
Ludwell Cl. Wint 37 E3
Ludwells Orch. Paul 131 F3
Lullington Rd. Bris 64 A1
Lulsgate Rd. Bris 79 D4
Lulworth Cres. Mang 51 F4
Lulworth Rd. Keyn 81 F2
Lurgan Wlk. Bris 63 E1
Luvers La. Blag 110 B1
Lux Furlong. Bris 48 A4
Luxton St. Bris 64 A4
Lychgate Park. Lock 106 A2
Lydbrook Cl. Yate 39 E4
Lyddington Rd. Bris 49 F4
Lyddon Rd. W-S-M 89 D2
Lydford Wlk. Bris 63 E1
Lydiard Croft. Kingsw 65 E2
Lydney Rd. Bris 49 E4
Lydney Rd. Kingsw 51 F2
Lydstep Terr. Bris 63 E2
Lye Cross Rd. Wring 93 E1
Lye Hole La. Wring 93 E1
Lyefield Rd. W-S-M 88 C2
Lyme Gdns. Bath 101 D4
Lyme Rd. Bath 101 D4
Lymore Ave. Bath 101 E3
Lymore Gdns. Bath 101 E3
Lymore Terr. Bath 101 E2
Lympsham Green. Bath 118 B4
Lympsham Rd. Lymp 122 A1
Lynbrook La. Bath 101 F2
Lynbrook. Lo Ash 61 F1
Lynch Cl. W-S-M 88 C2
Lynch Cres. Wins 124 C4
Lynch Ct. Kingsw 65 F2
Lynch Hill. Chil 137 D2
Lynch The. Wins 124 C4

Lynchmead. Wins 124 C4
Lyncombe Hill. Bath 102 A3
Lyncombe Vale Rd. Bath .. 102 A2
Lyncombe Vale. Bath 102 A2
Lyncombe Wlk. Bris 51 D1
Lyndale Ave. Bris 48 B3
Lyndale Rd. Bris 64 B4
Lyndale Rd. Yate 27 E1
Lynde Cl. Bris 79 D2
Lyndhurst Rd. Bath 101 E3
Lyndhurst Rd. Bris 48 C4
Lyndhurst Rd. Keyn 81 F2
Lyndhurst Rd. Rod 138 A4
Lyndhurst Rd. W-S-M 104 C2
Lynfield Park. Bath 84 B1
Lynmouth Cl. W-S-M 89 D1
Lynmouth Rd. Bris 50 A1
Lynn Rd. Bris 50 B3
Lynton Cl. Portis 45 F2
Lynton Pl. Bris 64 B4
Lynton Rd. Rod 138 A4
Lynton Way. Bris 37 D1
Lynton. Kingsw 66 A4
Lynwood Cl. Rod 138 A4
Lynx Cres. W-S-M 105 D1
Lyons Court Rd. Bris 80 B4
Lyons Ct. W-S-M 104 C4
Lyppiatt Rd. Bris 64 B4
Lyppincourt Rd. Bris 35 D2
Lysander Rd. Bris 35 E3
Lysander Wlk. St Gif 36 C3
Lytchet Dr. Mang 51 F4
Lytes Cary Rd. Keyn 82 A2
Lytton Gdns. Bath 101 D2
Lytton Gr. Bris 50 A4
Lytton Gr. Keyn 82 A3
Lyveden Gdns. Bris 79 D3
Lyvedon Way. Lo Ash 62 A1

Macaulay Bldgs. Bath 102 B2
Macauley Rd. Bris 50 A4
Macey's Rd. Bris 79 E2
Machin Cl. Bris 34 C2
Machin Rd. Bris 34 C2
Machley La. N St P 135 F2
Macies The. Bath 84 A2
Mackie Ave. Bris 36 A1
Mackie Gr. Bris 36 A1
Mackie Rd. Bris 36 A1
Macleod Cl. Cleve 57 D1
Madam La. W-S-M 88 C1
Madam La. W-S-M 89 D2
Madam's Paddock. Ch Mag 96 A2
Maddocke House. Bris 79 E2
Madeira Rd. Cleve 57 E2
Madeira Rd. W-S-M 87 E1
Madeline Rd. Bris 50 C1
Madison Cl. Yate 27 E1
Maesbury Rd. Keyn 82 A1
Maesbury. Kingsw 65 F3
Maesknoll La. Whit 97 D4
Maesknoll Rd. Bris 64 A1
Magdalen Ave. Bath 101 F3
Magdalen Rd. Bath 101 F3
Magdalen Way. W-S-M 89 D2
Magdalene Pl. Bris 49 F1
Magdalene Rd. Rad 133 E1
Magellan Cl. W-S-M 88 C2
Maggs Folly. Paul 115 E1
Maggs La. Whit 80 B2
Magnolia Ave. W-S-M 89 D1
Magnolia Rd. Rad 132 C1
Magpie Bottom La. Bris 65 E3
Magpie Bottom La. Kingsw . 65 E3
Magpie Cl. W-S-M 105 F4
Maiden Way. Avon 47 E4
Maidenhead Rd. Bris 79 E2
Maidstone Gr. W-S-M 105 D1
Maidstone St. Bris 63 F2
Main Rd. Back 76 C4
Main Rd. Brock 75 F1
Main Rd. Lock 105 F1
Main Rd. Puck 52 B3
Main St. Paul 131 D2
Main View. Fr Cot 38 B4
Maisemore Ave. St Gif 24 A1
Maisemore. Yate 39 F3
Makin Cl. Kingsw 66 B3
Malago Rd. Bris 63 E2
Malago Vale Est. Bris 63 E2
Malago Wlk. Bris 78 C2
Maldowers La. Bris 65 D4
Mall The. Bath 102 A3
Mall The. Bris 62 C4
Mallard Cl. Bris 50 C1
Mallard Cl. Ch Sod 40 A4
Mallard Cl. St Gif 24 B1
Mallard Wlk. W-S-M 105 F4
Mallow Cl. Cleve 57 F1
Mallow Cl. Thorn 8 B1
Malmains Dr. Bris 37 D1
Malmesbury Cl. Bris 49 D1
Malmesbury Cl. Kingsw 65 F3
Maltings Ind Est The. Bath 101 D4
Maltings The. W-S-M 88 C1
Maltlands. W-S-M 105 E4
Maltravers Cl. St Gif 36 B4
Malvern Bldgs. Bath 85 D1

Malvern Ct. Bris 64 C4
Malvern Dr. Kingsw 66 B3
Malvern Dr. Thorn 15 E4
Malvern Rd. Bris 64 B2
Malvern Rd. Bris 64 C4
Malvern Rd. W-S-M 104 C3
Mancroft Ave. Bris 47 F4
Mandy Meadows. Mid No .. 131 F1
Mangotsfield Rd. Mang 52 A3
Manilla Pl. W-S-M 87 E1
Manilla Rd. Bris 63 D4
Manmoor La. Cleve 58 A1
Manor Cl The. Ab Lei 62 A4
Manor Cl. E in G 47 D2
Manor Cl. Fr Cot 38 B3
Manor Cl. Olve 14 B1
Manor Cl. Paul 131 D2
Manor Cl. Well 118 B1
Manor Copse Rd. Rad 133 E1
Manor Court Dr. Bris 49 F4
Manor Ct. Back 76 A3
Manor Ct. Bris 50 C2
Manor Dr. Bathf 86 A1
Manor Farm Cl. W-S-M 105 D1
Manor Farm Cres. W-S-M . 105 D1
Manor Farm. St Gif 36 B4
Manor Gdns. Farm 115 F3
Manor Gdns. Lock 106 A2
Manor Gdns. Paul 131 D2
Manor Gdns. W-S-M 88 A2
Manor Gr. Kingsw 52 A2
Manor Gr. St Gif 24 A1
Manor Grange. Blea 122 A4
Manor La. Ab Lei 61 F4
Manor La. Char 11 D2
Manor La. Wint 37 F4
Manor Park. Bath 101 D4
Manor Park. Bris 49 D2
Manor Park. Olve 14 A1
Manor Park. Rad 133 E1
Manor Pl. Bris 37 E1
Manor Rd. Ab Lei 61 F4
Manor Rd. Bath 84 B1
Manor Rd. Bris 49 F2
Manor Rd. Bris 50 C3
Manor Rd. Bris 79 D3
Manor Rd. Ir Act 27 D4
Manor Rd. Keyn 82 A1
Manor Rd. Kingsw 52 A2
Manor Rd. Rad 133 E1
Manor Rd. W-S-M 105 D4
Manor Rd. Wick 67 E3
Manor Rd. Wickw 27 D4
Manor Terr. Rad 133 E1
Manor Valley. W-S-M 88 A1
Manor Villas. Bath 84 B1
Manor Way. Ch Sod 28 A1
Manor Way. Wrax 61 E2
Manor Wlk. Thorn 8 A2
Mansel Cl. Keyn 82 B2
Mansfield Ave. W-S-M 105 D4
Mansfield St. Bris 63 D1
Manston Cl. Bris 80 B4
Manvers St. Bath 102 A3
Manworthy Rd. Bris 64 B2
Manx Rd. Bris 49 F4
Maple Ave. Bris 51 E2
Maple Ave. Thorn 8 B1
Maple Cl. Bris 80 B2
Maple Cl. Kingsw 66 A2
Maple Cl. St Gif 36 B4
Maple Cl. W-S-M 105 D4
Maple Dr. Rad 132 C1
Maple Gdns. Bath 101 F2
Maple Gr. Bath 101 F2
Maple Leaf Ct. Bris 63 D4
Maple Rd. Bris 49 E3
Maple Rd. Bris 64 B3
Maple Wlk. Keyn 81 E2
Maple Wlk. Puck 53 E3
Maplecroft. Bris 80 C3
Mapleleaze. Bris 64 B2
Maplemeade. Bris 49 E2
Mapleridge La. Hort 28 B4
Mapleridge La. Yate 28 B4
Maples The. Nail 59 E1
Maplestone Rd. Bris 80 A2
Marbeck Rd. Bris 35 D1
Marchfields Way. W-S-M .. 105 D3
Marconi Rd. Portis 44 C3
Mardale Cl. Bris 35 E1
Marden Rd. Keyn 82 A2
Mardon Rd. Bris 64 B3
Mardyke Ferry Rd. Bris 63 D3
Marfield Wlk. Bris 78 C2
Margaret Rd. Bris 78 C2
Margaret's Bldgs. Bath 101 F4
Margaret's Hill. Bath 102 A4
Margate St. Bris 63 F2
Marguerite Rd. Bris 78 C3
Marigold Wlk. Bris 63 D1
Marina Gdns. Bris 50 C2
Marindin Dr. W-S-M 89 D2
Marine Hill. Cleve 57 E2
Marine Par. Cleve 57 E2
Marine Par. E in G 47 E3
Marine Par. W-S-M 104 B3
Mariner's Cl. W-S-M 88 B1
Mariner's Way. E in G 47 E3

Mariners Cl. Back 76 A3
Mariners Dr. Back 76 A3
Mariners Dr. Bris 48 B2
Marion Way. Kingsw 65 D2
Marion Wlk. Bris 65 D4
Marissal Cl. Bris 34 C2
Marissal Rd. Bris 34 C2
Mariston Way. Kingsw 66 B3
Mark La. Bris 63 E3
Market Ind Est. Yatt 74 A1
Market Pl. Marsh 70 A4
Market Pl. Win 94 C4
Market Sq. Bris 51 E2
Markham Cl. Bris 47 E4
Marksbury Rd. Bris 63 E1
Marksbury. Marks 99 D3
Marlborough Ave. Bris 50 C2
Marlborough Bldgs. Bath .. 101 F4
Marlborough Dr. Bris 37 D1
Marlborough Dr. W-S-M 89 D1
Marlborough Hill Pl. Bris ... 63 E4
Marlborough Hill. Bris 63 E4
Marlborough La. Bath 101 F4
Marlborough St. Bath 101 F4
Marlborough St. Bris 50 C2
Marlborough St. Bris 63 E4
Marlepit Gr. Bris 78 C3
Marling Rd. Bris 64 C4
Marlwood Dr. Bris 35 D2
Marmaduke St. Bris 63 F2
Marmion Cres. Bris 34 C2
Marne Cl. Bris 80 B2
Marsden Rd. Bath 101 E2
Marsh Cl. Wint 37 F3
Marsh Comm. Piln 22 B3
Marsh La. Bris 63 D1
Marsh La. Bris 64 B3
Marsh La. Clut 115 D1
Marsh La. E in G 46 C3
Marsh La. Paul 131 D2
Marsh Rd. Bris 62 C2
Marsh Rd. Rode 136 C1
Marsh St. Avon 47 E4
Marsh St. Bris 63 E3
Marshacre La. Aust 13 F3
Marsham Way. Kingsw 65 F2
Marshfield La. Bitt 67 E1
Marshfield Rd. Bris 51 E2
Marshfield Rd. Mang 51 E4
Marshfield Rd. Tor 41 F1
Marshfield Way. Bath 85 D1
Marshwall La. Alm 23 F3
Marson Rd. Cleve 57 E2
Marston Rd. Bris 64 A2
Martin Cl. Bris 35 F4
Martin St. Bris 63 D2
Martin's Rd. Kingsw 65 E3
Martindale Ct. W-S-M 105 E4
Martindale Rd. W-S-M 105 E4
Martingale Rd. Bris 64 B2
Martins Cl. Kingsw 65 E3
Martins Gr. W-S-M 88 C1
Martock Cres. Bris 63 E1
Martock Rd. Bris 63 E1
Martock Rd. Keyn 82 A2
Martock. W-S-M 104 C1
Martor Ind Est. Marsh 56 A1
Marwood Rd. Bris 79 F4
Mary Carpenter Pl. Bris 49 F1
Mary St. Bris 64 B4
Marybush La. Bris 63 F4
Marygold Leaze. Kingsw ... 66 A2
Mascot Rd. Bris 63 E2
Masefield Way. Bris 50 A4
Maskelyne Ave. Bris 49 E4
Masons View. Wint 37 F4
Matchells Cl. Bris 64 C3
Materman Rd. Bris 80 C3
Matford Cl. Bris 35 E2
Matford Cl. Wint 37 F3
Matford La. Stone 3 F2
Matthew's Rd. Bris 64 B4
Matthews Cl. Bris 80 C3
Maules La. St Gif 36 C1
Maunsell Rd. Bris 34 A1
Maurice Rd. Bris 49 F1
Max Mill La. Wins 124 B3
Maxse Rd. Bris 64 A2
May St. Bris 51 E1
May Tree Cl. Nail 59 E1
May Tree Rd. Rad 132 C1
May Tree Wlk. Keyn 81 E2
May's La. Pux 90 B2
Maybank Rd. Yate 27 E1
Maybec Gdns. Bris 65 D3
Maybourne. Bris 65 D1
Maybrick Rd. Bath 101 E3
Maycliffe Park. Bris 49 F1
Mayfair Ave. Nail 59 F1
Mayfield Ave. W-S-M 88 C1
Mayfield Pk N. Bris 51 D1
Mayfield Pk S. Bris 51 D1
Mayfield Rd. Bath 101 E3
Mayfields. Keyn 81 F3

Mayflower Gdns. Nail 60 A1
Maynard Cl. Bris 79 E3
Maynard Cl. Cleve 57 F2
Maynard Rd. Bris 79 E3
Maynard Terr. Clut 115 D2
Maypole Cl. Clut 114 C2
Maysfield Cl. Portis 45 E2
Maysgreen Rd. Pux 90 A2
Maysmead La. Chur 109 E3
Maytree Ave. Bris 79 D4
Maytree Cl. Bris 79 D4
Mayville Ave. Bris 36 A2
Maywood Ave. Bris 51 D2
Maywood Cres. Bris 51 D2
Maywood Rd. Bris 51 E2
Maze St. Bris 64 A3
McAdam Way. Bris 62 C3
Mead Cl. Bath 101 F2
Mead Cl. Bris 47 F3
Mead La. Keyn 82 C2
Mead La. Keyn 83 D2
Mead La. Winsc 107 F2
Mead Lands. Cor 100 A4
Mead Rd. Ch Sod 28 A1
Mead Rd. Portis 45 E1
Mead Rd. St Gif 36 C3
Mead Rise. Bris 63 F3
Mead St. Bris 63 F3
Mead The. Alve 15 D3
Mead The. Bris 36 A4
Mead The. Chil 137 F1
Mead The. Clut 114 C2
Mead The. Dun 78 B1
Mead The. Farm 116 A3
Mead The. Ship 125 F4
Mead The. Tims 116 B2
Mead The. Win 95 D3
Mead The. Winsl 120 C4
Mead Vale. W-S-M 105 F4
Mead Way. Thorn 15 D4
Meadow Cl. Back 76 A3
Meadow Cl. Mang 51 F4
Meadow Cl. Nail 59 F2
Meadow Cl. Portis 44 C3
Meadow Court Dr. Kingsw .. 66 B2
Meadow Croft. W-S-M 105 D1
Meadow Dr. Lock 106 A2
Meadow Dr. W in G 44 C1
Meadow Gdns. Bath 84 A1
Meadow Gr. Bris 47 E4
Meadow La. Bath 85 E1
Meadow Mead. Fr Cot 38 A4
Meadow Rd. Ch Sod 28 A1
Meadow Rd. Cleve 57 F2
Meadow Rd. Crom 10 A2
Meadow Rd. Paul 131 F2
Meadow St. Avon 33 D1
Meadow St. Axb 125 E1
Meadow St. Bris 63 F4
Meadow St. W-S-M 104 C4
Meadow Vale. Bris 51 D1
Meadow View. Fr Cot 38 B4
Meadow View. Rad 133 D1
Meadow Villas. W-S-M 104 C4
Meadow Way. St Gif 36 C4
Meadowbank. W-S-M 88 C2
Meadowland Rd. Bris 34 C2
Meadowland. Yatt 74 A1
Meadowlands. Lock 89 E1
Meadows The. Kingsw 65 E2
Meadowside Dr. Bris 80 A2
Meadowside. Thorn 15 E4
Meadowsweet Ave. Bris 36 A2
Meads The. Burt 43 D2
Meads The. Mang 51 F4
Meadway Ave. Nail 59 E1
Meadway. Bris 48 B3
Meadway. Clut 114 C1
Meadway. Farm 116 A3
Mearcombe La. Blea 122 C3
Meardon Rd. Bris 80 C3
Meare Rd. Bath 102 A1
Meare. W-S-M 104 C1
Mede Cl. Bris 63 F3
Medical Ave. Bris 63 E4
Medina Cl. Thorn 15 E4
Medway Cl. Keyn 82 A2
Medway Ct. Thorn 15 E4
Medway Dr. Fr Cot 38 A4
Medway Dr. Keyn 82 A2
Meere Bank. Bris 34 A1
Meetinghouse La. Brock 75 D1
Meetinghouse La. Paul 131 D1
Meg Thatchers Cl. Bris 65 D4
Meg Thatchers Gdns. Bris .. 65 D4
Melbourne Dr. Ch Sod 28 A1
Melbourne Rd. Bris 49 E2
Melbourne Terr. Cleve 57 E1
Melbury Rd. Bris 64 A1
Melcombe Rd. Bath 101 E3
Melita Rd. Bris 49 F2
Mellent Ave. Bris 79 E2
Mells Cl. Keyn 82 A1
Mells La. Kilm 133 D1
Mells La. Rad 133 D1
Melrose Ave. Bris 63 D4
Melrose Ave. Yate 28 A1

Melrose Cl. Yate

Melrose Cl. Yate 28 A1
Melrose Gr. Bath 101 D2
Melrose Pl. Bris 63 D4
Melton Cres. Bris 50 A4
Melville Rd. Bris 49 D1
Melville Terr. Bris 63 E2
Memorial Cl. Kingsw 65 D2
Memorial Cotts. Bath 84 B1
Memorial Rd. Kingsw 65 D2
Memorial Rd. Wring 92 C1
Mendip Cl. W-S-M 88 C1
Mendip Cl. Axb 125 E1
Mendip Cl. Keyn 81 E3
Mendip Cl. Nail 59 F1
Mendip Cl. Paul 131 F2
Mendip Cl. Yatt 91 D4
Mendip Cres. Mang 52 A4
Mendip Edge. W-S-M 121 F4
Mendip Gdns. Bath 118 B4
Mendip Gdns. Yatt 91 D4
Mendip Rd. Bris 63 E2
Mendip Rd. Portis 45 D3
Mendip Rd. W-S-M 105 D4
Mendip Rd. Yatt 91 D4
Mendip Rise. Lock 106 A2
Mendip View Ave. Bris 51 D2
Mendip View. Wick 67 E4
Mendip Villas. Co Mar 127 F4
Mendip Way. 132 C2
Menlea. Blag 110 B2
Merchant St. Bris 63 F4
Merchants Cl. Bris 63 D3
Merchants Quay. Bris 63 E3
Merchants Rd. Bris 63 D3
Merchants Rd. Bris 63 D4
Mercia Dr. Bris 50 A1
Mercier Cl. Yate 27 F1
Meredith Ct. Bris 63 D3
Merfield Rd. Bris 64 A1
Meridian Pl. Bris 63 D4
Meridian Rd. Bris 49 E1
Meridian Vale. Bris 63 D4
Meriet Ave. Bris 79 D2
Merioneth St. Bris 63 F2
Meriton St. Bris 64 A3
Merlin Cl. Bris 48 C4
Merlin Cl. W-S-M 105 F4
Merlin Park. Portis 45 D2
Merlin Rd. Bris 35 E3
Merlin Ridge. Puck 53 E2
Merlin Way. Ch Sod 39 F4
Merrimans Rd. Bris 47 E4
Merryweathers. Bris 64 C1
Merrywood Cl. Bris 63 E2
Merrywood Rd. Bris 63 E2
Merstham Rd. Bris 50 A1
Merton Rd. Bris 49 F3
Mervyn Rd. Bris 49 F2
Metford Gr. Bris 49 D2
Metford Pl. Bris 49 E2
Metford Rd. Bris 49 E2
Methwyn Cl. W-S-M 105 E4
Mews The. Bath 101 D4
Michaels Mead. Bath 84 A1
Middle Ave. Bris 63 E3
Middle La. Bath 85 D1
Middle La. K Sey 73 D2
Middle Rd. Kingsw 51 F2
Middle St. E Harp 128 C2
Middle Stoke. Li St 120 A3
Middle Yeo Green. Nail 59 E2
Middledown Rd. Marsh 55 E1
Middleford House. Bris 79 E2
Middlemead. Chil 137 F2
Middlepiece La. Keyn 99 D4
Middleton Rd. Bris 47 F4
Midford Hill. Hin Cha 119 E2
Midford La. Hi Cha 120 A3
Midford La. Li St 119 F4
Midford Rd. Bath 101 F1
Midford Rd. Sosto 119 D4
Midford. W-S-M 104 C1
Midhaven Rise. W-S-M 88 C2
Midland Bridge Rd. Bath ... 101 F3
Midland Rd. Bath 101 E4
Midland Rd. Bris 63 F4
Midland Rd. Kingsw 51 F2
Midland Terr. Bris 50 C2
Midland Way. Thorn 15 D4
Midsomer Enterprise Park.
        Mid No 132 B1
Midsummer Bldgs. Bath 85 D1
Milbourn Cl. Winsl 120 B4
Milburn Rd. W-S-M 104 C4
Mildred St. Bris 64 B4
Mile Wlk. Bris 80 A3
Miles Ct. Kingsw 65 F2
Miles Rd. Bris 49 D1
Miles St. Bath 102 A3
Miles's Bldgs. Bath 101 F4
Milestone Ct. Lock 89 E1
Milford Ave. Wick 67 D4
Milford St. Bris 63 E2
Milk St. Bath 101 F3
Mill Ave. Bris 63 F4
Mill Cl. Fr Cot 38 B4
Mill Cl. Portb 46 B1
Mill Cres. West 39 D2

Mill Hill. Well 118 C1
Mill La. Bath 85 F1
Mill La. Bath 101 D3
Mill La. Bath 119 F4
Mill La. Bitt 66 C1
Mill La. Bitt 82 C4
Mill La. Bris 63 E2
Mill La. But 111 D4
Mill La. Ch Sod 28 A1
Mill La. Ch Sod 40 C3
Mill La. Ch St 112 B4
Mill La. Co Mar 128 A4
Mill La. Cong 91 B2
Mill La. Falf 9 F4
Mill La. Fr Cot 26 A1
Mill La. Kingsw 66 B3
Mill La. Olve 14 A1
Mill La. Portb 46 C1
Mill La. Pris 117 D4
Mill La. Tims 116 A1
Mill La. Wring 109 F4
Mill Leg. Cong 91 F2
Mill Pool Ct. Bris 35 D1
Mill rd. Mid No 133 D1
Mill Rd. Wint 37 D2
Mill Stream Cl. Axb 125 D1
Millard Cl. Bris 35 E1
Millard's Hill. Mid No 132 A2
Millbank Cl. Bris 64 C2
Millbrook Ave. Bris 64 C2
Millbrook Pl. Bath 102 A3
Millbrook Rd. Yate 27 D1
Millcross. Cleve 73 E4
Millers Cl. E in G 47 E2
Millers Dr. Kingsw 66 B3
Millers Rise. W-S-M 89 D2
Millfield Dr. Kingsw 66 B3
Millfield. Mid No 137 F4
Millfield. Thorn 8 B1
Millground Rd. Bris 78 C3
Millier Rd. Brock 92 A4
Milliman Cl. Bris 79 E3
Millmead House. Bris 79 E2
Millmead Rd. Bath 101 E3
Millpond St. Bris 50 A1
Millward Gr. Bris 51 E2
Milner Green. Kingsw 66 A3
Milner Rd. Bris 49 F3
Milsom St. Bath 101 F4
Milsom St. Bris 64 A4
Milton Ave. Bath 101 F2
Milton Ave. W-S-M 105 D4
Milton Brow. W-S-M 88 A1
Milton Cl. Nail 59 F2
Milton Cl. Yate 27 E1
Milton Green. W-S-M 88 B1
Milton Hill. W-S-M 88 A1
Milton Park Rd. W-S-M 88 B1
Milton Pk. Bris 64 B4
Milton Rd. Bris 49 F3
Milton Rd. Rad 132 B1
Milton Rd. Yate 27 E1
Milton Rise. W-S-M 88 B1
Miltons Cl. Bris 79 E2
Milverton. W-S-M 104 C1
Milward Rd. Keyn 81 F3
Mina Rd. Bris 50 A1
Minehead Rd. Bris 64 A1
Minerva Gdns. Bath 101 E2
Minor's La. Avon 34 A4
Minsmere Rd. Keyn 82 A2
Minster Way. Bath 102 B4
Minto Rd. Bris 50 A1
Minto Road Ind Centre. Bris 49 F1
Mission Rd. Ir Act 27 D2
Mitchell Cl. Bris 63 F3
Mitchell La. Bris 63 F3
Mitford-Slade Ct. Yatt 90 A1
Mivart St. Bris 50 A1
Mizzymead Cl. Nail 59 E1
Mizzymead Rd. Nail 59 F1
Mizzymead Rise. Nail 59 E1
Modecombe Gr. Bris 34 C2
Mogg St. Bris 50 A1
Molesworth Cl. Bris 79 D2
Molesworth Dr. Bris 79 D2
Molesworth Dr. Bris 79 D2
Molly Cl. Clut 130 C4
Monger Rd. Bris 49 E2
Monk Rd. Bris 49 E2
Monk's Park Ave. Bris 49 F4
Monks Ave. Bris 65 D4
Monks Hill. W-S-M 88 A2
Monksdale Rd. Bath 101 E2
Monkton Ave. W-S-M 105 D1
Monkton Farleigh. Mon Far 103 F4
Monkton Rd. Bris 65 D3
Monmouth Cl. Portis 44 C2
Monmouth Hill. Alm 23 F2
Monmouth Paddock. N St P 135 F2
Monmouth Pl. Bath 101 F3
Monmouth Rd. Bris 49 E2
Monmouth Rd. E in G 47 E3
Monmouth Rd. Keyn 81 F3
Monmouth St. Bath 101 F3
Monmouth St. Bris 63 F2
Monsdale Cl. Bris 35 D2

Monsdale Dr. Bris 35 D1
Montague Cl. St Gif 36 C3
Montague Hill S. Bris 63 E4
Montague Hill. Bris 63 E4
Montague Pl. Bris 63 E4
Montague Rd. Keyn 82 B1
Montague Rd. Well 133 F3
Montague St. Bris 63 E4
Montgomery St. Bris 63 F2
Montpelier E. W-S-M 87 F1
Montpelier. W-S-M 104 C4
Montreal Ave. Bris 50 A4
Montrose Ave. Bris 49 E1
Montrose Dr. Kingsw 66 A3
Montrose Pk. Bris 64 B1
Montroy Cl. Bris 49 E3
Moon St. Bris 63 F4
Moor Croft Dr. Kingsw 65 F2
Moor Croft Rd. Lock 105 F2
Moor End Spout. Nail 59 E1
Moor Gr. Bris 48 A4
Moor Green. Axb 125 E1
Moor La. Back 75 F3
Moor La. Cleve 58 A1
Moor La. Lock 105 E2
Moor La. Nail 58 C2
Moor La. Olve 24 A4
Moor La. Piln 23 F4
Moor La. W in G 45 F1
Moor La. W-S-M 105 F4
Moor Park. Cleve 57 F1
Moor Rd. Ban 107 D3
Moor Rd. Yatt 74 A1
Moordell Cl. Yate 27 E1
Moorend Gdns. Bris 47 F4
Moorend Rd. Wint 37 E2
Moorfield Rd. Back 76 A3
Moorfields Cl. Bath 101 E2
Moorfields Ct. Nail 59 E1
Moorfields Rd. Bath 101 E2
Moorfields Rd. Nail 59 E1
Moorham Rd. Wins 108 A1
Moorhill St. Bris 50 A1
Moorhouse La. Avon 34 A4
Moorings The. E in G 47 E2
Moorland Rd. Bath 101 E3
Moorland Rd. W-S-M 104 C2
Moorland Rd. Yate 27 E1
Moorland St. Axb 125 E1
Moorlands Cl. Nail 59 E1
Moorlands Rd. Bris 50 C2
Moorlands Rd. Bris 51 D1
Moorledge La. Ch Mag 96 B1
Moorledge La. Pens 113 F4
Moorledge Rd. Ch Mag 96 A1
Moorpark Ave. Yate 27 E1
Moorsfield. Clut 114 C2
Moorside Ct. Cleve 57 F1
Moorside Villas. Cleve 57 E1
Moorslade La. Falf 3 E1
Moorslade La. Stone 3 E1
Moravian Ct. Kingsw 65 E4
Moravian Rd. Kingsw 65 E4
Morden Wlk. Bris 80 B4
Moreton Cl. Bris 80 A2
Moreton St. Bris 63 F4
Morford St. Bath 101 F4
Morgan Cl. Keyn 82 B1
Morgan St. Bris 49 F1
Morgan's La. E Harp 128 C2
Morgans Hill Cl. Nail 75 E4
Morley Ave. Kingsw 52 A2
Morley Cl. Kingsw 51 E2
Morley Cl. St Gif 36 B4
Morley Rd. Bris 63 E2
Morley Rd. Kingsw 51 E2
Morley Sq. Bris 49 F2
Morley St. Bris 49 F1
Morley St. Bris 64 A4
Morley Terr. Kingsw 51 E1
Morley Terr. Mid No 133 D2
Mornington Rd. Bris 49 D1
Morpeth Rd. Bris 79 E4
Morris La. Bathe 86 A2
Morris Rd. Bris 50 A3
Morse Rd. Bris 64 B4
Mortimer Cl. Bath 84 A1
Mortimer Rd. Bris 36 A1
Mortimer Rd. Bris 63 D4
Morton St. Bris 64 A4
Morton St. Thorn 8 B2
Morton Way. Thorn 8 B1
Moseley Gr. W-S-M 104 C1
Mount Beacon Row. Bath ... 84 C1
Mount Beacon. Bath 85 D1
Mount Cl. Fr Cot 37 F4
Mount Cres. Wint 37 F3
Mount Gdns. Kingsw 65 E3
Mount Gr. Bath 101 D2
Mount Hill Rd. Kingsw 65 E3
Mount Pleasant Terr. Bris ... 63 E2
Mount Pleasant. Bath 102 B1
Mount Pleasant. E in G 47 E3
Mount Pleasant. Rad 133 D1
Mount Rd. Bath 101 D2
Mount Rd. Bath 101 F4
Mount View. Bath 101 D2
Mountain Ash. Bath 84 B1

Mountain Wood. Bathf 86 B1
Mountbatten Cl. W-S-M 88 C2
Mountbatten Cl. Yate 27 E2
Mounteney's La. Kings 18 B4
Mow Barton. Bris 78 C3
Mow Barton. Yate 27 E1
Mowbray Rd. Bris 80 B4
Mowcroft Rd. Bris 79 E2
Moxham Dr. Bris 79 E2
Mud La. Yatt 74 C1
Muddy La. W ST L 89 D4
Muirfield. Kingsw 66 A3
Muirfield. Yate 39 F4
Mulberry Cl. Back 76 A3
Mulberry Cl. Kingsw 65 F4
Mulberry Dr. Kingsw 51 F1
Mulberry La. Blea 122 B3
Mulberry Rd. Cong 91 F2
Mulberry Wlk. Bris 48 B4
Mule St. N Nib 4 A2
Mulberry Cl. W-S-M 89 D1
Muller Ave. Bris 49 F2
Muller Rd. Bris 50 A2
Mulready Cl. Bris 50 B3
Mumbleys Hill. Thorn 14 C4
Mumbleys La. Thorn 14 C4
Murford Ave. Bris 79 D2
Murford Wlk. Bris 79 D2
Murray St. Bris 63 E2
Musgrove Cl. Bris 34 B1
Myrtle Dr. Bris 47 F3
Myrtle Hill. E in G 47 E2
Myrtle Rd. Bris 63 E4
Myrtle St. Bris 63 D2
Myrtles The. Lock 105 E1

Nags Head Hill. Bris 65 D4
Nailsea Cl. Bris 79 D4
Nailsea Park Cl. Nail 59 F1
Nailsea Park. Nail 59 F1
Nailsea Wall. Nail 74 B4
Nailsea Wall. Yatt 74 B4
Nailsworth Dr. Yate 27 F1
Naish Hill. Wrax 59 F4
Naish La. Ba Gu 77 E2
Naish's Cross. Chil 137 E2
Naishcombe Hill. Wick 67 E4
Naishes Ave. P St J 133 E4
Naite The. O-on-S 7 E3
Nanny Hurn's La. Bi Sut 114 A1
Nanny Hurn's La. Clut 130 A4
Napier Ct. Bris 63 D3
Napier Miles Rd. Bris 48 A4
Napier Rd. Avon 33 D1
Napier Rd. Bath 84 A2
Napier Rd. Bris 49 D1
Napier Rd. Bris 50 A1
Napier Sq. Avon 33 D1
Napier St. Bris 64 A3
Narrow La. Kingsw 51 F2
Narrow Plain. Bris 63 F3
Narrow Quay. Bris 63 E3
Narrowyas Rd. Bris 50 A2
Naseby Wlk. Bris 50 C1
Nash Cl. Keyn 82 A3
Nash Dr. Bris 50 B4
Nates La. Wring 92 C1
Naunton Way. W-S-M 88 A1
Neath Rd. Bris 64 B4
Nelson Cl. W-S-M 88 C2
Nelson Pl W. Bath 101 F3
Nelson Pl. Bath 102 A4
Nelson Rd. Mang 51 E2
Nelson St. Bris 63 D1
Nelson St. Bris 63 E4
Nelson Terr. Bath 102 A4
Nelson Villas. Bath 101 F3
Nempnett St. But 111 E3
Neston Wlk. Bris 79 F4
Netham Park Ind Est. Bris ... 64 B3
Netham Rd. Bris 64 B4
Netham View Ind Park. Bris 64 B4
Netherways. Cleve 57 D1
Nettlestone Cl. Bris 34 C2
Nettleton Rd. Burt 43 D2
Neva Rd. W-S-M 104 C3
Nevalan Dr. Bris 65 D3
Nevil Rd. Bris 49 F2
Neville Rd. Kingsw 51 F1
New Bldgs. Bris 50 C2
New Bldgs. P St J 133 D4
New Bond St. Bath 102 A3
New Bond Street Pl. Bath .. 102 A3
New Bristol Rd. W-S-M 88 C1
New Brunswick Ave. Bris 65 D4
New Charlotte St. Bris 63 E2
New Cheltenham Rd.
        Kingsw 51 F1
New Cut Bow. K Sey 73 D3
New Fosseway Rd. Bris 80 A3
New John St. Bris 63 E2
New King St. Bath 101 F3
New Kingsley Rd. Bris 63 F3
New La. Alve 15 E3
New Leaze St. Gif 24 B2
New Orchard St. Bath 102 A3
New Queen St. Bris 63 F2
New Queen St. Bris 65 D4

Noble Ave. Kingsw

New Rd. Bathf 86 B1
New Rd. Bris 36 A2
New Rd. Bris 36 B2
New Rd. Chur 108 C2
New Rd. E in G 47 E2
New Rd. Farm 115 E2
New Rd. Hi Cha 120 A3
New Rd. Kilm 139 E2
New Rd. N Nib 5 F2
New Rd. Olve 14 A1
New Rd. Paul 115 E2
New Rd. Pens 97 E2
New Rd. Ship 108 C2
New Rd. Tyth 16 B2
New Rd. W-u-E 11 F3
New Rd. Wickw 27 D4
New Rd. Wring 93 F2
New Rd. Yate 17 E1
New Rock Ind Est. Chil 137 E1
New St. Bath 101 F4
New St. Bris 63 F4
New St. Char 11 D3
New Station Rd. Bris 51 D2
New Thomas St. Bris 63 F3
New Tyning La. Hort 29 E2
New Walls. Bris 63 F2
New Wlk. Kingsw 65 E4
Newark St. Bath 102 A3
Newbolt Cl. W-S-M 105 E4
Newbourne Rd. W-S-M 105 E4
Newbridge Cl. Bris 64 B4
Newbridge Ct. Bath 101 D4
Newbridge Gdns. Bath 101 D4
Newbridge Hill. Bath 101 D4
Newbridge Rd. Bath 101 D4
Newbridge Rd. Bris 64 C3
Newbury Rd. Bris 50 A4
Newchurch Rd. W-S-M 104 B1
Newcombe Dr. Bris 48 B2
Newcombe Rd. Bris 48 C4
Newditch La. Ba Gu 77 E1
Newent Ave. Bris 65 D2
Newfields. Blag 126 B4
Newfoundland Rd. Bris 63 F4
Newfoundland St. Bris 63 F4
Newfoundland Way. Bris 49 F1
Newgate. Bris 63 F4
Newhaven Pl. Portis 44 C2
Newhaven Rd. Portis 44 B2
Newland Dr. Bris 79 D2
Newland Rd. Bris 79 D2
Newland Rd. W-S-M 104 C3
Newland Wlk. Bris 79 D2
Newlands Ave. Fr Cot 38 B4
Newlands Green. Cleve 57 F1
Newlands Hill. Portis 45 E2
Newlands Rd. Keyn 81 E2
Newlands The. Bris 51 D4
Newlyn Ave. Bris 48 B3
Newlyn Way. Yate 27 F1
Newlyn Wlk. Bris 64 A1
Newman Cl. West 39 D2
Newmans La. Tims 116 A1
Newmarket Ave. Bris 63 E4
Newnham Cl. Bris 80 B4
Newnham Pl. Bris 23 F1
Newpit La. Bitt 66 C1
Newport Cl. Cleve 57 E1
Newport Cl. Portis 44 C2
Newport Rd. E in G 47 E3
Newport St. Bris 63 F2
Newquay Rd. Bris 63 F1
Newry Wlk. Bris 63 F1
Newsome Ave. E in G 47 E2
Newton Cl. E Harp 128 C3
Newton Cl. Kingsw 52 A1
Newton Dr. Kingsw 66 A3
Newton Green. Nail 75 E4
Newton Rd. Bath 100 C4
Newton Rd. Kingsw 66 A3
Newton Rd. W-S-M 104 C3
Newton St. Bris 64 A4
Newton's Rd. W-S-M 88 C2
Newtown. Char 11 D3
Niblett Cl. Kingsw 65 F3
Niblett's Hill. Bris 65 D3
Nibley La. Ir Act 26 C2
Nibley Rd. Bris 47 F3
Nichol's Rd. Portis 44 C3
Nicholas La. Bris 65 D3
Nicholas Rd. Bris 50 A1
Nicholas St. Bris 63 F2
Nicholettes. Kingsw 66 B3
Nicholls La. Wint 37 F3
Nigel Park. Bris 47 F4
Nightingale Cl. Fr Cot 38 A3
Nightingale Cl. Thorn 8 B1
Nightingale Cl. W-S-M 88 C1
Nightingale Gdns. Nail 59 E1
Nightingale La. Wint 38 A4
Nightingale Rise. Portis 44 C2
Nightingale Way. Rad 138 A4
Nine Tree Hill. Bris 49 F1
Ninth Ave. Bris 36 A1
Nippors Way. Wins 124 C4
Nithsdale Rd. W-S-M 104 C2
Noble Ave. Kingsw 66 B2

Nomis Park. Cong 91 F1
Nore Gdns. Portis 45 E3
Nore Park Dr. Portis 44 C3
Nore Rd. Portis 45 D3
Norfolk Ave. Bris 49 F1
Norfolk Ave. Bris 63 F4
Norfolk Bldgs. Bath 101 F3
Norfolk Cres. Bath 101 F3
Norfolk Gr. Keyn 81 E2
Norfolk Pl. Bris 63 E2
Norfolk Rd. Portis 45 F2
Norland Rd. Bris 62 C4
Norley Rd. Bris 49 F4
Norman Gr. Bris 51 E1
Norman Rd. Bris 50 A1
Norman Rd. Keyn 82 C2
Norman Rd. Sist 66 A4
Normanby Rd. Bris 50 A1
Normanton Rd. Bris 49 D1
Norrisville Rd. Bris 49 F1
North Croft. Kingsw 66 B2
North Devon Rd. Bris 51 D3
North Down Cl. Ship 125 F4
North Down La. Ship 125 F4
North East Rd. Thorn 8 B1
North End Rd. Yatt 73 F2
North End. Yatt 74 A1
North Gr. E in G 47 E2
North Green St. Bris 62 C3
North Hills Cl. W-S-M 105 D1
North La. Bath 102 B3
North La. Nail 59 D1
North La. W-S-M 104 C4
North Leaze. Lo Ash 62 A1
North Meadows. P St J 133 F4
North Par. Bath 102 A3
North Par. Yate 27 F1
North Parade Bldgs. Bath . 102 A3
North Parade Pas. Bath 102 A3
North Parade Rd. Bath 102 A3
North Pk. Kingsw 51 F1
North Rd. Ban 107 D2
North Rd. Bath 102 B1
North Rd. Bath 102 B3
North Rd. Bris 49 F1
North Rd. Bris 62 B4
North Rd. Bris 63 D2
North Rd. Ir Act 27 D2
North Rd. Lymp 122 B1
North Rd. Mid No 132 A1
North Rd. St Gif 36 C2
North Rd. Thorn 8 B1
North Rd. Tims 116 A1
North Rd. Wint 37 F4
North Rd. Yate 27 D2
North Side Rd. Wring 94 A4
North St. Bris 63 D2
North St. Bris 63 F4
North St. Kingsw 66 B2
North St. Mang 51 F3
North St. N St P 135 F2
North St. Nail 59 D1
North St. W-S-M 104 C4
North St. Wickw 18 A3
North Stoke La. Bitt 83 D4
North View Cl. Bath 101 D3
North View Dr. Ban 107 D1
North View. Bris 49 D2
North View. Kingsw 51 E2
North View. Mang 51 F3
North View. Rad 133 D1
North Way. Bath 101 D3
North Way. Mid No 132 A1
North Wlk. Yate 27 F1
Northampton Bldgs. Bath .. 101 F4
Northampton House. Wrax .. 60 B2
Northampton St. Bath 101 F4
Northavon Bsns Centre.
  Yate 27 E2
Northcote Rd. Bris 48 C1
Northcote Rd. Bris 64 C4
Northcote Rd. Mang 51 F3
Northcote St. Bris 50 A1
Northdown Rd. Paul 132 C3
Northend Ave. Kingsw 51 E1
Northend Gdns. Kingsw 51 E1
Northend Rd. Kingsw 51 F1
Northern Way. Cleve 57 F2
Northfield Ave. Kingsw 65 E3
Northfield Rd. Bris 65 D3
Northfield Rd. Portis 44 C2
Northfield. Mid No 133 D2
Northfield. Tims 116 B2
Northfield. Winsl 120 C4
Northfield. Yate 39 E4
Northfields Cl. Bath 84 C1
Northfields. Bath 84 C1
Northgate St. Bath 102 A3
Northleach Wlk. Bris 47 F3
Northleigh Ave. W-S-M 88 B1
Northmead Ave. Mid No .. 131 F1
Northmead Cl. Mid No .. 131 F1
Northmead La. Ir Act 26 B3
Northmead Rd. Mid No .. 131 F1
Northover Rd. Bris 35 D1
Northridge Bsns Centre.
  Yate 27 E1

Northumberland Pl. Bath ... 102 A3
Northumberland Rd. Bris ... 49 E1
Northumbria Dr. Bris 49 D3
Northville Rd. Bris 36 A1
Northway. Bris 36 A2
Northwick Gdns. Bi Sut 113 E2
Northwick Rd. Bris 49 F4
Northwick Rd. Ch Mag 96 B4
Northwick Rd. Piln 22 B4
Northwick Rd. Whit 96 B4
Northwoods Wlk. Bris 35 E2
Norton Cl. Ch Mag 96 A2
Norton Cl. Kingsw 65 F4
Norton La. Ch Mag 96 B3
Norton La. Hin Cha 135 E4
Norton La. W St L 88 B2
Norton La. Well 135 E4
Norton La. Whit 80 B1
Norton La. Whit 96 B3
Norton Rd. Bris 64 C2
Nortons Wood La. Cleve 58 A3
Norwich Dr. Bris 64 C3
Norwood Ave. Bath 102 C3
Norwood Gr. Portis 44 C3
Notgrove Cl. W-S-M 88 A1
Nottingham Rd. Bris 49 F2
Nottingham St. Bris 63 F2
Nova Scotia Pl. Bris 63 D3
Novers Cres. Bris 79 E4
Novers Hill Trading Est. Bris 63 E4
Novers Hill. Bris 79 E4
Novers La. Bris 79 E4
Novers Park Dr. Bris 79 E4
Novers Park Rd. Bris 79 E4
Novers Rd. Bris 79 E4
Nugent Hill. Bris 49 E1
Nunney Cl. Keyn 82 A1
Nupdown Rd. O-0n-S 1 C3
Nupdown Rd. Rock 2 A2
Nursery Gdns. Bris 35 D2
Nursery The. Bris 63 D2
Nutfield Gr. Bris 36 A1
Nutgrove Ave. Bris 63 F2
Nutgrove La. Ch Mag 96 A2
Nuthatch Dr. Bris 50 C3
Nutwell Rd. W-S-M 88 C1
Nutwell Sq. W-S-M 88 C1
Nye Rd. Winsc 107 F3
Nympsfield. Kingsw 51 F1

Oak Ave. Bath 101 E2
Oak Cl. St Gif 36 B4
Oak Cl. Yate 27 E2
Oak Dr. Portis 45 D2
Oak Gr. E in G 47 E3
Oak La. Bris 50 C1
Oak Rd. Bris 49 F3
Oak Rd. Col 70 C3
Oak Rd. Wins 125 D4
Oak St. Bath 101 F3
Oak Terr. Rad 132 B1
Oak Tree Ave. Puck 53 D2
Oak Tree Cl. Kingsw 65 E2
Oak Tree Wlk. Keyn 81 E2
Oakdale Ave. Mang 51 E4
Oakdale Cl. Mang 51 F4
Oakdale Ct. Mang 51 F4
Oakdale Gdns. W-S-M 88 C1
Oakdale Rd. Bris 80 A4
Oakdale Rd. Mang 51 F4
Oakdene Ave. Bris 50 B2
Oakenhill Wlk. Bris 64 C1
Oakes La. Tor 42 A3
Oakfield Dr. Bris 63 D4
Oakfield Pl. Bris 63 D4
Oakfield Rd. Bath 101 E4
Oakfield Rd. Bris 63 D4
Oakfield Rd. Keyn 81 D3
Oakfield Rd. Kingsw 65 E4
Oakford Ave. W-S-M 104 C4
Oakford La. Marsh 70 A1
Oakhanger Dr. Bris 34 A1
Oakhill Ave. Kingsw 66 B1
Oakhill Cl. Nail 60 A1
Oakhill Rd. Bath 101 F1
Oakhill. Bris 34 B2
Oakhill. W-S-M 105 D1
Oakhurst Rd. Bris 48 C3
Oakland Dr. Lock 105 F2
Oakland Rd. Bris 49 D1
Oakland Rd. Bris 64 C4
Oaklands Cl. Mang 52 A3
Oaklands Dr. Alm 24 A2
Oaklands Dr. Bris 51 D4
Oaklands Dr. Kingsw 66 B1
Oaklands Rd. Mang 52 A3
Oaklands. Clut 114 C1
Oaklands. Paul 131 F2
Oakleaze Rd. Thorn 8 B1
Oakleaze. Fr Cot 38 B4
Oakleigh Ave. Bris 64 B4
Oakleigh Cl. Back 76 A3
Oakleigh Gdns. Kingsw 66 B1
Oakley Rd. Bris 49 F4
Oakley. Bath 102 C3
Oakley. Cleve 73 D4
Oakmead Pk. Bris 64 A1
Oakridge Cl. Kingsw 66 A4

Oakridge Cl. Wins 125 D4
Oakridge La. Wins 125 D4
Oaks The. Win 94 C4
Oaksey Gr. Nail 60 A1
Oaktree Cres. St Gif 24 B1
Oaktree Ct. Bris 47 F4
Oaktree Gdns. Bris 78 C3
Oakwood Ave. Bris 49 D3
Oakwood Rd. Bris 49 D3
Oatlands Ave. Bris 80 A3
Oberon Ave. Bris 50 C1
Oclite Rd. Bath 101 E1
Odins Rd. Bath 101 E1
Okebourne Cl. Bris 35 D2
Okebourne Rd. Bris 35 D2
Old Ashley Hill. Bris 49 F1
Old Banwell Rd. Lock 106 A2
Old Barn La. But 94 A3
Old Barrow Hill. Bris 47 E4
Old Bond St. Bath 101 F3
Old Bread St. Bris 63 F3
Old Bristol Rd. Priddy 128 A2
Old Bristol Rd. W-S-M 89 D1
Old Chelsea La. Wrax 61 E2
Old Church Rd. Axb 125 E1
Old Church Rd. Cleve 57 E2
Old Church Rd. Nail 75 E4
Old Church Rd. W-S-M 104 B1
Old Coach Rd. Co Bi 124 C2
Old Down Rd. Ch Sod 42 B4
Old Down Rd. Gr Bad 30 C1
Old England Way. P St J ... 133 F4
Old Farm La. Bris 65 D3
Old Ferry Rd. Bath 101 E3
Old Fosse Rd. Bath 101 E1
Old Fosse Way. Mid No 132 C3
Old Frome Rd. Bath 118 C4
Old Gloucester Rd. Alve 15 D3
Old Gloucester Rd. Alve 25 E2
Old Gloucester Rd. Bris 37 D1
Old Gloucester Rd. Fr Cot .. 25 E2
Old Gloucester Rd. St Gif .. 37 D2
Old Gloucester Rd. St Gif .. 37 D3
Old Gloucester Rd. Thorn 9 D1
Old Gloucester Rd. Wint 37 D4
Old Hill. Win 94 B3
Old Hill. Wring 92 C2
Old King St Ct. Bris 63 F4
Old King St. Bath 101 F4
Old La. Farm 116 A3
Old La. Nail 59 E3
Old Manor Cl. Char 11 D3
Old Market St. Bris 63 F4
Old Midford Rd. Sosto 119 D4
Old Mill Rd. Portis 45 E3
Old Millard's Hill. Mid No . 132 A2
Old Mills Ind Est. Paul 131 F1
Old Mills La. Paul 131 E2
Old Newbridge Hill. Bath .. 101 D4
Old Orchard St. Bath 102 A3
Old Orchard. Bath 102 A4
Old Park Hill. Bris 63 E4
Old Park Rd. Bris 47 E4
Old Park Rd. Cleve 57 F2
Old Park. Bris 63 E4
Old Pit Terr. Mid No 132 C2
Old Post Office La. W-S-M 104 B4
Old Priory Rd. E in G 47 D2
Old Quarry Rd. Bris 47 F4
Old Quarry Rise. Bris 47 F4
Old Quarry. Bath 101 E1
Old Rd. Rad 133 E1
Old Rectory Rd. Kings 11 F2
Old School La. Blea 122 B3
Old Sneed Ave. Bris 48 B2
Old Sneed Park. Bris 48 B2
Old Sneed Rd. Bris 48 B2
Old St. Cleve 57 F2
Old Station Cl. Wring 92 B1
Old Tarnwell. Pens 97 D1
Old Track. Li St 119 F4
Old Vicarage Green. Keyn .. 81 F3
Old Wall. Blea 121 E3
Old Water Gdns The. Blag 110 C1
Old Wells Rd. Bath 101 F2
Old Weston Rd. Back 77 D4
Old Weston Rd. Cong 91 D3
Oldacre Rd. Bris 80 A2
Oldbridge Rd. Whit 80 B2
Oldbury Chase. Kingsw 66 A1
Oldbury Court Dr. Bris 51 D3
Oldbury Court Rd. Bris 51 D3
Oldbury La. Thorn 8 A2
Oldbury La. Wick 67 E3
Oldfield La. Bath 101 F2
Oldfield Pl. Bris 62 C3
Oldfield Rd. Bath 101 F3
Oldfield Rd. Bris 62 C3
Oldfield Rd. Bris 63 D3
Oldfield. Cleve 57 F1
Oldfields La. Alve 25 E4
Oldlands Ave. Fr Cot 38 B3
Oldmead Wlk. Bris 78 C4
Oldmixon Cres. W-S-M 105 D2
Oldmixon Rd. W-S-M 105 D1
Oldmixon Rd. W-S-M 105 D1
Oldown Hill. Olve 14 B1

Oldville Ave. Cleve 57 E1
Olive Gdns. Alve 14 C2
Olveston Rd. Bris 49 F3
Olympus Cl. St Gif 36 B3
Olympus Rd. Bris 35 E4
Oolite Gr. Bath 118 B4
Oram Ct. Kingsw 65 F2
Orange Gr. Bath 102 A3
Orange St. Bris 63 F4
Orchard Ave. Bris 63 E3
Orchard Ave. Mid No 131 F1
Orchard Ave. Nail 58 C2
Orchard Ave. Thorn 8 B1
Orchard Bvd. Kingsw 66 A2
Orchard Cl. Back 77 D4
Orchard Cl. Ban 107 D2
Orchard Cl. Bi Sut 113 E2
Orchard Cl. Bris 48 C3
Orchard Cl. Char 11 D3
Orchard Cl. Keyn 81 E3
Orchard Cl. Kingsw 65 F4
Orchard Cl. Portis 45 E3
Orchard Cl. W-S-M 88 A2
Orchard Cl. W-S-M 88 C1
Orchard Cl. Westw 120 C2
Orchard Cl. Win 94 B4
Orchard Cl. Wring 92 C1
Orchard Cl. Yate 27 F1
Orchard Cres. Bris 47 E4
Orchard Dr. Aust 13 D4
Orchard Dr. Bris 79 D3
Orchard Dr. Wins 108 A2
Orchard End. E Harp 128 C2
Orchard Gdns. Kingsw 65 F4
Orchard Grange. Thorn 8 A1
Orchard La. Bris 63 E3
Orchard Lea. Alve 15 D3
Orchard Lea. E in G 47 E2
Orchard Pl. W-S-M 104 C4
Orchard Rd. Axb 125 E1
Orchard Rd. Back 76 A3
Orchard Rd. Bris 49 F2
Orchard Rd. Bris 64 C4
Orchard Rd. Cleve 57 E1
Orchard Rd. Fr Cot 38 B4
Orchard Rd. Kingsw 65 F4
Orchard Rd. Lo Ash 61 F1
Orchard Rd. Lock 105 E1
Orchard Rd. Nail 59 E1
Orchard Rd. Paul 131 F3
Orchard Rd. Puck 53 D3
Orchard Rise. Olve 14 A2
Orchard St. Bris 63 E3
Orchard St. W-S-M 104 C4
Orchard Terr. Bath 101 D3
Orchard The. Ban 107 D2
Orchard The. E in G 47 E2
Orchard The. Fr Cot 38 B4
Orchard The. Hi Cha 120 B3
Orchard The. Lock 106 A3
Orchard The. Pens 97 D1
Orchard The. Pens 97 E2
Orchard The. St Gif 36 C3
Orchard The. Tyth 16 A3
Orchard Vale. Kingsw 65 F4
Orchard Vale. Mid No 131 F1
Orchard Wlk. Chur 108 C2
Orchard Wlk. Kings 11 F2
Orchards The. Kingsw 65 F4
Oriel Gdns. Bath 85 E1
Oriel Gr. Bath 101 D2
Orion Dr. St Gif 36 B3
Orland Way. Kingsw 66 A2
Orlebar Gdns. Bris 34 A1
Orme Dr. Cleve 57 E3
Ormerod Rd. Bris 48 C3
Ormonds Cl. St Gif 24 C1
Ormsley Cl. St Gif 36 B4
Orpen Gdns. Bris 50 A3
Orpen Park. St Gif 24 B2
Orpheus Ave. St Gif 36 B3
Orwell Dr. Keyn 81 F2
Orwell St. Bris 63 F2
Osborne Ave. Bris 49 F2
Osborne Ave. W-S-M 104 C4
Osborne Cl. St Gif 36 B2
Osborne Rd. Bath 101 D3
Osborne Rd. Bris 49 D1
Osborne Rd. Bris 63 E2
Osborne Rd. Piln 22 A4
Osborne Rd. W-S-M 104 C4
Osborne Terr. Bris 63 D1
Osborne Villas. Bris 63 E4
Oslings La. Bathf 86 A1
Osprey Ct. Bris 79 E3
Osprey Gdns. W-S-M 88 C1
Osprey Pk. Thorn 8 B2
Osprey Rd. Bris 64 B4
Ottawa Rd. W-S-M 104 C2
Otter Rd. Cleve 57 F1
Otterford Cl. Bris 80 A3
Ottery Cl. Bris 34 A1
Ottrells Mead. St Gif 24 B2
Oval The. Bath 101 D2
Over La. Alm 23 F1
Overdale. Mid No 132 C3
Overdale. Tims 116 C2
Overhill. E in G 47 E2

Overndale Rd. Mang 51 E3
Overnhill Ct. Mang 51 E3
Overnhill Rd. Mang 51 E3
Overnhurst Ct. Mang 51 E3
Overton Rd. Bris 49 F1
Owen Dr. Wrax 61 D2
Owen Gr. Bris 49 D3
Owen St. Bris 64 A4
Owls Head Rd. Kingsw 65 F4
Oxbarton. St Gif 36 C3
Oxen Leaze. St Gif 24 C1
Oxford Pl 102
Oxford Pl. Bris 50 A1
Oxford Pl. Bris 62 C3
Oxford Pl. W-S-M 104 B4
Oxford St. Bris 63 E4
Oxford St. Bris 63 F2
Oxford St. Bris 64 A3
Oxford St. Bris 64 C3
Oxford St. W-S-M 104 B4
Oxhouse La. Win 94 B3
Oxhouse La. Wrax 61 D3
Oxlease. Bris 79 E4
Oxleaze La. Bris 78 C2
Ozleworth. Kingsw 51 F1

Pack Horse La. Sosto 119 D4
Paddock Cl. St Gif 24 B1
Paddock Gdn. Bris 79 F2
Paddock Gdns. Alve 15 D3
Paddock The. Ban 107 D2
Paddock The. Cleve 57 E1
Paddock The. Portis 45 E2
Paddock Woods. Bath 102 B3
Paddocks The. Bath 102 A1
Paddocks The. Chur 108 B2
Paddocks The. Thorn 8 B1
Paddocks The. W-S-M 104 B1
Padfield Cl. Bath 101 D3
Padleigh Hill. Bath 101 D1
Padmore Ct. Bris 64 B4
Padstow Rd. Bris 79 F4
Pagans Hill. Ch Mag 95 E1
Pagans Hill. Ch St 95 E1
Page Rd. Kingsw 51 E2
Page's Ct. Yatt 91 E4
Pages Mead. Avon 47 E4
Painswick Ave. St Gif 36 A4
Painswick Dr. Yate 27 F1
Palace Yd Mews. Bath 101 F3
Palmdale Cl. Kingsw 66 A2
Palmer Row. W-S-M 104 C4
Palmer St. W-S-M 104 C4
Palmers Cl. Kingsw 66 B3
Palmers Leaze. St Gif 37 D4
Palmers Way. Lock 105 E1
Palmerston Rd. Bris 49 E2
Palmerston St. Bris 63 D1
Palmyra Rd. Bris 63 D1
Par The. Bath 101 D3
Parade The. Bris 23 F1
Parade The. Bris 47 F3
Parade The. Ch Sod 28 A1
Paradise Row. Pens 98 A3
Paragon The. Bris 62 C3
Paragon The. Bris 87 E1
Parfitt's Hill. Bris 64 C3
Park Ave. Bath 101 F3
Park Ave. Bris 50 B2
Park Ave. Bris 63 F2
Park Ave. Bris 64 C4
Park Ave. Fr Cot 38 B4
Park Ave. St Gif 24 A1
Park Ave. Wint 37 F4
Park Ave. Yatt 74 A1
Park Batch. Blag 110 C2
Park Cl. Keyn 81 E3
Park Cl. Kingsw 65 F4
Park Cl. Kingsw 66 A4
Park Cres. Bris 37 E1
Park Cres. Bris 64 B4
Park Cres. Kingsw 66 A3
Park Farm Ct. Kingsw 65 F2
Park Gdns. Bath 101 E4
Park Gr. Bris 49 E3
Park Hill. Bris 47 F3
Park La. Bath 101 E4
Park La. Blag 110 C2
Park La. Bris 63 E3
Park La. Faulk 134 A1
Park La. Fr Cot 38 A3
Park La. N Nib 5 F4
Park Pl. Bath 101 F4
Park Pl. Bris 50 C2
Park Pl. Bris 63 D4
Park Pl. W-S-M 104 B4
Park Rd. Bath 101 D4
Park Rd. Bris 36 A1
Park Rd. Bris 47 F3
Park Rd. Bris 63 D3
Park Rd. Cleve 57 F2
Park Rd. Cong 91 F2
Park Rd. Crom 10 A2
Park Rd. Keyn 81 F2
Park Rd. Kingsw 65 E4
Park Rd. Kingsw 66 A3
Park Rd. Mang 51 F3

Park Rd. Paul 131 E3
Park Rd. Thorn 8 A1
Park Row. Bris 63 E4
Park Row. Fr Cot 38 A4
Park St Ave. Bris 63 E4
Park St Mews. Bath 101 F4
Park St. Bath 101 F4
Park St. Bris 63 E4
Park St. Bris 64 A2
Park St. Bris 64 C4
Park St. H Up 20 A1
Park St. Ir Act 26 B2
Park The. Bitt 66 A1
Park The. Bris 37 D1
Park The. Keyn 81 F3
Park The. Kingsw 65 F4
Park The. St Gif 24 B2
Park The. Yatt 74 A1
Park View Ave. Thorn 8 B1
Park View Terr. Bris 64 C4
Park View. Kingsw 65 F4
Park View. Paul 131 E3
Park Way. Kingsw 66 A3
Park Way. Mid No 138 A4
Park Wood Cl. Bris 79 F2
Parker Cl. Bris 63 D2
Parkers Ave. Wick 67 E4
Parkers Barton. Bris 64 A3
Parkers Cl. Bris 35 E2
Parkfield Ave. Bris 64 B4
Parkfield Gdns. Bi Sut 113 E2
Parkfield Rd. Axb 125 E1
Parkfield Rd. Puck 53 D3
Parkhouse La. Keyn 81 E1
Parkhurst Ave. Bris 51 D2
Parkhurst Rd. W-S-M 105 D4
Parkland Way. Thorn 8 B2
Parklands Ave. W-S-M 88 C2
Parklands Rd. Bris 62 C2
Parklands. Kingsw 65 F4
Parklands. Paul 115 E1
Parkside Ave. Wint 37 F3
Parkside Gdns. Bris 50 A2
Parkstone Ave. Bris 49 F3
Parkwall Cres. Kingsw 66 A2
Parkwall Rd. Kingsw 66 A3
Parkway La. Tims 116 B2
Parkway. Tims 116 C1
Parliament St. Bris 64 A2
Parnall Cres. Yate 27 E2
Parnall Rd. Bris 51 D2
Parry Cl. Bath 101 D2
Parry's Cl. Bris 48 C3
Parry's La. Bris 48 C3
Parslow Barton. Bris 65 D4
Parson St. Bris 63 E1
Parsonage Cl. Win 94 C3
Parsonage La. Bath 101 F3
Parsonage La. Ched 125 F1
Parsonage La. Chil 137 E2
Parsonage La. Pens 97 E3
Parsonage La. Win 94 C3
Parsonage Rd. Lo Ash 62 B1
Parsons Ave. St Gif 36 C3
Parsons Gn. Cleve 73 E4
Parsons Green. W-S-M 89 D2
Parsons Mead. Back 76 C4
Parsons Paddock. Bris 80 A4
Parsons Way. Wins 124 B3
Partis College. Bath 101 D4
Partis Way. Bath 101 D4
Partition St. Bris 63 E3
Partridge Cl. W-S-M 88 C1
Partridge Cl. Yate 27 F2
Partridge Rd. Puck 53 E2
Passage Leaze. Bris 47 E3
Passage Rd. Bris 35 D1
Passage Rd. Bris 35 D2
Passage Rd. Bris 35 D3
Passage St. Bris 63 F3
Pastures The. Westw 120 C2
Patch Croft. Cleve 73 E4
Patch Elm La. Wickw 26 C4
Patch La. Wickw 27 D4
Patchway Trading Est. Bris 35 F4
Paul St. Bris 63 E4
Paulman Gdns. Lo Ash 77 F4
Paulto' Hill. Paul 132 A3
Paulton Dr. Bris 49 E2
Paulton La. Tims 132 B4
Paulton Rd. Mid No 131 F1
Paulton Rd. Paul 131 D4
Paulton Rd. Paul 131 E3
Paultow Ave. Bris 63 F2
Paultow Rd. Bris 63 F2
Paulwood Rd. Clut 114 C1
Pavey Cl. Bris 79 E2
Pavey Rd. Bris 79 E2
Pawlett Rd. Bris 79 E2
Pawlett Wlk. Bris 79 E2
Pawlett. W-S-M 105 D1
Paybridge Rd. Bris 78 C2
Payne Dr. Bris 64 A4
Payne Rd. Lock 105 E1
Peach Rd. Mang 51 F3
Peacock La. Kingsw 65 E4

Pear Tree Hey. Yate 27 F3
Pear Tree Rd. St Gif 24 B2
Pearces Hill. Bris 51 D4
Pearl St. Bris 63 D2
Pearsall Rd. Kingsw 65 F1
Pearse Cl. W-S-M 89 D3
Peart Cl. Bris 78 C3
Peart Dr. Bris 78 C2
Peartree La. Bris 65 D3
Peartree La. Kingsw 51 F1
Pedder Rd. Cleve 57 E1
Peel St. Bris 63 F4
Pegasus Rd. Bris 35 E4
Pelican Cl. W-S-M 105 F4
Pemberton Ct. Bris 51 E3
Pembery Rd. Bris 63 D2
Pembroke Ave. Bris 47 F3
Pembroke Gr. Bris 63 D4
Pembroke Pl. Bris 63 D3
Pembroke Rd. Bris 47 F3
Pembroke Rd. Bris 63 D4
Pembroke Rd. Bris 63 E2
Pembroke Rd. Kingsw 51 F1
Pembroke Rd. Portis 44 C2
Pembroke Rd. W-S-M 104 C2
Pembroke St. Bris 63 F4
Pembroke Vale. Bris 63 D4
Pen Park Rd. Bris 35 E1
Penard Way. Kingsw 65 F4
Penarth Dr. W-S-M 105 D1
Pendennis Ave. Mang 51 E2
Pendennis Pk. Bris 64 B1
Pendennis Rd. Mang 51 E3
Pendlesham Gdns. W-S-M 88 A1
Pendock Cl. Kingsw 66 B1
Pendock Rd. Wint 37 F3
Penfield Rd. Bris 50 A1
Penlea Ct. Bris 47 E4
Penn Gdns. Bath 101 D4
Penn Hill Rd. Bath 84 A1
Penn Lea Rd. Bath 84 A1
Penn Lea Rd. Bath 101 D4
Penn St. Bris 63 F4
Penn Way. Axb 125 E1
Pennard Ct. Bris 80 A3
Pennard Green. Bath 101 D3
Pennard. W-S-M 105 D1
Penngrove. Kingsw 66 A2
Pennine Gdns. W-S-M 88 A1
Pennine Rd. Kingsw 66 B2
Pennlea. Bris 79 E4
Penns The. Cleve 57 F1
Pennycress. W-S-M 105 E4
Pennyquick View. Bath 100 C3
Pennyquick. Cor 100 B3
Pennyroyal Gr. Bris 50 C2
Pennywell Rd. Bris 64 A4
Penpole Ave. Bris 47 F3
Penpole Cl. Bris 47 E4
Penpole La. Bris 47 F4
Penpole Pl. Bris 47 F3
Penrice Cl. W-S-M 88 B1
Penrith Gdns. Bris 49 E4
Penrose. Bris 79 F4
Pensfield Park. Bris 35 E2
Pensford Ct. Bris 80 B3
Pensford Hill. Pens 97 E3
Pensford La. Pens 97 D1
Pensford Old Rd. Pens 97 F2
Pentagon The. Bris 48 A3
Pentire Ave. Bris 79 D4
Pentland Ave. Thorn 15 F4
Peppershells La. Co Dan 98 B3
Pepys Cl. Keyn 82 B1
Pera Pl. Bath 102 A4
Pera Rd. Bath 102 A4
Percival Rd. Bris 62 C4
Percy St. Bris 63 E2
Peregrine Cl. W-S-M 88 C1
Perrin Cl. Clut 130 C4
Perrings The. Nail 75 F4
Perrinpit Rd. Fr Cot 25 F1
Perrott Rd. Kingsw 52 A1
Perry Cl. Wint 37 E3
Perry Rd. Bris 63 E4
Perry St. Bris 64 A4
Perrycroft Ave. Bris 79 D3
Perrycroft Rd. Bris 79 D3
Perrymans Cl. Bris 51 D3
Perrymead. Bath 102 A2
Perrymead. W-S-M 89 D3
Perrys Lea. St Gif 24 B1
Pesley Cl. Bris 79 D2
Peter's Terr. Bris 64 A4
Petercole Dr. Bris 79 D3
Peterside. Clut 130 C4
Peterson Sq. Bris 79 E2
Petersway Gdns. Bris 65 D3
Petherton Cl. Kingsw 65 F4
Petherton Gdns. Bris 80 A4
Petherton Rd. Bris 80 A4
Peto Gr. Westw 120 C2
Pettigrove Gdns. Kingsw 65 F4
Pettigrove Rd. Kingsw 65 F4
Pevensey Wlk. Bris 79 E4
Peverell Cl. Bris 34 C2
Peverell Dr. Bris 34 C2

Philadelphia Ct. Bris 63 F4
Philip St. Bris 63 E2
Philip St. Bris 64 A3
Philippa Cl. Bris 80 A4
Phillips Rd. W-S-M 105 D3
Phillis Hill. Paul 131 F2
Phippen St. Bris 63 F3
Phipps St. Bris 63 D2
Phoenix Gr. Bris 49 E3
Piccadilly Pl. Bath 102 A4
Pickedmoor La. O-on-S 7 E3
Pickwick Rd. Bath 85 D1
Picton La. Bris 49 F1
Picton St. Bris 49 F1
Pier Rd. Portis 45 F4
Pierrepont Pl. Bath 102 A3
Pierrepont St. Bath 102 A3
Pigeon La. Wring 93 F1
Pigott Ave. Bris 79 D2
Pilgrims Way. Avon 47 E4
Pilgrims Way. Ch St 112 B4
Pilgrims Way. Mang 51 E4
Pilgrims Way. W-S-M 88 C2
Pilgrims Wharf. Bris 64 C4
Pilkington Cl. Bris 36 B1
Pill Rd. Ab Lei 47 F1
Pill St. E in G 47 E2
Pill Way. Cleve 57 D1
Pillingers Rd. Kingsw 65 E4
Pilning St. Piln 23 E4
Pimm's La. W-S-M 88 A1
Pinchay La. Win 95 D2
Pinckney Green. Mon Far 103 F3
Pincots La. Wickw 18 A2
Pine Cl. Thorn 8 B1
Pine Cl. W-S-M 88 B1
Pine Cl. Ch Mag 96 A2
Pine Ct. Keyn 81 E2
Pine Ct. Rad 133 D1
Pine Gr. Bris 36 A1
Pine Grove Pl. Bris 49 E2
Pine Hill. W-S-M 88 B1
Pine Lea. Blea 122 A4
Pine Rd. Bris 35 D2
Pine Ridge Cl. Bris 48 B2
Pine Wlk. Rad 132 C1
Pinecroft. Bris 79 F4
Pinecroft. Portis 44 C3
Pines Cl. Chil 137 E2
Pines La. Olve 14 B2
Pines Rd. Kingsw 66 B1
Pines Way. Bath 101 F3
Pines Way. Rad 133 D1
Pinewood Ave. Mid No 131 F1
Pinewood Cl. Bris 49 D4
Pinewood Gr. Mid No 131 F1
Pinewood Rd. Mid No 131 F1
Pinewood Way. Col 70 C4
Pinewood. Kingsw 51 F1
Pinhay Rd. Bris 79 D3
Pinkhams Twist. Bris 80 A3
Pioneer Ave. Bath 101 F1
Pipe La. Bris 63 E3
Pipe La. Bris 63 E3
Pipehouse La. Hi Cha 120 A2
Pipehouse La. Hin Cha 119 F2
Piper Rd. Yate 27 F2
Pippin Cl. P St J 133 E4
Pippin Cl. Kingsw 65 F2
Pit La. Back 76 A2
Pit La. Win 111 F3
Pit Rd. Mid No 132 A1
Pitch And Pay La. Bris 48 C2
Pitch And Pay Park. Bris 48 C2
Pitch La. Bris 49 E1
Pitchcombe Gdns. Bris 48 B4
Pitchcombe. Yate 39 E4
Pitcot La. Hol 138 A1
Pithay Ct. Bris 63 E4
Pithay The. Bris 63 E4
Pithay The. Paul 131 F3
Pitman Ct. Bath 85 E1
Pitman Rd. W-S-M 104 C3
Pitt Rd. Bris 49 F3
Pittville Cl. Thorn 8 B2
Pitville Pl. Bris 63 D1
Pitway Cl. Paul 130 C2
Pitway La. Paul 130 B2
Pixash Bsns Centre. Keyn 82 A3
Pixash La. Keyn 82 A3
Pizey Ave. Cleve 57 D1
Pizey Cl. Cleve 57 D1
Plain The. N St P 135 F2
Plain The. Thorn 8 A1
Players St. St Gif 37 D2
Playford Gdns. Bris 47 F4
Pleasant Pl. Bathf 86 B1
Pleasant Rd. Mang 51 E3
Pleshey Cl. W-S-M 88 B1
Ploughed Paddock. Nail 59 E1
Plover Cl. W-S-M 88 C1
Plover Cl. Yate 27 E1
Plovers Rise. Mid No 133 D2
Plumbers Hill. Bris 64 C4
Plumers Cl. Cleve 57 F1
Plumpton Ct. Mang 37 F1
Plumptre Cl. Paul 131 F3
Plumptre Rd. Paul 131 F3

Plumtree Cl. Wins 108 A1
Plunder St. Brock 92 A4
Podium The. Bath 102 A3
Poets Cnr. Rad 132 B1
Poets' Cl. Bris 64 B4
Polden Cl. Nail 59 F1
Polden Rd. Portis 45 D3
Polden Rd. W-S-M 104 C4
Police Station Hill. Puck 53 D2
Polly Barnes Cl. Kingsw 65 D3
Polly Barnes Hill. Kingsw 65 D3
Polygon Rd. Bris 63 D3
Polygon The. Bris 62 C3
Pomfret House. Bris 79 E2
Pomfret Gdns. Bris 80 C3
Pomphrey Hill. Mang 52 A2
Ponsford Rd. Bris 80 A4
Ponting Cl. Bris 51 D1
Pool La. Win 95 D1
Pool Rd. Kingsw 51 F2
Poole Court Dr. Yate 27 F1
Poole St. Avon 47 D4
Poolemead Rd. Bath 100 C3
Poor Hill. Farm 115 F3
Pope's Wlk. Bath 102 A2
Poplar Ave. Bris 48 B3
Poplar Cl. Bath 101 E2
Poplar Cl. Kingsw 66 B3
Poplar Dr. Puck 53 D3
Poplar La. Wickw 18 A2
Poplar Pl. Bris 51 D2
Poplar Pl. W-S-M 104 C4
Poplar Rd. Bris 36 C1
Poplar Rd. Bris 65 D3
Poplar Rd. Bris 78 C4
Poplar Rd. Kingsw 66 B3
Poplar Way. Col 70 C3
Poplar Wlk. Lock 105 F3
Poplars The. E in G 47 D2
Poplars The. W-S-M 89 D1
Pople's La. Kilm 139 F1
Popular Terr. Kingsw 65 F4
Porlock Cl. Cleve 57 F1
Porlock Cl. W-S-M 104 C1
Porlock Gdns. Nail 59 F1
Porlock Rd. Bath 102 A1
Porlock Rd. Bris 63 E2
Port Elizabeth House. Bris 35 D1
Port View. E in G 47 E3
Portbury Comm. Portis 45 F2
Portbury Gr. Bris 47 E3
Portbury Hundred The.
  Portb 46 B2
Portbury La. Wrax 60 C3
Portbury Way. Portb 46 C3
Portbury Wlk. Bris 47 E3
Portishead Rd. W-S-M 89 D2
Portishead Way. Bris 62 C2
Portland Cl. Nail 59 E1
Portland Ct. Bris 63 D3
Portland Dr. Portis 45 F2
Portland Pl. Bath 101 F4
Portland Pl. Kingsw 51 E2
Portland Sq. Bris 63 F4
Portland St. Bris 62 C4
Portland St. Bris 63 E4
Portland St. Kingsw 51 E2
Portmeade Dro. Axb 125 E1
Portmeirion Cl. Bris 80 A3
Portview Rd. Avon 47 D4
Portwall La E. Bris 63 F3
Portwall La. Bris 63 F3
Portway La. Ch Sod 29 D1
Portway. Bris 48 B2
Post Office La. Back 76 C4
Post Office La. Blag 110 B2
Poston Way. Winsl 120 C4
Pottery Cl. W-S-M 105 D3
Potts Cl. Bathe 85 F2
Pound Dr. Bris 50 C3
Pound La. Bris 50 C2
Pound La. Nail 59 E2
Pound Mead. Win 94 B4
Pound Rd. Kingsw 51 F1
Pound The. Alm 24 A3
Pound The. O-on-S 7 D2
Pound The. Wring 93 E2
Pountney Dr. Bris 64 A4
Pow's Hill. Paul 132 B3
Pow's Orch. Mid No 132 A1
Pow's Rd. Kingsw 65 E4
Powis Cl. W-S-M 88 B1
Powlett Rd. Bath 102 A4
Poyntz Ct. Bris 79 F4
Poyntz Rd. Bris 79 F2
Pratten's La. Mang 51 E2
Preanes Green. W-S-M 89 D1
Preddy's La. Bris 65 D3
Prescot Cl. W-S-M 88 A1
Prescott. Yate 39 E4
Press Moor Dr. Kingsw 65 F2
Prestbury. Yate 39 E4
Preston Wlk. Bris 64 A1
Prestwick Cl. Bris 64 B1
Pretoria Rd. Bris 35 F4
Prewett St. Bris 63 F3
Priddy Cl. Bath 101 D2
Priddy Ct. Bris 80 A3

Priddy Dr Bris 80 A3
Priests Way. W-S-M 88 B1
Priestwood Cl. Bris 35 D2
Primrose Cl. Bris 65 E4
Primrose Cl. St Gif 24 B1
Primrose Dr. Thorn 8 B1
Primrose Hill. Bath 84 B1
Primrose La. Bris 51 E1
Primrose La. Mid No 132 A1
Primrose Terr. Bris 65 E3
Prince St. Bris 63 E3
Prince's Pl. Bris 49 E2
Prince's Rd. Cleve 57 E2
Prince's St. Bris 63 F4
Prince's St. Mid No 132 C3
Princes Ct. Kingsw 65 F2
Princes St. Bath 101 F3
Princes' La. Bris 62 C3
Princess Cl. Keyn 81 F2
Princess Gdns. Bris 50 B3
Princess Row. Bris 63 F4
Princess St. Bris 63 F2
Princess St. Bris 64 A4
Princess Victoria St. Bris 62 C4
Priors Hill. Tims 116 A1
Priors Lea. Yate 27 E2
Priory Ave. Bris 49 D4
Priory Cl. Bath 102 A1
Priory Cl. Mid No 132 A1
Priory Court Rd. Bris 49 D4
Priory Ct. Kingsw 65 E2
Priory Dene. Bris 49 D4
Priory Gdns. Bris 47 E4
Priory Gdns. Bris 49 D4
Priory Gdns. E in G 47 D2
Priory Park Rd. Bath 102 A3
Priory Rd. Bris 47 E3
Priory Rd. Bris 63 E4
Priory Rd. Bris 64 A1
Priory Rd. E in G 47 D2
Priory Rd. Keyn 81 F4
Priory Rd. Portb 46 B2
Priory Rd. W-S-M 105 D4
Priory Wlk. Portb 46 B2
Priston Cl. W-S-M 89 D3
Priston La. Pris 117 D3
Priston Rd. Engl 117 E3
Priston Rd. Pris 117 E3
Pritchard St. Bris 63 F4
Probyn Cl. Bris 51 D4
Proctor Cl. Bris 64 B1
Prospect Ave. Bris 51 D1
Prospect Cl. Alm 22 C1
Prospect Cl. Alm 23 D1
Prospect Cl. Fr Cot 37 F4
Prospect Cl. Wint 37 F2
Prospect Cres. Kingsw 51 F1
Prospect Gdns. Bathe 85 F3
Prospect La. Fr Cot 37 F4
Prospect Pl. Bath 84 B1
Prospect Pl. Bathf 86 B1
Prospect Pl. Bris 63 E2
Prospect Pl. Bris 64 B4
Prospect Pl. W-S-M 104 C4
Prospect Rd. Bath 102 B2
Prospect Rd. Piln 22 A3
Providence La. Lo Ash 61 F1
Providence Pl. Bris 63 E2
Providence St. Bris 63 E2
Prowse's La. Axb 125 D1
Prudham St. Bris 50 B1
Publow La. Pens 97 F3
Pucklechurch Trading Est.
  Puck 53 D3
Pudding Pie Cl. Chur 109 D3
Pudding Pie La. Chur 109 D3
Puffin Cl. W-S-M 105 F4
Pullen's Green. Thorn 8 A1
Pullin Ct. Kingsw 66 B3
Pulteney Ave. Bath 102 A3
Pulteney Bridge. Bath 102 A3
Pulteney Gdns. Bath 102 A3
Pulteney Gr. Bath 102 A3
Pulteney Mews. Bath 102 A4
Pulteney Rd. Bath 102 A3
Pump La. Bathf 86 A1
Pump La. Bris 63 F3
Pump La. Olve 14 B2
Pump La. Wring 93 F2
Pump Sq. E in G 47 E3
Purcell Wlk. Bris 79 E4
Purdey Rd. Bris 50 C2
Purdue Cl. W-S-M 89 D2
Purn La. W-S-M 122 A4
Purn Rd. W-S-M 121 F4
Purn Way. Blea 122 A4
Purplewent Dr. Bath 84 B1
Pursey Dr. St Gif 36 C3
Purton Cl. Kingsw 65 F3
Purton Rd. Bris 49 E1
Purving Row La. Lymp 122 B1
Purving Row. Lymp 122 B1
Puttingthorpe Dr. W-S-M 105 E4
Puxley Cl. Bris 80 C3
Puxton La. Ban 90 B2
Puxton La. Pux 90 B2
Puxton Rd. Ban 90 B1
Puxton Rd. Pux 90 B1

Pye Cnr. Chur

Pye Cnr. Chur 108 B2
Pye Croft. St Gif 24 C2
Pyecroft Ave. Bris 49 E4
Pylewell La. Ship 108 B1
Pyne Point. Cleve 57 E2
Pynne Cl. Bris 80 C3
Pynne Rd. Bris 80 C3
Pyracantha Wlk. Bris 80 A3

Quadrangle The. West 39 E2
Quadrant E. Bris 51 E2
Quadrant The. Bris 49 D2
Quadrant The. St Gif 24 A2
Quadrant W. Bris 51 E2
Quadrant. St Gif 24 A2
Quaker La. Thorn 8 A1
Quaker's Cl. Mang 51 E4
Quaker's Rd. Mang 51 F4
Quakers' Friars. Bris 63 F4
Quantock Cl. Kingsw 66 B3
Quantock Rd. Bris 63 E2
Quantock Rd. Portis 45 D3
Quantock Rd. W-S-M 104 C3
Quantocks. Bath 102 A1
Quarries The. Alm 24 B3
Quarrington Rd. Bris 49 F3
Quarry Barton. Wint 37 E2
Quarry Cl. Bath 101 F1
Quarry Hay. Ch St 112 B4
Quarry Head. Alve 14 C3
Quarry La. Wint 37 F2
Quarry Rd. Alve 14 C3
Quarry Rd. Bath 102 B3
Quarry Rd. Bris 51 E4
Quarry Rd. Ch Sod 28 A1
Quarry Rd. Kingsw 65 E3
Quarry Rd. Wins 108 A1
Quarry Stps. Bris 49 D1
Quarry Way. Bris 50 C3
Quarry Way. Nail 59 E1
Quay St. Bris 63 E4
Quayside. Bris 64 C3
Quedgeley. Yate 39 E4
Queen Ann Rd. Bris 64 A3
Queen Charlotte St. Bris 63 E3
Queen Charlton La. Co Dan 80 C1
Queen Charlton La. Whit 80 C1
Queen Sq Ave. Bris 63 E3
Queen Sq Pl. Bath 101 F4
Queen Sq. Bath 101 F4
Queen Sq. Bris 63 E3
Queen Sq. Keyn 82 C2
Queen St. Avon 33 D1
Queen St. Bath 101 F4
Queen St. Bris 50 B2
Queen St. Bris 63 F4
Queen St. Bris 65 D4
Queen Victoria Rd. Bris 49 D2
Queen Victoria St. Bris 64 A3
Queen's Ave. Bris 63 D4
Queen's Ave. Portis 45 E3
Queen's Dr. Bath 102 A1
Queen's Dr. Bris 49 E3
Queen's Par Pl. Bath 101 F4
Queen's Par. Bris 63 E3
Queen's Rd. Bris 49 F3
Queen's Rd. Bris 63 D4
Queen's Rd. Bris 64 C4
Queen's Rd. Bris 78 C2
Queen's Rd. Cleve 57 E2
Queen's Rd. Kingsw 66 A2
Queen's Rd. Nail 59 E1
Queen's Rd. Portis 44 C2
Queen's Rd. Puck 53 D3
Queen's Rd. Rad 133 D1
Queen's Rd. W-S-M 87 E1
Queen's Way. Portis 44 C2
Queen's Way. W-S-M 89 D2
Queens Down Gdns. Bris 64 B2
Queens Dr. Kingsw 65 D2
Queens Par. Bath 101 F4
Queens Rd. Ban 107 D2
Queens Rd. Bris 64 B1
Queens Rd. Keyn 81 E2
Queens Wlk. Thorn 8 A2
Queensdale Cres. Bris 64 A1
Queenshill Rd. Bris 64 A1
Queensholm Ave. Mang 37 F1
Queensholm Cl. Mang 37 F1
Queensholm Dr. Mang 37 F1
Queensway. St Gif 36 B3
Queenwood Ave. Bath 85 D1
Quickthorn Cl. Bris 80 A3
Quiet St. Bath 101 F3
Quilter Gr. Bris 79 E4

Raby Mews. Bath 102 A4
Rackfield Pl. Bath 101 D3
Rackham Cl. Bris 50 A3
Rackhay. Bris 63 E3
Rackley La. Co Bi 124 A1
Rackvernal Rd. Mid No 132 A1
Radford Hill. Paul 131 E4
Radford Hill. Tims 116 B1
Radley Rd. Bris 51 D2
Radnor Rd. Bris 37 D3
Radnor Rd. Bris 49 F3

Radstock Rd. Mid No 132 B1
Raeburn Rd. Bris 65 D3
Rag Hill. P St J 133 E3
Rag La. Wickw 17 E3
Raglan Cl. Chil 137 E2
Raglan La. Bris 65 D4
Raglan La. Win 94 C4
Raglan Pl. Bris 49 E2
Raglan Pl. Thorn 15 D4
Raglan Pl. W-S-M 87 E1
Raglan Rd. Bris 49 E2
Ragland La. Bath 85 D1
Ragland St. Bath 85 D1
Railton Jones Cl. St Gif 36 C2
Railway Pl. Bath 102 A3
Railway St. Bath 102 A3
Railway Terr. Bris 51 E2
Railway View Pl. Mid No 132 A1
Rainham Ct. W-S-M 87 E1
Rains Batch. Priddy 126 C3
Raleigh Cl. Keyn 82 B1
Raleigh Rd. Bris 63 D2
Raleigh Rise. Portis 45 D3
Ralph Allen Dr. Bath 102 B2
Ralph Rd. Bris 49 F2
Ram Hill. West 38 B2
Ramscombe La. Bathe 85 F3
Ramsey Cl. W-S-M 88 C2
Ramsey Rd. Bris 49 F4
Ranchways. Portis 44 C2
Randall Cl. Kingsw 51 F1
Randall Rd. Bris 63 D3
Randolph Ave. Bris 79 D3
Randolph Ave. Yate 27 E3
Randolph Cl. Bris 79 D3
Rangers Wlk. Kingsw 65 E2
Rankers La. Co Dan 98 B3
Rannoch Rd. Bris 35 F1
Ranscombe Ave. W-S-M 88 B1
Ransford. Cleve 57 D1
Raphael Ct. Bris 63 F3
Ratcliffe Dr. St Gif 36 C3
Rathbone Cl. Fr Cot 38 B3
Raven Cl. W-S-M 88 C1
Ravendale Dr. Kingsw 66 A1
Ravenglass Cres. Bris 35 E1
Ravenhead Dr. Bris 80 A4
Ravenhill Ave. Bris 63 F1
Ravenhill Rd. Bris 63 F1
Ravens Wood. Kingsw 66 A2
Ravenscourt Rd. Bris 36 A4
Ravenswood Rd. Bris 49 E1
Rawlins Ave. W-S-M 89 D3
Rayens Cl. Lo Ash 61 F1
Rayens Cross Rd. Lo Ash 61 F1
Rayleigh Rd. Bris 48 C4
Raymend Rd. Bris 63 F2
Raymend Wlk. Bris 63 F1
Raymill. Bris 65 D1
Raymore Rise. Lo Ash 61 F1
Raynes Rd. Bris 63 D2
Reach Hill La. Ch St 112 B3
Rector's Way. W-S-M 104 C3
Rectory Cl. Farm 116 A3
Rectory Cl. Yate 27 F2
Rectory Dr. Yatt 91 E4
Rectory La. Bris 36 A2
Rectory La. Co Mar 128 A3
Rectory La. Crom 17 D4
Rectory La. Tims 116 B1
Rectory Rd. E in G 47 D2
Rectory Rd. Fr Cot 38 A4
Rectory Way. Lymp 121 F1
Rectory Way. Yatt 91 E4
Red Hill. Tims 116 C1
Red Hill. Wring 93 E1
Red House La. Alm 24 A2
Red House La. Bris 48 C3
Red Rd. Berr 121 D1
Redacre. Wring 93 E2
Redcatch Rd. Bris 63 F1
Redcliff Backs. Bris 63 F3
Redcliff Hill. Bris 63 F3
Redcliff Mead La. Bris 63 F3
Redcliff St. Bris 63 F3
Redcliffe Cl. Portis 44 C2
Redcliffe Par E. Bris 63 F3
Redcliffe Par W. Bris 63 F3
Redcliffe Way. Bris 63 F3
Redcroft. Wring 93 E2
Redcross La. Bris 63 F4
Redcross St. Bris 63 F4
Redding Pit La. Win 94 C2
Reddings The. Co Mar 128 A4
Reddings The. Kingsw 51 F1
Redfield Gr. Mid No 138 A4
Redfield Hill. Bitt 66 C3
Redfield Rd. Bris 36 A4
Redfield Rd. Mid No 132 A1
Redford Cres. Bris 78 C2
Redford La. Puck 53 E2
Redford Wlk. Bris 78 C2
Redham La. Piln 23 D4
Redhill Cl. Bris 50 C2
Redhill Dr. Bris 50 C2
Redhill La. Aust 13 D4
Redland Ave. E in G 46 C3

Redland Court Rd. Bris 49 E1
Redland Gr. Bris 49 E1
Redland Green Rd. Bris 49 E2
Redland Hill. Bris 49 D1
Redland Park. Bath 100 C3
Redland Park. Bris 49 E1
Redland Rd. Bris 49 D1
Redland Terr. Bris 49 E1
Redlands Terr. Mid No 137 F4
Redlynch La. Co Dan 81 E1
Redshard La. Chur 109 D4
Redshelf Wlk. Bris 35 E2
Redwick Cl. Bris 34 B1
Redwick Gdns. Piln 22 B4
Redwick Rd. Piln 22 B4
Redwing Dr. W-S-M 88 C1
Redwood Cl. Kingsw 66 A2
Redwood Cl. Nail 60 A1
Redwood Cl. Rod 138 C4
Redwoods The. Keyn 81 E3
Reed Ct. Kingsw 65 F2
Reed's Row. Hill 19 E4
Reedley Rd. Bris 48 C3
Reedling Cl. Bris 50 C3
Regency Dr. Bris 65 D1
Regent Rd. Bris 63 E2
Regent St. Kingsw 65 E4
Regent St. W-S-M 104 B4
Regents Cl. Thorn 8 A1
Regents St. Bris 63 D4
Regil La. Win 94 C2
Regil La. Win 95 D3
Remenham Dr. Bris 49 D3
Remenham Park. Bris 49 D3
Rendcomb Cl. W-S-M 88 A2
Rene Rd. Bris 50 A1
Repton Rd. Bris 64 B2
Retort Rd. Avon 33 E2
Retreat The. Faulk 133 F2
Reubens Cl. W-S-M 88 C2
Reynold's Wlk. Bris 50 A4
Reynolds Cl. Keyn 82 A3
Rhode Cl. Keyn 82 A2
Rhodyate Hill. Brock 92 A4
Rhodyate Hill. Cong 91 F3
Rhodyate La. Brock 92 A4
Rhodyate The. Ban 107 E1
Rhodyate. Blag 110 B1
Rhyne Terr. W-S-M 104 B1
Ribblesdale. Thorn 15 E4
Richards Cl. W-S-M 89 D2
Richeson Cl. Bris 34 C1
Richeson Wlk. Bris 34 C1
Richmond Ave. Bris 49 F1
Richmond Ave. St Gif 36 C3
Richmond Cl. Bath 84 C1
Richmond Cl. Keyn 81 E2
Richmond Cl. Portis 45 F3
Richmond Dale. Bris 49 D1
Richmond Green. Nail 59 F1
Richmond Hill Ave. Bris 63 D4
Richmond Hill. Bath 84 C1
Richmond Hill. Bris 63 D4
Richmond Hts. Bath 84 C1
Richmond La. Bath 84 C1
Richmond La. Bris 63 D4
Richmond Park Rd. Bris 63 D4
Richmond Pl. Bath 84 C1
Richmond Rd. Bath 84 C1
Richmond Rd. Bris 64 C4
Richmond Rd. Mang 52 A3
Richmond Rd. W-S-M 104 B4
Richmond St. Bris 63 F2
Richmond St. W-S-M 104 B4
Richmond Terr. Avon 33 D1
Richmond Terr. Bris 63 D4
Ricketts La. W-S-M 89 D1
Rickford La. Blag 110 A2
Rickford Rd. Nail 59 F1
Rickford Rise. Blag 110 A2
Rickyard Rd. Wring 92 C1
Ride The. Kingsw 52 A1
Ridge Cl. Portis 45 D2
Ridge Cres. E Harp 128 C3
Ridge La. E Harp 128 B3
Ridge The. Bris 47 F4
Ridge The. Fr Cot 38 B4
Ridge The. Yatt 91 D4
Ridge View. Lo Ash 62 A1
Ridgehill. Bris 49 E3
Ridgemeade. Bris 80 A2
Ridgeway Ave. W-S-M 104 C3
Ridgeway Cl. E Harp 128 C3
Ridgeway Ct. Bris 35 D1
Ridgeway Gdns. Bris 80 B3
Ridgeway La. Bris 80 B3
Ridgeway Par. Bris 50 C2
Ridgeway Rd. Bris 50 C2
Ridgeway Rd. Lo Ash 62 A1
Ridgeway The. Bris 35 D1
Ridgeway The. W-S-M 88 A1
Ridgeway. Fr Cot 38 B4
Ridgeway. Nail 59 E1
Ridgeway. Yate 27 F1
Riding Barn Hill. Wick 67 D4
Ridingleaze. Bris 34 A1
Ridings Cl. Ch Sod 28 A1

Ridings Rd. Fr Cot 38 B3
Ridings The. Bris 78 C2
Ridings The. Fr Cot 38 B3
Ringspit La. Pens 97 F4
Ringswell Gdns. Bath 85 E1
Ringwell La. N St P 135 F2
Ringwell. N St P 135 F2
Ringwood Cres. Bris 35 E1
Ringwood Gr. W-S-M 88 A1
Ringwood Rd. Bath 101 E3
Ripley Rd. Bris 51 D1
Ripon Ct. Mang 37 F1
Ripon Rd. Bris 64 C3
Ripple The. Nail 59 E2
Rippleside Rd. Cleve 57 F3
Rippleside. Portis 45 E3
Risdale Rd. Bris 62 C1
Risedale Rd. Wins 125 D4
Rivendell. W-S-M 89 D2
River Rd. Ch Sod 28 A1
River St. Bris 63 F4
River Terr. Keyn 81 F3
River View. Bris 50 C3
Riverland Dr. Bris 78 C3
Riverleaze. Bris 48 A3
Riverleaze. Portis 44 C3
Rivers Rd. Bath 85 D1
Rivers St Mews. Bath 101 F4
Rivers St. Bath 101 F4
Riverside Bsns Park. Bris ... 64 B3
Riverside Cl. Bris 47 D3
Riverside Cl. Cleve 57 D1
Riverside Cl. Mid No 137 F4
Riverside Cotts. Kingsw 65 D1
Riverside Cotts. Rad 133 D1
Riverside Ct. Bath 101 F3
Riverside Ct. Bris 63 F4
Riverside Gdns. Mid No 137 F4
Riverside Mews. Bris 64 C3
Riverside Rd. Bath 101 F3
Riverside Rd. Mid No 137 F4
Riverside Way. Kingsw 65 E2
Riverside Wlk. Mid No 137 F4
Riverside. Ban 107 D3
Riverway. Nail 59 F2
Riverwood Rd. Bris 37 E1
Riviera Cres. Kingsw 51 F2
Roach's La. Gr Bad 30 B1
Road Hill. Col 70 B1
Road Two. Avon 22 A2
Roath Rd. Portis 45 E3
Robbins Cl. Marsh 69 F4
Robbins Cl. St Gif 36 C3
Robel Ave. Fr Cot 37 F4
Robert St. Bris 50 A1
Robert St. Bris 64 A4
Robertson Rd. Bris 50 B1
Robin Cl. Rod 138 A4
Robin Cl. W-S-M 105 F4
Robin Dr. Lock 105 F1
Robin La. Cleve 57 E3
Robin Way. Ch Sod 40 A4
Robinia Wlk. Bris 80 A4
Robinson Cl. Back 76 A3
Robinson Way. Back 76 A3
Rochester Cl. W-S-M 105 D1
Rochester Rd. Bris 64 C3
Rock Ave. Nail 59 E1
Rock Cl. Bris 64 C1
Rock Hall La. Bath 102 A1
Rock La. Bath 102 A1
Rock La. St Gif 36 C3
Rock Rd. Chil 137 E1
Rock Rd. Mid No 132 A1
Rock Rd. Wick 67 E4
Rock Rd. Yatt 91 E4
Rock St. Thorn 15 D4
Rock The. Bris 64 C2
Rockhill Est. Keyn 81 F2
Rockingham Gr. W-S-M 88 A1
Rockland Gr. Bris 50 B3
Rockland Rd. Mang 51 E4
Rockleaze Ave. Bris 48 C2
Rockleaze Rd. Bris 48 C2
Rockliffe Ave. Bath 102 A4
Rockliffe Rd. Bath 102 A4
Rocks La. Ba Gu 77 F1
Rocks La. Win 77 F1
Rockside Ave. Mang 51 F4
Rockside Dr. Bris 49 E3
Rockside Gdns. Fr Cot 38 B4
Rockside Gdns. Mang 51 F4
Rockstowes Way. Bris 35 E2
Rockwell Ave. Bris 34 A1
Rodborough Way. Kingsw 66 A4
Rodborough. Yate 39 E4
Rodbourne Rd. Bris 49 F3
Rode Hill. Rode 136 C1
Rodford Way. Yate 39 E4
Rodfords Mead. Bris 80 A4
Rodmead Wlk. Bris 79 D2
Rodmoor Rd. Portis 45 E3
Rodney Ave. Bris 65 D4
Rodney Cres. Bris 36 A2
Rodney Pl. Bris 63 D4
Rodney Rd. Back 76 A3
Rodney Rd. Bris 65 D4

Rows The. W-S-M

Rodney Rd. Keyn 82 C1
Rodney Wlk. Bris 51 D1
Rodney. W-S-M 105 D1
Rodway Hill Rd. Kingsw 52 A2
Rodway Hill. Sist 52 A2
Rodway Rd. Bris 36 A4
Rodway Rd. Mang 52 A3
Rodway View. Kingsw 51 F2
Roebuck Cl. W-S-M 89 D2
Roegate Dr. Bris 64 C3
Rogers Cl. Clut 114 C2
Rogers Cl. Kingsw 66 A3
Rokeby Ave. Bris 49 E1
Roman Rd. Bris 50 A1
Roman Rd. Winsc 107 F2
Roman Way. Bris 48 B2
Roman Way. Paul 131 E3
Roman Wlk. Bris 64 B2
Roman Wlk. St Gif 36 C3
Romney Ave. Bris 50 A3
Ronald Rd. Bris 50 C3
Ronayne Wlk. Bris 51 E3
Rook Rd. Keyn 81 F3
Rookery Cl. W-S-M 88 C2
Rookery La. Doyn 53 F2
Rookery La. Piln 23 D3
Rookery Rd. Bris 64 A2
Rookery Way. Bris 79 F2
Rooksbridge Wlk. Bath 101 D3
Roper's La. Wring 92 C2
Rose Acre. Bris 35 D2
Rose Cl. Wint 37 F2
Rose Gdns. W-S-M 89 D2
Rose Green Cl. Bris 50 C1
Rose Green Rd. Bris 50 C1
Rose Hill. Bath 85 E2
Rose La. Fr Cot 38 B3
Rose Mead. Bris 50 A4
Rose Meare Gdns. Bris 78 C4
Rose Oak La. Fr Cot 38 B4
Rose Rd. Bris 64 C4
Rose St. Bris 63 F3
Rose Wlk. Bris 51 E2
Rosebay Mead. Bris 50 C2
Roseberry Pk. Bris 64 B4
Roseberry Rd. Bath 101 E3
Roseberry Rd. Bris 64 B4
Rosebery Ave. Bris 50 A1
Rosedale Ave. W-S-M 105 D4
Rosedale Rd. Bris 51 E2
Roselarge Gdns. Bris 35 D1
Rosemary La. Bris 50 B1
Rosemary La. Hi Cha 120 A2
Rosemont Terr. Bris 63 D3
Rosemount La. Bath 102 A2
Rosery Cl. Bris 49 D4
Rosery The. Bris 51 E2
Rosevear. Bris 64 A4
Roseville Ave. Kingsw 66 A1
Rosewarn Cl. Bath 101 D2
Rosewell Ct. Bath 101 F3
Rosewood Gdns. Alve 14 C3
Rosling Rd. Bris 49 F3
Roslyn Ave. W-S-M 88 B1
Roslyn Rd. Bris 49 E1
Rossall Ave. St Gif 36 B3
Rossall Rd. Bris 64 B2
Rossendale Cl. W-S-M 88 C2
Rossiter Rd. Bath 102 A3
Rossiter's La. Bris 65 D3
Rosslyn Rd. Bath 101 D4
Rosslyn Way. Thorn 8 B2
Rotcombe La. Paul 115 E1
Rotcombe Vale. Paul 115 E1
Rounceval St. Ch Sod 28 A1
Roundhill Park. Bath 101 D2
Roundhill. Bath 101 D2
Roundmoor Cl. Keyn 82 B2
Roundmoor Gdns. Bris 80 B4
Roundways. Fr Cot 38 B3
Rousham Rd. Bris 50 A2
Row La. Faulk 135 E1
Row Of Ashes La. But 94 A2
Row Of Ashes La. Wring 93 F2
Row The. Aust 13 D4
Rowacres. Bath 101 D2
Rowacres. Bris 79 F3
Rowan Cl. Bris 51 D1
Rowan Cl. Nail 60 A1
Rowan Cl. Rad 132 C1
Rowan Way. Chur 109 D3
Rowan Way. Kingsw 65 D2
Rowan Wlk. Keyn 81 E2
Rowans The. Bris 37 D1
Rowans The. Portis 45 E2
Rowberrow La. Ship 108 C1
Rowberrow La. Ship 125 F4
Rowberrow Way. Nail 59 F1
Rowberrow. Bris 79 F4
Rowland Ave. Bris 50 B2
Rowlands Cl. Bathf 86 A1
Rowlandson Gdns. Bris 50 A3
Rowley St. Bris 63 E2
Rownham Cl. Bris 63 D3
Rownham Hill. Lo Ash 62 C3
Rownham Mead. Bris 63 D3
Rows The. W-S-M 88 C1

Roy King Gdns. Kingsw 66 B3
Royal Albert Rd. Bris 49 D2
Royal Ave. Bath 101 F4
Royal Cl. Bris 34 B2
Royal Cres. Bath 101 F4
Royal Cres. W-S-M 104 B4
Royal Fort Rd. Bris 63 E4
Royal Park. Bris 63 D4
Royal Portbury Dock Rd.
 E in G 46 C3
Royal Prom. Bris 63 D4
Royal York Cres. Bris 62 C3
Royal York Cres. Bris 63 D3
Royate Hill. Bris 50 B1
Roycroft Rd. Bris 36 A1
Royston Wlk. Bris 35 E1
Rozel Rd. Bris 49 F3
Rubens Cl. Keyn 82 A3
Ruby St. Bris 63 D2
Ruddymead. Cleve 57 E1
Rudford Cl. St Gif 24 A1
Rudgeway Park. Alve 14 C1
Rudgeway Rd. Paul 131 F2
Rudgewood Cl. Bris 79 E2
Rudgleigh Ave. E in G 47 E2
Rudgleigh Rd. E in G 47 E2
Rudhall Gr. Bris 49 F4
Rudhall Green. W-S-M 89 D2
Rudmore Park. Bath 101 D4
Rudthorpe Rd. Bris 49 F3
Ruffet Rd. West 38 B2
Rugby Rd. Bris 64 B2
Runnymead Ave. Bris 64 B1
Runnymede. Kingsw 51 F1
Runswick Rd. Bris 64 B2
Rupert St. Bris 63 E4
Rupert St. Bris 64 B4
Rurdown Rd. Bris 49 F3
Rush Cl. St Gif 24 B1
Rush Hill. Bath 101 D1
Rush Hill. Paul 130 C2
Rush Hill. Ston E 130 C2
Rushgrove Gdns. Bi Sut 113 E2
Rushmead La. Marsh 55 F1
Rushmoor Gr. Back 76 A3
Rushmoor La. Back 76 A3
Rushmoor. Cleve 57 D1
Rushton Dr. Fr Cot 38 B4
Rushway. Blag 110 A2
Rushy. Kingsw 66 A2
Ruskin Gr. Bris 50 A4
Ruskin Rd. Rad 132 B1
Russ St. Bris 63 F3
Russell Ave. Kingsw 65 F4
Russell Cl. Win 95 D3
Russell Gr. Bris 49 E3
Russell Rd. Bris 49 D2
Russell Rd. Bris 51 D1
Russell Rd. Cleve 57 E2
Russell St. Bath 101 F4
Russell Town Ave. Bris 64 A4
Russet Cl. Olve 14 A2
Russet Ct. Kings 11 F2
Russet Way. P St J 133 E4
Russett Cl. Back 76 A3
Russett Gr. Nail 75 E4
Rutherford Cl. Kingsw 66 A2
Ruthven Rd. Bris 79 F4
Rutland Ave. Kingsw 66 A1
Rutland Cl. W-S-M 105 E4
Rutland Rd. Bris 49 F2
Rydal Ave. Lock 106 A2
Rydal Rd. W-S-M 104 C2
Ryde Rd. Bris 64 A1
Rye Cl. Bris 78 C3
Ryecroft Ave. W-S-M 88 C1
Ryecroft Rd. Fr Cot 38 B4
Ryecroft Rise. Lo Ash 62 A1
Ryedown La. Bitt 66 B1
Ryland Pl. Bris 50 A1
Rylestone Cl. Fr Cot 37 F4
Rylestone Gr. Bris 48 C3
Rysdale Rd. Bris 48 C3

Sabrina Way. Bris 48 B2
Sadbury Cl. W-S-M 89 D2
Sadlier Cl. Bris 48 A4
Saffron Ct. Bath 102 A4
Saffrons The. W-S-M 89 D2
Sage Cl. Portis 44 C2
Sailsburt St. Bris 64 C4
Sailsbury Rd. Bris 64 B3
St John's Rd. Back 76 A3
St Agnes Ave. Bris 63 F1
St Agnes Cl. Nail 60 A1
St Agnes Wlk. Bris 63 F1
St Aidan's Cl. Bris 65 D3
St Aidan's Rd. Bris 65 D3
St Alban's Rd. Bris 49 D2
St Aldams Dr. Puck 53 D3
St Aldwyn's Cl. Bris 49 F4
St Andrew's Cl. Cong 91 E2
St Andrew's Dr. Cleve 57 D1
St Andrew's Par. W-S-M 104 C2
St Andrew's Rd. Avon 33 D2
St Andrew's Terr. Bath 101 F1
St Andrews Cl. Nail 60 A1

St Andrews Cl. W-S-M 88 C2
St Andrews Rd. Back 76 A3
St Andrews Trading Est.
 Avon 33 E1
St Andrews. Kingsw 66 A3
St Ann's Way. Bath 102 A3
St Anne's Ave. Keyn 81 E3
St Anne's Cl. Kingsw 66 A2
St Anne's Ct. Keyn 81 E3
St Anne's Dr. Fr Cot 38 B3
St Anne's Dr. Wick 67 D4
St Anne's Park Rd. Bris 64 C3
St Anne's Rd. Bris 65 D3
St Anne's Rd. Bris 64 C3
St Anne's Terr. Bris 64 C3
St Annes Dr. Kingsw 66 B2
St Anthony's Dr. Wick 67 D4
St Anthonys Cl. Mid No 132 A1
St Anway. Kingsw 66 B1
St Aubin's Ave. Bris 64 C2
St Aubyn's Ave. W-S-M 104 B1
St Augustine's Cl. Portis 44 C2
St Augustine's Par. Bris 63 E3
St Augustine's Pl. Bris 63 E3
St Austell Cl. Nail 76 A4
St Austell Rd. W-S-M 105 D4
St Barnabas Cl. Bris 63 F1
St Barnabas Cl. Mid No 132 A2
St Barnabas Cl. Sist 66 B4
St Bartholomew's Rd. Bris .. 49 F2
St Bede's Rd. Bris 51 E1
St Bernard's Rd. Bris 47 F3
St Brelades Gr. Bris 64 C3
St Brendan's Way. Avon 33 D1
St Briavels Dr. Yate 39 E4
St Bridges Cl. W St L 88 A3
St Catherine's Cl. Bath 102 B3
St Catherine's Ind Est. Bris . 63 E2
St Catherine's Mead.
 E in G 47 E2
St Catherine's Pl. Bris 63 E2
St Chad's Ave. Mid No 132 A1
St Chad's Green. Mid No .. 132 A1
St Charles Cl. Mid No 132 A1
St Christophers Cl. Bath 102 B4
St Clements Ct. Keyn 81 F2
St Clements Rd. Keyn 81 F2
St David's Ave. Kingsw 66 A3
St David's Cl. W-S-M 88 A1
St David's Cres. Bris 64 C3
St Dunstan's Rd. Bris 63 E1
St Edward's Rd. Bris 63 D3
St Edyth's Rd. Bris 48 B3
St Fagans Ct. Kingsw 66 A1
St Francis Dr. Wick 67 D4
St Francis Dr. Wint 37 F3
St Francis Rd. Bris 63 D2
St Francis Rd. Keyn 81 E3
St Gabriel's Rd. Bris 64 A4
St George's Hill. Bath 102 B4
St George's Hill. E in G 47 D2
St George's Rd. Bris 63 E3
St George's Rd. E in G 46 C4
St George's Rd. Keyn 81 E3
St Giles Barton. Hill 19 E4
St Gregory's Rd. Bris 49 F4
St Gregory's Wlk. Bris 49 F4
St Helen's Wlk. Bris 51 D1
St Helena Rd. Bris 49 D2
St Helens Dr. Kingsw 66 B1
St Helens Dr. Wick 67 E4
St Helier Ave. Bris 64 C2
St Hilary Cl. Bris 48 B3
St Ivel Way. Kingsw 66 B3
St Ives Cl. Nail 60 A1
St Ives Rd. W-S-M 105 D3
St James Cl. Thorn 8 B2
St James Ct. St Gif 24 B2
St James St. W-S-M 104 B4
St James' Barton. Bris 63 F4
St James's Par. Bath 101 F3
St James's Park. Bath 101 F4
St James's Pl. Mang 52 A3
St James's Sq. Bath 101 F4
St James's St. Bath 101 F4
St James's St. Mang 52 A3
St John St. H Up 20 A2
St John St. Thorn 8 B2
St John's Ave. Cleve 57 E2
St John's Bridge. Bris 63 E4
St John's Cl. P St J 133 D4
St John's Cl. W-S-M 87 E1
St John's Cres. Bris 63 F1
St John's Cres. Mid No 132 A1
St John's La. Bris 63 F1
St John's Pl. Bath 101 F3
St John's Rd. Bath 101 F3
St John's Rd. Bath 102 A4
St John's Rd. Bris 63 E2
St John's Rd. Cleve 57 E2
St John's Rd. Bris 63 E2
St John's Steep. Bris 63 E4
St Johns Ct. Keyn 81 F3
St Johns Way. Ch Sod 28 A1
St Jonhs Rd. Bris 49 D1
St Jonhs Rd. Tims 116 A1
St Joseph's Rd. Bris 35 D2

St Joseph's Rd. W-S-M 87 F1
St Jude's Terr. W-S-M 88 B1
St Julian's Rd. Well 133 F3
St Kenya Ct. Keyn 81 F3
St Keyna Rd. Keyn 81 F3
St Kilda's Rd. Bath 101 E3
St Ladoc Rd. Keyn 81 E3
St Laud Cl. Bris 48 B3
St Leonard's Rd. Bris 49 F3
St Leonard's Rd. Bris 50 B1
St Lucia Cl. Bris 49 F4
St Lucia Cres. Bris 49 F4
St Luke St. Bris 64 A4
St Luke's Cres. Bris 63 F2
St Luke's Gdns. Bris 64 C1
St Luke's Rd. Bath 101 F2
St Luke's Rd. Bris 63 F2
St Luke's Rd. Mid No 131 F1
St Margaret's Cl. Back 76 A3
St Margaret's Cl. Keyn 81 E3
St Margaret's Dr. Bris 49 E3
St Margaret's La. Back 76 A3
St Margaret's Terr. W-S-M 104 B4
St Mark's Gr. Bris 50 A1
St Mark's Rd. Bath 102 A3
St Mark's Rd. Bris 50 A1
St Mark's Rd. Mid No 132 A1
St Mark's Terr. Bris 50 A1
St Marks Cl. Keyn 81 F3
St Marks Rd. W-S-M 89 D2
St Martin's Cl. Bris 64 A1
St Martin's Ct. Bath 101 F1
St Martin's Gdns. Bris 64 A1
St Martin's La. Marsh 69 F4
St Martin's Park. Marsh 69 F4
St Martin's Rd. Bris 64 A1
St Martin's Wlk. Bris 64 A1
St Martins Ct. W-S-M 88 C2
St Mary St. Thorn 15 D4
St Mary's Bldgs. Bath 101 F3
St Mary's Cl. Bath 102 A3
St Mary's Cl. Tims 116 A1
St Mary's Ct. W-S-M 105 D1
St Mary's Gdns. Chur 109 D3
St Mary's Gr. Nail 75 E4
St Mary's Park Rd. Portis 45 E2
St Mary's Park. Nail 75 E4
St Mary's Rd. Bris 47 E4
St Mary's Rd. Lo Ash 62 B3
St Mary's Rd. Lock 105 E1
St Mary's Rd. Portis 45 E2
St Mary's Rise. Bath 133 E1
St Mary's St. Axb 125 E1
St Mary's Way. Yate 27 F1
St Mary's Wlk. Bris 47 E3
St Marys Cl. Lock 105 E1
St Marys Way. Thorn 8 A1
St Matthew's Cl. W-S-M 87 E1
St Matthew's Rd. Bris 63 E4
St Matthias Park. Bris 63 F4
St Michael's Ave. Cleve 57 E1
St Michael's Cl. Wint 37 F4
St Michael's Hill. Bris 63 E4
St Michael's Park. Bris 63 E4
St Michael's Rd. Bath 101 E4
St Michaels Ct. Bris 65 D4
St Michaels Rd. Bath 101 D3
St Micheal's Ave. W-S-M 89 D2
St Nicholas Cl. Winsl 120 B4
St Nicholas Park. Bris 85 F1
St Nicholas Rd. Bris 50 A1
St Nicholas Rd. W-S-M 104 B1
St Nicholas Rd. Whit 80 B2
St Nicholas St. Bris 63 F3
St Nicholas' Rd. Bris 49 F1
St Oswald's Ct. Bris 49 D2
St Oswald's Rd. Bris 49 D2
St Patrick's Ct. Bath 102 A3
St Patricks Ct. Keyn 81 F3
St Paul St. Bris 63 F4
St Paul's Rd. Bris 63 D4
St Paul's Rd. Bris 63 E2
St Paul's Rd. W-S-M 104 C3
St Pauls Pl. Bath 101 F3
St Pauls Pl. Mid No 132 A1
St Peter's Ave. W-S-M 87 E1
St Peter's Cres. Fr Cot 38 A4
St Peter's Rd. Rod 138 B4
St Peter's Rise. Bris 79 D4
St Peter's Wlk. Bris 49 D3
St Peters Rd. Portis 45 E2
St Phillips Causeway. Bris .. 64 A3
St Phillips Rd. Bris 64 A4
St Pierre Dr. Kingsw 66 A3
St Ronan's Ave. Bris 49 E1
St Saviour's Rd. Bath 85 E1
St Saviours Way. Bath 85 E1
St Silas St. Bris 64 A3
St Stephen's Ave. Bris 63 E3
St Stephen's Cl. Bath 101 F4
St Stephen's Cl. Bris 50 A3
St Stephen's Rd. Kingsw 51 E1
St Stephen's St. Bris 63 E3
St Stephens Bsns Centre.
 Kingsw 66 B3
St Stephens Cl. Kingsw 51 F2
St Stephens Rd. Bath 101 F4
St Swithin's Pl. Bath 102 A4

St Thomas Rd. Mid No 132 A1
St Thomas St E. Bris 63 F3
St Thomas St. Bris 63 F3
St Vincent's Hill. Bris 49 D1
St Vincent's Rd. Bris 63 D3
St Werburgh's Park. Bris 50 A1
St Werburgh's Rd. Bris 49 F1
St Whytes Rd. Bris 79 E4
St Winifreds Dr. Bath 102 B1
Salcombe Gdns. W-S-M 89 D1
Salcombe Rd. Bris 64 A1
Salem Rd. Wint 37 F4
Salisbury Ave. Bris 65 D4
Salisbury Gdns. Mang 51 F3
Salisbury Rd. Bath 85 D1
Salisbury Rd. Bris 49 E1
Salisbury Rd. Mang 51 F3
Salisbury Rd. Paul 131 F2
Salisbury Rd. W-S-M 105 E4
Salisbury St. Bris 64 A3
Salisbury Terr. W-S-M 104 B4
Sally In The Wood Rd.
 Bathf 103 E3
Sallybarn Cl. Kingsw 65 F1
Sallys Way. Wint 37 F4
Sallysmead Cl. Bris 79 D2
Saltford Ct. Keyn 82 C2
Salthouse Ct. Cleve 57 D1
Salthouse Rd. Cleve 57 D1
Salthrop Rd. Bris 49 F2
Saltings Cl. Cleve 57 D1
Saltmarsh Dr. Bris 34 A1
Saltwell Ave. Whit 80 B3
Sambourne La. E in G 47 E2
Sampsons Rd. Bris 79 E2
Samian Way. St Gif 36 C3
Samuel St. Bris 64 B4
Samuel White Rd. Kingsw 65 E2
Samuel Wright Cl. Kingsw 66 B3
Sanctuary Gdns. Bris 48 B2
Sand Farm La. W St L 88 A3
Sand Hill. Bris 64 B2
Sand Rd. W St L 88 A3
Sandbach Rd. Bris 64 B2
Sandbed Rd. Bris 50 A1
Sandburrows Rd. Bris 78 C3
Sandburrows Wlk. Bris 78 C3
Sandcroft Ave. W-S-M 104 B1
Sandcroft. Bris 79 F3
Sandford Cl. Cleve 57 D1
Sandford Rd. Bris 63 D3
Sandford Rd. W-S-M 105 D4
Sandford Rd. Winsc 107 F1
Sandgate Rd. Bris 64 B2
Sandholm Rd. Bris 64 B2
Sandholme Cl. Mang 51 F4
Sandhurst Cl. St Gif 24 A1
Sandhurst Rd. Bris 64 B2
Sandhurst. Yate 39 E4
Sandling Ave. Bris 50 A4
Sandmead Rd. Wins 108 A2
Sandown Cl. Mang 37 F1
Sandown Rd. Bris 36 B2
Sandown Rd. Bris 64 B2
Sandpiper Dr. W-S-M 88 C1
Sandpits La. H Up 19 F1
Sandringham Park. Mang 51 F4
Sandringham Rd. Bris 64 B2
Sandringham Rd. Kingsw 65 F1
Sandringham Rd. St Gif 36 B2
Sandringham Rd. W-S-M .. 104 C3
Sands Hill. Dyrh 54 C2
Sands La. Fr Cot 25 F1
Sandwich Rd. Bris 64 B2
Sandy Cl. St Gif 36 C3
Sandy La. Ab Lei 61 E4
Sandy La. Aust 13 D4
Sandy La. Bris 50 B2
Sandy La. Pens 96 C2
Sandy La. Wrax 47 D1
Sandy La. Wrax 61 E4
Sandy Lodge. Yate 39 F4
Sandy Park Rd. Bris 64 B2
Sandyleaze. Bris 48 C4
Sarabeth Dr. Pris 117 D2
Saracen St. Bath 102 A4
Sarah St. Bris 64 A4
Sargent St. Bris 63 F2
Sarum Cres. Bris 35 E1
Sassoon Ct. Kingsw 65 E1
Satchfield Cl. Bris 34 C1
Satchfield Cres. Bris 34 C1
Sates Way. Bris 49 E3
Saunders Rd. Kingsw 51 F2
Saunton Wlk. Bris 79 F4
Savages Wood Rd. St Gif 36 B4
Savages Wood Rd. St Gif 36 C4
Savernake Rd. W-S-M 88 C2
Saville Cres. W-S-M 105 E4
Saville Gate Cl. Bris 48 C2
Saville Pl. Bris 63 D3
Saville Rd. Bris 48 C2
Saville Rd. W-S-M 105 E4
Saville Row. Bath 101 F4
Savoy Rd. Bris 64 B2
Saw Cl. Bath 101 F3
Saw Mill La. Thorn 8 A1

Sawyers Ct. Cleve 57 F2
Saxby Cl. Cleve 57 D1
Saxby Cl. W-S-M 89 D2
Saxon Rd. Bris 50 A1
Saxon Rd. W-S-M 105 E4
Saxon Way. St Gif 24 B1
Saxon Way. Winsl 120 C4
Says La. Chur 109 D2
Sbi Centre. Kingsw 65 D3
Scandrett Cl. Bris 34 C1
Scaurs The. W-S-M 88 C1
School Cl. Bris 79 F2
School Cl. Hill 19 F4
School Cl. St Gif 36 B4
School La. Ba Gu 77 E3
School La. Bathe 85 F2
School La. Bris 50 C3
School La. Ch St 112 B4
School La. Paul 131 D2
School La. Ship 109 D1
School La. Wring 94 A4
School Rd. Bris 64 A2
School Rd. Bris 64 C2
School Rd. Fr Cot 38 A4
School Rd. Kingsw 65 E4
School Rd. Kingsw 66 B2
School Rd. Wring 92 C1
School Way. Piln 22 A3
School Wlk. Bris 50 B1
School Way. Yate 27 F1
Scobell Rise. Paul 115 E1
Score La. Blag 110 C1
Score The. Blag 110 C1
Scot La. Ch St 95 E1
Scotch Horn Cl. Nail 59 F1
Scotch Horn Way. Nail 59 F1
Scots Pine Ave. Nail 60 A1
Scott Ct. Kingsw 65 F3
Scott Lawrence Cl. Bris 51 D4
Scott Rd. W-S-M 105 D2
Scott Way. Ch Sod 39 F4
Scumbrun La. Farm 115 E1
Scumbrun La. Paul 115 E1
Sea Bank Rd. E in G 32 C1
Sea Mills La. Bris 48 B3
Seabrook Rd. W-S-M 88 B1
Seagry Cl. Bris 35 F1
Searl Court Ave. Bris 64 C2
Searle Cres. W-S-M 105 D3
Seaton Rd. Bris 50 B1
Seavale Rd. Cleve 57 E2
Seaview Rd. Portis 44 C2
Seaview Rd. Portis 44 C3
Seawalls Rd. Bris 48 B1
Seawalls. Bris 48 B1
Second Ave. Bath 101 E3
Second Ave. Rod 138 B4
Second Way. Avon 33 E1
Seddon Rd. Bris 50 A1
Sedgefield Gdns. Mang 37 F1
Sedgemoor Cl. Nail 75 F4
Sedgemoor Rd. Bath 101 F1
Sedgemoor Rd. W-S-M 87 F1
Sefton Park Rd. Bris 49 F2
Selbourne Rd. Bris 49 F3
Selbourne Rd. W-S-M 104 C2
Selbrooke Cres. Bris 51 E3
Selby Rd. Bris 50 C1
Selden Rd. Bris 80 C3
Selkirk Rd. Bris 51 E1
Selley Wlk. Bris 79 D3
Selwood Cl. W-S-M 105 E4
Selworthy Cl. Keyn 81 E3
Selworthy Gdns. Nail 59 F1
Selworthy Rd. Bris 64 A1
Selworthy Rd. W-S-M 105 D2
Selworthy. Kingsw 65 F4
Seneca Pl. Bris 64 B4
Seneca St. Bris 64 B4
Sercombe Park. Cleve 57 F1
Serlo Ct. W-S-M 88 C2
Seven Acres La. Bathe 85 F3
Seventh Ave. Bris 36 A1
Severn Ave. W-S-M 104 C3
Severn Cl. Char 11 D2
Severn Dr. Thorn 8 A1
Severn Grange. Bris 34 B2
Severn Rd. Avon 33 E2
Severn Rd. Avon 33 F4
Severn Rd. Bris 47 E3
Severn Rd. E in G 47 E3
Severn Rd. Piln 22 A3
Severn Rd. Portis 45 E3
Severn View Rd. Thorn 8 B1
Severn Way. Bris 23 F1
Severn Way. Keyn 81 F2
Severnmeade. Portis 44 C3
Severnwood Gdns. Piln 22 A3
Sevier Rd. Blea 123 E2
Sevier St. Bris 50 A1
Seville Rd. Portis 45 F4
Seward Terr. Rad 133 E1
Seymour Ave. Bris 49 F2
Seymour Cl. Cleve 57 F2
Seymour Cl. W-S-M 88 C2
Seymour Rd. Bath 102 A4

ymour Rd. Bris 49 F2
ymour Rd. Bris 50 A1
ymour Rd. Kingsw 51 F1
ymour Rd. Kingsw 51 F2
yton Wlk. St Gif 36 C3
ackleton Ave. Yate 39 F4
adwell Rd. Bris 49 E2
aft Rd. Bath 102 B1
aft Rd. Piln 22 A4
aftesbury Ave. Bris 49 F1
aftesbury Rd. Bath 101 E3
aftesbury Rd. W-S-M 105 D4
aftesbury Terr. Bris 64 B4
aftesbury Terr. Mid No .. 133 D2
aftsbury Ave. Bath 101 E4
akespeare Ave. Bath 101 F2
akespeare Ave. Bris 50 A4
akespeare Rd. Rad 132 B1
aldon Rd. Bris 50 A2
allows The. Keyn 82 C2
am Castle La. Bath 102 B4
amrock Rd. Bris 50 B2
anklin Dr. Bris 36 A2
annon Ct. Thorn 15 E4
apcott Cl. Bris 64 A1
aplands. Bris 48 C3
arland Cl. Bris 48 C2
aw Cl. Bris 64 A4
aws Way. Bath 101 D3
aymoor La. Alm 23 D2
eene La. Bris 63 E2
eep Fair La. Marsh 69 F4
eeps Croft. Bris 79 D3
eepway. Portb 46 B3
eepwood Cl. Bris 35 D1
eepwood Rd. Bris 35 D1
eldare Barton. Bris 65 D4
eldon Cl. Cleve 57 F1
eldrake Dr. Bris 50 C3
ellards La. Alve 15 E2
ellards Rd. Kingsw 65 F2
elley Ave. Cleve 57 E1
elley Cl. Bris 64 C4
elley Rd. Bath 101 F2
elley Rd. Rad 132 B1
elley Rd. W-S-M 105 D2
ellmor Ave. St Gif 24 A1
ellmor Cl. St Gif 24 B1
elly Way. Bris 50 A4
epherds Cl. Mang 51 F3
eppard Rd. Bris 51 E3
eppards Gdns. Bath 84 A1
epperdine Rd. O-0n-S 1 B1
eppy's Mill. Cong 91 E3
epton Wlk. Bris 63 E1
epton. W-S-M 105 D1
erbourne Ave. St Gif 36 C4
erbourne Cl. Kingsw 51 F1
erbourne St. Bris 64 C4
erbourne's Brake. St Gif . 36 C4
eridan Rd. Bath 100 C3
eridan Ave. Bris 50 A4
eridan Way. Kingsw 66 A1
erin Way. Bris 78 C2
errings The. St Gif 36 A4
erston Cl. Bris 51 D3
erston Cl. Nail 60 A1
erston Rd. Bris 49 F4
erston Rd. Luck 31 F3
erwell Rd. Bris 64 B2
erwood Cl. Keyn 81 F3
erwood Cres. W-S-M 88 C2
erwood Rd. Bris 51 D1
erwood Rd. Keyn 81 F3
etland Rd. Bris 35 E1
etland Way. Nail 60 A1
ickle Gr. Bath 101 E1
ields Ave. Bris 36 A1
iels Dr. St Gif 36 B4
ilton Cl. Kingsw 65 F4
imsey Cl. Bris 51 E3
ip La. Bris 63 F3
ipham Cl. Bris 80 A3
ipham Cl. Nail 75 F4
ipham La. Ship 108 A1
ipham La. Wins 108 A1
iplate Rd. Blea 122 C3
ipley Rd. Bris 49 D4
ire Gdns. Bris 47 E4
ire Hill. Tor 56 A3
ire Way. Yate 39 E3
irehampton Rd. Bris 48 B3
ockerwick La. Bathf 86 B3
op La. Gr Bad 30 C1
ophouse Rd. Bath 101 D3
oredtich. Ch St 112 B4
ort La. Litt 129 F1
ort La. Lo Ash 62 A1
ort St. Bris 64 A3
ort Way. Thorn 15 D4
ort Way. Wrax 61 D2
orthill Rd. West 39 E2
ortlands Rd. Bris 34 A1
ortwood Hill. Puck 52 C2

Shortwood Rd. Bris 79 F2
Shortwood Rd. Puck 53 D3
Shortwood View. Kingsw .. 65 F4
Shortwood Wlk. Bris 79 F2
Showering Rd. Bris 80 B3
Shrubbery Ave. W-S-M 87 E1
Shrubbery Cotts. Bris 49 D1
Shrubbery Rd. Mang 51 E3
Shrubbery Rd. W-S-M 87 E1
Shrubbery Terr. W-S-M 87 E1
Shrubbery Wlk W. W-S-M .. 87 E1
Shrubbery Wlk. W-S-M 87 E1
Shuter Rd. Bris 78 C3
Sibland Cl. Thorn 15 E4
Sibland Rd. Thorn 15 E4
Sibland Way. Thorn 15 E4
Sibland. Thorn 15 E4
Sidcot La. Wins 125 D4
Sidcot. Bris 65 D1
Sideland Cl. Bris 80 C3
Sidelands Rd. Bris 51 E3
Sidings The. Char 11 D3
Sidings The. Co Mar 127 E4
Sidmouth Gdns. Bris 63 E1
Sidmouth Rd. Bris 63 F1
Sidney Hill Cottage Homes.
   Chur 108 C2
Signal Rd. Kingsw 51 F2
Silbury Rd. Bris 62 C1
Silbury Rise. Keyn 82 A1
Silcox Rd. Bris 79 E2
Silklands Gr. Bris 48 B4
Silver Birch Cl. St Gif 36 B4
Silver Ct. Nail 59 E1
Silver Mead. Cong 91 E1
Silver Moor La. Ban 106 C4
Silver St. Bris 63 E4
Silver St. Ch Mag 96 A2
Silver St. Cong 91 E1
Silver St. Hol 138 B1
Silver St. Kilm 139 D3
Silver St. Mid No 138 A4
Silver St. Nail 59 E1
Silver St. Rod 138 A4
Silver St. W in G 44 C1
Silver St. Wring 92 C1
Silverberry Rd. W-S-M 89 D1
Silverhill Rd. Bris 34 C2
Silverlow Rd. Nail 59 E1
Silverstone Way. Cong 91 E2
Silverthorne La. Bris 64 A3
Silverthorne Wharf. Bris 64 A3
Silverton Ct. Bris 63 F1
Simon's Cl. Paul 131 F3
Simons Cl. W-S-M 89 D1
Simplex Ind Est The.
   Kingsw 66 B2
Singapore Rd. W-S-M 104 C2
Single Hill. Well 134 A3
Sion Hill Pl. Bath 84 C1
Sion Hill. Bath 84 C1
Sion Hill. Bath 101 E4
Sion Hill. Bris 62 C4
Sion La. Bris 62 C4
Sion Pl. Bris 62 C4
Sion Rd. Bath 84 C1
Sion Rd. Bris 63 E2
Sir John's La. Bris 50 A3
Siskin Wlk. W-S-M 105 F4
Siston Centre The. Kingsw .. 52 A1
Siston Cl. Sist 52 A1
Siston Comm. Sist 52 A1
Siston La. Puck 52 C1
Siston Park. Sist 52 A1
Six Ways. Cleve 57 E2
Sixpence. Paul 115 E1
Sixth Ave. Bris 36 A1
Sixty Acres Cl. Wrax 61 D2
Skinner's Hill. Tims 132 C4
Skinners La. Chur 108 C2
Skippon Ct. Kingsw 65 F3
Sladacre La. Blag 110 C1
Slade La. Ba Gu 77 E2
Slade La. Lymp 122 A1
Slade Rd. Portis 45 E3
Sladebrook Ave. Bath 101 E2
Sladebrook Rd. Bath 101 D2
Slate La. Co Dan 98 A4
Sleep La. Whit 80 B2
Slimbridge Cl. Ch Sod 39 F4
Sloan St. Bris 64 B4
Slough La. Co Ash 68 C3
Slymbridge Ave. Bris 35 D2
Small Down End. Winsc 107 F1
Small La. Bris 50 C3
Small St. Bris 63 E4
Small St. Bris 64 A3
Smallbrook La. Co Dan 98 A3
Smallcombe Cl. Mid No 132 C3
Smallcombe Rd. Mid No 132 C2
Smallway. Cong 91 E3
Smarts Green. Ch Sod 40 B4
Smeaton Rd. Bris 62 C3
Smithcourt Dr. St Gif 36 B3
Smithmead. Bris 79 D3
Smoke La. Avon 33 E4
Smyth Rd. Bris 63 D2
Smythe Croft. Bris 80 A2

Smyths Cl. Avon 33 D1
Snow Hill. Bath 85 D1
Snowberry Cl. W-S-M 89 D1
Snowberry Wlk. Bris 50 C1
Snowdon Cl. Bris 50 C2
Snowdon Rd. Bris 50 C2
Snowdon Vale. W-S-M 88 A1
Sodbury Rd. Wickw 18 A2
Solent Way. Thorn 15 E4
Solsbury Cl. St Bathe 85 F2
Solsbury Way. Bath 85 D1
Somer Ave. Mid No 131 F1
Somer Lea. Chil 137 E3
Somer Rd. Mid No 131 F1
Somerby Cl. St Gif 36 B4
Somerdale Ave. Bath 101 E1
Somerdale Ave. Bris 64 A1
Somerdale Ave. W-S-M 105 E4
Somerdale Cl. W-S-M 105 E4
Somerdale Rd N. Keyn 81 F4
Somerdale Rd. Keyn 81 F4
Somerdale View. Bath 101 E1
Somermead. Bris 63 E1
Somerset Ave. Yate 27 F2
Somerset Cres. St Gif 36 C3
Somerset Folly. Tims 116 A1
Somerset La. Bath 84 C1
Somerset Mews. W-S-M .. 104 C3
Somerset Pl. Bath 84 C1
Somerset Rd. Bris 64 A2
Somerset Rd. Cleve 57 F2
Somerset Rd. Portis 44 C3
Somerset Sq. Bris 63 E3
Somerset Sq. Nail 59 F1
Somerset St. Bris 63 E3
Somerset St. Bris 63 F3
Somerset Terr. Bris 63 E2
Somerset Way. Paul 131 F3
Somerton Cl. Kingsw 65 F4
Somerton Rd. Bris 49 E1
Somerton Rd. Cleve 57 F1
Somerton. W-S-M 105 D1
Somervale Rd. Rad 132 C1
Somerville Cl. Keyn 82 C1
Somerville Rd. Wins 108 A2
Sommerille Rd S. Bris 49 F1
Sommerville Rd. Bris 49 F2
Sophia Gdns. W-S-M 89 D2
Sorrel Cl. Thorn 8 B1
Soundwell Rd. Bris 65 E4
Soundwell Rd. Kingsw 51 E1
South Ave. Bath 101 E3
South Ave. Portis 45 E3
South Ave. Yate 27 D1
South Combe. Blea 122 A3
South Croft. Bris 49 E4
South Croft. Winsc 107 F1
South Dene. Bris 48 C3
South Gr. Bris 49 E3
South Gr. E in G 47 E2
South Green St. Bris 62 C3
South Hayes. Bris 50 A2
South Hill. Winsc 107 F1
South Lawn Cl. Lock 105 F2
South Lawn. Lock 105 F2
South Lea Rd. Bath 101 D4
South Liberty La. Bris 62 C1
South Meadows. Wring 92 C1
South Par. Bath 102 A3
South Par. Ch Mag 96 A2
South Par. W-S-M 104 B4
South Par. Yate 27 F1
South Rd. Alve 24 C3
South Rd. Bris 48 C3
South Rd. Bris 63 E2
South Rd. Kingsw 65 E4
South Rd. Lymp 122 A1
South Rd. Mid No 132 A1
South Rd. Portis 45 D4
South Rd. Tims 116 A1
South Rd. W-S-M 87 E1
South Rock Ind Est. Chil .. 137 E1
South Side. Cong 91 F3
South St. Bris 63 D2
South St. Chil 137 F1
South Terr. Bris 49 D1
South Terr. W-S-M 104 B4
South View Cres. Fr Cot 38 B3
South View Pl. Mid No 132 A1
South View Rd. Bath 101 E3
South View Rise. Fr Cot 38 B3
South View Terr. Yatt 74 A1
South View. Fr Cot 38 A4
South View. Kilm 139 D2
South View. Mang 51 F3
South View. Mid No 132 C3
South View. Portis 45 D4
South View. Tims 116 A1
South Wlk. Yate 27 F1
Southbourne Gdns. Bath .. 85 D1
Southcot Pl. Bath 102 A3
Southdown Ave. Bath 101 D2
Southdown Rd. Bath 101 D2
Southdown Rd. Bris 48 C4
Southdown. W-S-M 88 C2
Southend Rd. W-S-M 104 C2
Southern Way. Cleve 57 D1

Southernhay Ave. Bris 63 D3
Southernhay. Bris 63 D3
Southernhay. Kingsw 51 E2
Southey Ave. Kingsw 51 F1
Southey Ct. Kingsw 51 E1
Southey Rd. Cleve 57 E1
Southey St. Bris 49 F1
Southfield Ave. Kingsw 51 F1
Southfield Cl. Nail 59 F2
Southfield Cl. W-S-M 104 B1
Southfield Ct. Bris 49 D4
Southfield Pl. Bris 63 E2
Southfield Rd. Bris 49 D4
Southfield Rd. Bris 49 E1
Southfield Rd. Nail 59 F2
Southfield Road Trading Est.
   Nail 59 F2
Southfield. N St P 135 F2
Southfield. Rad 133 D1
Southgate. Bath 102 A3
Southlands Dr. Tims 116 A1
Southlands Way. Cong 91 F3
Southlands. Bath 84 A1
Southlands. Tyth 16 A2
Southleaze. Wins 125 D3
Southleigh Rd. Bris 63 D4
Southmead Rd. Bris 35 F1
Southmead Rd. W-S-M 105 D4
Southmead. Wins 125 D4
Southover Cl. Bris 49 D4
Southover Rd. Paul 115 E1
Southridge Hts. W-S-M 122 A4
Southsea Rd. Bris 36 A4
Southside Cl. Bris 48 A4
Southside Cres. W St L 88 A2
Southside. W-S-M 104 C4
Southstoke La. Sosto 118 C4
Southstoke Rd. Bath 101 F1
Southview Cl. Lock 105 F1
Southville Rd. Bris 63 E2
Southville Rd. W-S-M 104 C2
Southway Dr. Kingsw 66 B3
Southwell St. Bris 63 E4
Southwood Ave. Bris 48 B4
Southwood Dr E. Bris 48 B4
Southwood Dr. Bris 48 A4
Sovereign Gdns. Bris 48 C2
Spa La. Bath 85 E1
Spalding Cl. Bris 50 A2
Spaniorum View. Alm 22 C1
Spar Rd. Avon 33 E2
Spar Rd. Yate 27 E1
Spartley Dr. Bris 78 C3
Spartley Wlk. Bris 78 C3
Specklemead. Paul 131 E3
Speedwell Ave. Bris 64 B4
Speedwell Cl. Thorn 8 B1
Speedwell Rd. Bris 51 D1
Spencer Dr. W-S-M 89 D2
Spey Cl. Thorn 15 E4
Spider La. W-S-M 104 B4
Spindleberry Gr. Nail 60 A1
Spinners End. W-S-M 89 D2
Spinney Croft. Bris 78 C3
Spinney The. Fr Cot 38 A4
Spinney The. W-S-M 104 C1
Spires View. Bris 50 C3
Spratts Bridge. Ch Mag 96 A2
Spring Cres. Bath 102 A3
Spring Gardens Rd. Bath .. 102 A4
Spring Gardens Rd. Bath .. 102 A4
Spring Gdns. Bris 64 A1
Spring Ground Rd. Paul 131 F3
Spring Hill Dr. W-S-M 88 C1
Spring Hill. Bris 63 E4
Spring Hill. Kingsw 51 F1
Spring Hill. W-S-M 88 B1
Spring La. Bath 85 D1
Spring Rise. Portis 45 E2
Spring St Pl. Bris 63 F2
Spring St. Bris 63 F2
Spring Terr. W-S-M 88 B1
Spring Valley. W-S-M 88 B1
Springfield Ave. Bris 47 E3
Springfield Ave. Mang 52 A4
Springfield Ave. W-S-M 88 B1
Springfield Bldgs. Mid No .. 133 D2
Springfield Bldgs. Paul 131 E1
Springfield Cl. Bath 101 D1
Springfield Cl. Mang 52 A4
Springfield Cres. Mid No 133 D2
Springfield Gdns. Ban 107 D2
Springfield Gr. Bris 49 E3
Springfield Hts. Mid No 132 C1
Springfield Lawns. Bris 47 E3
Springfield Pl. Mid No 132 C2
Springfield Rd. Bris 49 E1
Springfield Rd. E in G 47 E2
Springfield Rd. Mang 52 A4
Springfield Rd. Portis 45 D3
Springfield. P St J 133 E4
Springfield. Thorn 15 E4
Springfields. Bris 36 A1
Springhill Cl. Paul 131 E3
Springleaze. Bris 64 A1
Springleaze. Mang 52 A4
Springville Cl. Kingsw 66 A2

Springwater Park Ind Est.
   Bris 64 C4
Springwell. N St P 135 F2
Springwood Dr. Bris 34 B2
Spruce Way. Bris 35 F4
Square The. Alve 15 D2
Square The. Axb 125 E1
Square The. Ban 107 D2
Square The. Blag 109 F2
Square The. Bris 64 A1
Square The. Clut 114 C1
Square The. Mang 51 F2
Square The. Ship 125 F4
Square The. Tims 116 A1
Square The. Well 118 B1
Square The. Wins 124 C3
Squire La. Co Mar 111 E1
Squires Ct. Kingsw 65 F2
Squires Leaze. Thorn 8 B1
Stabbins Cl. W-S-M 89 D3
Stable Yd. Bath 101 E3
Stackpool Rd. Bris 63 E2
Staddlestones. Mid No 137 F4
Stadium Rd. Bris 49 E3
Stafford Cres. Thorn 8 A1
Stafford Pl. W-S-M 104 C4
Stafford Rd. Bris 50 A1
Stafford Rd. Portis 45 F2
Stafford Rd. W-S-M 104 C4
Stafford St. Bris 63 E2
Staffords Ct. Kingsw 66 A3
Stainer Cl. Bris 79 E4
Stalcombe La. Co Dan 99 D2
Stall St. Bath 102 A3
Stambrook Park. Bathe 85 F3
Stanbridge Cl. Mang 51 F3
Stanbridge Rd. Mang 51 F3
Stanbury Ave. Bris 51 E3
Stanbury Rd. Bris 63 F2
Stancombe La. Back 76 C4
Standfast Rd. Bris 34 C2
Standish Ave. St Gif 24 B1
Standish Cl. Bris 34 C1
Standon Way. Bris 35 E4
Stane Way. Avon 47 E4
Stanfield Cl. Bris 50 B3
Stanford Cl. Fr Cot 37 F4
Stanford Pl. Bris 79 E4
Stanhope Pl. Bath 101 F3
Stanhope Rd. Kingsw 65 F1
Stanhope Rd. W-S-M 104 C2
Stanhope St. Bris 64 A3
Stanier Rd. Bath 101 F3
Stanle Hill. Bris 64 A2
Stanley Ave. Bris 36 A1
Stanley Ave. Bris 49 F2
Stanley Chase. Bris 50 C1
Stanley Cres. Bris 36 A1
Stanley Ct. Mid No 132 A1
Stanley Gdns. Kingsw 66 A2
Stanley Gr. W-S-M 104 C4
Stanley Mead. St Gif 24 C1
Stanley Park Rd. Kingsw .. 51 F2
Stanley Park. Bris 50 B1
Stanley Rd W. Bath 101 E3
Stanley Rd. Bris 49 E1
Stanley Rd. Kingsw 66 A4
Stanley St N. Bris 63 E2
Stanley St S. Bris 63 E1
Stanley St. Bris 63 E1
Stanley Terr. Bris 63 E1
Stanley Terr. Mid No 133 D2
Stanshalls Cl. Win 94 B4
Stanshalls Dr. Win 94 B4
Stanshalls Rd. Win 94 B4
Stanshaw Cl. Bris 51 D4
Stanshaw Rd. Bris 51 D4
Stanshawe Cres. Yate 27 F1
Stanshawes Dr. Yate 27 E1
Stanshawes Ct. St Gif 24 B1
Stanton Cl. Kingsw 51 F1
Stanton La. Pens 97 E2
Stanton Rd. Bris 35 F1
Stanton Wick La. Pens 97 D1
Stanway Cl. Bath 101 E1
Staple Gr. Keyn 81 E3
Staple Grove Cres. Bris 65 D3
Staplehill Rd. Bris 51 E2
Staples Cl. Cleve 57 F1
Staples Green. W-S-M 89 D2
Staples Hill. Hi Cha 120 B2
Staples Rd. Yate 27 E1
Stapleton Cl. Bris 50 B3
Stapleton Rd. Bris 50 A1
Stapleton Rd. Bris 50 B2
Star Barn Rd. Wint 37 F4
Star La. Bris 50 C2
Starcross Rd. W-S-M 89 D1
Starling Cl. W-S-M 105 F4
Starrs Cl. Axb 125 D1
Station App. Pens 97 E3
Station App. W-S-M 104 C4
Station Cl. Bris 51 D2
Station Cl. Ch Sod 40 B4
Station Cl. Kingsw 66 B4
Station La. Bris 50 A2
Station Rd. Alm 22 C2
Station Rd. Axb 125 E1

Station Rd. Back ... 76 A3
Station Rd. Back ... 77 D4
Station Rd. Bath ... 101 C2
Station Rd. Blag ... 110 C2
Station Rd. Bris ... 34 C2
Station Rd. Bris ... 36 A1
Station Rd. Bris ... 36 A2
Station Rd. Bris ... 47 E3
Station Rd. Bris ... 49 F1
Station Rd. Bris ... 49 F2
Station Rd. Bris ... 51 D2
Station Rd. Bris ... 64 B1
Station Rd. Char ... 11 D3
Station Rd. Cleve ... 57 E2
Station Rd. Clut ... 114 C2
Station Rd. Cong ... 91 E2
Station Rd. E in G ... 47 E2
Station Rd. Fr Cot ... 38 B3
Station Rd. Gr Bad ... 30 C1
Station Rd. Hi Cha ... 120 B3
Station Rd. Ir Act ... 26 B2
Station Rd. Keyn ... 81 F3
Station Rd. Kingsw ... 51 F2
Station Rd. Kingsw ... 66 B4
Station Rd. Lock ... 89 E1
Station Rd. Mid No ... 132 A1
Station Rd. Nail ... 59 F1
Station Rd. Piln ... 22 C2
Station Rd. Portb ... 46 B2
Station Rd. Portis ... 45 E3
Station Rd. St Gif ... 36 B4
Station Rd. W-S-M ... 88 C1
Station Rd. W-S-M ... 104 C4
Station Rd. Winsc ... 107 F2
Station Rd. Wint ... 37 F2
Station Rd. Wring ... 92 B1
Station Rd. Yate ... 27 E1
Station Rd. Yatt ... 74 A1
Station R d. Wickw ... 18 A4
Staunton Fields. Whit ... 80 B2
Staunton La. Whit ... 80 B2
Staunton Rd. Ch Mag ... 96 A2
Staunton Way. Whit ... 80 B2
Staveley Cres. Bris ... 35 E1
Staverton Cl. St Gif ... 24 B1
Staverton Way. Kingsw ... 66 A4
Stavordale Gr. Bris ... 80 A3
Steam Mills. Mid No ... 137 F4
Stean Bridge Rd. St Gif ... 36 C3
Steel Ct. Kingsw ... 65 F2
Steel Mills. Keyn ... 81 F2
Stella Gr. Bris ... 63 D1
Stephen St. Bris ... 64 B4
Stephens Dr. Kingsw ... 65 F3
Stepney Rd. Bris ... 50 B1
Stepney Wlk. Bris ... 50 B1
Stepping Stones The. Bris ... 64 C3
Sterncourt Rd. Bris ... 51 D4
Stevens Cres. Bris ... 63 F2
Steway La. Lymp ... 122 B2
Stibbs Ct. Kingsw ... 65 F2
Stibbs Hill. Bris ... 65 D4
Stickland. Cleve ... 57 E1
Stidcot La. Tyth ... 16 B3
Stidcote La. Wickw ... 16 C3
Stile Acres. Bris ... 34 A1
Stilemead La. Co Mar ... 111 E1
Stillhouse La. Bris ... 63 E2
Stillingfleet Rd. Bris ... 79 E3
Stillman Cl. Bris ... 78 C2
Stinchcombe. Yate ... 27 F1
Stirling Cl. Yate ... 27 E2
Stirling Rd. Bris ... 64 B2
Stirling Way. Keyn ... 81 F2
Stirtingale Ave. Bath ... 101 E2
Stirtingale Rd. Bath ... 101 E2
Stitchings La. Engl ... 117 E4
Stitchings Shord La. Bi Sut ... 113 E2
Stock Hill. Thorn ... 7 D1
Stock La. Chur ... 109 D4
Stock La. Cong ... 91 F1
Stock Way N. Nail ... 59 F1
Stock Way S. Nail ... 59 F1
Stockhill Cl. Chil ... 137 E2
Stockhill Rd. Chil ... 137 E1
Stockmead. Chur ... 109 D3
Stockton Cl. Bris ... 79 F2
Stockton Cl. Kingsw ... 66 A2
Stockwell Ave. Mang ... 52 A4
Stockwell Cl. Mang ... 51 F4
Stockwell Dr. Mang ... 52 A3
Stockwell Glen. Mang ... 52 A4
Stockwood Cres. Bris ... 63 F1
Stockwood Hill. Keyn ... 81 E4
Stockwood La. Bris ... 80 C3
Stockwood La. Whit ... 80 C3
Stockwood Rd. Bris ... 81 D4
Stodelegh Cl. W-S-M ... 89 D2
Stoke Bridge Ave. St Gif ... 36 B3
Stoke Hamlet. Bris ... 48 C3
Stoke Hill. Bris ... 48 C2
Stoke Hill. Ch St ... 112 B4
Stoke La. Bris ... 48 C3
Stoke La. Bris ... 50 C4
Stoke La. St Gif ... 36 B4
Stoke Mead. Li St ... 119 F4
Stoke Meadows. St Gif ... 24 B1

Stoke Paddock Rd. Bris ... 48 B3
Stoke Park Rd S. Bris ... 48 C2
Stoke Park Rd. Bris ... 48 C2
Stoke Rd. Bris ... 49 D1
Stoke Rd. Portis ... 45 E3
Stoke View Rd. Bris ... 50 C2
Stoke View. Bris ... 36 A2
Stokefield Cl. Thorn ... 8 A1
Stokeleigh Wlk. Bris ... 48 B3
Stokemead. St Gif ... 36 B4
Stokes Croft. Bris ... 63 F4
Stokes Ct. Kingsw ... 66 A2
Stone La. Wint ... 37 F2
Stone's Cross. Mid No ... 132 A1
Stoneable Rd. Mid No ... 133 D2
Stoneage La. P St J ... 117 D1
Stoneberry Rd. Bris ... 80 A3
Stonebridge Park. Bris ... 50 C1
Stonebridge Rd. W-S-M ... 104 C2
Stonebridge. Cleve ... 57 E1
Stonechat Gdns. Bris ... 50 C3
Stonehenge La. Nail ... 59 F2
Stonehill. Kingsw ... 65 F2
Stonehouse Cl. Bath ... 102 A1
Stonehouse La. Bath ... 102 A1
Stoneleigh Cres. Bris ... 64 A1
Stoneleigh Rd. Bris ... 64 A1
Stoneleigh Wlk. Bris ... 64 A1
Stoneleigh. Ch Mag ... 96 A2
Stonewell Dr. Cong ... 91 E2
Stonewell Gr. Cong ... 91 E2
Stonewell La. Cong ... 91 E2
Stonewell Park Rd. Cong ... 91 E2
Stoney Steep. Wrax ... 60 A2
Stoney Stile Rd. Alve ... 15 D3
Stoneyard La. Litt ... 129 E1
Stoneyfield Cl. E in G ... 47 D3
Stoneyfields. E in G ... 47 D2
Stores Rd. Avon ... 33 E2
Stormont Cl. W-S-M ... 104 C2
Stothard Rd. Bris ... 50 A4
Stottbury Rd. Bris ... 50 A2
Stoulton Gr. Bris ... 35 D2
Stourden Cl. Bris ... 51 D4
Stourton Dr. Kingsw ... 65 F2
Stover Rd. Yate ... 27 D1
Stover Trading Est. Yate ... 27 D1
Stowel Hill Rd. Tyth ... 16 A3
Stowey Bottom. Bi Sut ... 113 F3
Stowey Park. Yatt ... 91 E4
Stowey Rd. Yatt ... 91 E4
Stowick Cres. Bris ... 34 B1
Stradbrook Ave. Bris ... 65 D4
Stradling Ave. W-S-M ... 104 C3
Stradling Rd. Bris ... 34 B1
Straight St. Bris ... 63 F3
Straits Par. Bris ... 51 D3
Stratford Cl. Bris ... 79 F2
Stratford La. Co Mar ... 112 C1
Strathmore Rd. Bris ... 49 F3
Stratton Cl. St Gif ... 36 B4
Stratton Rd. Keyn ... 82 C2
Stratton St. Bris ... 63 F4
Strawberry Cl. Nail ... 59 E1
Strawberry Gdns. Nail ... 75 E4
Strawberry Hill. Cleve ... 57 F2
Strawberry La. Dun ... 78 C4
Strawbridge Rd. Bris ... 64 A4
Stream Cl. Bris ... 35 E2
Stream Side. Mang ... 51 F3
Stream The. Bris ... 37 D1
Streamcross. Yatt ... 74 C1
Streamleaze Ct. Thorn ... 15 D4
Streamleaze. Ch Mag ... 96 A2
Streamleaze. Thorn ... 15 E4
Streamside Rd. Ch Sod ... 28 A1
Streamside. Ch Mag ... 96 A2
Streamside. Cleve ... 57 F2
Street End La. Blag ... 110 B1
Street End. Blag ... 110 B1
Street The. Alve ... 15 D3
Street The. Bi Sut ... 113 F2
Street The. Ch St ... 112 B4
Street The. Chil ... 137 E3
Street The. Co Mar ... 111 E1
Street The. Co Mar ... 128 A4
Street The. Farm ... 115 F3
Street The. Luck ... 31 F2
Street The. N Nib ... 5 E2
Street The. Olve ... 14 A2
Street The. Rad ... 132 B1
Street The. Win ... 94 C1
Stretford Ave. Bris ... 64 B4
Stretford Rd. Bris ... 64 B4
Stride Cl. Piln ... 22 A3
Strode Comm. Alve ... 14 C3
Strode Gdns. Alve ... 14 C3
Strode Rd. Cleve ... 57 E1
Stroud Rd. Bris ... 35 F4
Stroud Rd. Bris ... 47 F3
Stuart Pl. Bath ... 101 E3
Stuart Rd. W-S-M ... 105 D3
Stuart St. Bris ... 64 B4
Stumpwell La. N Nib ... 5 F1
Sturden La. Bris ... 37 E2
Sturdon Rd. Bris ... 63 D2
Sturmer Cl. Yate ... 27 F2
Sturminster Cl. Bris ... 80 B3

Sturminster Rd. Bris ... 80 B4
Sullivan Cl. Bris ... 79 E3
Sumerlin Dr. Cleve ... 57 F2
Summer Hill. Bris ... 64 A2
Summer La N. W-S-M ... 89 D1
Summer La. Ban ... 106 C2
Summer La. Bath ... 102 B1
Summer La. Lock ... 89 D1
Summer La. W-S-M ... 89 D1
Summer St. Bris ... 63 E2
Summerfield Rd. Bath ... 85 D1
Summerfield. W-S-M ... 89 D2
Summerhayes. Kingsw ... 66 B3
Summerhill Rd. Bath ... 84 B1
Summerhill Rd. Bris ... 64 C4
Summerhill Terr. Bris ... 64 C4
Summerhouse. Nail ... 59 E2
Summerlands Rd. W-S-M . 105 D4
Summerlands. Back ... 76 A3
Summerlea. Pris ... 117 D3
Summerleaze. Bris ... 51 E2
Summerleaze. Keyn ... 81 F4
Summers Dr. Doyn ... 54 A1
Summers Mead. Yate ... 27 E1
Summers Rd. Bris ... 50 A1
Summers Terr. Bris ... 50 A1
Sundays Hill. Alm ... 24 A2
Sunderland Pl. Bris ... 63 D4
Sunderland St. Bath ... 102 A4
Sundridge Park. Yate ... 39 F4
Sunfield Rd. Lock ... 105 F2
Sunningdale Cl. Nail ... 60 A1
Sunningdale Dr. Kingsw ... 66 A3
Sunningdale Rd. W-S-M ... 88 C2
Sunningdale. Bris ... 63 D4
Sunningdale. Yate ... 39 F4
Sunny Bank. Bris ... 51 D1
Sunny Hill. Bris ... 48 B4
Sunny Wlk. Bris ... 51 D1
Sunnybank. Mang ... 51 F3
Sunnydene. Bris ... 64 B2
Sunnyhill Dr. Bris ... 47 F3
Sunnymead. Keyn ... 81 F2
Sunnymead. Mid No ... 131 F1
Sunnymeade Rd. Nail ... 59 E2
Sunnyside Cres. Cleve ... 57 E2
Sunnyside La. Yate ... 27 E1
Sunnyside Rd N. W-S-M ... 104 C3
Sunnyside Rd. Cleve ... 57 E2
Sunnyside Rd. W-S-M ... 104 C3
Sunnyside View. P St J ... 133 E4
Sunnyside. Bris ... 48 C3
Sunnyside. Clut ... 115 D2
Sunnyside. Fr Cot ... 38 A4
Sunnyvale Dr. Kingsw ... 66 A2
Sunnyvale. Cleve ... 57 D1
Sunnyvale. Tims ... 132 C4
Sunridge Cl. Mid No ... 137 F4
Sunridge Park. Mid No ... 137 F4
Sunridge. Mang ... 51 E3
Sunrise Gr. Bris ... 64 B2
Surrey Rd. Bris ... 49 F2
Surrey St. Bris ... 63 F4
Sussex Pl. Bris ... 49 F1
Sussex St. Bris ... 64 A3
Sutherland Ave. Mang ... 51 F4
Sutherland Ave. Yate ... 27 E2
Sutherland Dr. Lock ... 105 E1
Sutherland Pl. Bris ... 49 D1
Sutton Ave. Bris ... 64 B2
Sutton Hill Rd. Bi Sut ... 113 E4
Sutton La. Wring ... 93 F1
Sutton Park. Bi Sut ... 113 E2
Sutton St. Bath ... 102 A4
Swainswick Gdns. Bath ... 85 E1
Swainswick La. Bathe ... 85 E2
Swainswick. Bris ... 79 F3
Swaish Dr. Kingsw ... 66 A2
Swallow Cl. W-S-M ... 105 F4
Swallow Dr. Bris ... 35 F4
Swallow Park. Thorn ... 8 B2
Swallow St. Bath ... 102 A3
Swallows Ct. St Gif ... 36 C2
Swan Cl. W-S-M ... 105 F4
Swan La. Fr Cot ... 25 D1
Swan La. Wint ... 37 F4
Swancombe. Blag ... 110 C1
Swancombe. W in G ... 59 F4
Swane Rd. Bris ... 80 C3
Swangrove. Wint ... 37 F3
Swanley La. Newp ... 4 A3
Swanmoor Cres. Bris ... 35 D2
Sweets Cl. Kingsw ... 51 F1
Sweets Rd. Kingsw ... 51 F1
Swift Cl. W-S-M ... 88 C1
Swinhay La. N Nib ... 5 E1
Swiss Dr. Bris ... 62 C1
Swiss Rd. Bris ... 62 C1
Swiss Rd. W-S-M ... 104 C4
Sycamore Cl. Bris ... 50 C1
Sycamore Cl. Kingsw ... 65 D2
Sycamore Cl. Nail ... 59 F1
Sycamore Cl. Ship ... 125 F4
Sycamore Cl. W-S-M ... 105 D4
Sycamore Dr. Bris ... 35 F4

Sycamore Rd. Rad ... 133 D1
Sydenham Bldgs. Bath ... 101 F3
Sydenham Hill. Bris ... 49 E1
Sydenham La. Bris ... 49 F1
Sydenham Rd. Bath ... 101 F3
Sydenham Rd. Bris ... 49 E1
Sydenham Rd. Bris ... 64 A2
Sydenham Way. Kingsw ... 65 E2
Sydney Bldgs. Bath ... 102 A3
Sydney House. E in G ... 47 E2
Sydney Mews. Bath ... 102 A4
Sydney Pl. Bath ... 102 A4
Sydney Rd. Bath ... 102 A4
Sydney Row. Bris ... 63 D3
Sydney Wharf. Bath ... 102 A4
Sylvan Way. Bris ... 48 B4
Sylvia Ave. Bris ... 63 F2
Symes Ave. Bris ... 79 E2
Symington Rd. Bris ... 51 D3
Syston Way. Kingsw ... 51 E1

Tabernacle Rd. Kingsw ... 65 E3
Tackley Rd. Bris ... 50 A2
Tadwick La. Bathe ... 84 C4
Tailor's Ct. Bris ... 63 E4
Talbot Ave. Bris ... 51 E1
Talbot Rd. Bris ... 64 A1
Talgarth Rd. Bris ... 49 F2
Tallis Gr. Bris ... 79 E3
Tamar Cl. Thorn ... 15 E4
Tamar Dr. Keyn ... 82 A2
Tamar Rd. Bris ... 64 B3
Tamar Rd. W-S-M ... 89 D1
Tamblyn Cl. Mid No ... 133 D2
Tamsin Ct. Keyn ... 81 F3
Tamworth Rd. Keyn ... 81 F2
Tanhouse La. Ir Act ... 27 E4
Tanhouse La. Yate ... 27 E4
Tankard's Cl. Bris ... 63 E4
Tanner Cl. Kingsw ... 65 F3
Tanners Ct. Bris ... 37 D1
Tanners Cl. Thorn ... 15 D4
Tanners La. Marsh ... 69 F4
Tanorth Cl. Bris ... 80 A2
Tanorth Rd. Bris ... 79 F2
Tanyard The. Kingsw ... 66 A1
Tapsters. Kingsw ... 66 A2
Tarnock Ave. Bris ... 80 A4
Tarnwell. Pens ... 97 D1
Taunton Rd. W-S-M ... 89 D2
Taunton Wlk. Bris ... 51 E1
Taveners Ind Est. Nail ... 59 F2
Taverner Cl. Bris ... 79 E4
Tavistock Rd. Bris ... 63 F1
Tavistock Rd. W-S-M ... 89 D1
Tavistock Wlk. Bris ... 63 F1
Tawny Way. W-S-M ... 105 F4
Taylor Cl. Kingsw ... 65 F4
Taylor Ct. W-S-M ... 89 D2
Taylor Gdns. Bris ... 78 C2
Tayman Cl. Bris ... 49 F3
Tayman Ridge. Bitt ... 82 B4
Taynton Cl. Kingsw ... 66 B1
Teal Cl. St Gif ... 24 B1
Teal Cl. W-S-M ... 88 C1
Teddington Cl. Bath ... 101 E2
Teesdale Cl. W-S-M ... 105 E4
Teewell Ave. Kingsw ... 51 F1
Teewell Cl. Kingsw ... 51 F2
Teewell Hill. Kingsw ... 51 F1
Teignmouth Rd. Bris ... 63 F1
Teignmouth Rd. Cleve ... 57 F2
Telephone Ave. Bris ... 63 E3
Telford Wlk. Bris ... 51 D1
Tellisford La. N St P ... 135 F2
Templar Rd. Yate ... 27 F1
Temple Back. Bris ... 63 F3
Temple Gate. Bris ... 63 F3
Temple St. Bris ... 63 D1
Temple St. Bris ... 63 F3
Temple St. Keyn ... 81 F3
Temple Way Underpass.
  Bris ... 63 F4
Temple Way. Bris ... 63 F4
Templeland Rd. Bris ... 78 C3
Tenby Rd. Keyn ... 81 E2
Tenby St. Bris ... 64 A4
Tennessee Dr. Bris ... 49 E3
Tennis Court Ave. Paul ... 131 E3
Tennis Court Rd. Paul ... 131 E3
Tennis Rd. Bris ... 64 A1
Tenniscourt Rd. Kingsw ... 52 A1
Tennyson Ave. Cleve ... 57 D1
Tennyson Cl. Keyn ... 81 F3
Tennyson Rd. Bath ... 101 E4
Tennyson Rd. Bris ... 49 E2
Tennyson Rd. W-S-M ... 105 D2
Tenterk Cl. Blea ... 122 A3
Tenth Ave. Bris ... 36 A1
Tereslake Green. Bris ... 35 E2
Terrace Wlk. Bath ... 102 A3
Terrell Gdns. Bris ... 64 B4
Terrell St. Bris ... 63 E4
Terry Hill. Kilm ... 139 E4
Tetbury Gdns. Nail ... 60 A1
Tetbury Rd. Bris ... 64 C4
Tetbury Rd. Bris ... 51 D4
Teviot Rd. Keyn ... 82 A2

Tewkesbury Rd. Bris ... 50 A4
Tewther Rd. Bris ... 79 E2
Teyfant Rd. Bris ... 79 F2
Teyfant Wlk. Bris ... 79 F2
Thackeray Ave. Cleve ... 57 D1
Thackeray Rd. Cleve ... 57 D1
Thackeray Wlk. Bris ... 50 A4
Thames Cl. Char ... 11 D3
Thanet Rd. Bris ... 63 D2
Thatcher Cl. Portis ... 45 E4
Thatchers Cl. Bris ... 65 D3
The Timbers. Rod ... 138 A1
The Triangle. Wring ... 92 B2
The Tyning. Hi Cha ... 120 A3
The Weal. Bath ... 84 B2
There-and-back-again La.
  Bris ... 63 E4
Theresa Ave. Bris ... 49 F2
Theynes Croft. Lo Ash ... 62 A1
Thicket Ave. Bris ... 51 E2
Thicket Rd. Bris ... 51 E3
Thicket Wlk. Thorn ... 8 B2
Thiery Rd. Bris ... 64 B1
Thingwall Park. Bris ... 50 C1
Third Ave. Bris ... 36 A1
Third Ave. Bris ... 36 A2
Third Ave. Rod ... 138 B1
Third Way. Avon ... 33 E3
Thirlmere Ct. Kingsw ... 66 B1
Thirlmere Rd. Bris ... 36 A1
Thirlmere Rd. W-S-M ... 105 E4
Thistle St. Bris ... 63 D2
Thomas Cl. Ban ... 107 D1
Thomas La. Bris ... 63 F3
Thomas Pring Wlk. Bris ... 51 D1
Thomas St. Bris ... 49 E1
Thomas St. Bath ... 102 A4
Thomas St. Bris ... 49 F4
Thomas St. Bris ... 63 F4
Thomas St. Bris ... 64 A4
Thompson Rd. Bris ... 80 C3
Thomson Rd. Bris ... 64 A4
Thorn Cl. W-S-M ... 89 D2
Thorn Cl. Yate ... 27 E1
Thornbank Pl. Bath ... 101 F3
Thornbury Dr. W-S-M ... 104 B4
Thornbury Rd. Alve ... 15 D3
Thornbury Rd. W-S-M ... 104 B4
Thorndale Cl. W-S-M ... 105 E4
Thorndale. Bris ... 63 D4
Thornhayes Cl. Fr Cot ... 38 A4
Thornleigh Rd. Bris ... 49 F3
Thornmead Gr. Bris ... 35 D3
Thornycroft Cl. Bris ... 50 A4
Three Queens' La. Bris ... 63 F3
Three Wells Rd. Bris ... 78 C2
Thrissell St. Bris ... 64 A4
Throgmorton Rd. Bris ... 79 F4
Thrubwell La. But ... 94 A2
Thrush Cl. W-S-M ... 105 F4
Thurlestone. Bris ... 80 A3
Thurlow Rd. Bris ... 50 A3
Thurston's Barton. Bris ... 50 B1
Tibberton. Kingsw ... 66 A1
Tibbott Rd. Bris ... 80 B3
Tibbott Wlk. Bris ... 80 B3
Tichborne Rd. Bris ... 64 B4
Tichborne Rd. W-S-M ... 87 F1
Tickenham Hill. Nail ... 59 F3
Tickenham Rd. Cleve ... 58 A1
Tide Gr. Bris ... 48 A4
Tidenham Way. Bris ... 23 F1
Tiffany Ct. Bris ... 63 F3
Tiledown Cl. Clut ... 114 C1
Tiledown. Clut ... 114 C1
Tilley Cl. Farm ... 116 A3
Tilley Cl. Keyn ... 82 A1
Tilley La. Farm ... 115 F3
Tilling Rd. Bris ... 49 F4
Tilling Wlk. Bris ... 49 F4
Tilting Rd. Thorn ... 8 A1
Timber Dene. Bris ... 50 B2
Timberscombe Wlk. Bris ... 80 B3
Timsbury Rd. Bris ... 63 F1
Timsbury Rd. Farm ... 116 A3
Timsbury Rd. Paul ... 115 E3
Timsbury Wlk. Bris ... 63 F1
Tindell Ct. Kingsw ... 65 F2
Tinker's La. Co Mar ... 128 A4
Tinker's La. Hol ... 139 D1
Tintagel Cl. Keyn ... 81 E2
Tintern Ave. Bris ... 64 B4
Tintern Cl. Kingsw ... 65 F3
Tippetts Rd. Kingsw ... 65 E3
Tirley Way. W-S-M ... 88 A1
Titan Barrow. Bathf ... 86 B1
Tiverton Gdns. W-S-M ... 89 D2
Tiverton Rd. Cleve ... 57 F1
Tiverton Wlk. Bris ... 51 D1
Tockington La. Alm ... 24 A4
Tockington La. Olve ... 24 A4
Tockington La. Piln ... 24 A4
Tockington Park La. Alve ... 24 C4
Toddington Cl. Yate ... 39 E4
Toghill La. Doyn ... 68 A4
Toll Down Way. Burt ... 43 D3
Toll Rd. W-S-M ... 121 F4
Tolland. W-S-M ... 105 D1

Tollbridge Rd. Bath — **Wardour Rd. Bris**

Street	Page	Grid
Tollbridge Rd. Bath	85	F2
Tone Rd. Cleve	57	E1
Top Rd. Ship	125	F4
Tor Cl. W-S-M	89	D1
Tormarton Cres. Bris	34	C2
Tormarton Rd. A Tur	42	C3
Tormarton Rd. Marsh	56	A2
Tormarton Rd. Marsh	70	A4
Tormynton Rd. W-S-M	88	C2
Toronto Rd. Bris	50	A4
Torpoint Rd. Bris	63	E1
Torridge Rd. Keyn	82	A2
Torrington Ave. Bris	79	F4
Torrington Cres. W-S-M	89	D1
Tortworth Rd. Bris	49	F3
Totnes Cl. W-S-M	89	D1
Totshill Dr. Bris	79	F2
Totshill Gr. Bris	79	F2
Totterdown La. W-S-M	105	D1
Totterdown Rd. W-S-M	104	C2
Touching End La. Marsh	69	F4
Touchstone Ave. St Gif	36	C3
Tovey Cl. W-S-M	88	C2
Tower Hill. Bris	63	F4
Tower La. Bris	63	E4
Tower La. Kingsw	66	A3
Tower Rd N. Kingsw	66	A3
Tower Rd S. Kingsw	66	A3
Tower Rd. Bris	51	E1
Tower Rd. Portis	45	D2
Tower St. Bris	63	F3
Tower Wlk. W-S-M	87	E1
Towerhead Rd. Ban	107	E2
Town Barton. N St P	135	F2
Town End. N St P	135	F2
Townsend Cl. Bris	80	C3
Townsend La. Alm	24	A3
Townsend Rd. Bris	80	C3
Townsend Rd. W-S-M	89	D3
Townsend. Alm	23	F2
Townsend. E Harp	129	D3
Townwell. Crom	10	A1
Tracy Wlk. Bris	79	F4
Trafalgar Rd. Bath	84	A1
Trafalgar Terr. Bris	63	D1
Tralee Wlk. Bris	78	C2
Tramway Rd. Bris	64	B2
Tranmere Ave. Bris	35	D2
Tranmere Gr. Bris	35	D2
Tranton La. Rock	2	B2
Tratman Wlk. Bris	34	C2
Travers Cl. Bris	79	E3
Travers Wlk. St Gif	36	C3
Trawden Cl. W-S-M	88	A1
Tredegar Rd. Bris	51	D2
Tree Leaze. Yate	27	F1
Treefield Pl. Bris	50	A1
Treefield Rd. Cleve	57	E1
Tregarth Rd. Bris	62	C1
Trelawn Cl. Lock	89	E1
Trelawney Ave. Bris	64	B4
Trelawney Park. Bris	64	B4
Trelawney Rd. Bris	49	E1
Tremlett Mews. W-S-M	89	D2
Trench La. St Gif	25	D1
Trenchard Rd. Keyn	82	B2
Trenchard St. Bris	63	E4
Trendlewood Park. Bris	50	C3
Trendlewood Way. Nail	60	A1
Trenleigh Dr. W-S-M	89	D1
Trent Dr. Thorn	15	E4
Trent Gr. Keyn	82	A2
Trentham Cl. Bris	50	A1
Tresham Cl. St Gif	24	B1
Trevanna Rd. Bris	62	C1
Trevelyan Rd. W-S-M	104	C4
Trevelyan Wlk. Bris	34	C2
Treverdowe Wlk. Bris	34	B2
Trevethin Cl. Kingsw	65	E4
Trevisa Gr. Bris	35	E2
Trewartha Cl. W-S-M	104	C4
Trewartha Park. W-S-M	104	C4
Trewint Gdns. Bris	79	F4
Triangle Centre The. Cleve	57	E2
Triangle E. Bath	101	E3
Triangle N. Bath	101	E3
Triangle South. Bris	63	D4
Triangle The. Cleve	57	E2
Triangle W. Bath	101	E3
Triangle West. Bris	63	D4
Trident Cl. Mang	38	A1
Trim Bridge. Bath	101	F3
Trim St. Bath	101	F3
Trin Mills. Bris	63	E3
Trinder Rd. E in G	47	D2
Trinity Cl. Bath	101	F3
Trinity Ct. Nail	59	E1
Trinity Pl. W-S-M	87	E1
Trinity Rd. Bath	102	A1
Trinity Rd. Bris	64	A4
Trinity Rd. Nail	59	E1
Trinity Rd. W-S-M	87	E1
Trinity St. Bath	101	F3
Trinity Wlk. Bris	64	A4
Tripps Cnr. Yatt	91	E4
Troon Dr. Kingsw	66	A3
Troon. Yate	39	F4
Troopers Hill Rd. Bris	65	D4
Trossachs Dr. Bath	102	B4
Trowbridge Rd. Bris	35	E1
Trowbridge Wlk. Bris	35	E1
Truro Rd. Bris	63	D2
Truro Rd. Nail	60	A1
Trym Cross Rd. Bris	48	B3
Trym Rd. Bris	49	D4
Trym Side. Bris	48	B3
Trymleaze. Bris	48	B3
Trymwood Cl. Bris	34	C1
Tucker St. Bris	63	F4
Tucker's La. Co Mar	127	F4
Tuckett La. Bris	51	E4
Tuckingmill La. Co Dan	98	C3
Tuckmill. Cleve	57	D1
Tudor Cl. Kingsw	66	B2
Tudor Mews. W-S-M	104	C4
Tudor Rd. Bris	49	F1
Tudor Rd. Bris	50	B1
Tudor Rd. Kingsw	65	E3
Tudor Rd. Portis	45	F2
Tudor Rd. W-S-M	89	D2
Tuffley Rd. Bris	49	E4
Tugela Rd. Bris	78	C4
Tuggy's La. Hin Cha	119	F1
Tunbridge Cl. Ch Mag	96	A1
Tunbridge Rd. Ch Mag	96	A1
Tunley Hill. Tims	116	C4
Tunley Rd. Pris	117	E2
Tunnel La. Chil	137	F3
Tunstall Cl. Bris	48	C2
Turley Rd. Bris	50	B1
Turnberry Wlk. Bris	64	B1
Turnberry. Kingsw	66	A3
Turnbridge Rd. Bris	35	E2
Turnbury Ave. Nail	60	A1
Turnbury Cl. W-S-M	88	C2
Turnbury. Yate	39	F4
Turner Cl. Keyn	82	A3
Turner Gdns. Bris	50	A3
Turner Way. Cleve	57	D1
Turner's Terr. Faulk	134	A1
Turners Ct. Kingsw	65	F2
Turnpike Gate. Wickw	18	A3
Turnpike Rd. Co Bi	124	C2
Turnpike Rd. Ship	125	F4
Turtlegate Ave. Bris	78	C2
Turtlegate Wlk. Bris	78	C2
Turville Dr. Bris	50	A3
Tutton Way. Cleve	57	F1
Tweed Cl. Thorn	15	E4
Tweed Rd. Cleve	57	E1
Tweeny La. Kingsw	66	B3
Twenty Acres Rd. Bris	35	D1
Twerton Farm Cl. Bath	101	D3
Twickenham Rd. Bris	49	E3
Twinhoe La. Well	118	C1
Two Acres Rd. Bris	80	A4
Two Mile Ct. Kingsw	65	E4
Two Stones La. Ch Sod	40	B4
Two Trees. Priddy	126	C4
Twomile Hill Rd. Bris	65	D4
Twynings The. Kingsw	51	F1
Tybalt Way. St Gif	36	C3
Tyler Cl. Kingsw	65	F3
Tyler Green. W-S-M	89	D2
Tyler St. Bris	64	A3
Tyler's La. Mang	51	E3
Tyndale Ave. Bris	51	D2
Tyndale Ave. Yate	27	E2
Tyndale Cl. N Nib	5	F2
Tyndale Rd. Kingsw	51	F1
Tyndall Ave. Bris	63	E4
Tyndall Rd. Bris	64	A4
Tyndall's Park Mews. Bris	63	E4
Tyndall's Park Rd. Bris	63	E4
Tyne Rd. Bris	49	E2
Tyne St. Bris	50	A1
Tyning Cl. Bris	80	A4
Tyning Cl. Yate	27	F1
Tyning End. Bath	102	A3
Tyning Hill. Mid No	133	D2
Tyning La. Bath	85	D1
Tyning Rd. Bath	85	F1
Tyning Rd. Bath	102	B1
Tyning Rd. Bris	63	F2
Tyning Rd. Keyn	82	C1
Tyning Rd. P St J	133	E4
Tyning Rd. Winsl	120	C4
Tyning The. Bath	102	A3
Tynings The. Cleve	57	D1
Tynings Way. Clut	114	C2
Tynings Way. Westw	120	C2
Tynte Ave. Bris	79	E2
Tyntesfield Rd. Bris	79	D4
Tyrone Wlk. Bris	79	F4
Tyrrel Way. St Gif	36	C3
Tytherington Rd. Alve	16	A3
Ubley Dr. Priddy	127	D4
Ullswater Cl. Kingsw	66	B3
Ullswater Cl. Yate	27	F1
Ullswater Dr. Bath	85	D1
Ulswater Rd. Bris	35	E1
Uncombe Cl. Back	76	B4
Under La. Wring	93	E1
Underbanks. E in G	47	E2
Underhill Ave. Mid No	131	F1
Underhill Dr. W-S-M	104	B1
Underhill La. Mid No	131	F1
Underhill La. Ston E	131	F1
Underhill Rd. Char	11	D3
Underleaf Way. P St J	133	E4
Undertown La. Co Mar	128	A4
Undertown. Co Mar	128	A4
Underwood Ave. W-S-M	88	A1
Underwood Cl. Alve	15	D2
Underwood End. Wins	108	A2
Underwood Rd. Portis	45	E2
Union Pas. Bath	102	A3
Union Pl. W-S-M	104	B4
Union St. Bath	102	A3
Union St. Bris	63	F4
Union St. Nail	59	E1
Union St. W-S-M	104	B4
Unity Ct. Keyn	82	A3
Unity Rd. Keyn	82	A3
Unity St. Bris	63	E3
Unity St. Bris	63	F4
Unity St. Bris	65	E4
University Cl. Bris	48	C2
University Rd. Bris	63	E4
University Wlk. Bris	63	E4
Uphill Dr. Bath	85	D1
Uphill Rd N. W-S-M	104	B2
Uphill Rd S. W-S-M	104	C1
Uphill Rd. Bris	49	F3
Uphill Way. W-S-M	104	B1
Upjohn Cres. Bris	79	E2
Uplands Cl. Li St	119	F4
Uplands Dr. Keyn	82	C1
Uplands Rd. Bris	51	E2
Uplands Rd. Keyn	82	C1
Uplands The. Nail	75	E4
Upper Bath Rd. Thorn	15	D4
Upper Belgrave Rd. Bris	49	D1
Upper Belmont Rd. Bris	49	F2
Upper Berkeley Pl. Bris	63	D4
Upper Bloomfield Rd. Bath	101	E1
Upper Borough Walls. Bath	101	F3
Upper Bristol Rd. Bath	101	E4
Upper Bristol Rd. Clut	114	B2
Upper Bristol Rd. W-S-M	88	A1
Upper Byron Pl. Bris	63	D4
Upper Chapel La. Fr Cot	38	B4
Upper Cheltenham Pl. Bris	49	F1
Upper Church La. Bris	63	E4
Upper Church La. Lock	105	E1
Upper Church Rd. W-S-M	87	E1
Upper Church St. Bath	101	F4
Upper Cranbrook Rd. Bris	49	D2
Upper East Hayes. Bath	85	E1
Upper Farm Cl. N St P	135	F2
Upper Hedgemead Rd. Bath	102	A4
Upper Lambridge St. Bath	85	E1
Upper Lansdown Mews. Bath	84	C1
Upper Maudlin St. Bris	63	E4
Upper Mount Pleasant. Hi Cha	120	A2
Upper Myrtle Hill. E in G	47	E2
Upper New Rd. Ched	125	E1
Upper Oldfield Park. Bath	101	F3
Upper Perry Hill. Bris	63	E2
Upper Pitching. Chil	137	E3
Upper Rd. Hin Ble	129	F3
Upper Sandhurst Rd. Bris	64	B3
Upper St. Bris	64	A2
Upper St. Dyrh	54	C2
Upper Stanton. Pens	97	D1
Upper Station Rd. Kingsw	51	E2
Upper Stone Cl. Fr Cot	38	B4
Upper Strode. Win	111	F4
Upper Sydney St. Bris	63	D3
Upper Tockington Rd. Olve	14	A1
Upper Town La. Win	94	B4
Upper Wells St. Bris	63	E4
Upper York St. Bris	63	F4
Upton La. Ch Mag	95	F4
Upton La. Dun	95	F4
Upton Rd. Bris	63	D2
Upton. W-S-M	105	D1
Urchinwood La. Cong	91	F2
Urfords Dr. Bris	51	E3
Vain End. W-S-M	88	C2
Valda Rd. W-S-M	88	B1
Vale Cres. Lock	89	E1
Vale End. Nail	59	E1
Vale La. Bris	79	E4
Vale St. Bris	64	A2
Vale The. Puck	52	C3
Vale View Terr. Bathe	85	F2
Vale View. Rad	133	D1
Valentine Cl. Bris	80	A3
Valerian Cl. Bris	47	F3
Valetta Cl. W-S-M	104	C2
Valley Cl. Nail	59	F1
Valley Gdns. Mang	51	F4
Valley Gdns. Nail	59	F1
Valley Rd. Bris	79	D4
Valley Rd. Cleve	57	F3
Valley Rd. Kingsw	66	B3
Valley Rd. Lo Ash	62	B4
Valley Rd. Mang	52	A3
Valley Rd. Portis	44	C2
Valley Rd. W in G	45	D1
Valley View Cl. Bath	85	D2
Valley View Rd. Bath	85	E2
Valley View Rd. Paul	131	F3
Valley Way Rd. Nail	59	F2
Valley Wlk. Mid No	132	A1
Valls The. St Gif	36	C3
Valma Rocks. Bris	65	D3
Van Diemen's La. Bath	84	C1
Vandyke Ave. Keyn	81	F3
Vane St. Bath	102	A4
Vassall Ct. Bris	51	D3
Vassall Rd. Bris	51	D3
Vattingstone La. Alve	14	C3
Vaughan Cl. Bris	34	C2
Vayre Cl. Ch Sod	28	A1
Veale The. Blea	122	B3
Vee La. Win	94	B4
Vellore La. Bath	102	A4
Ventnor Ave. Bris	64	C4
Ventnor Rd. Bris	36	A2
Ventnor Rd. Bris	50	C1
Venus La. Clut	114	C2
Venus St. Cong	91	F1
Vera Rd. Bris	50	C1
Verbena Way. W-S-M	89	D1
Vereland Rd. Lock	105	F2
Verlands. Cong	91	F3
Vernals La. N Nib	11	E4
Vernham Gr. Bath	101	E1
Vernon Cl. Keyn	82	B2
Vernon La. Co Bi	124	A2
Vernon Park. Bath	101	E3
Vernon St. Bris	63	F2
Vernon Terr. Bath	101	E3
Vernslade. Bath	84	A1
Verrier Rd. Bris	64	B4
Verwood Dr. Kingsw	66	B1
Vicarage Cl. W-S-M	89	D2
Vicarage Ct. Kingsw	65	D3
Vicarage Gdns. P St J	133	D4
Vicarage La. Ba Gu	77	E3
Vicarage La. Co Bi	124	A2
Vicarage La. Co Dan	98	B3
Vicarage La. Hill	19	E4
Vicarage La. N St P	135	F2
Vicarage La. Olve	14	A2
Vicarage Rd. Bris	63	D2
Vicarage Rd. Bris	64	B4
Vicarage Rd. Bris	79	D3
Vicarage Rd. Fr Cot	38	B3
Vicarage Rd. Kingsw	65	D3
Vicarage Rd. Lo Ash	62	B3
Vicarage Rd. Piln	22	B4
Vicars Cl. Bris	51	D2
Victor Rd. Bris	63	E2
Victor St. Bris	64	A3
Victoria Ave. Bris	64	B4
Victoria Bldgs. Bath	101	E3
Victoria Bridge Rd. Bath	101	F3
Victoria Cl. Bath	101	E3
Victoria Cl. Portis	45	E3
Victoria Cl. Thorn	8	A2
Victoria Cotts. Sosto	118	C4
Victoria Cres. Piln	22	A3
Victoria Ct. Portis	45	E3
Victoria Gdns. Bathe	85	F2
Victoria Gdns. Bris	49	E1
Victoria Gr. Bris	63	F2
Victoria Parade. Bris	64	B4
Victoria Park. Bris	51	D3
Victoria Park. Bris	51	E1
Victoria Park. W-S-M	87	E1
Victoria Pl. Bris	63	E2
Victoria Pl. Paul	131	E3
Victoria Pl. W-S-M	104	B4
Victoria Quadrant. W-S-M	104	C4
Victoria Rd. Avon	47	D4
Victoria Rd. Bath	101	E3
Victoria Rd. Bris	64	A3
Victoria Rd. Cleve	57	E2
Victoria Rd. Keyn	82	B2
Victoria Rd. Kingsw	65	D3
Victoria Rd. Kingsw	66	B3
Victoria Sq. Bris	63	D4
Victoria Sq. Portis	45	E3
Victoria Sq. W-S-M	104	B4
Victoria St. Bris	63	F3
Victoria Terr. Bath	101	E3
Victoria Terr. Bris	62	C3
Victoria Terr. Bris	64	A3
Victoria Terr. Paul	131	F3
Victoria Wlk. Bris	49	E1
Vigor Rd. Bris	79	D3
Village Cl. Yate	27	E1
Villice La. Co Mar	128	A4
Villiers Rd. Bris	50	A1
Vilner La. Thorn	15	D4
Vimpany Cl. Bris	34	C2
Vimpennys La. Alm	22	C1
Vincent Cl. Bris	34	B1
Vine Gdns. W-S-M	89	D1
Viner's La. A Tur	43	D3
Vinery The. Wins	125	D4
Vineyard La. Kings	11	F3
Vining Wlk. Bris	64	A4
Vinney Ave. Mang	52	A4
Vinney La. Hort	28	C4
Vintery Leys. Bris	49	D4
Virginia Cl. Ch Sod	28	A1
Vivian St. Bris	63	E2
Vivien Ave. Mid No	132	A1
Vowell Cl. Bris	79	D2
Vynes Cl. Nail	60	A1
Vynes Way. Nail	60	A1
Vyvyan Rd. Bris	63	D4
Vyvyan Terr. Bris	63	D4
Wade Rd. Yate	27	D2
Wade St. Bris	63	F4
Wadehurst Ind Pk. Bris	64	A4
Wades Rd. Bris	36	A2
Wadham Dr. Bris	37	D1
Wadham St. W-S-M	104	B4
Wagtail Gdns. W-S-M	105	F4
Wainbridge Cres. Piln	22	B4
Wainbrook Dr. Bris	50	B1
Wains Cl. Cleve	57	E1
Wainwright Cl. W-S-M	89	D2
Waits Cl. Ban	106	C2
Wakedean Gdns. Yatt	74	A1
Wakeford Rd. Mang	52	A4
Walcot Gate. Bath	102	A4
Walcot St. Bath	102	A4
Waldegrave House. Bris	79	E2
Waldegrave Rd. Bath	84	C1
Waldegrave Terr. Mid No	133	D2
Walden Rd. Keyn	82	A2
Walford Ave. Lock	89	D2
Walk Mill La. Kings	11	F2
Walk The. Kings	11	F3
Walker Cl. Bris	64	A4
Walker Cl. Mang	52	A4
Walker St. Bris	63	E4
Walker Way. Thorn	15	D4
Wall Green. Axb	125	E1
Wallace La. E Harp	128	C2
Wallace Rd. Bath	85	D1
Wallenge Cl. Paul	131	F3
Wallenge Dr. Paul	131	F3
Walley La. Ch Mag	113	D2
Wallingford Rd. Bris	79	E4
Walliscote Ave. Bris	49	E3
Walliscote Grove Rd. W-S-M	104	C4
Walliscote Rd S. W-S-M	104	B2
Walliscote Rd. Bris	49	E3
Walliscote Rd. W-S-M	104	B3
Wallscourt Rd S. Bris	36	A1
Wallscourt Rd. Bris	36	A1
Wallsend La. Tor	55	E3
Wallycourt Rd. Ch St	112	C4
Walnut Ave. Yate	28	A1
Walnut Bldgs. Mid No	133	D2
Walnut Cl. Axb	125	D1
Walnut Cl. E in G	47	D2
Walnut Cl. Keyn	81	E2
Walnut Cl. Kingsw	51	F1
Walnut Cl. Nail	75	F4
Walnut Cl. Thorn	8	B1
Walnut Cl. W-S-M	105	D1
Walnut Cres. Kingsw	65	F4
Walnut Dr. Bath	101	F2
Walnut Dro. W in G	70	C3
Walnut La. Kingsw	66	A4
Walnut Tree Cl. Alm	24	A3
Walnut Wlk. Bris	79	D3
Walnut Wlk. Keyn	81	E2
Walsh Ave. Bris	80	A4
Walsh Cl. W-S-M	105	D1
Walshe Ave. Ch Sod	28	A1
Walsingham Rd. Bris	49	F1
Walter St. Bris	63	D3
Walton Ave. Bris	64	B3
Walton Cl. Keyn	81	E2
Walton Cl. Kingsw	51	F1
Walton Dro. W in G	58	B3
Walton Heath. Yate	39	F1
Walton Rd. Bris	47	E3
Walton Rd. Cleve	57	E1
Walton Rise. Bris	49	D4
Walton St. Bris	50	A1
Walton. W-S-M	105	D1
Walwyn Cl. Bath	101	D3
Walwyn Gdns. Bris	79	E2
Wansbeck Rd. Keyn	82	A2
Wansbrough Rd. W-S-M	89	D2
Wanscow Wlk. Bris	49	D3
Wansdyke Ct. Bris	80	A3
Wansdyke Rd. Bath	101	E3
Wapley Hill. West	39	F2
Wapping Rd. Bris	63	E3
Warden Rd. Bris	63	E2
Wardour Rd. Bris	79	E4

Wareham Cl. Nail

Wareham Cl. Nail 59 E1
Warleigh Dr. Bathe 86 A2
Warleigh La. Bathf 103 E3
Warleigh La. Mon Far 103 E3
Warman Cl. Bris 80 C3
Warman Rd. Bris 80 C3
Warmington Rd. Bris 80 B4
Warminster Rd. Bath 103 D3
Warminster Rd. Bris 50 A1
Warminster Rd. Hin Cha 119 F3
Warminster Rd. Li St 120 A4
Warne Park. W-S-M 105 D3
Warne Rd. W-S-M 105 D3
Warner Cl. Brock 92 A4
Warner Cl. Kingsw 65 F3
Warns The. Kingsw 66 A2
Warren Cl. Lock 105 E1
Warren Cl. St Gif 24 B2
Warren Croft. N Nib 5 F2
Warren Gdns. Bris 80 C3
Warren La. Lo Ash 61 F1
Warren Rd. Bris 36 A2
Warren Way. Yate 27 F2
Warrilow Cl. W-S-M 89 D3
Warrington Rd. Bris 64 B1
Warth La. W ST L 89 D4
Warwick Ave. Bris 50 A1
Warwick Cl. Kingsw 66 A1
Warwick Cl. Thorn 8 A1
Warwick Cl. W-S-M 105 E4
Warwick Gdns. Clut 114 B2
Warwick Rd. Bath 101 D4
Warwick Rd. Bris 49 D1
Warwick Rd. Bris 50 A1
Warwick Rd. Keyn 81 E2
Washing Pound La. Nail 59 D2
Washing Pound La. Whit 80 A2
Washingpool Hill Rd. Olve .. 14 B1
Washingpool La. Avon 33 F4
Washington Ave. Bris 50 B1
Washpool La. Engl 100 C1
Watch Elm Cl. St Gif 36 C3
Watchhouse Rd. E in G 47 E2
Watchill Ave. Bris 78 C3
Watchill Cl. Bris 78 C3
Water La. Bris 63 F2
Water La. Bris 63 F3
Water La. Bris 64 B1
Water La. E in G 47 E2
Water La. Kingsw 65 D1
Water La. Mid No 132 A2
Water St. E Harp 128 C2
Water's La. Bris 49 D4
Waterbridge Rd. Bris 78 C3
Watercress Rd. Bris 49 F2
Waterdale Cl. Bris 49 E4
Waterdale Gdns. Bris 49 E4
Waterford Cl. Thorn 15 E4
Waterford Park. Rad 132 C1
Waterford Rd. Bris 49 D3
Waterloo Bldgs. Bath 101 D3
Waterloo Pl. Bris 64 A4
Waterloo Rd. Bris 63 F4
Waterloo Rd. Rad 133 D1
Waterloo St. Bris 62 C4
Waterloo St. Bris 63 F4
Waterloo St. W-S-M 104 B4
Watermore Cl. Fr Cot 38 B4
Waters Rd. Bris 65 E4
Waters Rd. Kingsw 65 E4
Waterside Cres. Rad 132 B1
Waterside Dr. St Gif 24 A1
Waterside La. Kilm 138 C3
Waterside Park. Portis 44 B2
Waterside Rd. Rad 132 B1
Waterside Way. Rod 138 B4
Watery La. Bath 101 D3
Watery La. Chil 138 A2
Watery La. Doyn 68 A4
Watery La. Nail 59 E1
Watery La. Win 95 D2
Wathen Rd. Bris 49 D4
Watkins Yd. Bris 49 D4
Watley's End Rd. Wint 37 F4
Watling Way. Bris 47 E4
Watson Ave. Bris 64 B2
Watson's Rd. Kingsw 65 F2
Watters Cl. Fr Cot 38 B3
Wavell Cl. Yate 27 E2
Waveney Rd. Keyn 82 A2
Waverley Rd. Back 76 A4
Waverley Rd. Bris 47 F3
Waverley Rd. Bris 49 E1
Waverley Rd. Ir Act 27 D1
Waverley Rd. W-S-M 104 C2
Waverley St. Bris 50 A1
Wayacre Dro. Blea 121 F3
Wayfield Gdns. Bathe 85 F2
Wayford Cl. Keyn 82 A2
Wayland Rd. W-S-M 88 C2
Wayleaze. Fr Cot 38 B4
Wayside Cl. Fr Cot 38 A4
Wayside Dr. Cleve 57 F3
Wayside. W-S-M 88 B1
Weare Ct. Bris 63 D3
Weatherley Ave. Bath 101 E1
Weavers Cl. Kings 11 F2
Webb St. Bris 64 A4

Webbington Rd. Co Bi 124 B2
Webbs Heath. Sist 66 C4
Webbs Wood Rd. St Gif 36 C3
Webbs Wood. St Gif 36 C4
Wedgewood Rd. Mang 37 E1
Wedgwood Cl. Bris 80 A3
Wedgwood Rd. Bath 101 D3
Wedmore Cl. Kingsw 65 F4
Wedmore Cl. W-S-M 104 C1
Wedmore Park. Bath 101 D2
Wedmore Rd. Cleve 57 D1
Wedmore Rd. Keyn 82 B2
Wedmore Rd. Nail 75 F4
Wedmore Vale. Bris 63 F1
Weedon Cl. Bris 50 A1
Weekesley La. Tims 116 B1
Weetwood Rd. Cong 91 F3
Weight Rd. Bris 64 B4
Weind The. W-S-M 88 B1
Weir La. Ab Lei 61 F3
Weir La. Marsh 69 F4
Weir Rd. Cong 91 F2
Well Cl. Lo Ash 62 A1
Well Cl. W-S-M 105 D1
Well Cl. Wins 125 D4
Well House Cl. Bris 48 C2
Well La. Yatt 91 E4
Well Park. Cong 91 F2
Welland Rd. Keyn 81 F2
Wellard Cl. W-S-M 89 D2
Wellgarth Rd. Bris 64 A1
Wellgarth Wlk. Bris 64 A1
Wellington Ave. Bris 49 F1
Wellington Bldgs. Bath 84 A1
Wellington Cres. Bris 49 F3
Wellington Dr. Bris 49 E3
Wellington Dr. Yate 27 D1
Wellington Hill W. Bris 49 E4
Wellington Hill. Bris 49 F3
Wellington La. Bris 49 F1
Wellington Mews. Bris 47 E3
Wellington Park. Bris 49 D1
Wellington Pl. Bris 37 D1
Wellington Pl. W-S-M 104 B4
Wellington Rd. Bris 63 F4
Wellington Rd. Kingsw 51 E1
Wellington Rd. Yate 27 F2
Wellington Terr. Cleve 57 E3
Wellington Wlk. Bris 49 E4
Wellow La. Hin Cha 119 E1
Wellow La. N St P 135 E3
Wellow La. P St J 133 E3
Wellow Mead. P St J 133 D4
Wellow Rd. Well 134 A4
Wellow Tyning. P St J 133 E4
Wells Cl. Bris 80 B3
Wells Cl. Nail 60 A1
Wells Rd. Bath 101 F3
Wells Rd. Bris 64 A1
Wells Rd. Bris 80 B4
Wells Rd. Ch Mag 95 F4
Wells Rd. Chil 137 F2
Wells Rd. Cleve 57 E1
Wells Rd. Dun 95 F4
Wells Rd. Mid No 132 B1
Wells Rd. N St P 135 E2
Wells Rd. Paul 131 D3
Wells Sq. Rad 132 B1
Wells St. Bris 63 D2
Wellsea Gr. W-S-M 105 D4
Wellstead Ave. Yate 27 E1
Wellsway. Bath 101 F1
Wellsway. Keyn 81 F2
Welsford Ave. Bris 50 B2
Welsford Rd. Bris 50 B2
Welsh Back. Bris 63 E3
Welton Gr. Mid No 132 A2
Welton Rd. Rad 132 C1
Welton Vale. Mid No 132 A1
Welton Wlk. Bris 51 E1
Wemberham Cres. Yatt 74 A1
Wemberham La. Yalt 90 C4
Wenmore Cl. Mang 37 E1
Wentforth Dr. Bris 51 E1
Wentwood Dr. W-S-M 105 D1
Wentworth Rd. Bris 49 E2
Wentworth. Kingsw 66 A3
Wentworth. Yate 27 F1
Wesley Ave. Kingsw 65 E3
Wesley Ave. Rad 132 B1
Wesley Cl. Kingsw 51 E2
Wesley Dr. W-S-M 89 D2
Wesley Hill. Kingsw 51 E1
Wesley La. Kingsw 66 A3
Wesley Pl. Bris 49 D1
Wesley Rd. Bris 49 F2
Wesley St. Bris 63 E2
Wessex Ave. Bris 49 F4
Wessex Rd. W-S-M 105 D1
West Ave. Bath 101 E3
West Broadway. Bris 49 E3
West Cl. Bath 101 D3
West Coombe. Bris 48 B3
West Croft. Bris 49 E4
West Croft. Cleve 57 D1
West Dene. Bris 48 C3
West Dundry La. Dun 78 C1
West End. Bris 63 E3

West End. Bris 63 E4
West Garston. Ban 107 D2
West Gr. Bris 49 F1
West Hay Rd. Wring 92 B2
West Hill Gdns. Portis 45 E3
West Hill Gdns. Rad 132 C1
West Hill Rd. Rad 132 B1
West Hill. Portis 45 E3
West Hill. Wrax 60 A3
West La. Win 94 A4
West Lea Rd. Bath 84 A1
West Leaze Pl. St Gif 36 C3
West Links Cl. W-S-M 88 A2
West Littleton Rd. Marsh 55 F1
West Mall. Bris 62 C4
West Par. Bris 48 B4
West Park Rd. Mang 51 F3
West Park. Bris 63 D4
West Point Row. St Gif 24 B2
West Priory Cl. Bris 49 D4
West Rd. Mid No 132 A2
West Rd. Lymp 122 A1
West Rd. Yatt 91 D4
West Ridge. Fr Cot 38 B4
West Rocke Ave. Bris 48 B3
West Rolstone Rd. Ban 89 F1
West Shrubbery. Bris 49 D1
West St. Axb 125 D1
West St. Ban 107 D2
West St. Bris 63 E2
West St. Bris 63 F4
West St. Kingsw 66 B2
West St. Kingsw 66 B2
West St. Tyth 16 A3
West St. W-S-M 104 B4
West Town Ave. Bris 64 B1
West Town Gr. Bris 80 B4
West Town La. Bris 64 B1
West Town Park. Bris 80 B4
West Town Rd. Back 76 A3
West Town Rd. Bris 47 E4
West Tyning. Marks 99 D1
West View Rd. Bathe 86 A2
West View Rd. Bris 63 D2
West View Rd. Keyn 81 F3
West View. Alve 14 C2
West Way. Bris 35 F2
West Way. Cleve 57 E2
West Wick. Lock 89 E1
West Wlk. Yate 27 F1
West. St Gif 24 A1
Westacre Cl. Bris 35 D1
Westaway Cl. Yatt 91 E4
Westaway Park. Yatt 91 E4
Westbourn Rd. Bris 64 A4
Westbourne Ave. Cleve 57 D1
Westbourne Ave. Keyn 81 F3
Westbourne Cres. Cleve 57 D1
Westbourne Gr. Bris 63 E2
Westbourne Pl. Bris 63 D4
Westbourne Rd. Mang 51 F4
Westbourne Terr. Bris 51 D4
Westbrook Park. Charl 84 A1
Westbrook Rd. Bris 80 B4
Westbrook Rd. W-S-M 88 B1
Westbrooke Ct. Bris 63 D3
Westbury Court Rd. Bris 49 D4
Westbury Cres. W-S-M 104 C1
Westbury Ct. Bris 49 D4
Westbury Hill. Bris 49 D4
Westbury La. Bris 48 B4
Westbury Park. Bris 49 D2
Westbury Rd. Bris 49 D2
Westcourt Dr. Kingsw 66 A2
Westcroft. Blag 110 C1
Westend La. O-on-S 7 D3
Westend Rd. Wickw 17 F3
Westend Rd. Yate 17 F3
Westering Cl. Mang 52 A3
Westerleigh Cl. Mang 51 F4
Westerleigh Rd. Bath 102 A1
Westerleigh Rd. Cleve 57 D1
Westerleigh Rd. Mang 52 A4
Westerleigh Rd. Puck 53 E4
Westerleigh Rd. West 39 E2
Westerleigh Rd. Yate 39 E4
Western Ave. Fr Cot 26 A1
Western Ct. Cleve 57 E2
Western Dr. Bris 79 F3
Western La. E Harp 128 B2
Western La. Priddy 128 B2
Western Rd. Bris 49 F3
Westfield Cl. Back 76 A3
Westfield Cl. Bath 101 F2
Westfield Cl. Keyn 81 E3
Westfield Cl. Kingsw 65 E3
Westfield Cl. W-S-M 104 B1
Westfield Cres. Ban 107 D2
Westfield Dr. Back 76 A3
Westfield Ind and Trading Est.
Rod 138 B4
Westfield La. St Gif 36 C2
Westfield Park S. Bath 101 D4
Westfield Park. Bath 101 D4
Westfield Park. Bris 49 D1
Westfield Pl. Bris 62 C4
Westfield Rd. Back 76 A3
Westfield Rd. Ban 107 D2

Westfield Rd. Bris 49 D4
Westfield Rd. W-S-M 104 B1
Westfield Terr. Rad 132 B1
Westfield Way. St Gif 24 B1
Westfield. Cleve 73 E4
Westgate Bldgs. Bath 101 F3
Westgate St. Bath 101 F3
Westhall Rd. Bath 101 E4
Westland Ave. Kingsw 66 B2
Westleigh Cl. Yate 27 E1
Westleigh Park. Bris 80 A4
Westleigh Rd. Bris 35 E1
Westmarch Way. W-S-M 89 D2
Westmarsh La. O-on-S 7 D3
Westmarsh. O-on-S 7 D3
Westmead Gdns. Charl 84 A1
Westmead Rd. Bris 65 D4
Westminster Cl. Bris 49 D4
Westminster Rd. Bris 64 B4
Westmoreland Dr. Bath 101 F3
Westmoreland Rd. Bath 101 F3
Westmoreland Rd. Bris 49 D2
Westmoreland St. Bath 101 F3
Westmoreland Station Rd.
Bath 101 F3
Westmorland Terr. Ch Sod . 41 E4
Weston Ave. Bris 64 B4
Weston Cl. Bris 48 B4
Weston Cres. Bris 49 F3
Weston Dro. W in G 58 C4
Weston Farm La. Bath 84 A1
Weston Ind Est. W-S-M 105 D2
Weston La. Bath 101 E4
Weston Park Court. Bath 84 B1
Weston Park E. Bath 84 B1
Weston Park W. Bath 84 B1
Weston Park. Bath 84 B1
Weston Rd. Bath 101 E4
Weston Rd. Berr 121 D3
Weston Rd. Cong 91 D3
Weston Rd. Lo Ash 77 E4
Weston Rd. Wrax 61 E2
Weston Way. Lock 105 F1
Weston Wood Rd. Portis 45 E2
Westons Way. Kingsw 65 F4
Westover Cl. Bris 34 C1
Westover Dr. Bris 35 D1
Westover Gdns. Bris 48 C4
Westover Rd. Bris 35 D1
Westover Rise. Bris 35 D1
Westview Orchard. Hi Cha 120 A3
Westview. Paul 131 E3
Westward Cl. Wring 92 B1
Westward Dr. E in G 47 E2
Westward Gdns. Lo Ash 62 A1
Westward Rd. Bris 78 C4
Westway. Nail 59 F1
Westwood Ave. Paul 115 E1
Westwood Cl. W-S-M 88 C1
Westwood Cres. Bris 64 B3
Westwood Ct. Westw 120 C2
Westwood Rd. Bris 80 B4
Westwoods. Bathe 86 A2
Wetherby Ct. Mang 37 F1
Wetherell Pl. Bris 63 D4
Wetlands La. Portis 45 E2
Wexford Rd. Bris 79 E4
Weymouth Rd. Bris 63 F1
Weymouth St. Bath 102 A4
Wharf La. Portb 46 A3
Wharf Rd. Bris 50 C2
Wharfedale. Thorn 15 E4
Wharfside. Lymp 121 F2
Wharnecliffe Cl. Bris 80 A3
Wharnecliffe Gdns. Bris 80 A3
Whatley Rd. Bris 49 D1
Wheatfield Dr. St Gif 24 B1
Wheathill Cl. Keyn 81 E3
Wheelers Cl. Mid No 132 B1
Wheelers Dr. Mid No 132 B1
Wheelers Rd. Mid No 132 B1
Whinchat Gdns. Bris 50 C3
Whippington Ct. Bris 63 E3
Whistley La. E Harp 128 C3
Whitby Rd. Bris 64 B3
Whitchurch La. Bris 79 F3
Whitchurch La. Bris 80 A2
Whitchurch La. Dun 79 E1
Whitchurch Rd. Bris 79 D3
White Cross Gate. Paul 130 C3
White Hill. Well 133 F3
White Horse Rd. Winsl 120 C4
White House La. Badg 123 D2
White House Rd. Yatt 91 F4
White Lodge Park. Portis 45 E3
White Lodge Rd. Kingsw 51 F3
White Ox Mead La. Well 117 F1
White St. Bris 63 F4
White Tree Rd. Bris 49 D2
Whitebrook La. P St J 133 D4
Whitebrook La. Tims 132 C4
Whitecroft Way. Kingsw 66 A4
Whitecross Ave. Bris 80 B3
Whitecross La. Ban 107 D2
Whitecross Rd. E Harp 128 C2
Whitecross Rd. W-S-M 104 C3
Whitefield Ave. Bris 51 D1
Whitefield Ave. Kingsw 65 E3

Whitefield Cl. Bathe 86 A2
Whitefield Cl. Kingsw 51 E3
Whitefield Rd. Bris 51 D1
Whitefields. Ch Sod 28 A1
Whitegate Cl. Blea 122 B3
Whitehall Ave. Bris 50 C1
Whitehall Gdns. Bris 64 B1
Whitehall Rd. Bris 64 B4
Whitehall Trading Est. Bris .. 64 B4
Whitehouse La. Bris 63 E2
Whitehouse La. Litt 129 F1
Whitehouse La. Wrax 60 A3
Whitehouse Pl. Bris 63 F2
Whitehouse Rd. Piln 22 B4
Whitehouse St. Bris 63 F2
Whiteladies Rd. Bris 49 D1
Whitelands Hill. Mid No 133 D2
Whiteleaze. Bris 49 E4
Whiteoak Way. Nail 75 E4
Whites Hill. Bris 65 D3
Whitesfield Rd. Nail 59 E1
Whiteshill. Wint 37 E2
Whitewall La. Thorn 8 C1
Whiteway Ave. Bath 101 D2
Whiteway Cl. Bris 64 C3
Whiteway Ct. Bris 65 D4
Whiteway Mews. Bris 65 D4
Whiteway Rd. Bath 101 D2
Whiteway Rd. Bris 51 D1
Whitewells Rd. Bath 85 D1
Whitewood Rd. Bris 50 C1
Whitfield Rd. Thorn 8 B1
Whiting Rd. Bris 79 D4
Whitland Ave. Bris 79 D3
Whitland Rd. Bris 79 D3
Whitley Cl. Yate 27 E2
Whitley Mead. St Gif 36 C2
Whitling St. Win 95 D1
Whitmead Gdns. Bris 79 E2
Whitmore Ave. Bris 65 D2
Whitson St. Bris 63 E4
Whitting Rd. W-S-M 104 C2
Whittington Dr. W-S-M 88 B1
Whittington Rd. Bris 51 E3
Whittock Rd. Bris 80 B3
Whittock Sq. Bris 80 B4
Whittucks Cl. Kingsw 65 E2
Whittucks Rd. Kingsw 65 E2
Whitwell Rd. Bris 80 A4
Whytes Cl. Bris 49 D4
Wick Cres. Bris 64 B2
Wick Ct. W-S-M 89 D1
Wick House Cl. Keyn 82 B2
Wick La. Bitt 67 D1
Wick La. Lymp 121 F1
Wick La. Pens 97 E2
Wick La. Tims 116 C1
Wick Rd. Berr 121 E1
Wick Rd. Bi Sut 113 E2
Wick Rd. Bris 64 B2
Wick Rd. Bris 64 C3
Wick Rd. Lymp 121 E1
Wick Rd. Piln 22 B4
Wickets The. Bris 35 F1
Wickets The. Kingsw 51 E1
Wickfield. Cleve 57 E1
Wickham Cl. Ch Sod 40 B4
Wickham Cl. Bris 50 B3
Wickham Glen. Bris 50 B3
Wickham Hill. Bris 50 B3
Wickham View. Bris 50 B3
Wicklow Rd. Bris 79 F4
Wigton Cres. Bris 35 E1
Wilbye Gr. Bris 79 E3
Wilcox Cl. Kingsw 65 E3
WildCountry La. Ba Gu 77 F3
Wildcountry La. Lo Ash 77 F3
Wildcroft Rd. Bris 49 D2
Wilder St. Bris 63 F4
Willada Cl. Bris 63 D1
William Daw Cl. Ban 106 C2
William Mason Cl. Bris 64 A4
William St. Bath 102 A4
William St. Bris 49 F1
William St. Bris 51 D2
William St. Bris 63 F2
William St. Bris 64 B4
Williams Cl. Kingsw 65 F2
Williamson Rd. Bris 49 F2
Williamstowe. Bath 102 B1
Willinton Rd. Bris 79 F4
Willis Rd. Kingsw 51 F1
Williton Cres. W-S-M 104 C2
Willment Way. Avon 33 E1
Willmott Cl. Bris 79 F2
Willoughby Cl. Alve 15 D3
Willoughby Cl. Bris 79 D4

165

Willoughby Rd. Bris — Zion Hill. Ston E

loughby Rd. Bris 49 F3
low Cl. Bris 35 F4
low Cl. Char 11 D2
low Cl. Cleve 57 F2
low Cl. Kingsw 66 B3
low Cl. Lo Ash 61 F1
low Cl. Lock 89 E1
low Cl. Portis 45 E2
low Cl. Rad 132 C1
low Cl. W-S-M 104 C1
low Cl. Wick 67 D3
low Dr. Blea 122 B3
low Dr. Lock 105 F1
low Dr. Lock 105 F3
low Gdns. Lock 89 E1
low Gr. Bris 51 E1
low Green. Bath 101 F2
low Rd. Kingsw 65 E2
low Way. Fr Cot 38 B3
low Wlk. Bris 35 D2
low Wlk. Keyn 81 E2
lowdown. W-S-M 88 C2
lowfalls The. Bath 85 F2
lows Shopping Centre The.
Mang 51 F3
lows The. Bris 37 D1
lows The. Nail 59 F2
lows The. St Gif 36 B4
lows The. Yate 27 E1
's Dr. Bris 64 A4
sbridge Hill. Kingsw 66 A1
way St. Bris 63 E2
way St. Bris 63 F4
mot Ct. Kingsw 66 A3
mots Way. E in G 47 E2
mott House. E in G 47 E2
son Pl. Bris 63 F4
son St. Bris 63 F4
ton Cl. Bris 35 E1
ton Gdns. W-S-M 104 B4
tons. Wring 92 B1
tshire Ave. Kingsw 65 E3
tshire Ave. Yate 28 A2
tshire Pl. Kingsw 51 F2
tshire Way. Bath 85 D1
verley Ind Est. Bris 64 C1
nbledon Rd. Bris 49 E3
nblestone Rd. Winsc 107 F1
nborne Rd. Bris 63 E1
nash Cl. Bris 80 B4
ncanton Cl. Nail 60 A1
nchcombe Cl. Nail 76 A4
nchcombe Gr. Bris 47 F3
nchcombe Rd. Fr Cot 38 A4
nchester Ave. Bris 64 B2
nchester Rd. Bath 101 E3
nchester Rd. Bris 64 B2
ncroft. Kingsw 66 B2
ndcliff Cres. Bris 47 F4
ndermere Rd. Bris 36 A4
ndermere Way. Kingsw 66 B3
ndmill Cl. Bris 63 F2
ndmill Farm Bsns Cen.
Bris 63 E2
ndmill Hill. Bris 63 E2
ndmill Hill. Lock 106 A1
ndmill La. Bris 34 B2
ndrush Cl. Bath 100 C2
ndrush Ct. Thorn 15 E4
ndrush Green. Keyn 82 A2
ndrush Rd. Keyn 82 A2
ndsor Ave. Bris 65 D3
ndsor Ave. Keyn 81 F2
ndsor Bridge Rd. Bath 101 E4
ndsor Cl. Cleve 57 E1
ndsor Cl. St Gif 36 C2
ndsor Cres. Bris 34 B2
ndsor Ct. Bath 101 E4
ndsor Ct. Bris 62 C3
ndsor Ct. Mang 51 F4
dsor Ct. Wick 67 E4
dsor Dr. Yate 27 E1
dsor Gr. Bris 64 A4
dsor Pl. Bris 62 C3
ndsor Pl. Mang 52 A3
ndsor Rd. Bris 49 F1
ndsor Rd. Kingsw 65 F1
ndsor Rd. W-S-M 88 B1
ndsor Terr. Bris 62 C3
ndsor Terr. Bris 63 F2
ndwhistle Circ. W-S-M 104 C2
ndwhistle La. W-S-M 104 C2
ndwhistle Rd. W-S-M 104 B2
ne St. Bath 102 A3
ne St. Bris 63 E4
neberry Cl. Bris 50 B1
nfield Rd. Sist 66 B4
nford Cl. Portis 45 F2
nford Gr. Bris 79 D4
nford La. Dun 78 B1
nford Rd. Ch Mag 95 F2
ngard Cl. W-S-M 104 B1
ngfield Rd. Bris 63 F1
nifred's La. Bath 84 C1
nkworth Pl. Bris 49 F1
nnowing End. Wins 108 A2
nsbury Way. St Gif 24 B1
nscombe Cl. Keyn 81 E3
Winscombe Dro. Ship 125 E3
Winscombe Dro. Wins 125 E3
Winscombe Hill. Wins 124 C3
Winscombe Rd. W-S-M 105 D4
Winsford St. Bris 64 A4
Winsham Cl. Bris 80 A3
Winsley Hill. Winsl 120 A3
Winsley Rd. Bris 49 E1
Wint Hill. Ban 107 D1
Winterbourne Hill. Wint 37 E3
Winterbourne Rd. St Gif 36 C3
Winterfield Park. Paul 131 F2
Winterfield Rd. Paul 131 F3
Winterstoke Cl. Bris 63 D1
Winterstoke Rd. Bris 62 C2
Winterstoke Rd. W-S-M 105 D2
Winterstoke Underpass. Bris 62 C2
Winton St. Bris 63 F2
Wistaria Ave. Ch Sod 28 A1
Wisteria Ave. Lock 105 E1
Witch Hazel Rd. Bris 79 F2
Witchell Rd. Bris 64 B4
Witcombe Cl. Kingsw 51 F1
Witcombe. Yate 39 E4
Witherlies Rd. Bris 50 C3
Withey Cl E. Bris 48 C3
Withey Cl W. Bris 48 C3
Witheys The. Whit 80 B2
Withies La. Mid No 138 A4
Withies Park. Mid No 137 F4
Withington Cl. Kingsw 66 B1
Withleigh Rd. Bris 64 A1
Withyditch La. Pris 117 E2
Withymead Rd. Marsh 70 A4
Withypool Gdns. Bris 80 A3
Withywood Gdns. Bris 78 C2
Withywood Rd. Bris 78 C2
Witney Cl. Keyn 82 B2
Woburn Cl. Kingsw 65 F3
Woburn Rd. Bris 50 A2
Wolferton Rd. Bris 49 F1
Wolfridge Gdns. Bris 35 D2
Wolfridge La. Alve 14 C2
Wolfridge Ride. Alve 14 C2
Wolseley Rd. Bris 49 E2
Wolvers Hill Rd. Ban 106 C3
Wolvers Hill Rd. Lock 106 C3
Wolvershill Park. Ban 107 D2
Wood End Wlk. Bris 48 B3
Wood Hill Park. Portis 45 D4
Wood Hill. Cong 91 F3
Wood Kilns The. Yatt 74 A1
Wood La. Axb 125 E1
Wood La. Hork 19 D1
Wood La. W in G 59 F4
Wood La. W-S-M 87 F1
Wood Rd. Kingsw 65 E4
Wood St. Bath 101 F3
Wood St. Bath 101 F3
Wood St. Bris 50 A1
Woodbine Rd. Bris 64 B4
Woodborough Cres. Wins 125 D4
Woodborough Dr. Wins 125 D4
Woodborough La. Mid No 133 D2
Woodborough Rd. Mid No 133 D2
Woodborough Rd. Wins 124 C4
Woodborough Rd. Wins 125 D4
Woodborough St. Bris 50 A1
Woodbridge Rd. Bris 64 A1
Woodbury La. Bris 49 D1
Woodchester Rd. Bris 49 E4
Woodchester. Kingsw 51 F2
Woodchester. Yate 39 F4
Woodcliff Ave. W-S-M 88 B1
Woodcliff Rd. W-S-M 88 B1
Woodcote Rd. Bris 51 D2
Woodcote Wlk. Bris 51 D1
Woodcote. Kingsw 65 E3
Woodcroft Ave. Bris 50 B1
Woodcroft Cl. Bris 64 C2
Woodcroft Rd. Bris 64 C2
Woodcroft. Bi Sut 113 E2
Woodend La. Rock 2 C1
Woodend Rd. Fr Cot 38 B4
Woodend. Kingsw 65 E3
Woodfield Rd. Bris 49 D1
Woodfinch Cres. Puck 53 E2
Woodford Cl. Nail 60 A1
Woodgrove Rd. Bris 34 B1
Woodhall Cl. Mang 51 F3
Woodhill Ave. Portis 45 E3
Woodhill Rd. Portis 45 D4
Woodhill Views. Nail 59 F2
Woodhouse Ave. Alve 24 B4
Woodhouse Cl. Alve 24 B3
Woodhouse Gr. Bris 49 F3
Woodhouse Rd. Bath 101 D3
Woodhurst Rd. W-S-M 105 D4
Woodington Ct. Kingsw 65 F2
Woodington Rd. Cleve 57 E1
Woodland Ave. Kingsw 51 E1
Woodland Cl. Wrax 61 D2
Woodland Cotts Winsl 120 B3
Woodland Glade. Cleve 57 F3
Woodland Gr. Bath 102 C3
Woodland Gr. Bris 48 B3
Woodland Rd. Bris 63 E4
Woodland Rd. Crom 10 A2
Woodland Rd. Nail 59 F2
Woodland Rd. W-S-M 104 B2
Woodland Terr. Bris 49 D1
Woodland Terr. Kingsw 65 F4
Woodland Way. Bris 51 E1
Woodland Way. Wrax 61 D2
Woodlands Ct. St Gif 24 A2
Woodlands Dr. Winsl 120 A3
Woodlands La. Alve 24 C3
Woodlands La. St Gif 24 B2
Woodlands Park. Bath 85 E1
Woodlands Park. St Gif 24 B2
Woodlands Rd. Char 11 D2
Woodlands Rd. Cleve 57 E2
Woodlands Rd. Portis 45 F4
Woodlands Rd. Tyth 16 A3
Woodlands Rise. Mang 51 E3
Woodlands The. Pris 116 C2
Woodlands. Mang 51 F3
Woodlands. St Gif 24 B2
Woodlands. Tyth 16 A3
Woodleaze. Bris 48 A3
Woodleigh Gdns. Bris 80 B3
Woodleigh. Thorn 8 B1
Woodmancote Rd. Bris 49 F1
Woodmancote. Yate 39 E4
Woodmans Cl. Ch Sod 40 A4
Woodmans Rd. Ch Sod 40 A4
Woodmans Vale. Ch Sod 40 B4
Woodmarsh Cl. Bris 80 A2
Woodmead Gdns. Bris 79 E2
Woodmead La. Doyn 54 A1
Woodmill. Yatt 74 A1
Woodpecker Ave. Rod 138 A4
Woodpecker Dr. W-S-M 105 F4
Woods Hill. Li St 120 A4
Woodside Ave. W-S-M 105 D1
Woodside Gdns. Portis 44 C3
Woodside Gr. Bris 34 B2
Woodside Rd. Bris 64 C3
Woodside Rd. Cleve 57 F3
Woodside Rd. Fr Cot 38 B4
Woodside Rd. Kingsw 65 E4
Woodside Rd. Mang 51 E4
Woodside. Bris 48 B2
Woodside. Mid No 131 F1
Woodspring Ave. W-S-M 88 A2
Woodspring Cres. W-S-M 88 A2
Woodstock Ave. Bris 49 E1
Woodstock Cl. Kingsw 65 F4
Woodstock Rd. Bris 49 E1
Woodstock Rd. Kingsw 65 F4
Woodstock Rd. W-S-M 105 D4
Woodview Cl. Bris 47 F4
Woodview Dr. Brock 92 A4
Woodview Terr. Nail 59 F1
Woodview Terr. W-S-M 105 D3
Woodview. Chil 137 F3
Woodview. Cleve 57 F2
Woodview. Paul 131 E3
Woodward Dr. Kingsw 65 F2
Woodwell Rd. Bris 47 F3
Woodyleaze Dr. Kingsw 65 E3
Wookey Cl. Nail 75 F4
Woolcot St. Bris 49 D1
Wooler Rd. W-S-M 104 C4
Woollard La. Pens 80 B1
Woollard La. Whit 80 B1
Woolley La. Charl 85 D2
Woolley Rd. Bris 80 C3
Wootton Cres. Bris 64 C3
Wootton Pk. Bris 64 A1
Wootton Rd. Bris 64 C3
Worcester Bldgs. Bath 85 D1
Worcester Cl. Bris 51 D1
Worcester Cres. Bris 63 D4
Worcester Gdns. Nail 75 E4
Worcester Park. Bath 85 D1
Worcester Pl. Bath 85 D1
Worcester Rd. Bris 63 D4
Worcester Rd. Kingsw 51 E1
Worcester Terr. Bris 63 D4
Worcester Villas. Bath 85 D1
Wordsworth Rd. Bris 50 A4
Wordsworth Rd. Cleve 57 E1
Wordsworth Rd. W-S-M 105 D2
Workshop Rd. Avon 33 E2
World's End La. Keyn 82 B3
Worldsend La. Stone 2 C4
Worle Ct. W-S-M 88 C2
Worle Parkway. W-S-M 89 D1
Worlebury Cl. W-S-M 88 A2
Worlebury Hill Rd. W-S-M 88 B2
Worlebury Park Rd. W-S-M 88 A1
Wormcliffe La. Box 86 C2
Worrall Rd. Bris 49 D1
Worrel's La. Wint 37 E2
Worsley St. Bris 64 B4
Worth Cl. Kingsw 65 F3
Worthies The. Lymp 122 A1
Worthing Rd. Bris 35 F4
Worthy Cres. Lymp 122 A1
Worthy La. W-S-M 104 C4
Worthy Pl. W-S-M 104 B4
Worthy Rd. Avon 33 F4
Worthys The. St Gif 37 D3
Wotton Rd. Char 11 D3
Wotton Rd. Ir Act 26 C3
Wotton Rd. W-u-E 11 F3
Wotton Rd. Wickw 27 D4
Wrangle Farm Green. Cleve 57 F1
Wraxall Gr. Bris 79 D4
Wraxall Hill. Wrax 60 B3
Wraxall Rd. Kingsw 66 A3
Wren Cl. W-S-M 105 E4
Wren Dr. Bris 51 D3
Wrenbert Rd. Mang 51 E3
Wrington Cl. St Gif 36 B4
Wrington Cres. Bris 79 D4
Wrington Hill. Cong 92 C3
Wrington Hill. Wring 92 C3
Wrington La. Cong 91 F3
Wrington Mead. Cong 91 F3
Wrington Rd. Cong 91 F3
Wroughton Dr. Bris 79 E2
Wroughton Gdns. Bris 79 E2
Wroxham Dr. St Gif 36 B4
Wyatt Ave. Bris 78 C3
Wyatt Cl. Bris 78 C3
Wyatt's Cl. Nail 59 E1
Wychwood. Kingsw 65 F3
Wyck Beck Rd. Bris 35 D2
Wycliffe Rd. Bris 49 D4
Wycombe Gr. Bris 64 B1
Wye Croft Cl. Bris 35 E2
Wye Ct. Thorn 15 E4
Wyedale Ave. Bris 48 A4
Wykis Ct. Kingsw 65 F3
Wyllie Ct. W-S-M 89 D3
Wymbush Cres. Bris 79 E3
Wymbush Gdns. Bris 79 E3
Wyndham Cres. Bris 65 D2
Wyndham Cres. E in G 47 D2
Wyndham Way. Portis 45 F3
Wynstones The. Kingsw 65 E4
Wynter Cl. W-S-M 89 D2
Wytham Rd. Keyn 82 A2

Yadley Cl. Wins 125 D4
Yadley La. Wins 125 D3
Yadley Way. Wins 125 D4
Yanleigh Cl. Dun 78 B3
Yanley La. Lo Ash 78 B4
Yarbury Way. W-S-M 89 D1
Yate Rd. Ir Act 26 C2
Yate Rocks. Yate 27 F4
Yelverton Rd. Bris 64 C1
Yeo Bank La. K Sey 72 C1
Yeo Cl. W-S-M 105 D3
Yeo Ct. Cong 91 E2
Yeo La. Lo Ash 61 F1
Yeo Moor. Cleve 57 F1
Yeo Way. Cleve 57 D1
Yeolands Dr. Cleve 57 D1
Yeoman's Cl. Bris 48 B3
Yeomans Orch. Wring 92 C2
Yeomanside Cl. Bris 80 B3
Yeomead. Nail 59 F2
Yeomeads. Lo Ash 61 F1
Yeoward Rd. Cleve 57 F1
Yew Tree Cl. Bi Sut 113 E2
Yew Tree Cl. Blag 109 F3
Yew Tree Cl. Nail 59 E1
Yew Tree Dr. Kingsw 51 F2
Yew Tree Gdns. E in G 47 E2
Yew Tree Gdns. Nail 59 E1
Yew Tree Gdns. Wins 108 A2
Yew Tree La. Co Mar 128 A4
Yew Tree La. K Sey 73 D1
Yew Tree Park. Cong 91 E2
Yewcroft Cl. Bris 80 A2
Yewtree Batch. But 94 A1
Yomede Park. Bath 101 D4
York Ave. Bris 49 F2
York Cl. Mang 37 F1
York Cl. St Gif 36 B2
York Cl. W-S-M 89 D2
York Cl. Yate 27 F2
York Gdns. Bris 62 C3
York Gdns. Bris 63 D3
York Gdns. Wint 37 F4
York Pl. Bris 63 D4
York Pl. Bris 63 E3
York Rd. Bris 49 F1
York Rd. Bris 50 B1
York Rd. Bris 63 F2
York Rd. Kingsw 51 F2
York St. Bath 102 A3
York St. Bris 49 D1
York St. Bris 50 A1
York St. Bris 63 F4
York St. Bris 64 B4
York St. W-S-M 104 B4

Zetland Rd. Bris 49 E1
Zig Zag. Cleve 57 E2
Zinc Rd. Avon 33 E2
Zion Hill. Ston E 137 D4